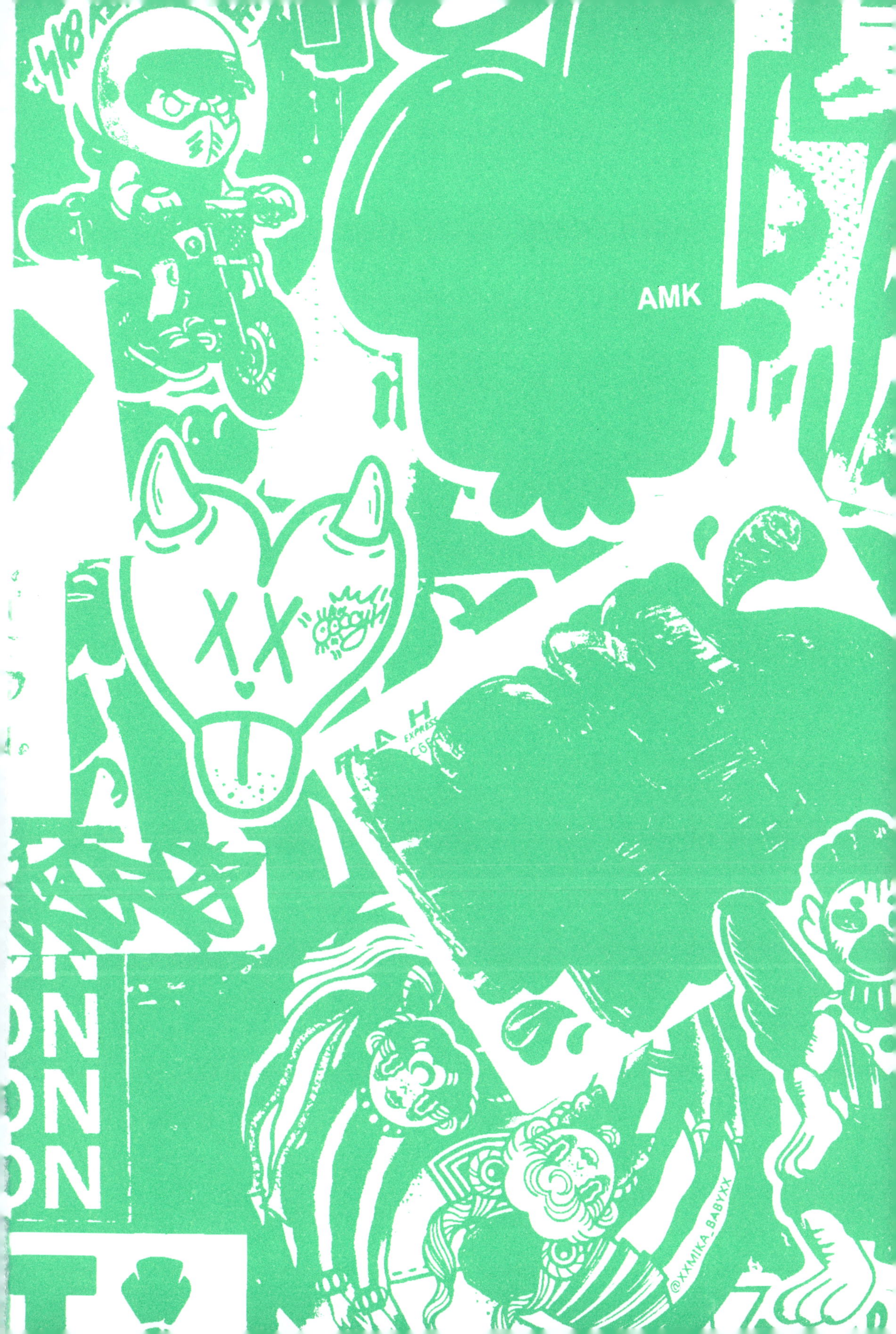
AMK
@XXMIKA_BABYXX

NSVANDALS
DEIO
DEIO
DEIO
malt

BANGKOK STREET ART AND GRAFFITI

HOPE FULL, HOPE LESS, HOPE WELL

FIRST PUBLISHED IN THAILAND IN 2022
BY RIVER BOOKS PRESS CO., LTD.

396/1 MAHARAJ ROAD,
PHRABOROMMAHARAJAWANG,
BANGKOK 10200.
TEL 66 2 6221900, 2254963, 2246686
E-MAIL: ORDER@RIVERBOOKSBK.COM
WWW.RIVERBOOKSBK.COM

BRITISH LIBRARY
CATALOGUING-IN-PUBLICATION DATA.
A CATALOGUE RECORD FOR THIS
BOOK IS AVAILABLE FROM THE BRITISH
LIBRARY.

ISBN: 978 616 451 061 6

PUBLISHER: NARISA CHAKRABONGSE
EDITORS: SARAH ROONEY, NARISA
CHAKRABONGSE
COVER DESIGN: STUDIO150, BANGKOK
ORIGINAL COVER ART: NEV3R, CRUDE,
POYD1
DESIGN: STUDIO150, BANGKOK

PRINTED AND BOUND IN THAILAND BY
SIRIVATANA INTERPRINT CO., LTD.

BANGKOK STREET ART AND GRAFFITI

HOPE FULL, HOPE LESS, HOPE WELL

TEXT AND
PHOTOGRAPHS
RUPERT MANN

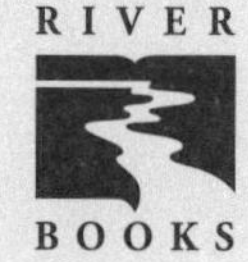

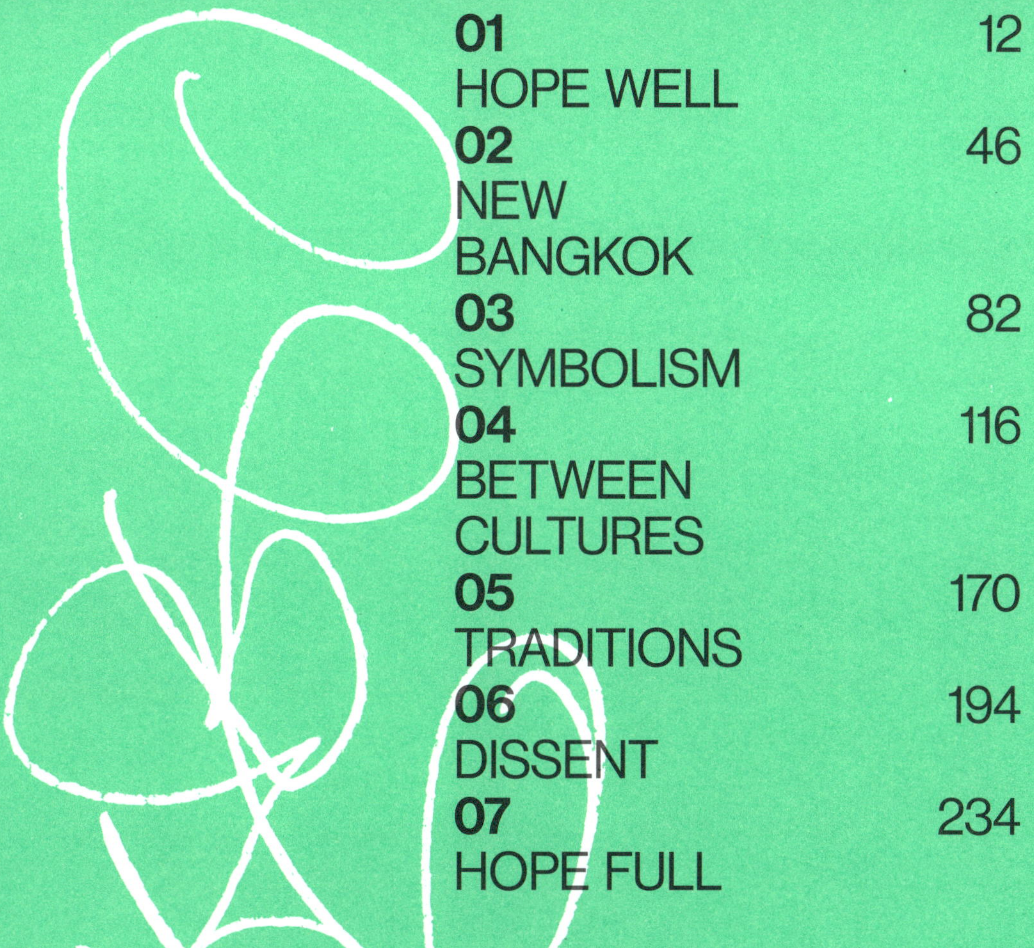

CONTENTS

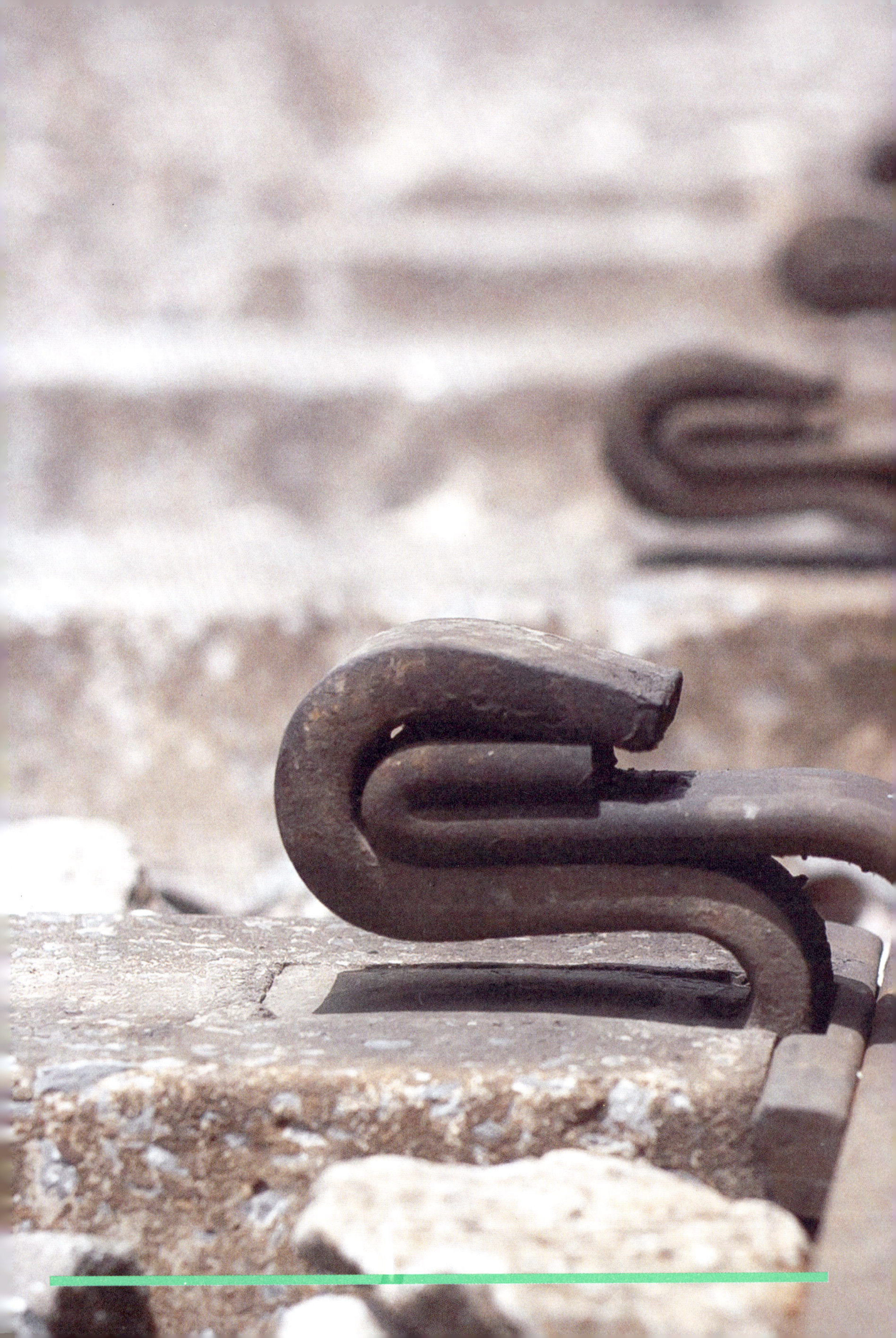

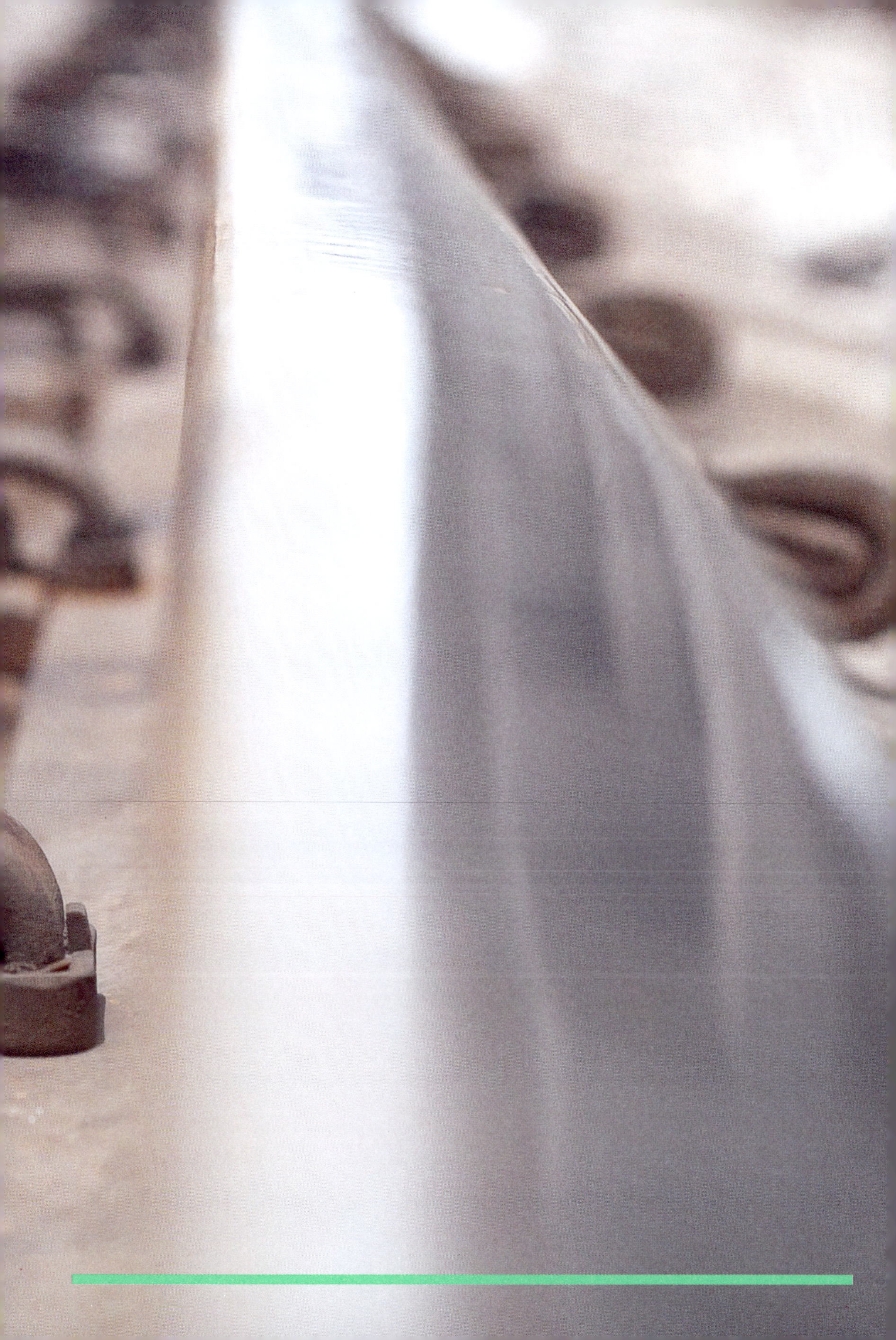

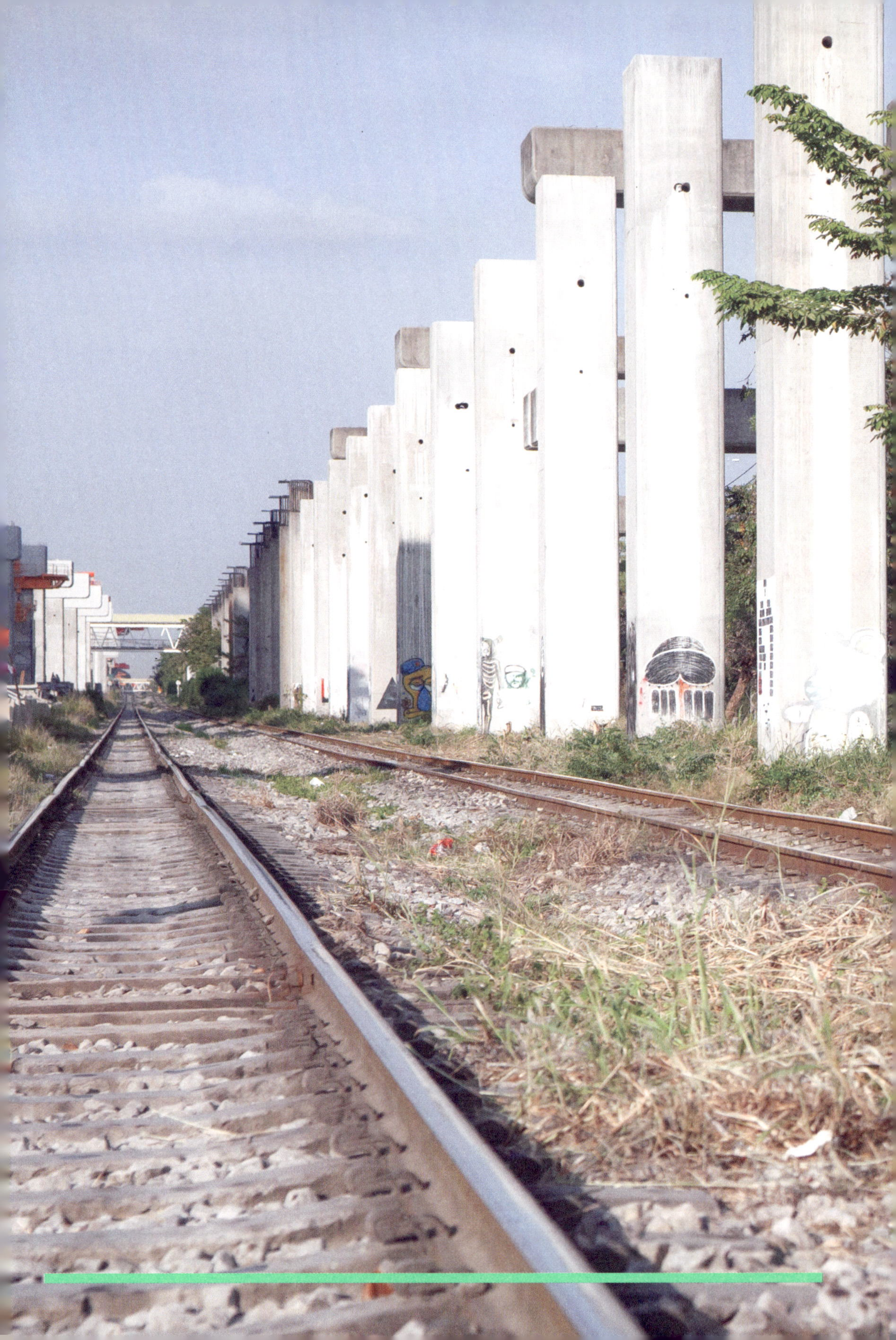

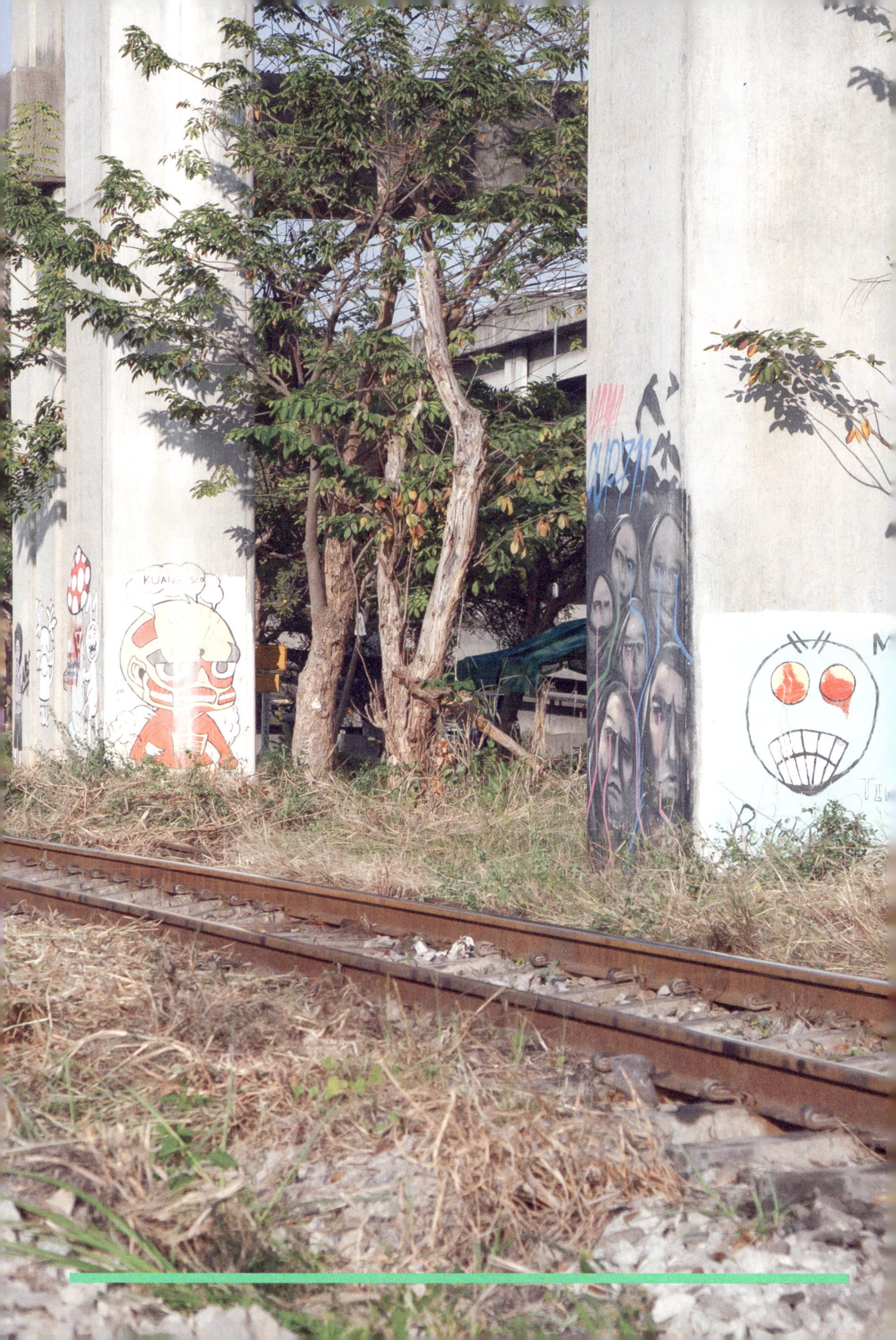

01

HOPE WELL

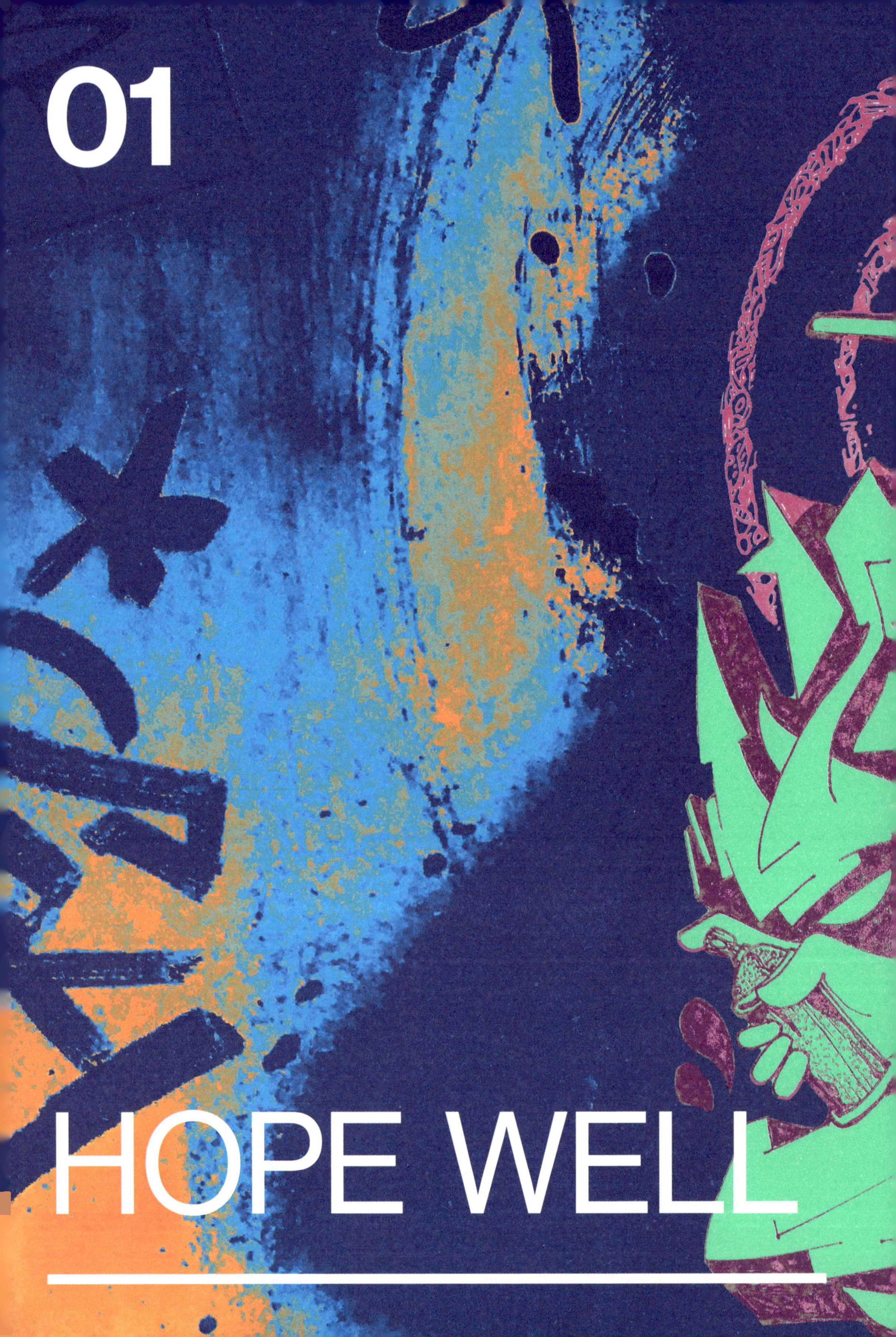

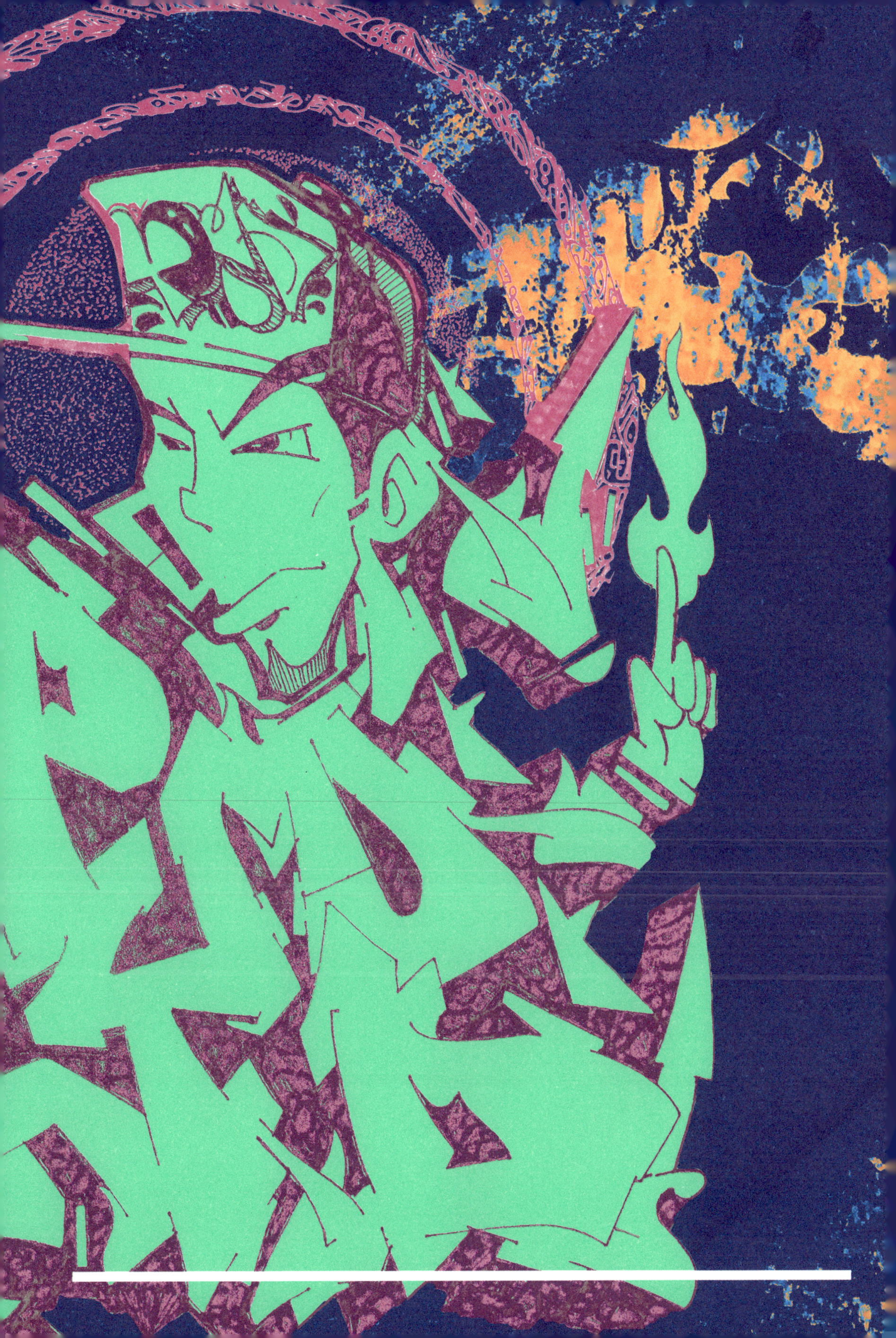

The just-completed nocturnal journey over Bangkok's highways still tunnels out of the back of my closed eyelids. I step off the motorbike into tungsten light – glad to walk a bit. A year before, in 2013, I'd first glimpsed this place while driving with a friend out through the back lots behind Klong Prem Prison. We passed across railway tracks within a forest of tall cement columns and, momentarily aligning with their very centre, I'd looked down the line. Within a heartbeat, the hundreds of columns and their overhead beams – illuminated with a fanciful menagerie of saints and monsters – created a tunnel of ever-diminishing frames surrounding a slender pyramid formed by the tracks merging on the horizon – Hopewell (see opposite).

This night, I was back, looking for more of what I'd seen. Leaving the bike and walking along the tracks, there were no columns, no street art, just a wide void. The culprit was nearby, a crooked 60-tonne excavator hibernated by a demountable shed. In its doorway a man sat under a cone of light. I'd waited too long. My heart fell away. What I'd hoped to photograph was already gone.

Dejected, I pushed further up the line, to unlit areas of track beyond the excavator. Declarations of despair and indignation emerged from the darkness as my eyes adjusted – contorted figures in lurid hues, creeping, warped faces and fine, elegant lines. Relieved, I saw there were still many columns adorned with art in the area. Some of the pieces were new. Artists were still working here – just ahead of the diesel-driven destruction that was rolling up the line by daylight. There was still a chance to record this place and its street art before it was lost.

As the first constructed attempt at rail mass transit in Thailand, the story of the Bangkok Elevated Road and Train System (the Hopewell Project) is part of Bangkok's urban heritage.

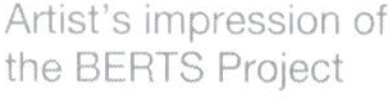

Artist's impression of the BERTS Project

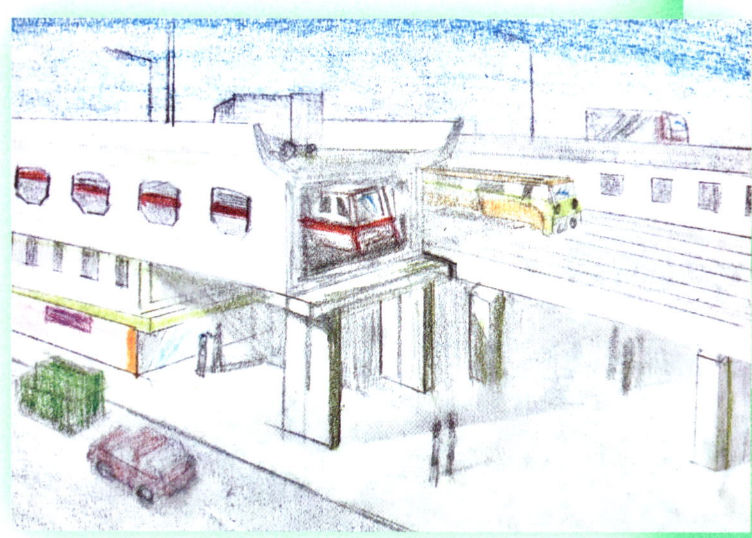

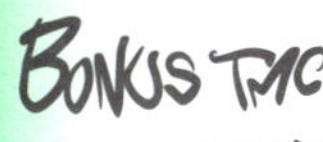

"Hopewell was the trace of former architecture. It had its own history."

With the construction boom of the 1960s and '70s, came a massive increase in the city's population. Transport systems failed to keep up. To alleviate terrible traffic congestion, the government focussed resources on expanding the road network – this didn't help. Belatedly, in the '80s, planning began on several public transport projects. Approved in 1990, the first of these to break ground was Hopewell. It is reported that Gordon Wu of Hopewell Holdings was awarded the contract based only on a two-page proposal. Hopewell was to construct the combined road and railway above existing State Rail Transport lines in return for development rights along the corridor.

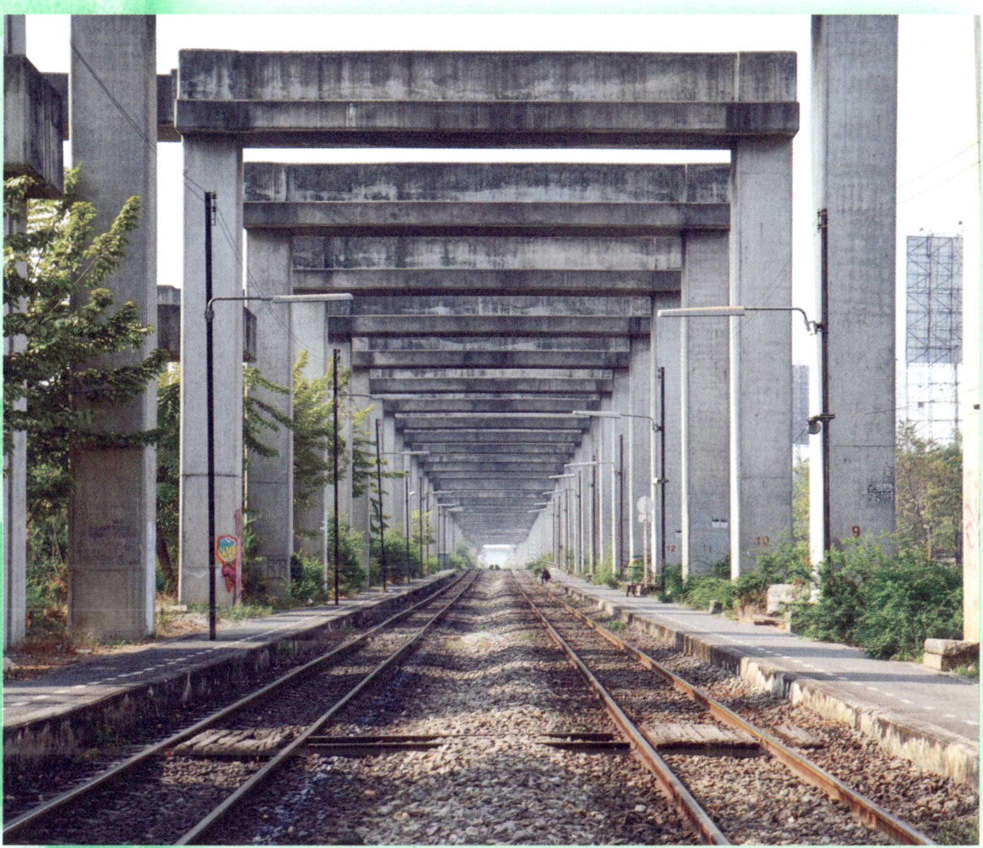

Originally, three lines were designed. The only one to move beyond planning was the northern section from Chatuchak to Don Mueang Airport, then Bangkok's international airport. Construction was ten percent complete when it was halted in 1997. Rumours of mismanagement and squandered funds surrounded the project.

In February 2013, it was finally announced that the columns would be removed to make way for an entirely new elevated rail project. By then, Hopewell had sat for years as a set of several hundred defunct columns, highly visible beside the Vibhavadi Rangsit Road.

Thailand changed a great deal over the years that the Hopewell columns sat, became a street art site and then were demolished – a long-reigning king died, elected governments fell, military coups were staged and the internet arrived. Reflecting these events, the columns absorbed meaning far beyond their origins. This symbolism and the news of their looming destruction, inspired dozens of street artists from across Thailand to come and work there. Between late 2012 and 2015, the site also became part of Bangkok's street art history – during a tipping point when, aided by social media, the scene became an accepted part of Thai popular culture and commerce. Tribal tensions flared between those loyal to the contrarian origins of the graffiti movement and those who pushed newer styles.

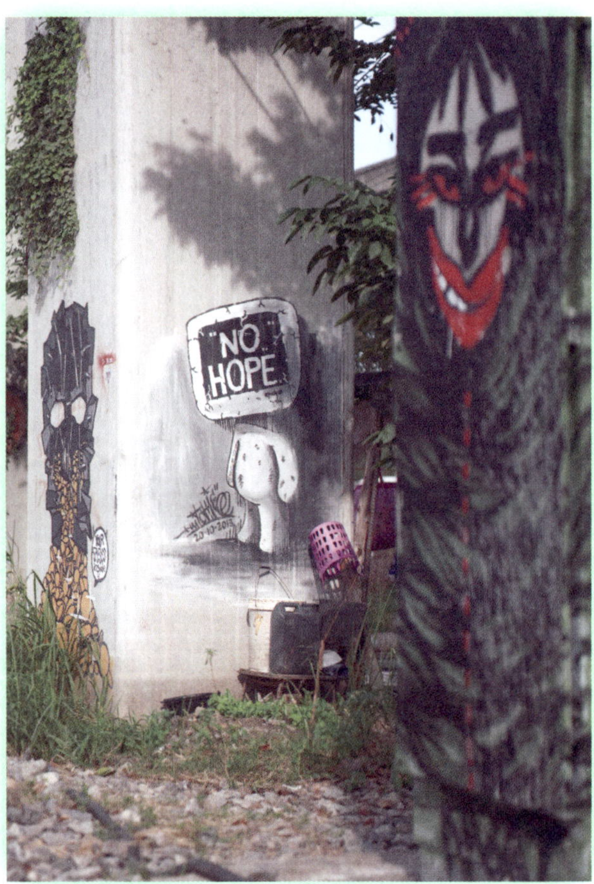

By laying at such a dense intersection, this single, charged space can speak of the impact of development, the cost of corruption, how nationhood is forged –

The tensions between old and new, between urban and rural – and the role of street art, graffiti, censorship and political dissent within modern Thailand. Hopewell offers a decorated gateway through which tracks of subcultural meaning can be followed to the hidden heart of contemporary Thailand.

The site's form was repetitious – hundreds of vertical cement columns spread across twelve kilometres. These easels created an open-air gallery. Artists had freedom to choose one of the columns, and on each column, one of four faces. This format demanded discipline. There was no possibility of putting something epic up. There were no heavens (inaccessible places that are high up and visible) to conquer, only a thousand identical cement faces. You chose one, and did your work on the same terms as anybody else. Each artist was creating variations on a theme. The physical theme was the form. The political theme was that of corruption. This was dictated by Bangkok's history. As they do elsewhere in the city, form and history curated Hopewell's street art.

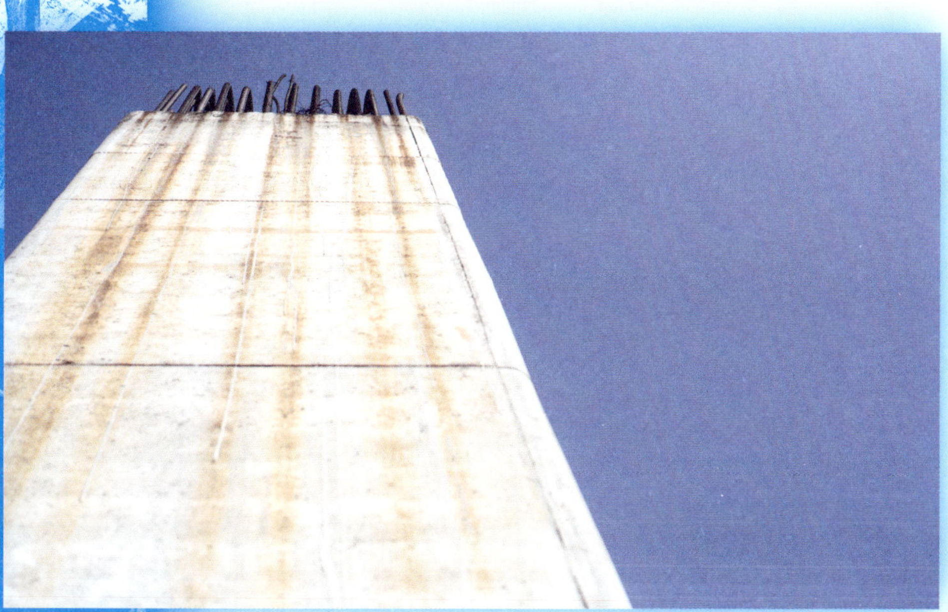

This book combines photography of the Hopewell site and other street art sites around Bangkok with interviews undertaken during 2019 with 18 of the city's graffiti writers and street artists, many of whom worked at Hopewell. The Hopewell art around Bang Khen Station was photographed between 2014 and 2015. The other street art sites were photographed between 2019 and 2021. These photographs also record how the informality and warmth of the old Bang Khen Station was superseded by the clean starkness of a new elevated Bang Khen Station, as another piece of old Bangkok succumbed to progress. This tale has been repeated many times since the 1960s – years of unprecedented change. What was once a collection of aquatic villages nestled beside canals around a land-based royal core has largely been obscured beneath a roiling storm of cement and steel.

Thailand's indigenous street art – the stencil and gang traditions of polytechnical students in Bangkok – mirrored how modern graffiti and street art were brought into existence by raucous urban kids in the 1960s, '70s and '80s. As a crumbling New York and Philadelphia were the global birthplaces of these movements, the New Bangkok, now a concrete maze, was the crucible of Thai graffiti and street art. Having found their way here through hip-hop and skateboarding cultures – outside traditions – the US styles would themselves be mutated by the ways of Thailand. And in Bangkok, the old, unstable balance between modernity and tradition continued to sway, this way and that.

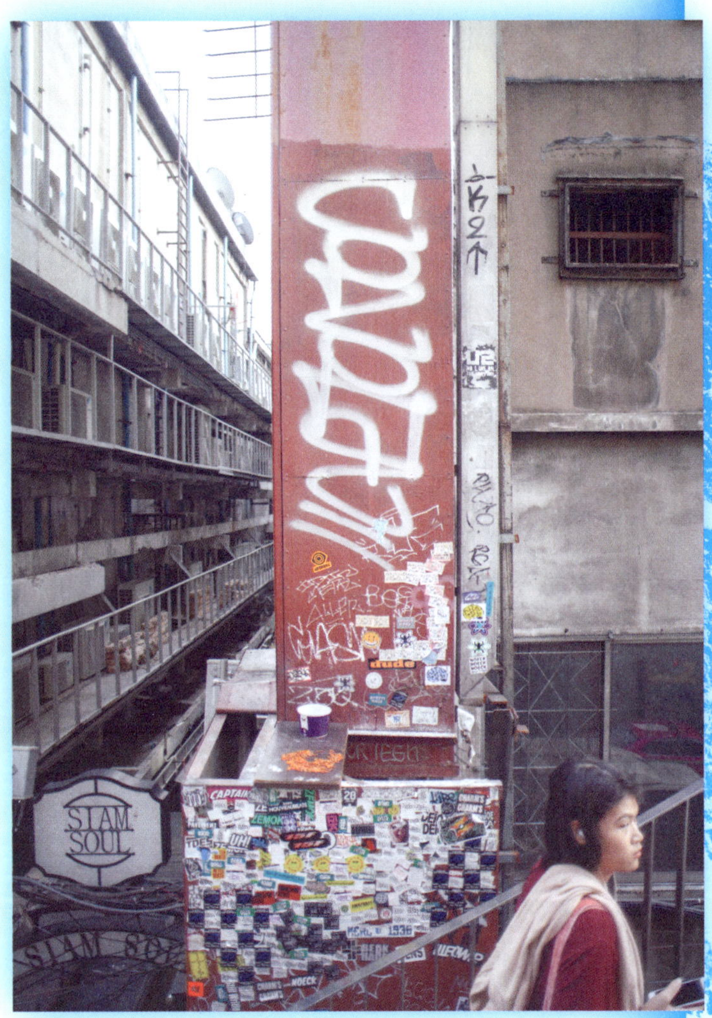

Graffiti and street art are created by people who contemplate the less pedestrian aspects of our existence and reveal threads that ordinarily remain concealed. Upon being created in the public realm, their words and images become a marker of that city's sub-history. Often, this contribution is fleeting. The work is painted over or the wall it adorns is torn down as the city consumes itself again and again.

It then lives in the memory of the people who saw it for a few weeks on their way to work or online. This transience makes record-keeping important for street art and graffiti – the scene subverts the traditions of history-making, but also relies on them to exist beyond their short lives.

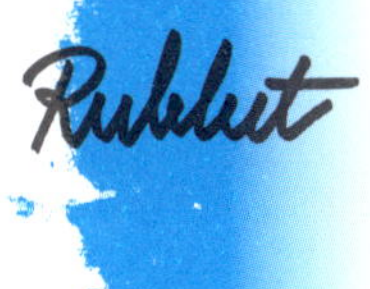

"Even though we didn't start street art, it is part of Thai culture. Every work created on the street is a memoir of its artist. Some artists like cartoon characters, some like graffiti. Each message is a historical record representing that moment in time. Street art is one of the ways to record the passing of time."

This book documents the gaze of a tiny set of subcultures within the massive populace of Bangkok – those of its street artists and graffiti writers. They tell many versions of the scene's history, sometimes conflicting and contradictory – the nature of underground movements, where the ways people work and the agendas they advance are not officially sanctioned. I hope the book will serve as a record of Hopewell's now lost street art and of the Thai heritage that Bangkok's scene represents. Also how urban decay – particularly the corpses of failed construction projects created by the Tom Yam Kung financial crisis – provide harbours for street art and graffiti in Bangkok. Regardless of whether the works depicted here are considered to be of high quality or not, they all burned for a year or two and hundreds of thousands of people saw them. That's reason enough to be written about – so may they burn a little longer.

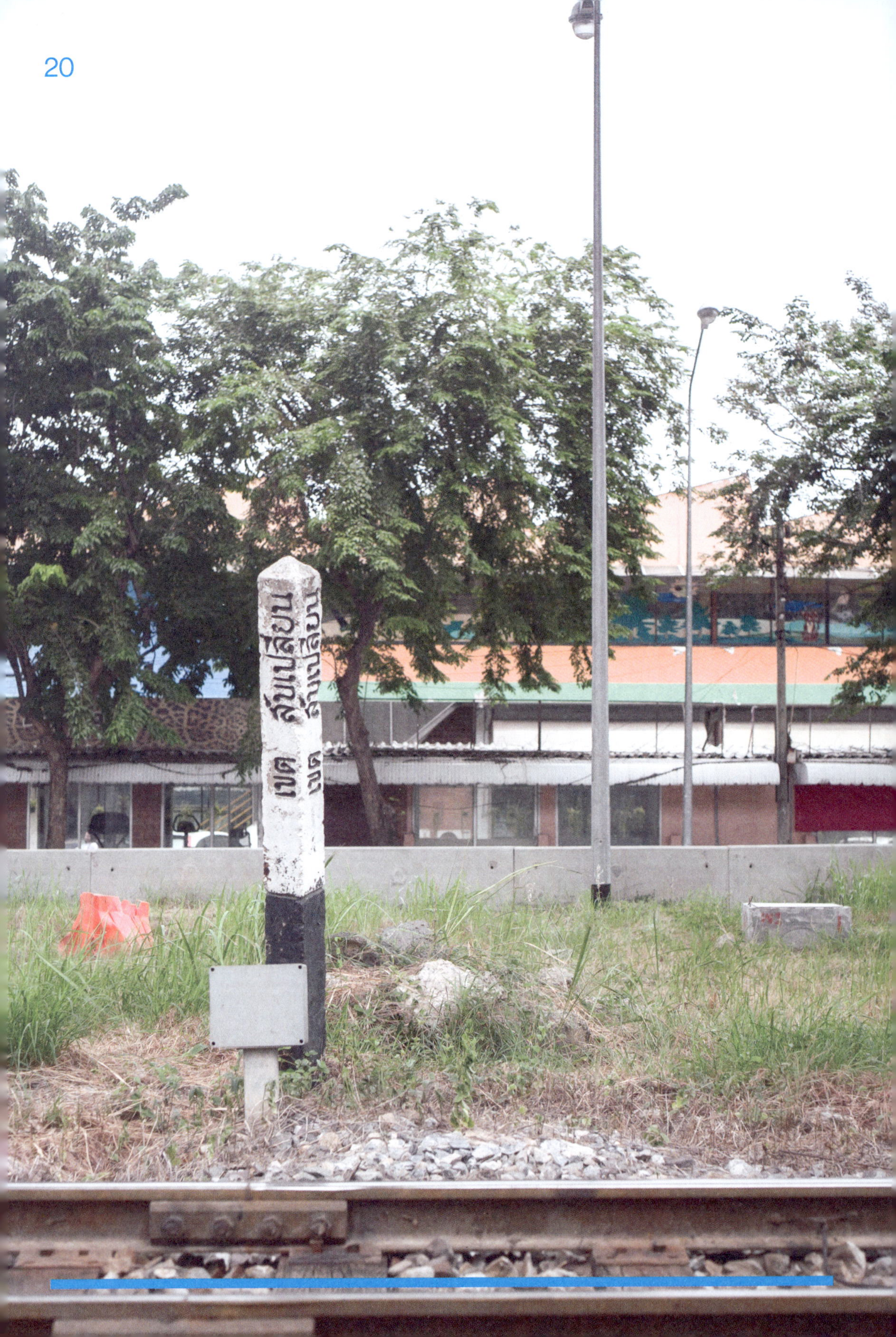

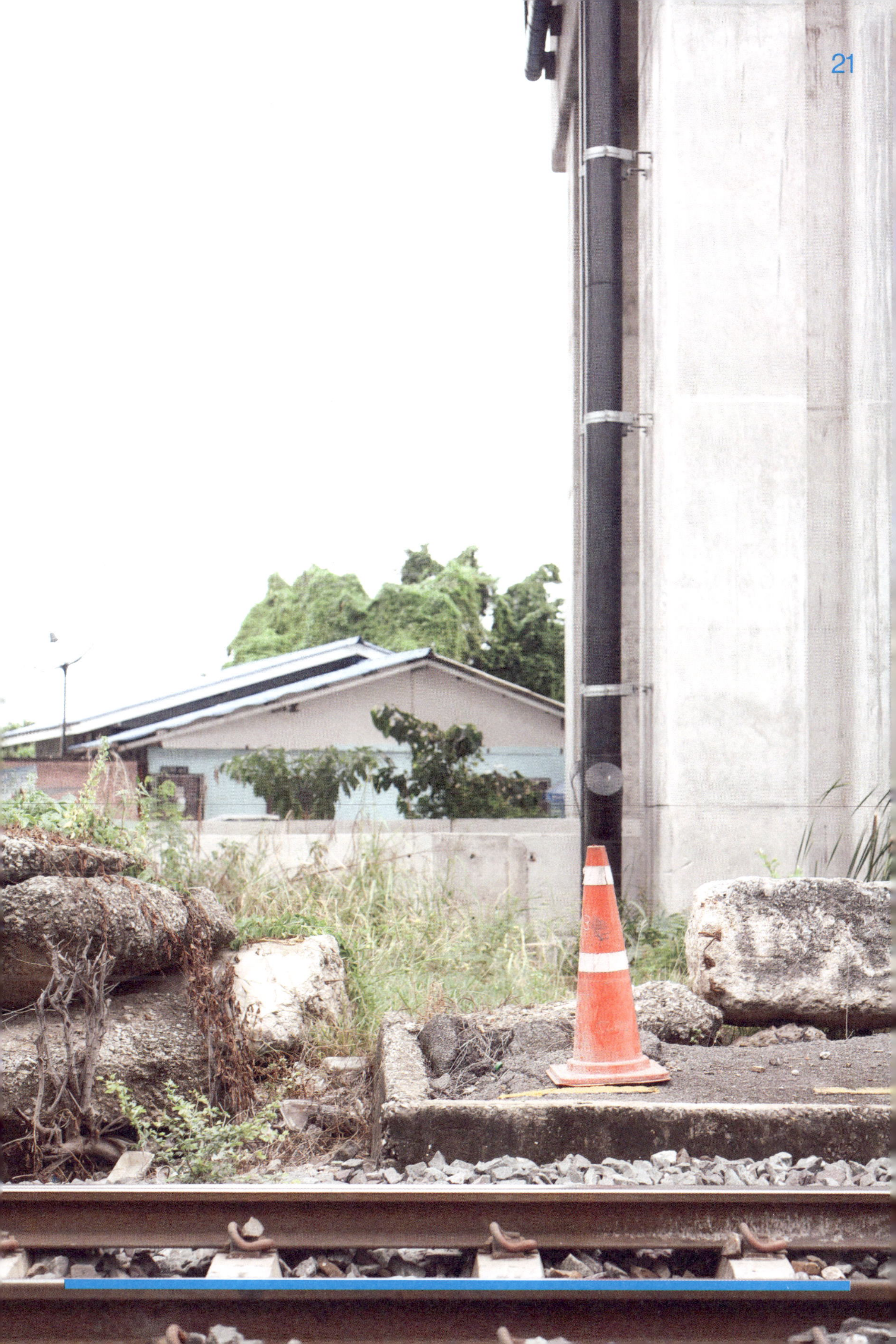

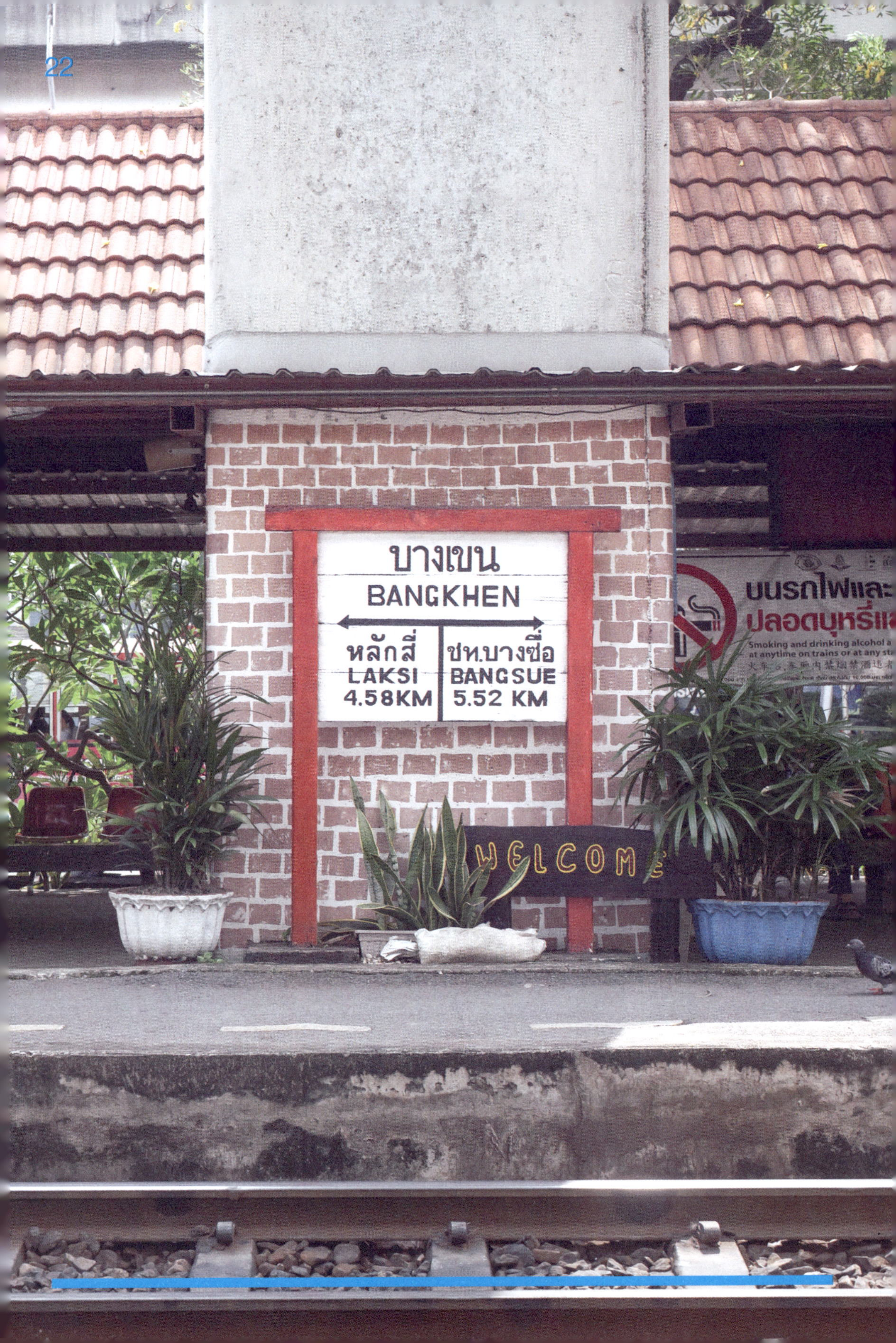
บางเขน
BANGKHEN
หลักสี่
LAKSI
4.58KM
ชท.บางซื่อ
BANGSUE
5.52 KM
WELCOME

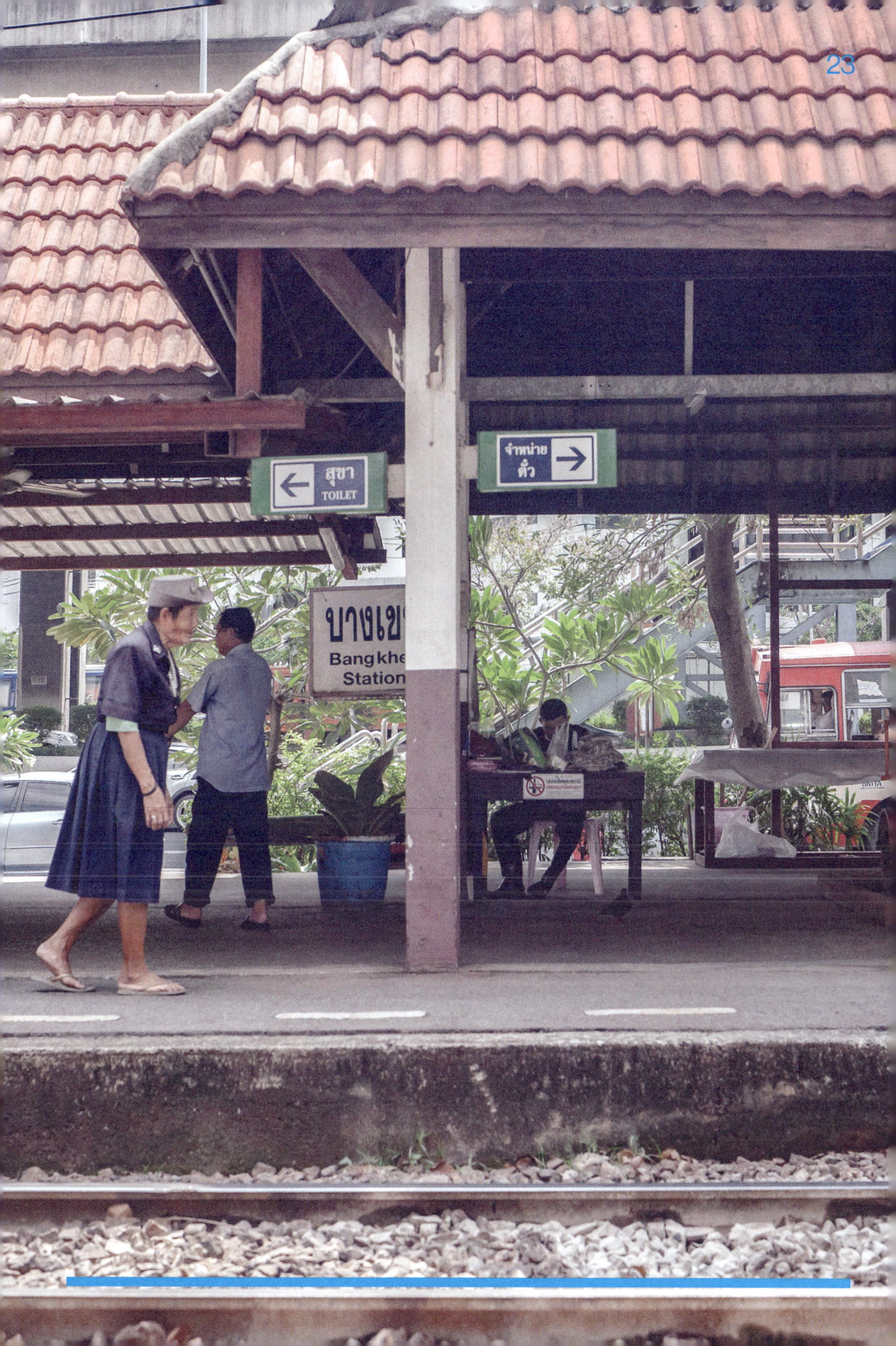
สุขา
TOILET
จำหน่าย
ตั๋ว
บางเข
Bangkhe
Station

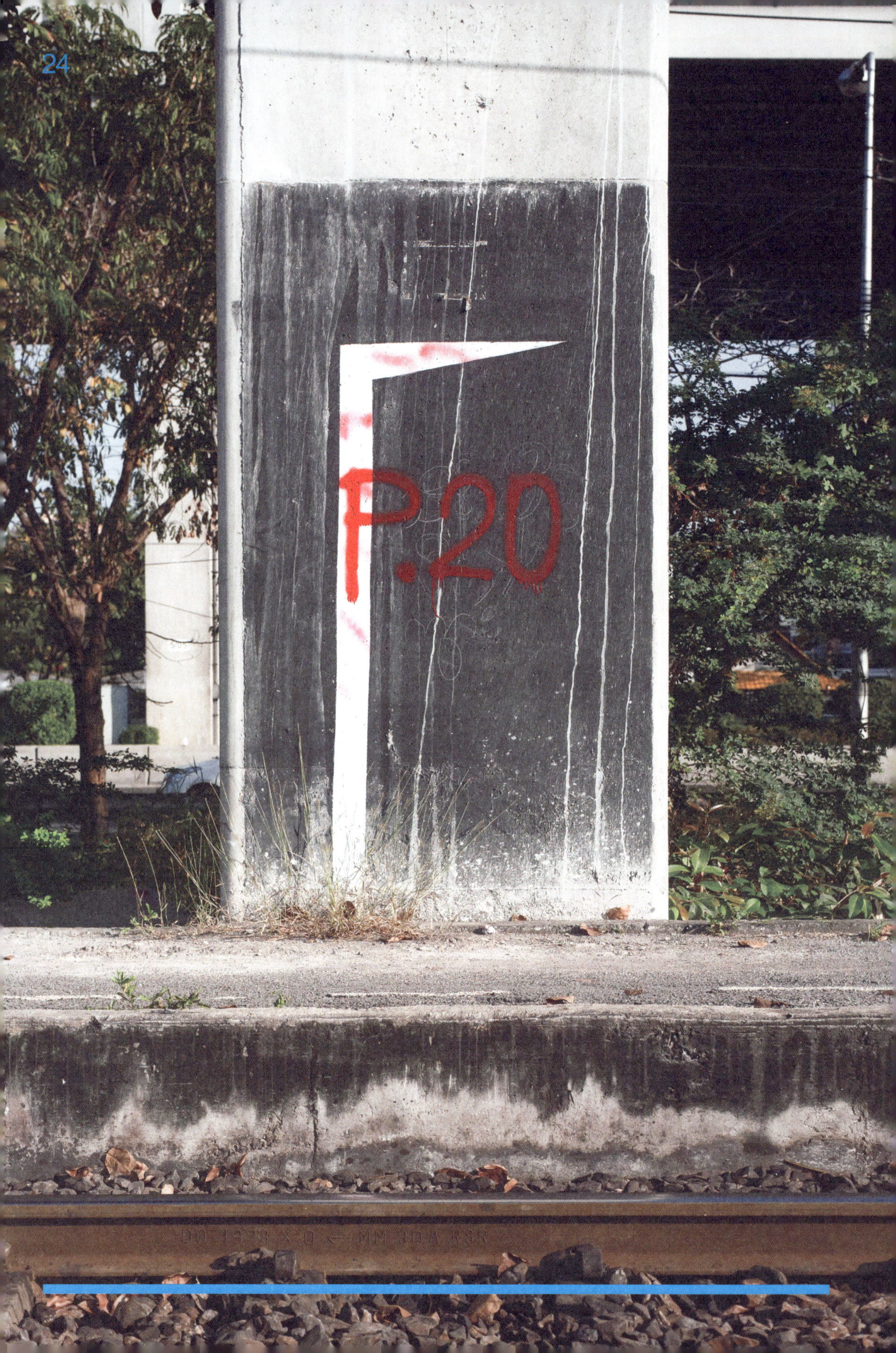
P.20

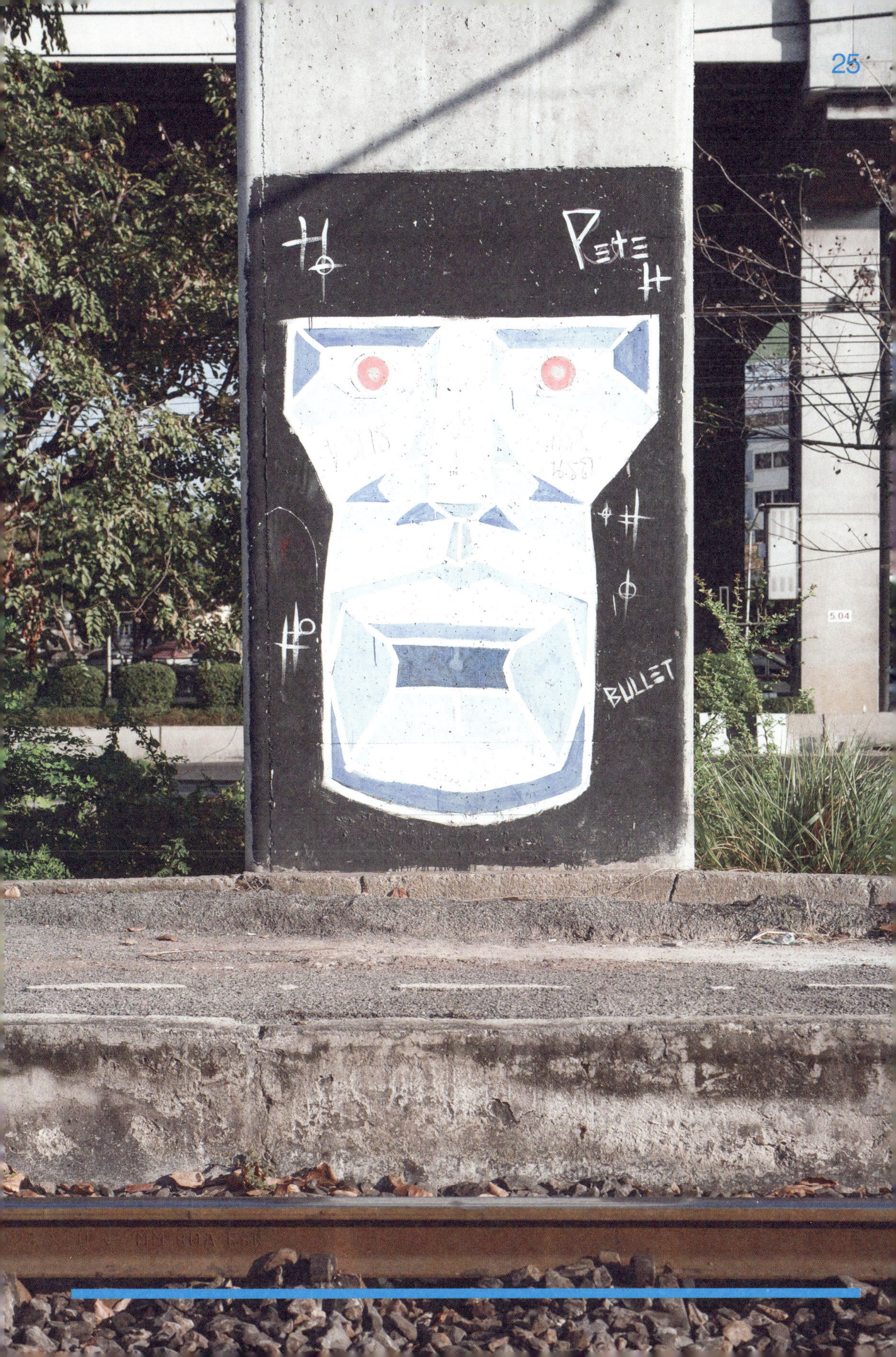
BULLET

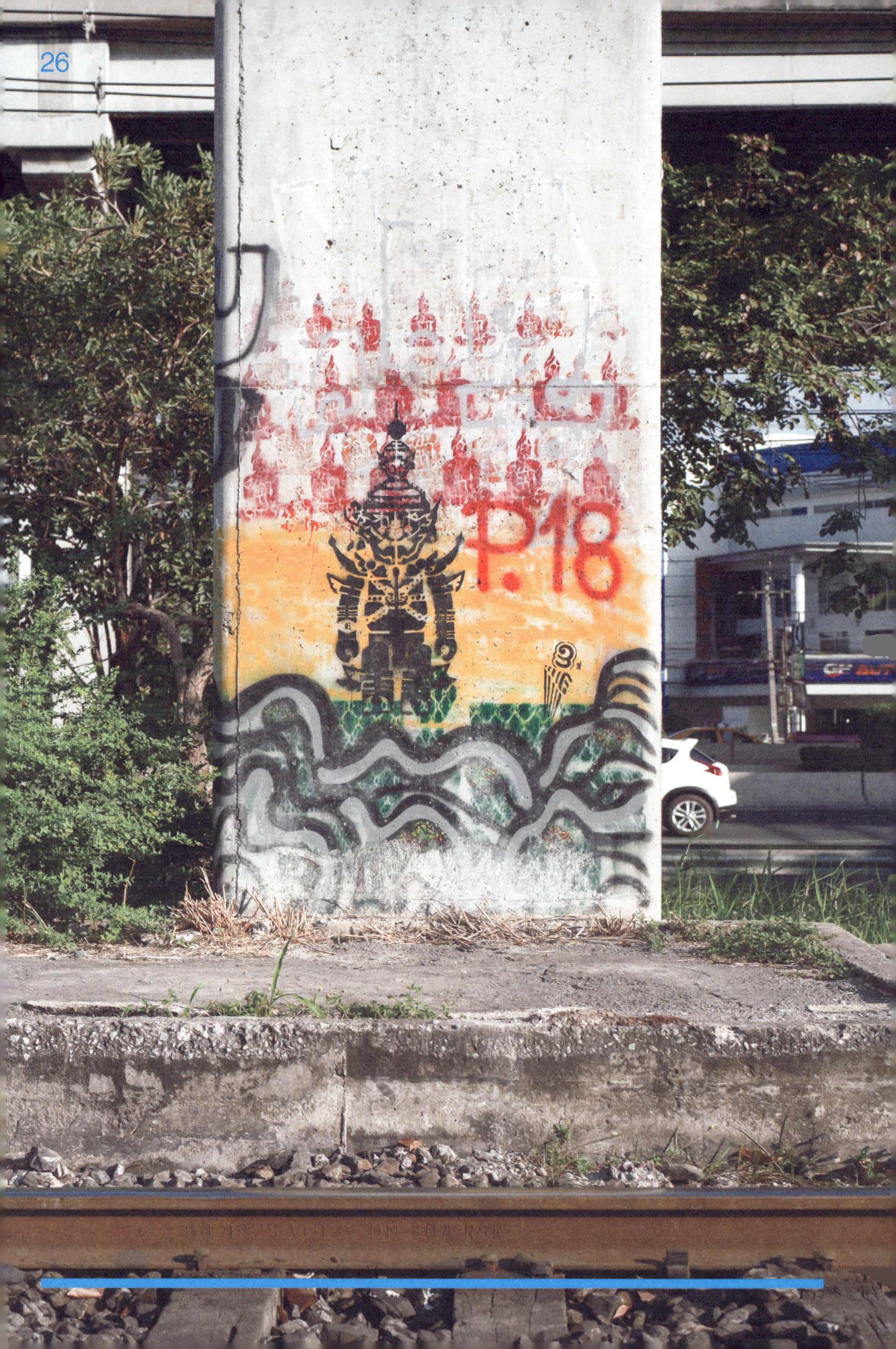
P.18

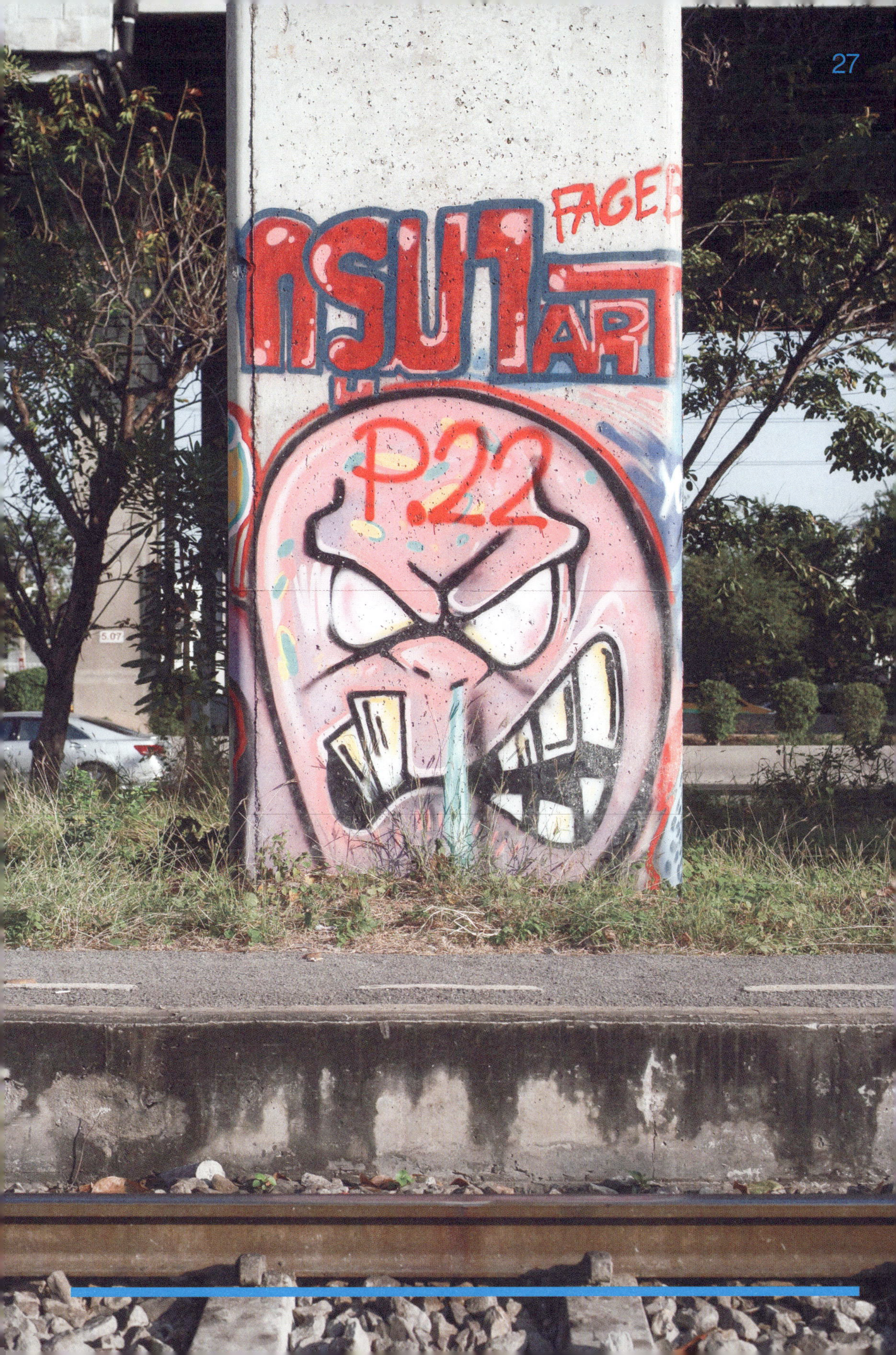
FACEB
ART
P.22

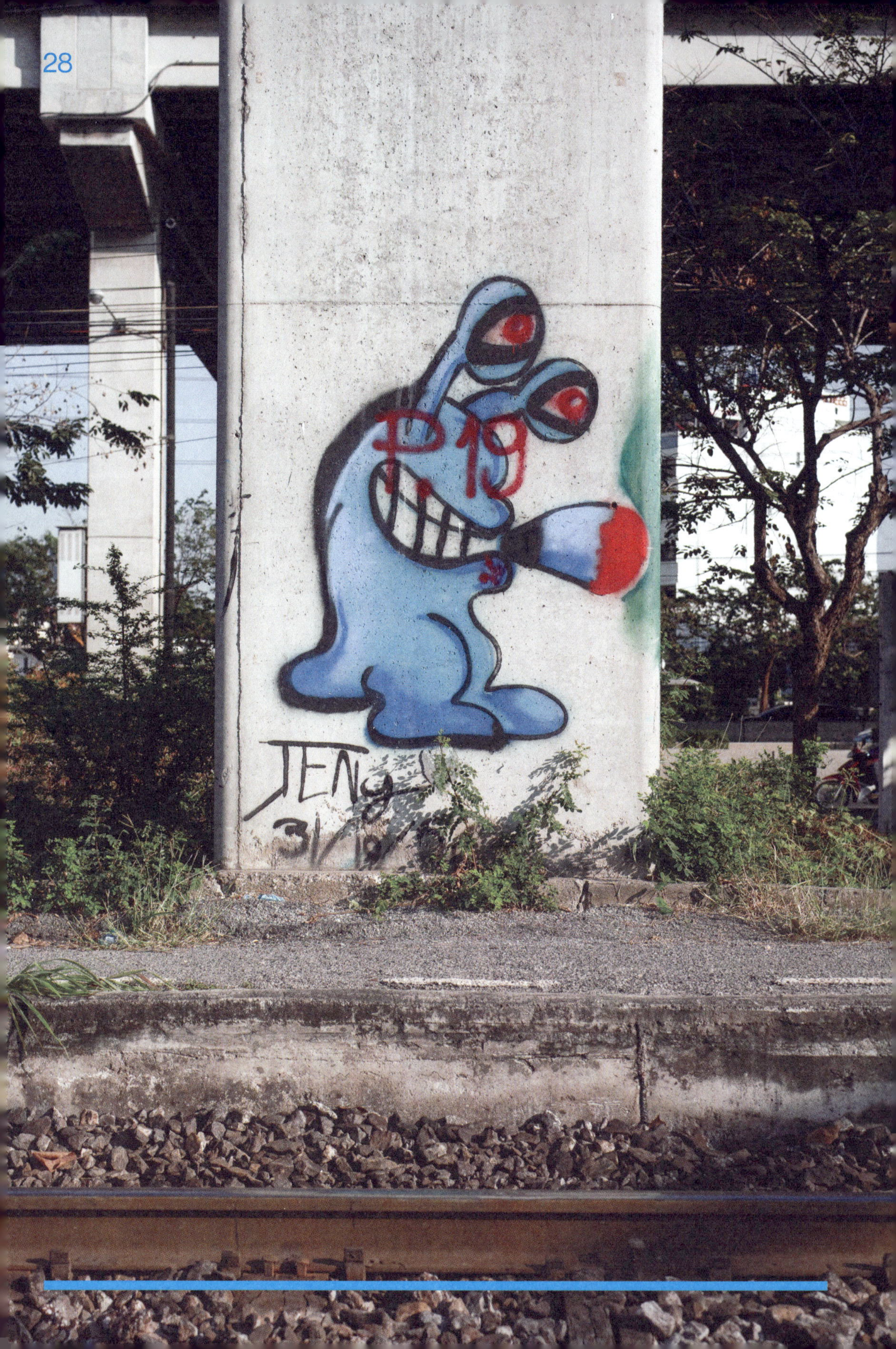
P.19
TENg

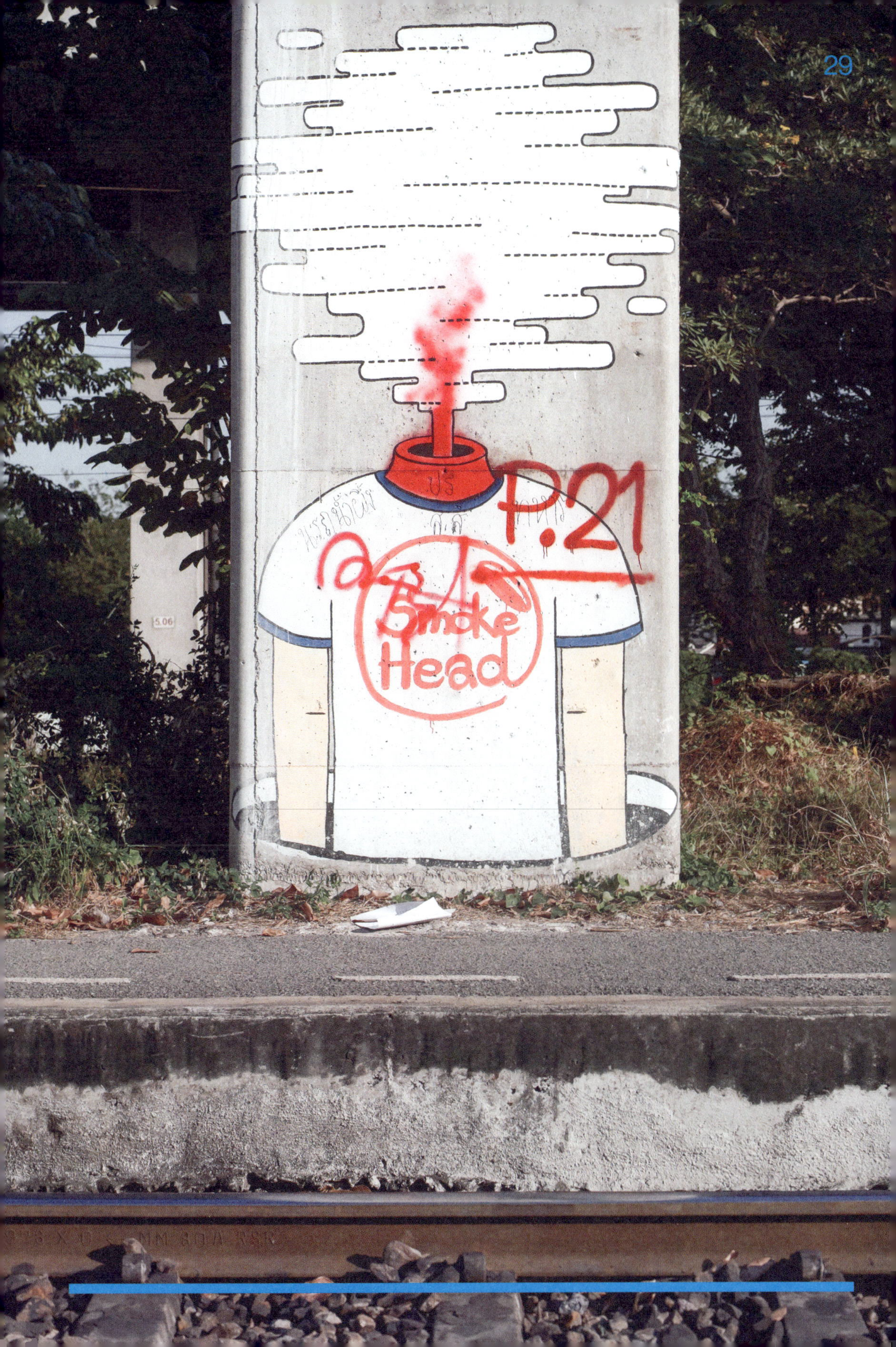
P.21
Smoke
Head

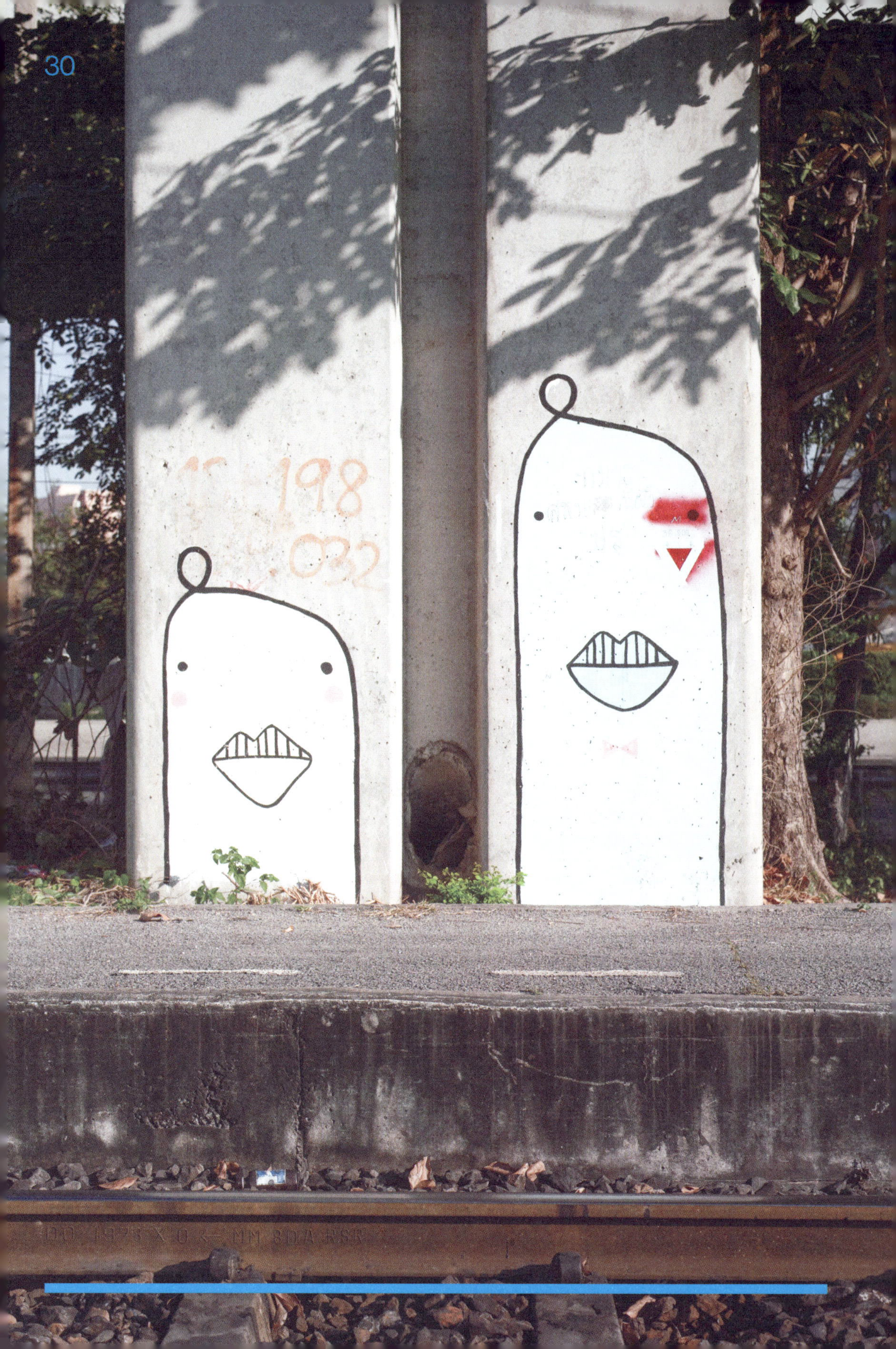
198
032

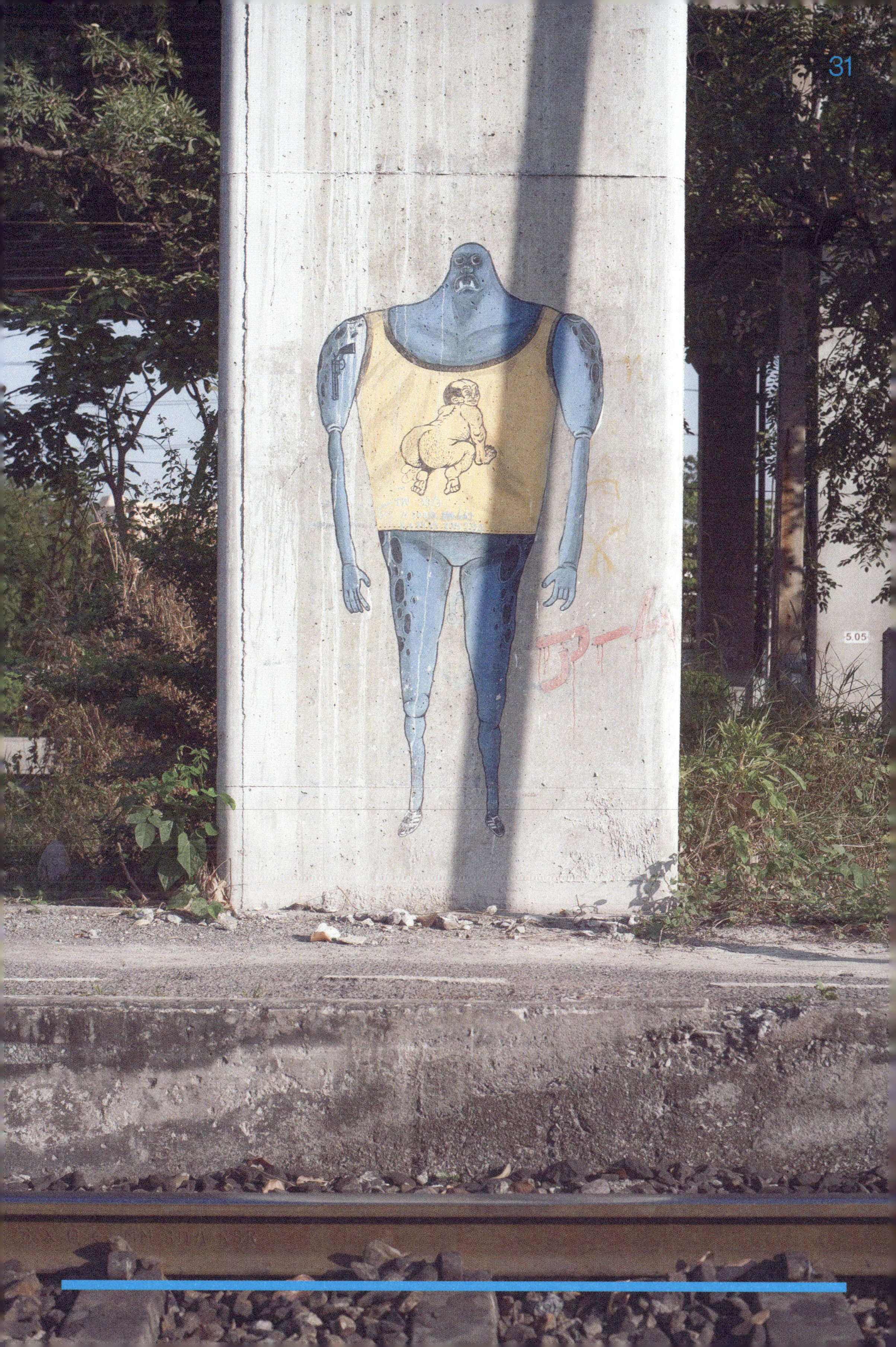

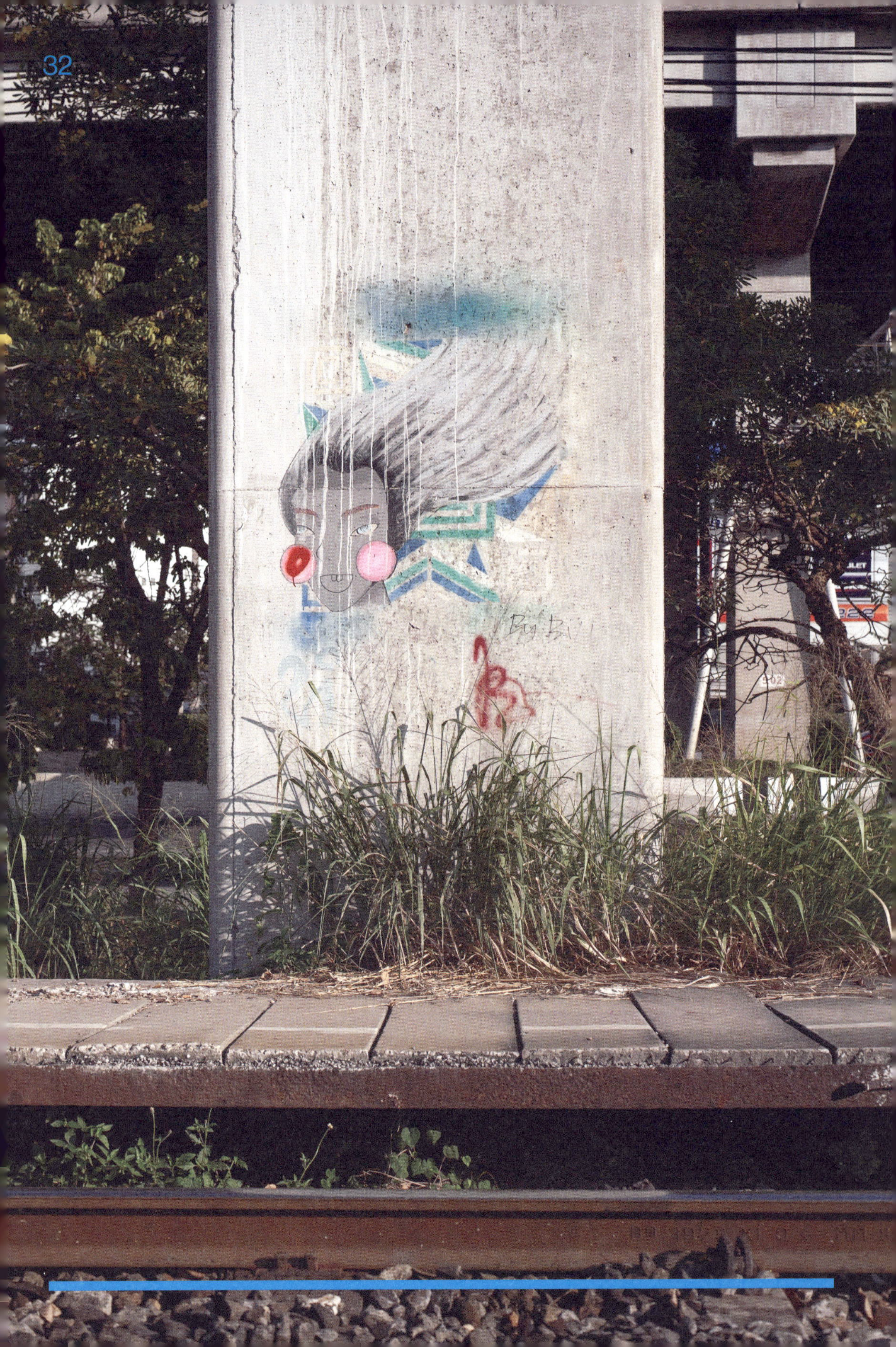

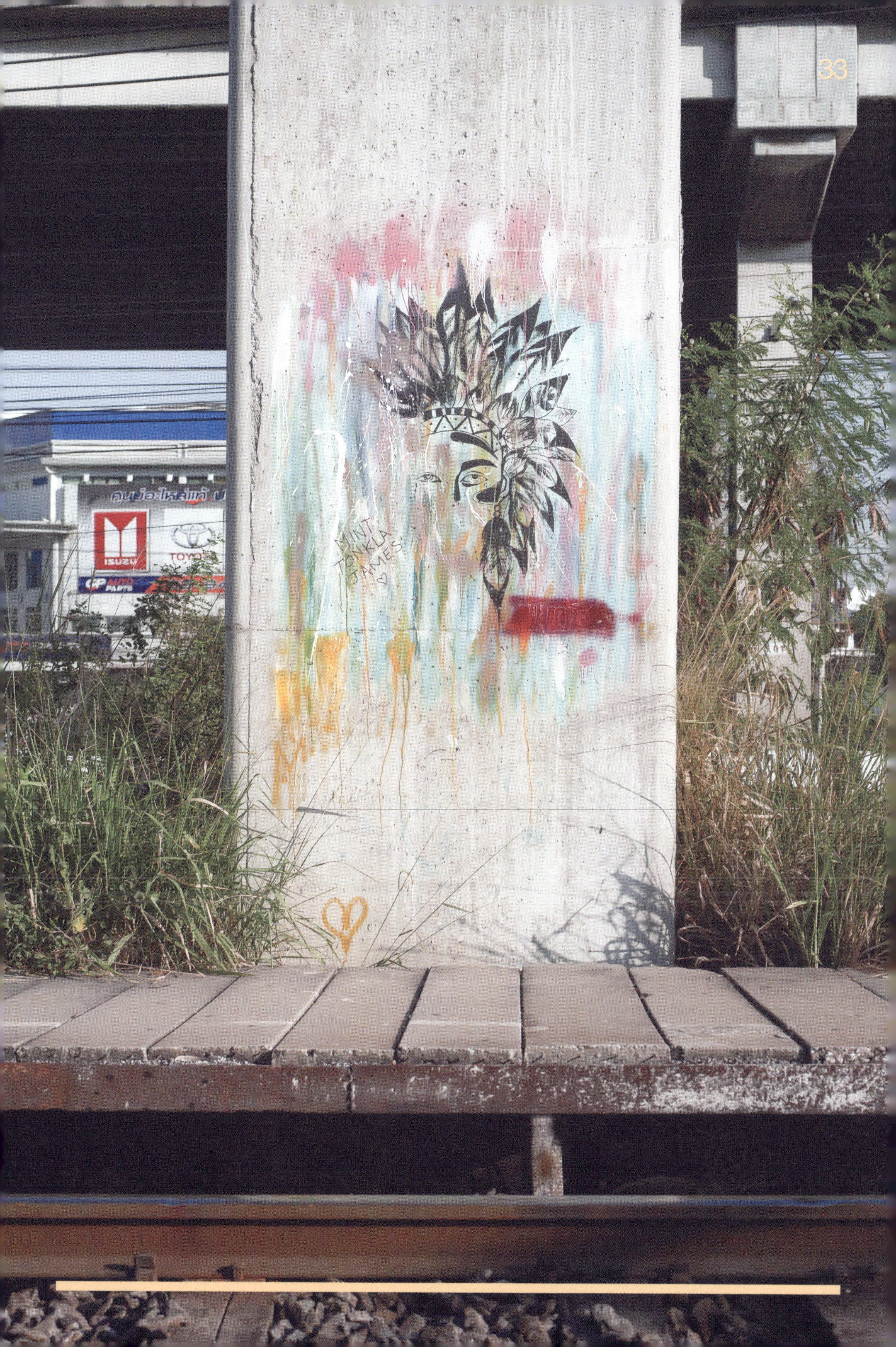
ISUZU
MINT
TONKLA
JAMES

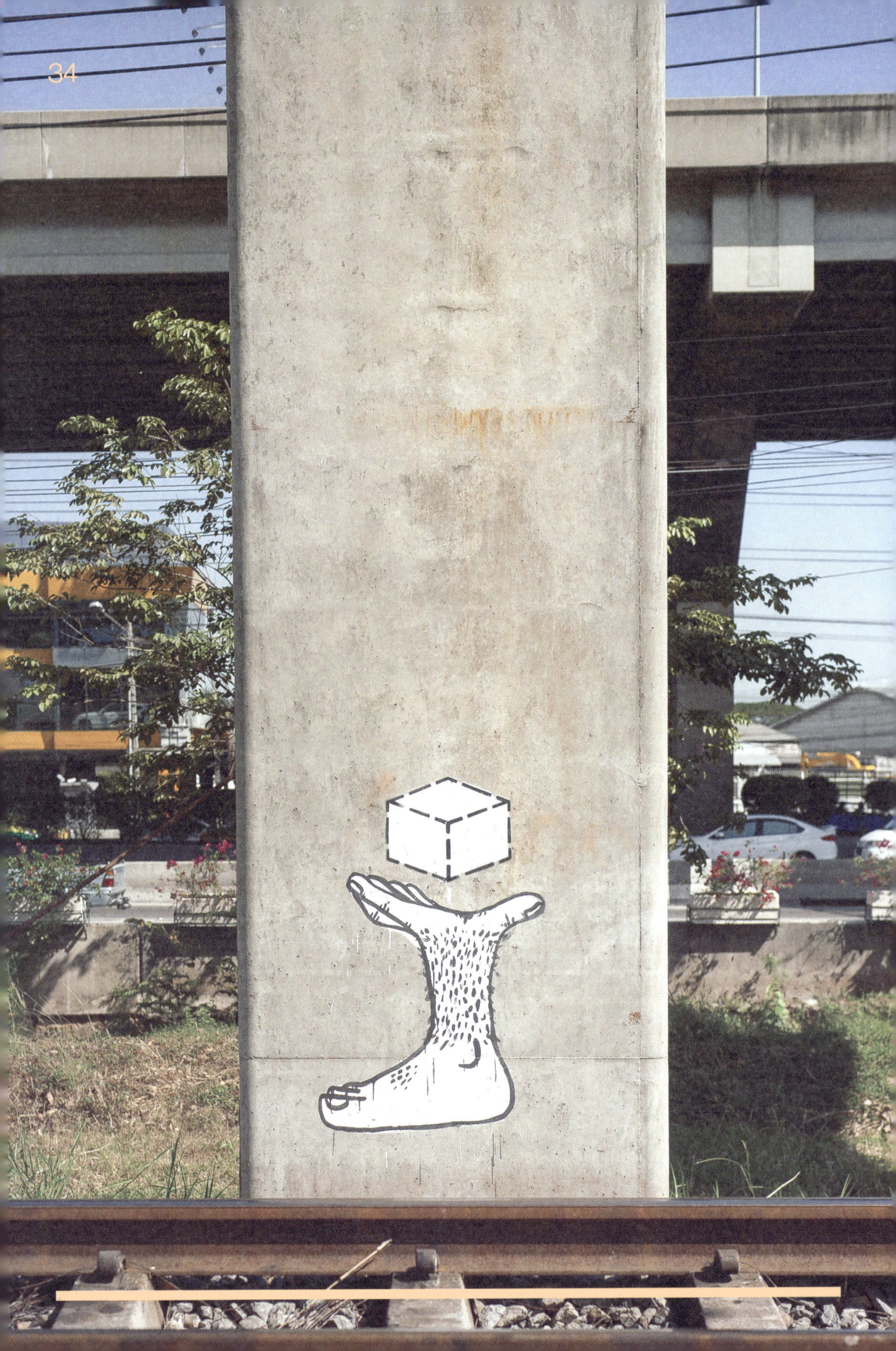

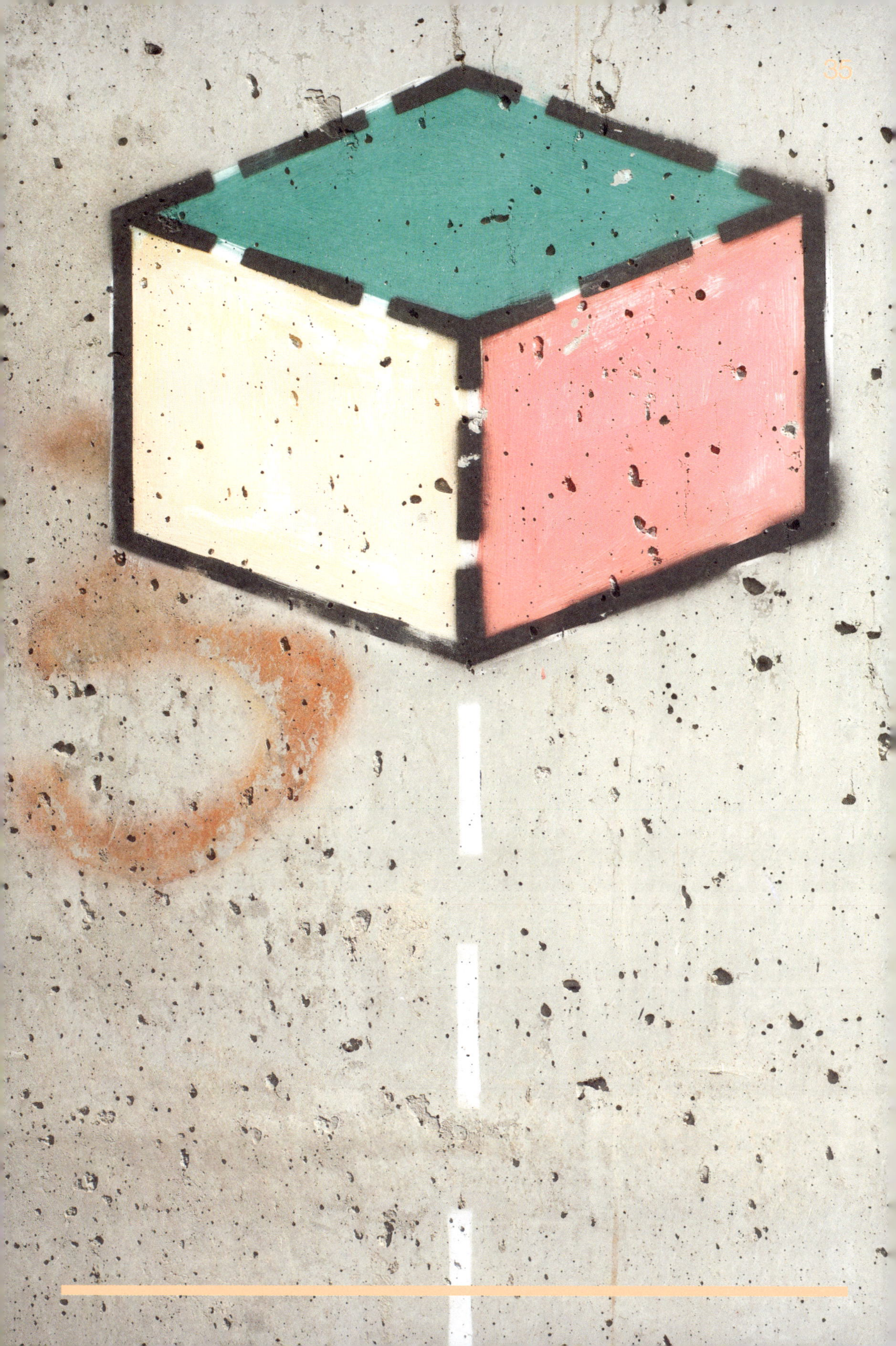

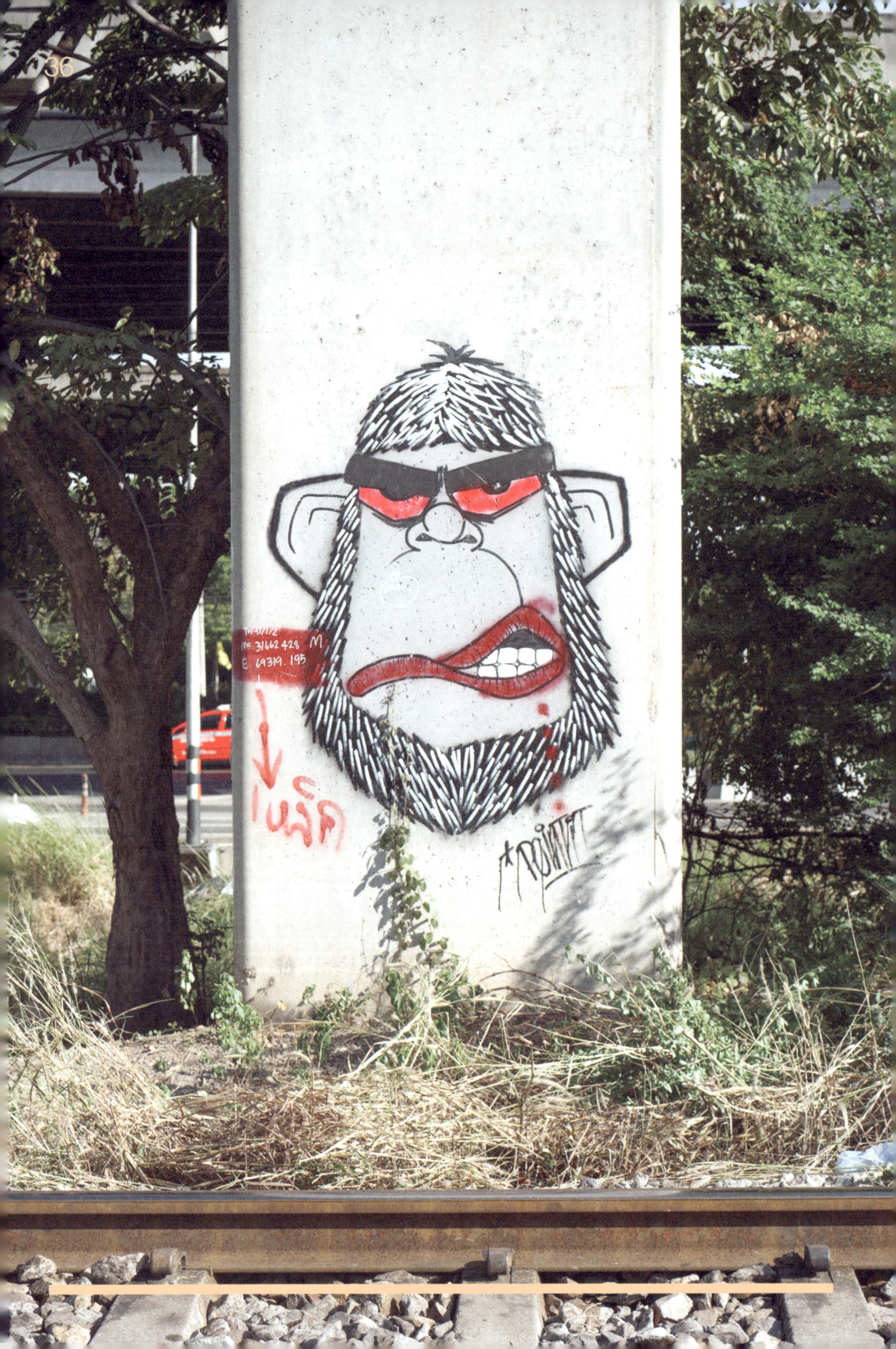
E 69319. 195
เหล็ก

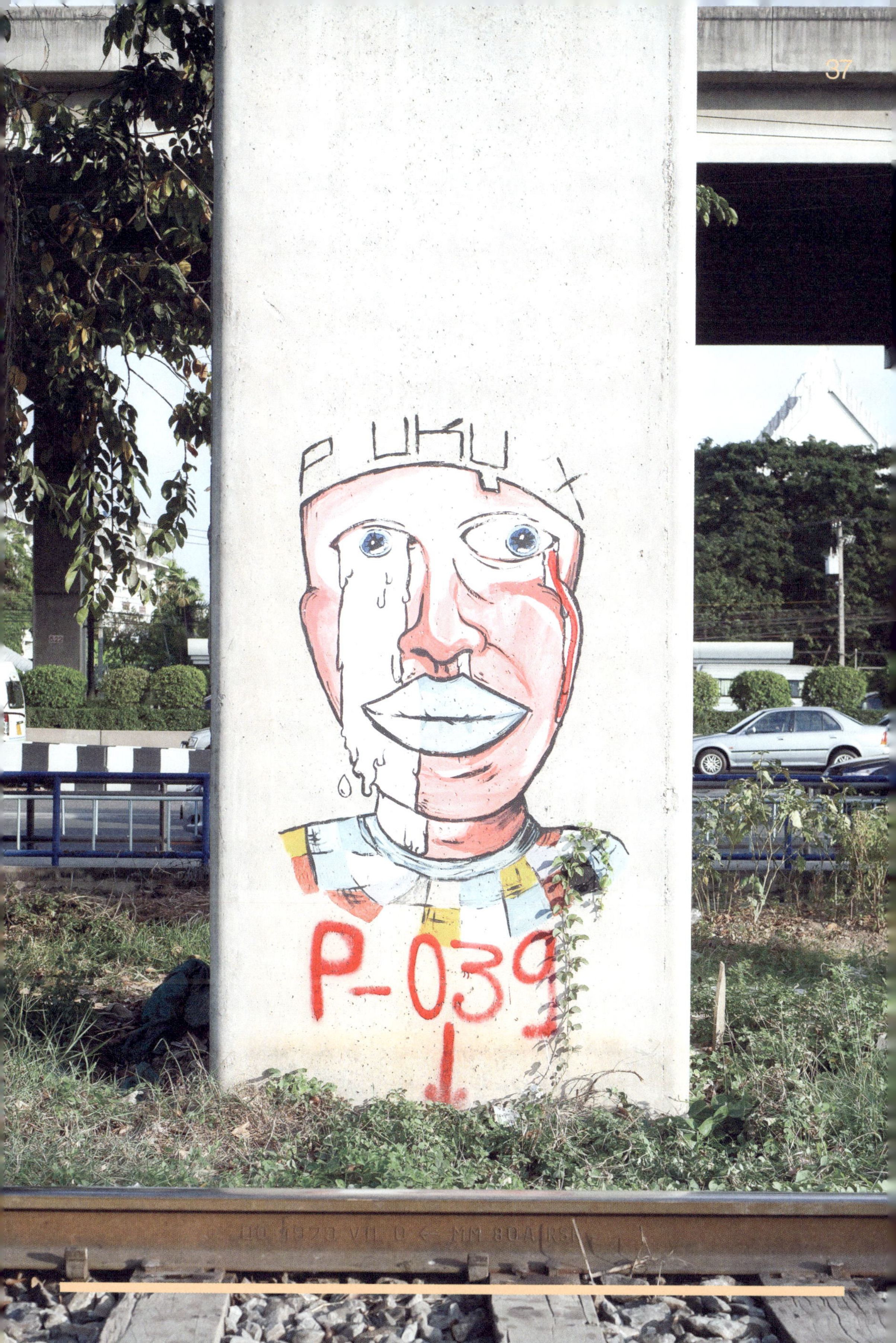
P-039

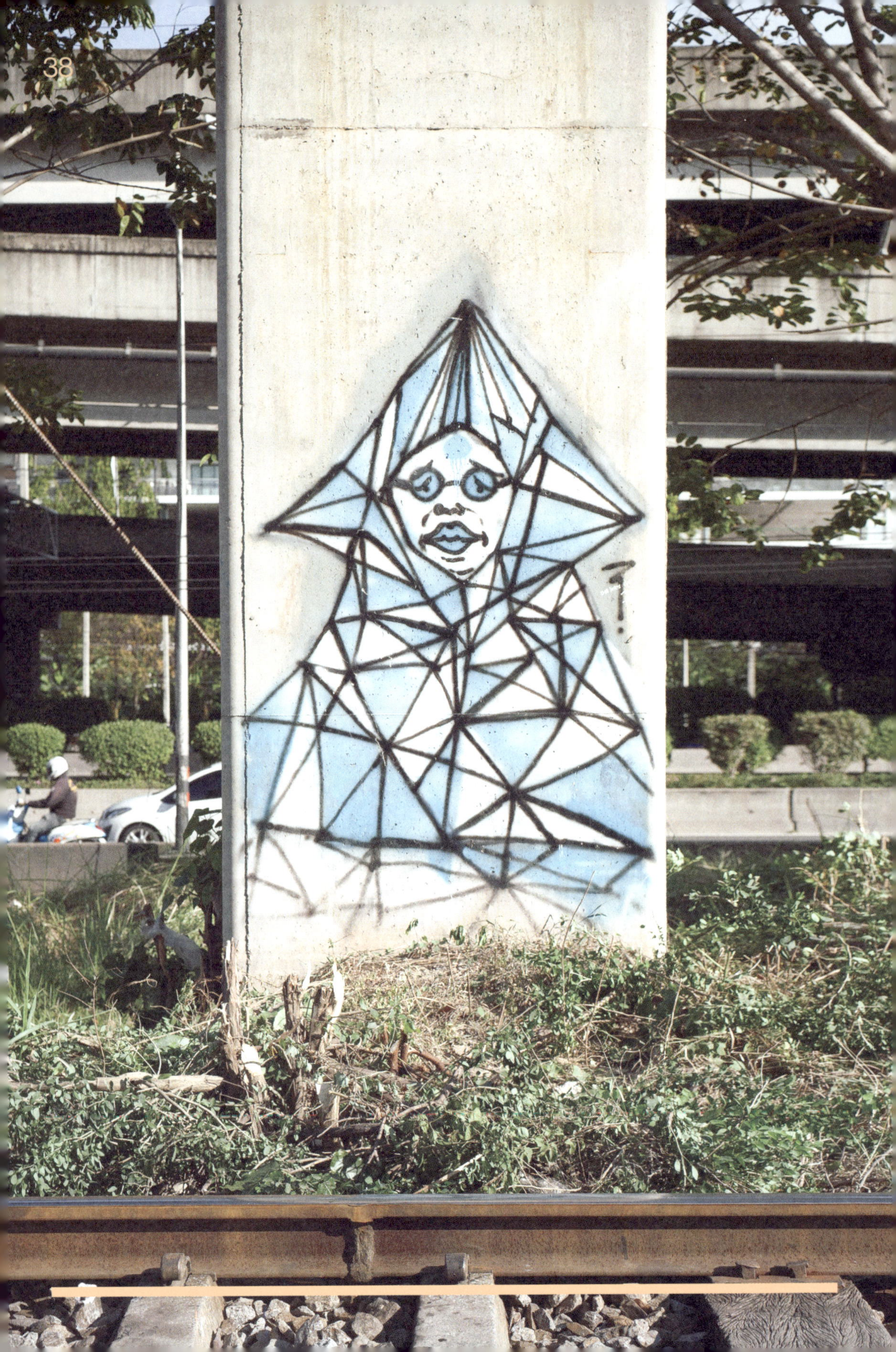

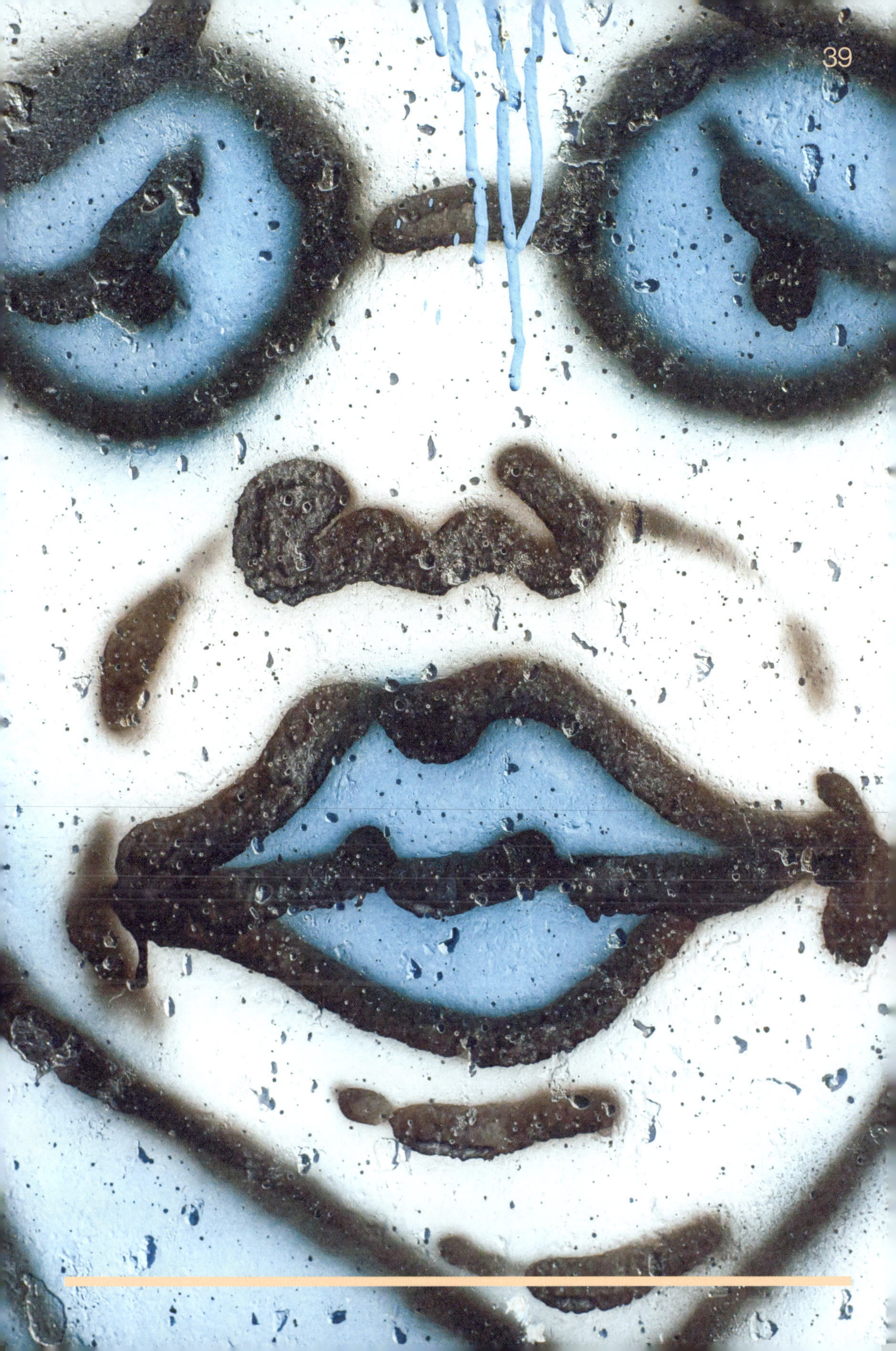

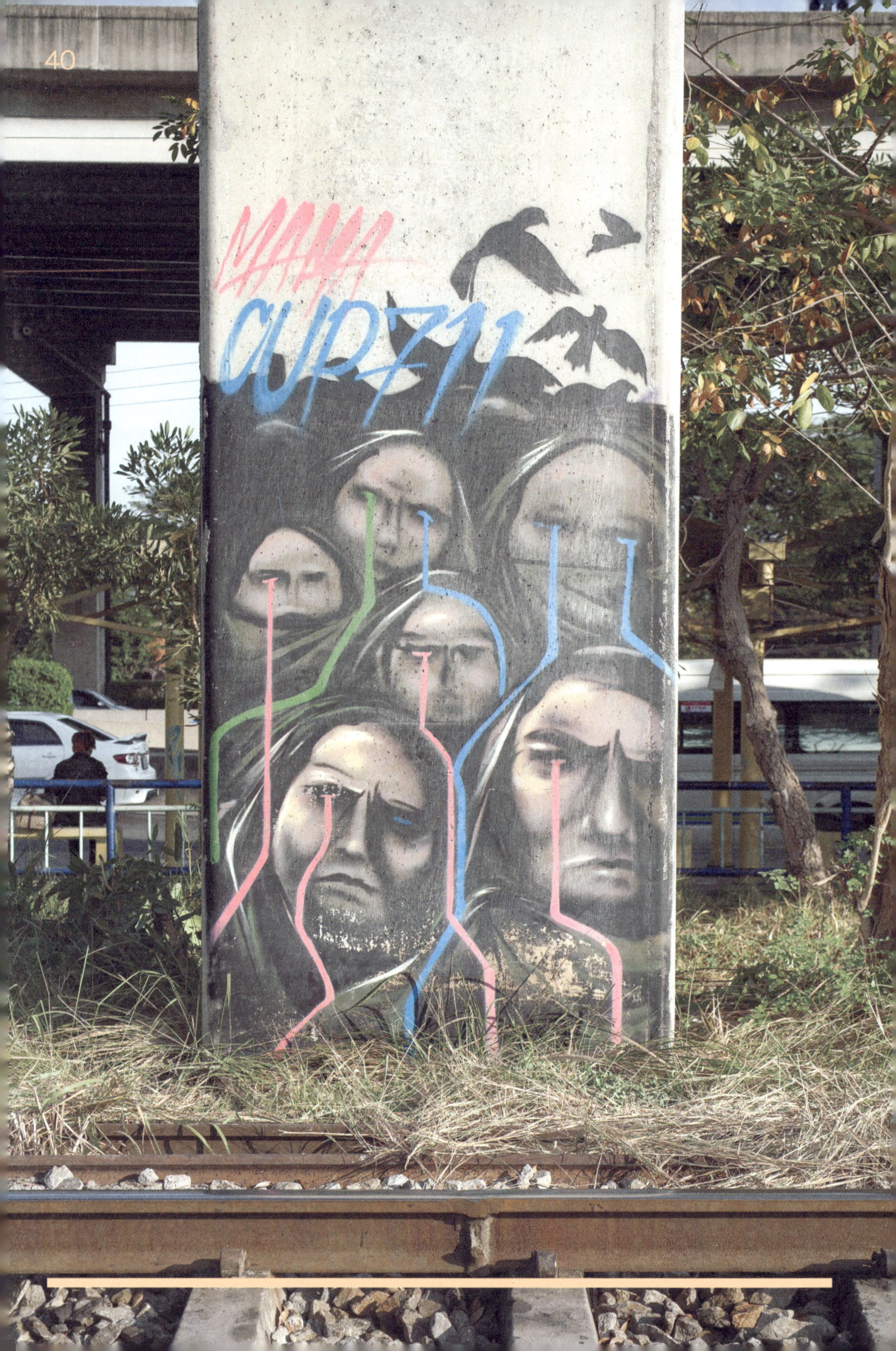

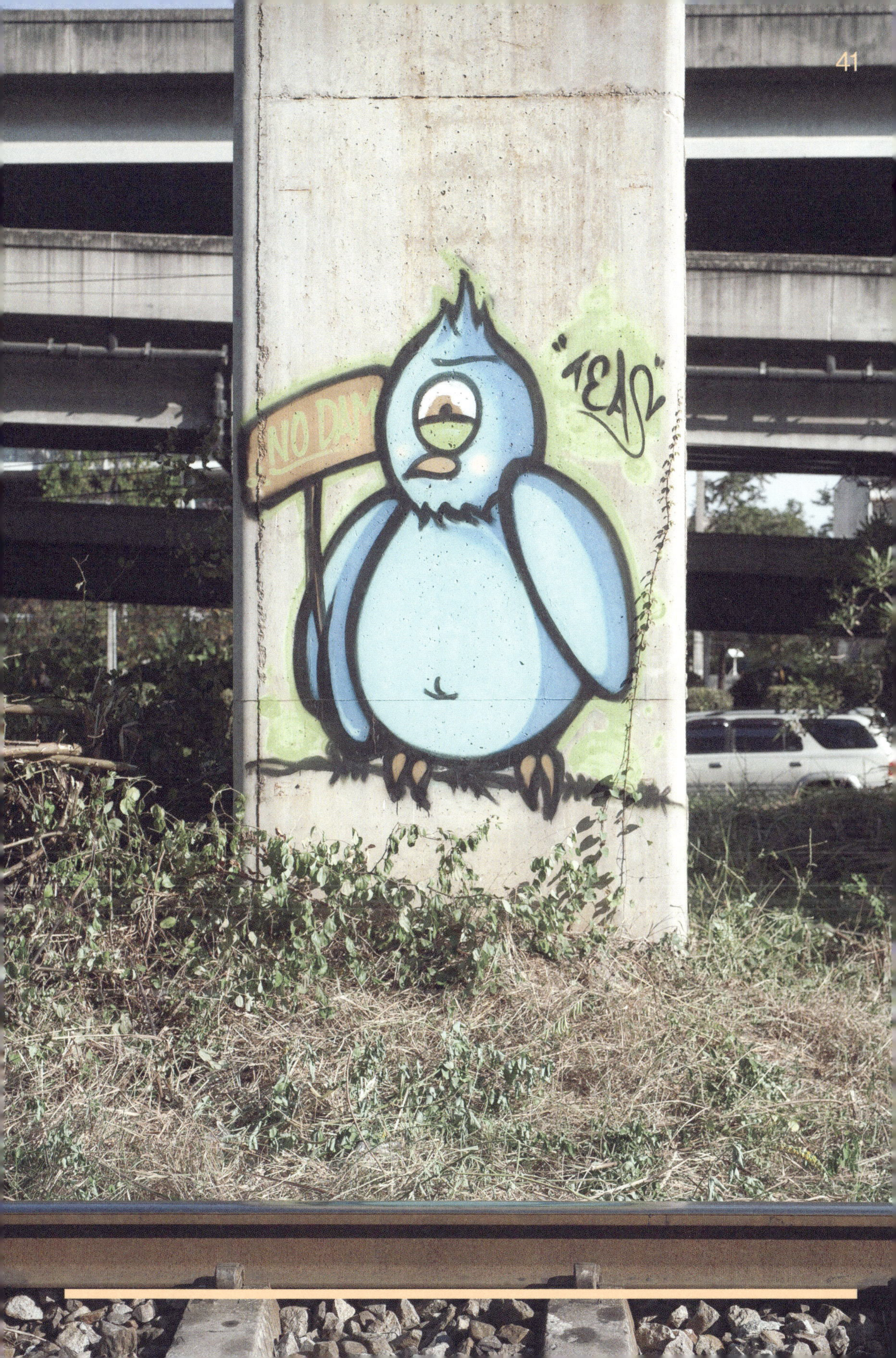
NO DAM

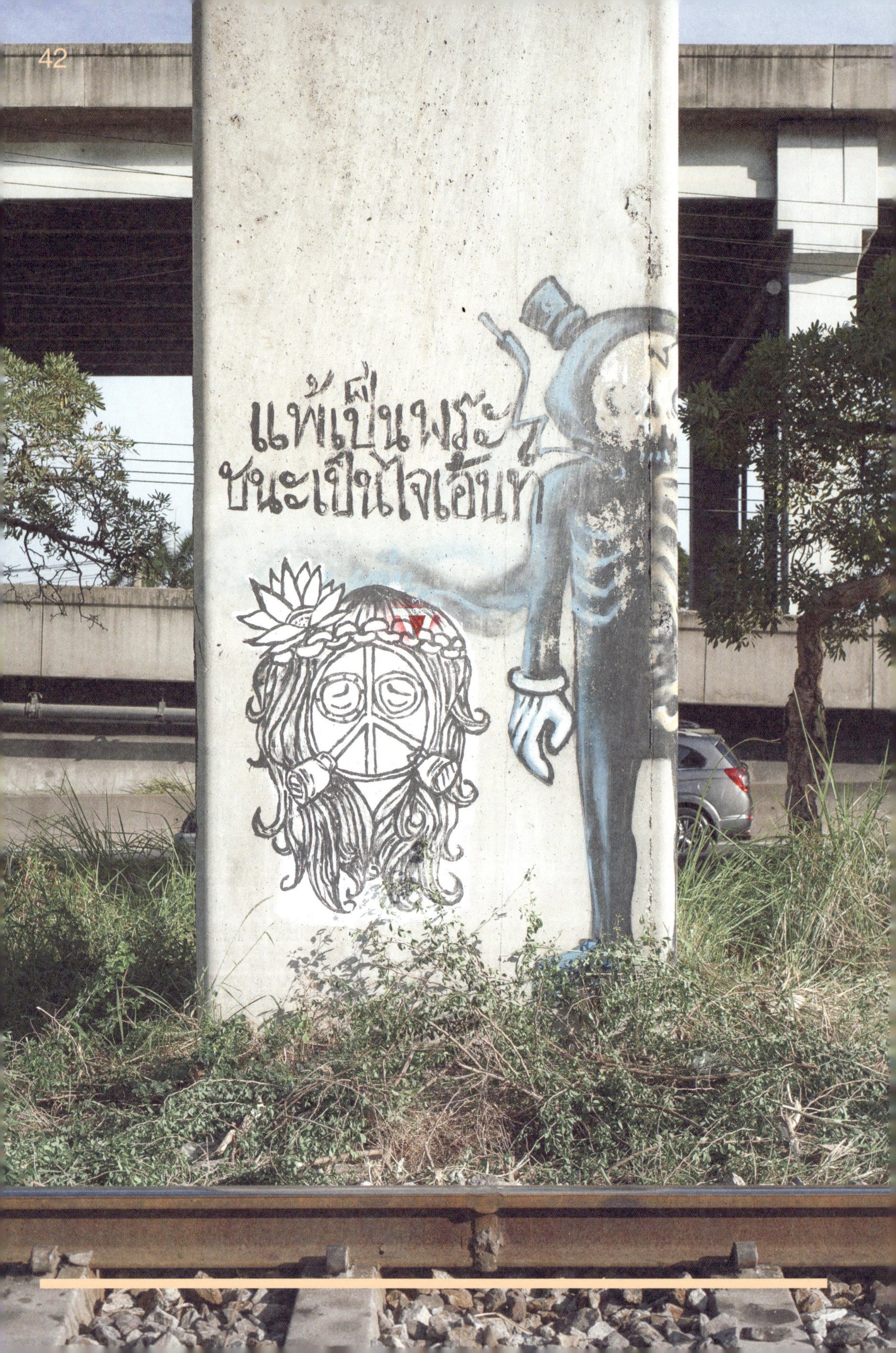
แพ้เป็นพระ
ชนะเป็นไจเอ็นท

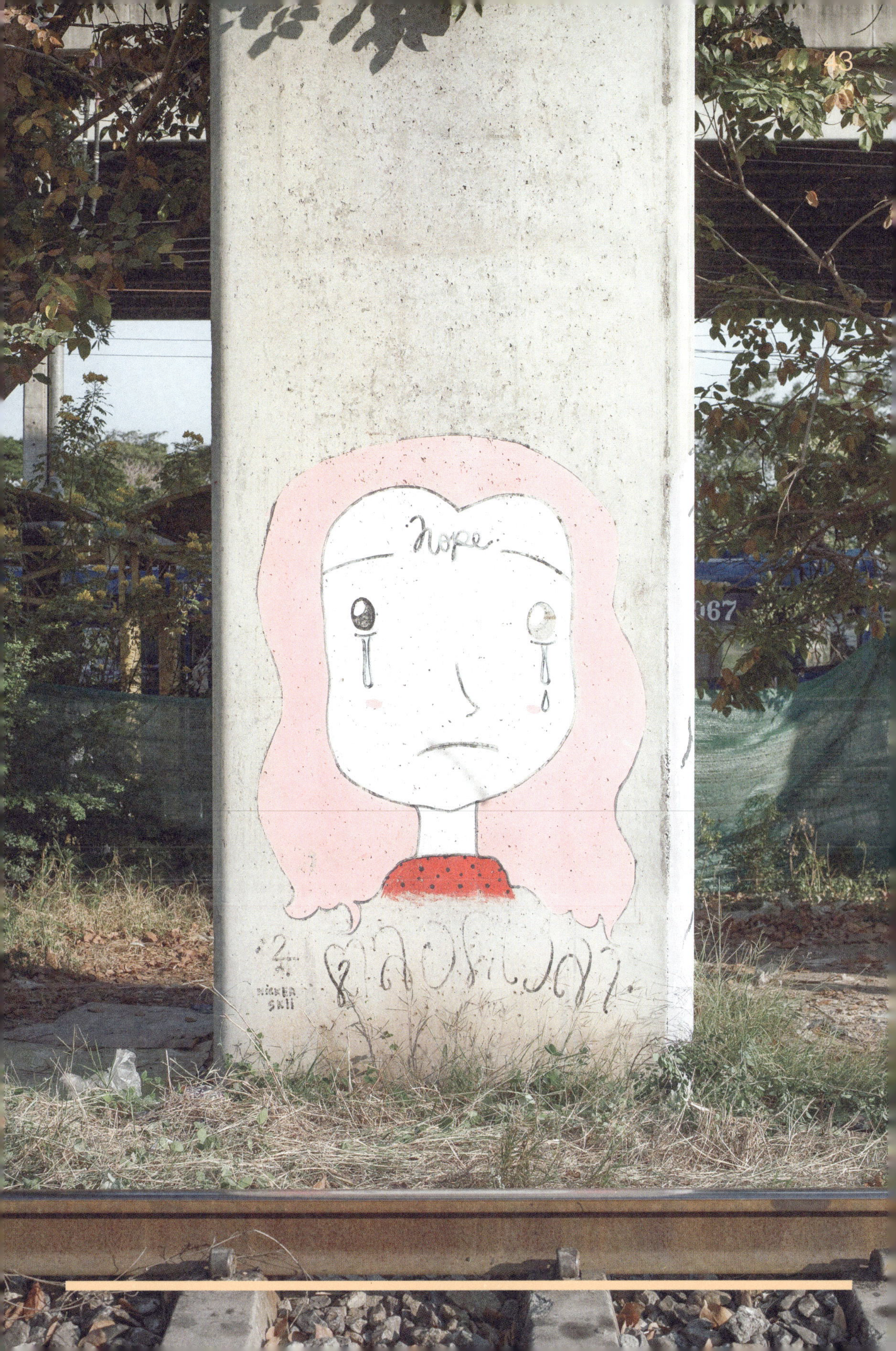
hope

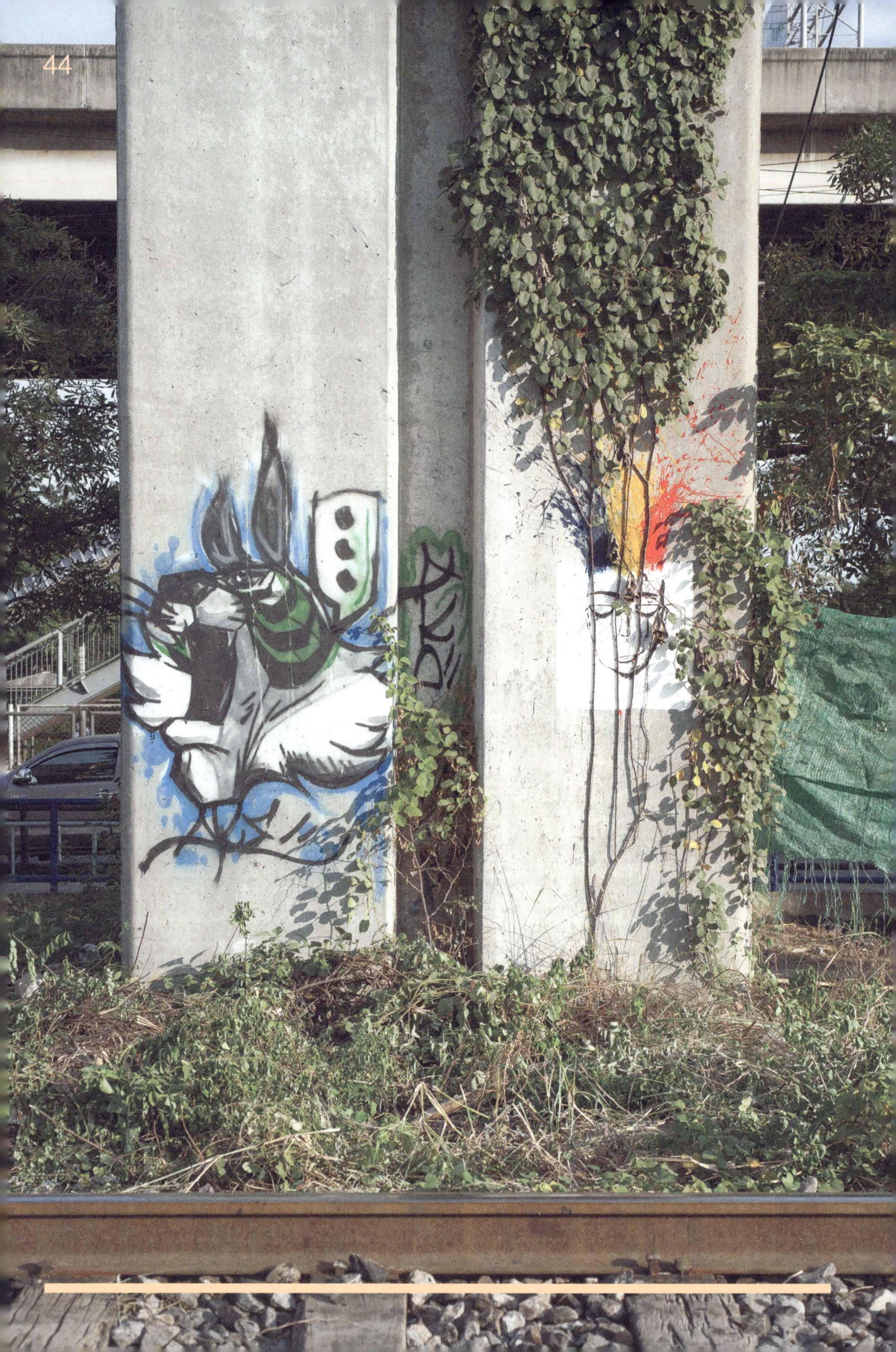

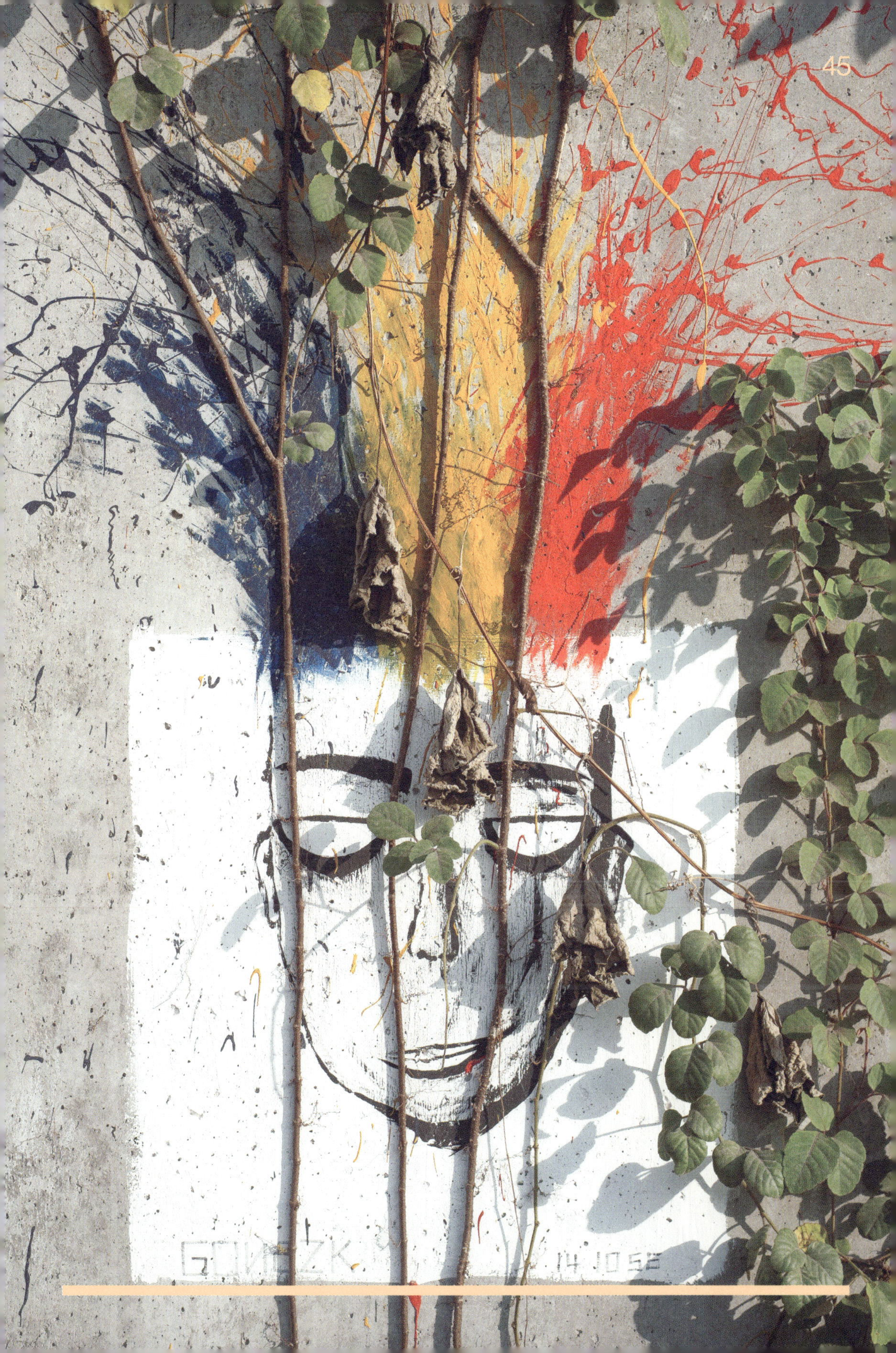

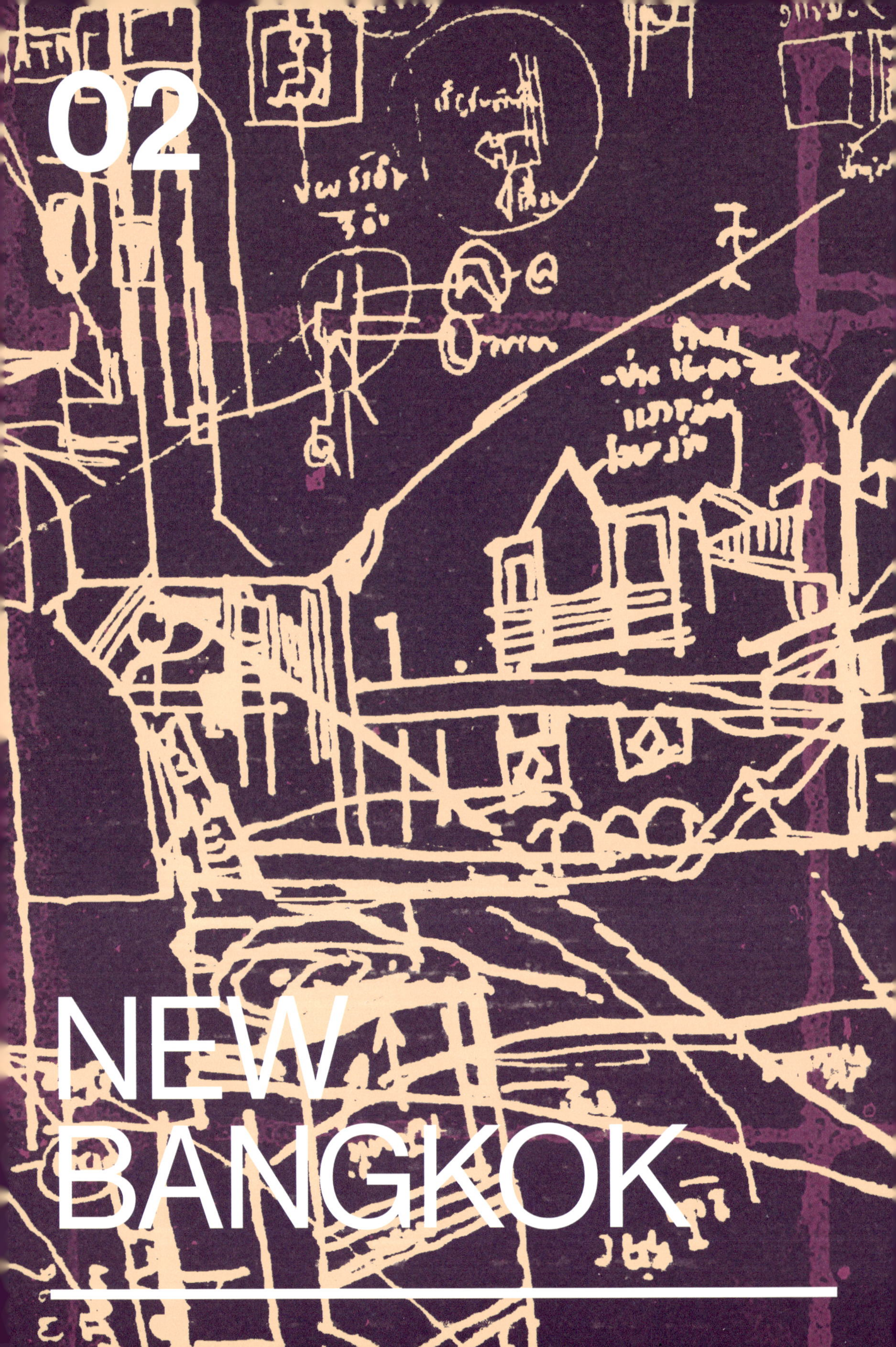
02
NEW
BANGKOK

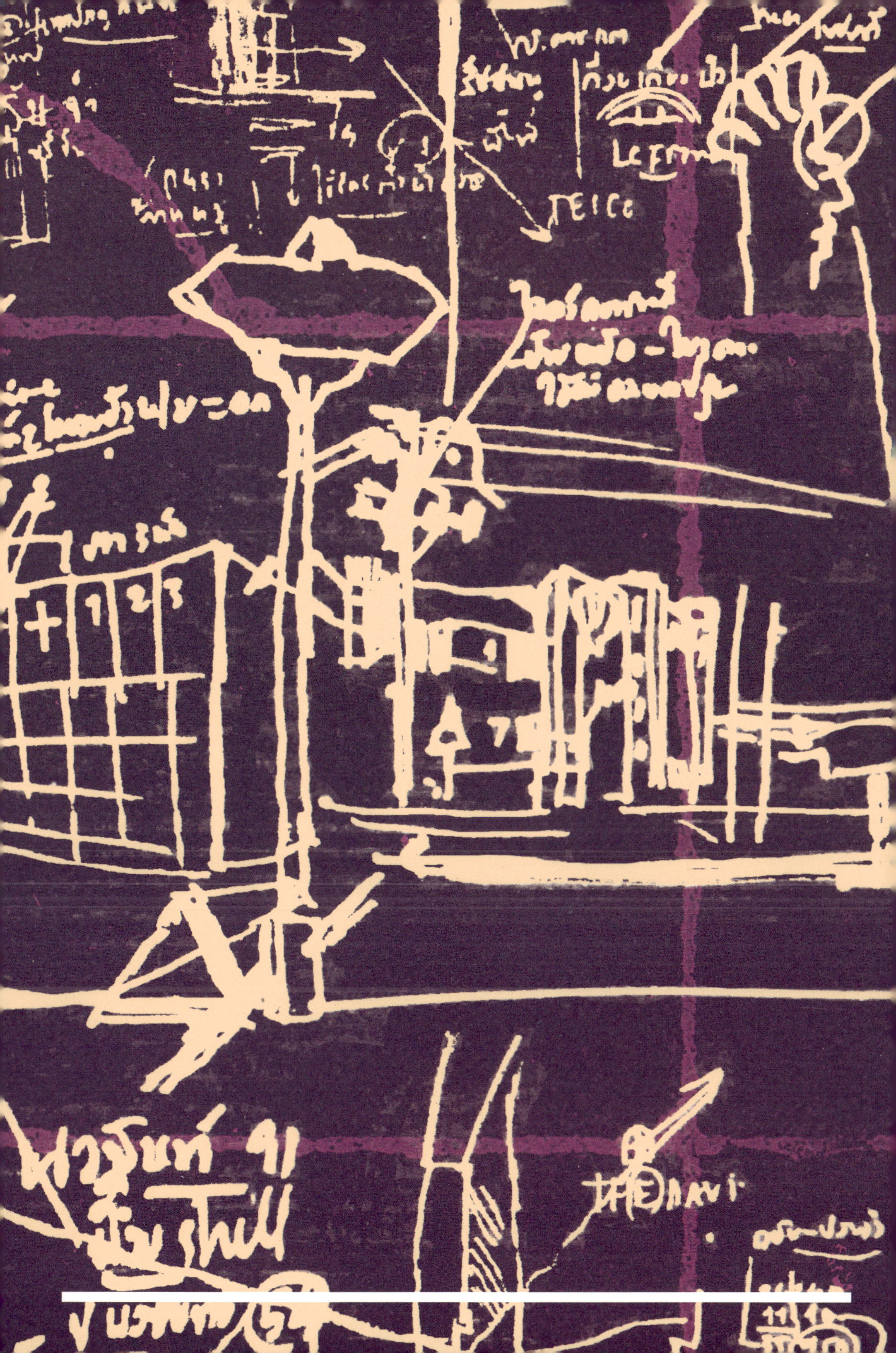

Much of Hopewell's street art was created around Bang Khen Station and Wat Samian Nari. Over several years, this area witnessed the construction of the new, State Railway of Thailand (SRT) elevated Dark Red Line. A series of new stations were built heading north from Chatuchak, including at Bang Khen during 2018 and 2019. The old Bang Khen Station has hand-painted signs, kept crisp with regular touch ups. Pot plants huddle at the feet of recycled-rail-line columns that hold up the station's rusty iron roof. Passengers buy tickets from a hole cut into the side of a demountable shed. Bits and pieces of railway apparatus lie about. The new Bang Khen Station was built just up the line. It's like any other of Bangkok's elevated rail line stations – bland. It's a facsimile of a thousand other railway stations across the world, projecting a vision of the future without the past. And, unlike the old station, which tolerated its strange street-art neighbours, this new station brought with it the erasure of the art depicted in this book – officially buffed to remove imperfection and complexity. Somehow, this transformation at Bang Khen Station is also the story of Bangkok – the old giving way to the new.

Bangkok, c. 1964

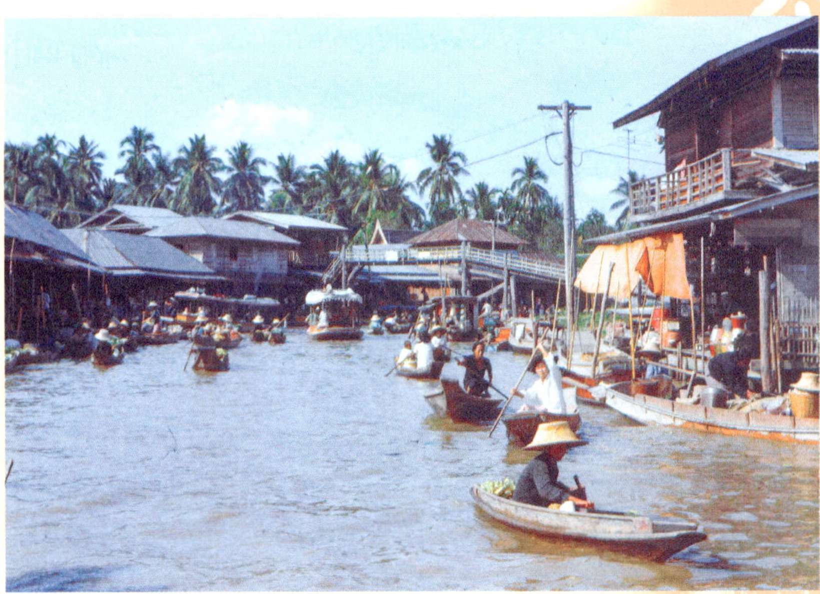

It was amongst this New Bangkok, torn by development, that Thai street art and graffiti laid their roots. The city's entrenched transport problems were what Hopewell was meant to have solved but, instead, came to symbolise. Street artists and graffiti writers have a honed view of Bangkok's character. They constantly scan the city for good places to create their art. They are attuned to the rolling nature of development. Bangkok's urban cementscape is their studio and their muse, its walls their canvas. They are usually people who have something to say, contrarians speaking outside the normal confines of visual art – museums, galleries, books. Some were born in Bangkok and others, like many of its residents, came here from the provinces, looking for what they couldn't find at home – drawn to the city's undeniable vitality and then becoming trapped by it.

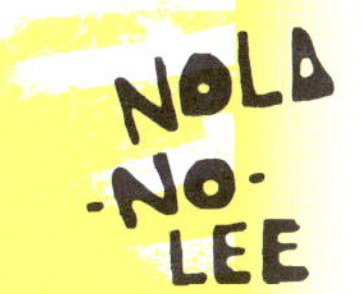

"I've lived in Bangkok for ten years and I love it so much. I like people-watching and love parties. I like witnessing city people. People who live in big cities are a little more aggressive. My street art is mostly to do with people. I retell these stories sarcastically and mockingly in my own style."

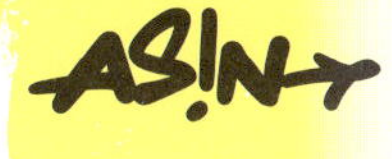

"I like and dislike Bangkok at the same time. I like the night time and long holidays when Bangkok locals leave town. I also like how charming Bangkok's old city is. There is beautiful architecture in Khao San, Ratchadamnoen and Sao Ching Cha. You walk past the Grand Palace and you will come across Khlong Lod, Trok Sake and then a slum. This is its charm. That's why I like it."

Bangkok was always a city of many faces. It started life split between a royal, administrative island and a surrounding water-based collection of *yan*, or small hamlets. These prenatal suburbs had particular industrial purposes. Locals lived in the same area they worked in. The royal core was separate from the rest of the city until the reign of King Rama V who emulated grand European capitals by building boulevards and shopping promenades out from the palaces. These roads were the beginning of the strip development that is seen today. At that time, people moved through the city along *khlongs* (canals) in shallow draught canoes (see opposite). These waterways were vital, tree-lined arteries, not merely drains as many are today. Bangkok truly was an urban jungle. Travelling along the low canals, you would hardly have been aware of the city at all. The trees enveloped everything. Many lived in timber huts huddled by the water's edge. People bathed, washed clothes and lived their lives connected via water. By the beginning of the 20th century, many people lived in one or two-storey timber and brick homes that allowed the sounds of neighbours and the outside world to bleed in. They were aware of the city around them, and of the lives of people living nearby. This kind of life is still known today in some areas, but for many of Bangkok's residents, it's a way of living relegated to the past.

Not many buildings rose taller than four storeys in the 1960s and early '70s. In the Old Bangkok, before 1960, intact webs of memory had spun out over generations, making up communities and traditions (see next page). During the '70s and '80s, entire areas of that city were replaced as Bangkok boomed. The first influx of development that arrived in the late '50s brought with it the tail end of international modernism, by then distilled into sparse brutality. The *khlongs* and their role receded. Their soft green banks were beaten back with cement walls that separated people from the water. In other areas, families were kicked off land they had occupied for generations, and, due to unclear land tenure, received little or no compensation. Lower-income families survived away from developed areas. As established communities were disrupted, the city also lost much of its built and cultural heritage – Bangkok's people were discovering what it meant for a traditional people to live in a modern city. Things had changed drastically and faster than anybody could control. In the late 1970s, attempts to moderate development came too late and did little to stop unplanned growth. As a result, this Old Bangkok is now buried.

Bangkok, 1951

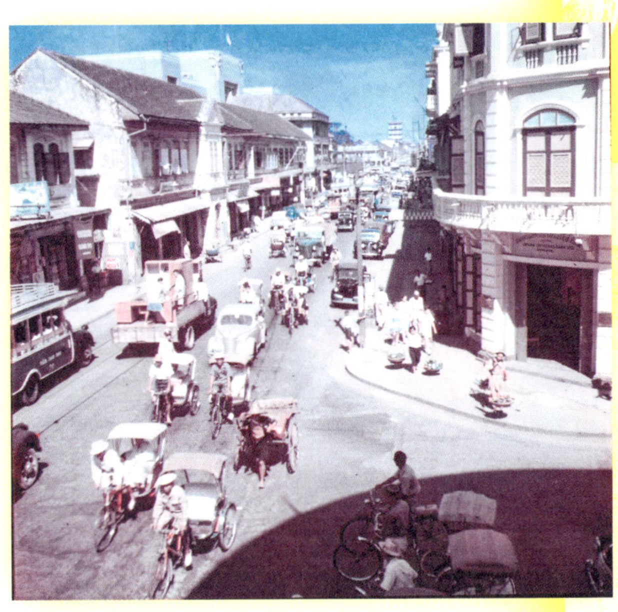

·MUEBON·

"The world is changing all the time. Everything evolves. Nothing lasts forever. We just need to understand that and come to terms with it. Personally, I am in favour of change if it makes people's lives better. The problem lies with the process of change, not with change itself. Ridiculous. For example, a one-hundred-year-old building was demolished just so it could be rebuilt to be the same as the old building. Why? They could have renovated it. But of course that would have required a smaller budget. They wanted a bigger budget. It's corruption. It's the process of change that is screwed up, in my opinion. This is people's taxes, after all."

Those with the most wealth shape much of the city. At the same time, large areas have been moulded by millions of powerless people. Entire neighbourhoods were created without permission. These two forces differ in the permanence of their impact. The monarchs, the government, the army and their business associates have created long-lasting features in stone, cement and steel. Those occupying what is leftover, create monuments of plastic, wood and discarded roofing – the planned and unplanned.

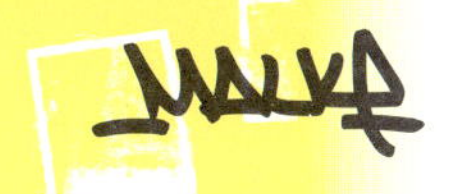

"Thailand has been a developing country for a very long time. Too long! This development has been without a clear direction or plan. There's been too little attention on the environment and the use of urban space."

Bangkok is typical of major commercial centres in the Asian region such as Manila, Jakarta, Hong Kong, Singapore, Kuala Lumpur and Phnom Penh. Such places were developed over the last five decades with little consideration of the costs of changing so much, so quickly. They often struggle with transport problems, lack of green space, an imbalance between informal street-based economies and shopping malls, and with defining their identities. Many of these cities now cling to the last remnants of their heritage, smothering authenticity.

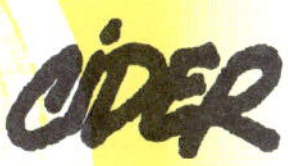

"Now, Bangkok is like any big city. It's like Shanghai or Hong Kong. You can buy the same things in Hong Kong as you can here. People look the same. Fashion, lifestyles, trends and even the people, they all look the same. Strange but true. So Bangkok is like any other big city, you know. The beauty of it? It's still got some temples going on. It's still got some old culture going on. But the young are forgetting the old culture due to globalization."

HEAD ACHE

"If you want to come to Bangkok, don't. Just stay in your country – it's the same thing, stay in your downtown."

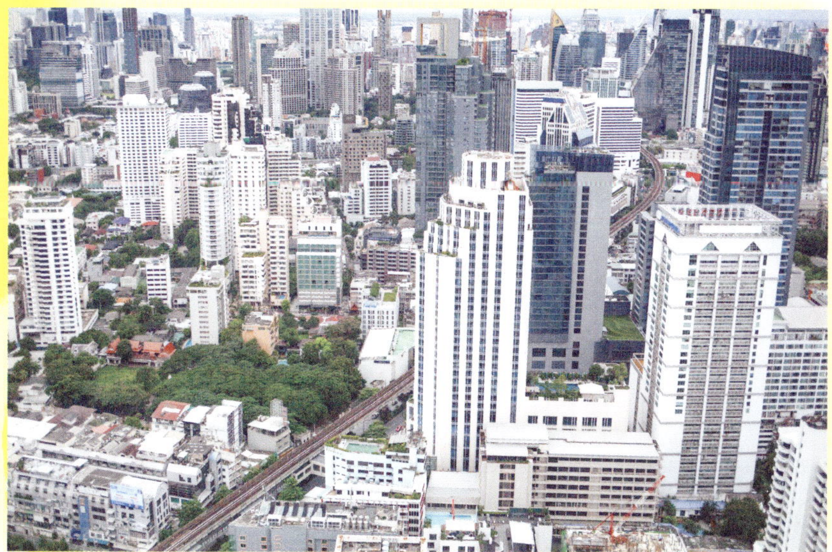

Bangkok, 2021

This New Bangkok (see previous page) hasn't entirely replaced the Old Bangkok. New development often presents a commercial face hiding more intimate neighbourhoods behind. Patches of meaning and character survive. Street vendors still work, despite government attempts to remove them. These conservationists of vibrancy retain their importance. The *paak soi* (mouth of the lane) is still a focus of community and commerce.

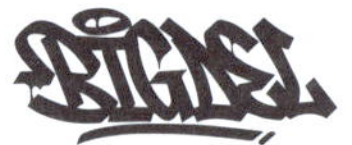

"Bangkok is changing a lot. Every city around the world is changing a lot. But in the process of changing there is still something there. Maybe you have the new Skytrain coming, but people still drive motorbikes the wrong way on the footpath. In the changing, there are also some things that are not changed. Things go forward and go backwards at the same time in Bangkok. Physically, some things are good but, mentally, things seem to be going backwards."

This New Bangkok fed unfamiliar lifestyles into Thailand. In the 1970s, as homes were built in the new suburbs, young couples rejoiced in their independence and fled family compounds – a tradition that saw several generations live on the same land. And so, a way of living was broken. High-rise development boomed. And in modern apartment towers, residents became compartmentalised, isolated in the sky and separated from the street and its sounds. Many of these towers turned their backs on the old *khlongs* and dominated small streets, which had once meandered organically through leafy residential neighbourhoods.

HEAD ACHE

"We never feel a brotherhood anymore. When I was young, I knew the house next door. I knew all the names of the people in there. Now people don't know the next house. People in Bangkok are living in a rush. You have to get up early to go out to work, come back home on the road, traffic for two hours. You reach home in the evening. You are fucking tired. You go to bed. No time to know anybody. But outside Bangkok they still know each other. They still have the village leader. When I was young, they had neighbourhood leaders in Bangkok, but not now. Now people have no family. You have no friends in the city. If I could choose, I would not stay here."

The trees that once made Bangkok part of the nation's wilderness, disappeared until much of the greenery left was strangled by cement and power cables or reduced to living ornaments for corporate forecourts. The generous ability of the city to shelter its residents during the hot months with a dense canopy was lost and air-conditioning became a necessity. As the city boomed, traffic congestion worsened. In response, highways were constructed without much planning. Putting cars before walking and cycling, resulted in an unwelcoming city.

American money flowed into Bangkok as Thailand became involved in the Cold War, and later, a base for the Vietnam War. This presence brought with it, an influx of American culture, music, clothes, fashion. This was the birth of Thailand's modern service industries. Along with hotels and clubs, the drug trade and sex industry also grew. Bangkok, and its new hybrid culture, was populated more and more by rural Thais who left behind older ways of living to find a job in the big city. As the city became busier, higher, less friendly and more maze-like, the shopping mall arrived.

Today, these malls are perhaps the most visible face of Bangkok, along with the palaces and temples – the commercial, the sacred and the royal. The malls that first arrived in the 1970s, were larger, contemporary expressions of the commercialism that had always been here. These new shopping places arrived very differently in a neighbourhood, though. The old shopping streets and markets had evolved organically, part of the city's history and people. Malls arrived in a year or so, synthetic and obliterating what went before. They contain collections of activities that would have previously been distributed across a neighbourhood – interwoven between homes, industries and places of worship. Where they do connect with the street, malls blur the delineation between public and private space. The streets around them are often co-opted into moving people quickly and easily from one mall to the next.

·MUEBON·

"If everywhere was filled with advertisements focussed on making people desire and consume, that would be a kind of never-ending brainwashing – keeping us deprived of liveliness and creativity. Public artworks are like an antidote to that. They help people who come across them by directly or indirectly broadening their imagination, stimulating the creative part of their brains, and increasing their sense of humour and awareness. The government should designate more public spaces for art rather than letting capitalism hypnotise people everywhere with advertisements."

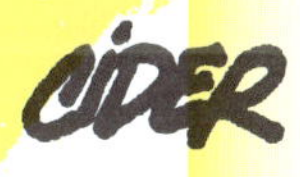

"Some people see development as a way for companies to make money out of Asia. The new takes over. You take over the country with a brand like McDonald's or Uniqlo, whatever."

In these commercial areas there is no place to stop. Those who dare to rest on a step, and don't look like customers, are moved on by security. Shopping malls like Icon Siam, Paragon, Central Lat Phrao and dozens of others sanitise the streets they exist on to make their interiors appear more inviting.

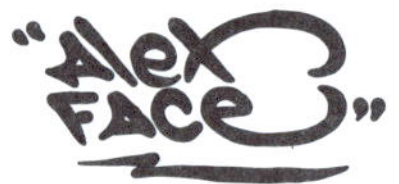

"I don't know if I like Bangkok or hate it. But I travel a lot, and when I fly back and step into Suvarnabhumi Airport I still feel, 'Yes! I'm here in Bangkok.' But when I live here, sometimes I'm like, 'Oh, I hate Bangkok.' I like Bangkok more than I hate it. If you're stuck in a traffic jam, yeah that's when you don't like it. But there are things I like about Bangkok – the food, and I can get anything I want. Bangkok is a really good place for art. I can make anything here. It's a really good place to make art. It's so big. I think I have to live in Bangkok forever."

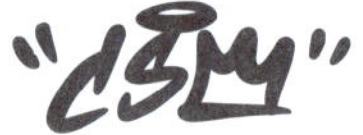

"Bangkok people are very individualistic. It's unique and diverse. Bangkok would be more liveable without corruption. Without corruption, roads and facilities would be so much better. I don't want to live in Bangkok, but we are all trapped. It has a lot of good things and potential. The uniqueness of Thai people is happiness. Most people are friendly. But because of the economic issues and the problems that occur in the city, it makes people stressed, and they struggle. The stress makes them unhappy. They don't smile or act in a friendly manner anymore."

HEAD ACHE

"Bangkok is full of sick things. People in Bangkok are angry because of the stress of living. Thai people drink and party all the time. We are a party country. We try to say we are a religious country, but we are a party country. Thai people are happy, Thai people smile. But we stopped smiling because of politics."

Aside from some surviving areas where long-standing communities have managed to cling to the fabric their ancestors gave them, Bangkok has changed so irrevocably that it's hard to tell what exactly has been lost and gained. Bit-by-bit, Old Bangkok, low-rise and leafy, gave way to New Bangkok, what we see today. It's in this city that graffiti was born in Thailand. This child of destruction is a remedy for the nausea of a commercially ruled cement city.

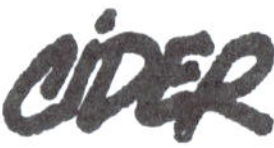

"Bangkok is a grey city. Everything has been sold over to make condos. You don't see any traditional buildings anymore. Unless you are really connected, you'll get bullied or they'll burn that shit down if you don't sell up. Bangkok has to develop, it has to grow."

• • •

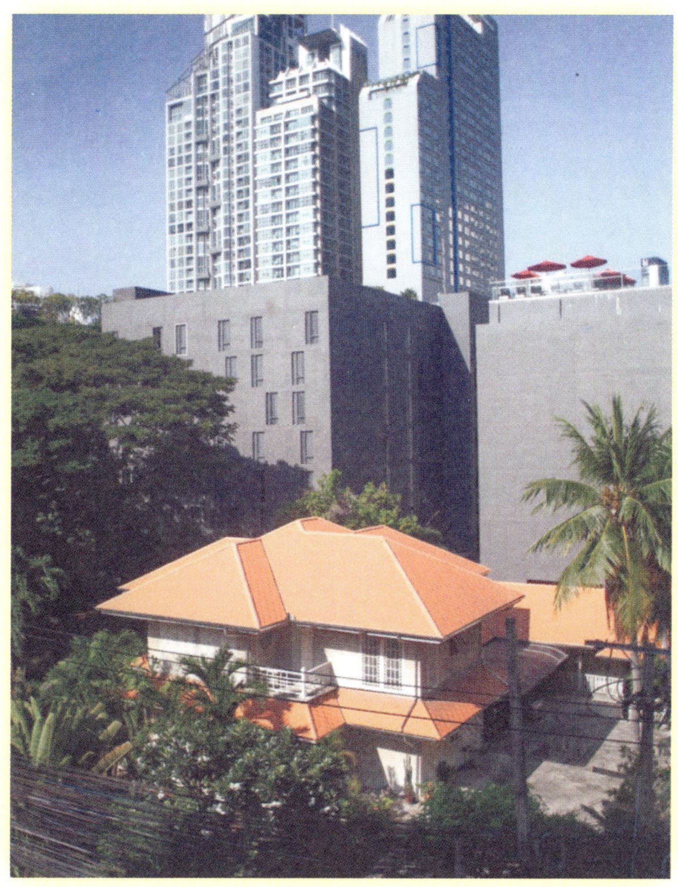

Despite such enormous change, Bangkok tells its story well (see above). Like its constantly changing graffiti and street art, the city is a jumble of superimpositions scribbled on top of one and other. Thailand's kaleidoscopic modern cultural history can be read here. It's the story of an ancient people propelled at speed into a future that most of them could never have imagined.

Rukkit

"I like Bangkok and its variety. I like how it's not very organised. An area might be well developed but right next to it there are holes on the street, water can't go down the drains. It is necessary to develop each area of Bangkok equally."

NOLA -NO- LEE

"I like the fakeness and pretentiousness in city people. They have so many charming qualities. When I take myself to different places, I find many stories to tell. Different places give me drawing ideas. I especially like Khao San and Silom. I'm an observer. I like to go where there are a lot of people and observe their behaviour."

Bangkok was built while the world grew connected through the mercantile and military expansion of the Chinese and later, the Europeans. The previous royal capital, Ayutthaya was destroyed by the Burmese in 1767. Away from the charred ruins of that great city, the new royal capital was established at Bangkok, after a brief interlude at Thonburi. The new founder of the Chakri Dynasty, Rama I, revived the smouldering symbols of the monarchy and re-defined national identity.

A fittingly auspicious name was given:

The City of Angels, Great City, the Residence of the Emerald Buddha, Capital of the World Endowed with Nine Precious Gems, the Happy City Abounding in Great Royal Palaces which Resembles the Heavenly Abode Wherein Dwell the Reincarnated Gods, A City Given by Indra and Built by Vishnukarn.

Its founding caught the end of the Chinese Junk trade that had dominated the region for centuries. The city did well out of it, and many peoples made a home there – Armenians, Burmese, Indians, Chinese and others. Soon, a new sun would rise in the west, the empire of the British with their guns, ships, and curiously effective way of breaking up and dominating much of the world. The Thai kings negotiated their way out of colonisation by opening their markets.

Over the coming centuries, Bangkok became a stage, trampled under foot, where the nation danced its identity. The footprints left can be tracked along pathways through Thai history – with graffiti and street art being some of the latest and most fascinating. By mixing various permutations of tradition and change, internal and external with attitudes, behaviours and symbols of what it means to be modern, Thainess is performed here.

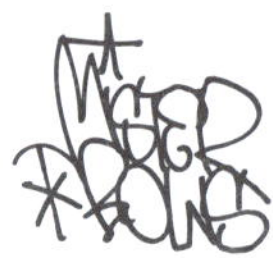

"I was born in this city and I love this city. I love how it evolves all the time. I started doing graffiti and meeting other artists in Bangkok and other provinces."

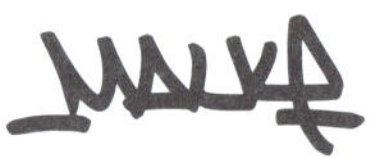

"Bangkok is a standout city when it comes to different art styles. Because it's a capital city, there is a variety of art to be seen. Also, Bangkok is suitable for modern art. Modern art is not going to fit well with rural Thailand. Bangkok is a perfect place for you to come and work with a clear goal in mind. For example, sometimes I just come to Bangkok for three days to paint a building and then return home."

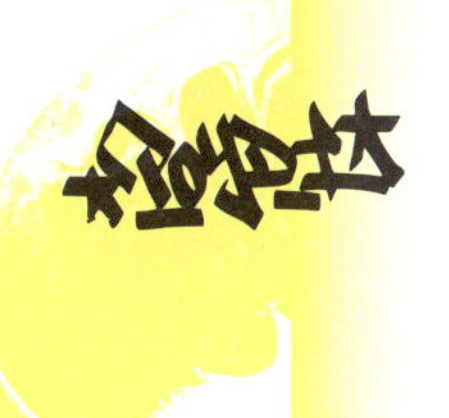

"There is an art museum in Bangkok, so I can look around and get inspired by pieces here. There are more opportunities to see works and meet artists here in Bangkok. There are lots of galleries. Bangkok is like the centre of everything in Thailand."

Experimentation with graffiti, hip-hop culture and modern street art, is a continuation of Bangkok's dual role as anchor and catalyst – itself an old tradition. The style and behaviours of those US-born art movements were modified in Thailand to become tools of history-making and part of what it takes to be fashionable. Fifty years of unprecedented change swept over Bangkok – the resulting loss of so many cultural anchor points left a chasm between those who have the power to imprint their story, and those who don't. As the focus where powerful people sanction nationhood, Bangkok is also where those outside that privileged troupe interject with their own movements. Graffiti writers and street artists interrupt the conventional governing of who speaks in public space and has the power to influence the Thai public.

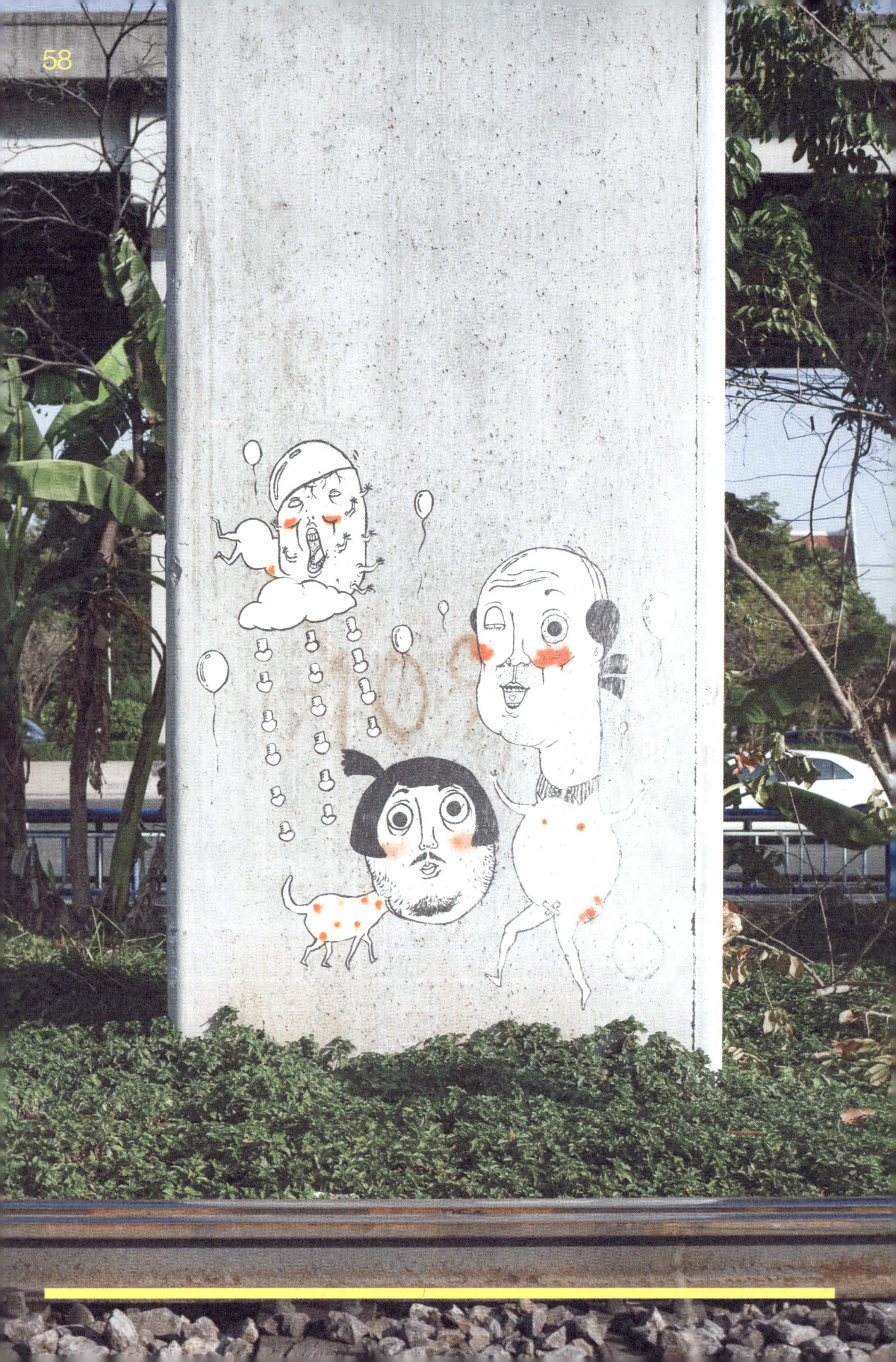

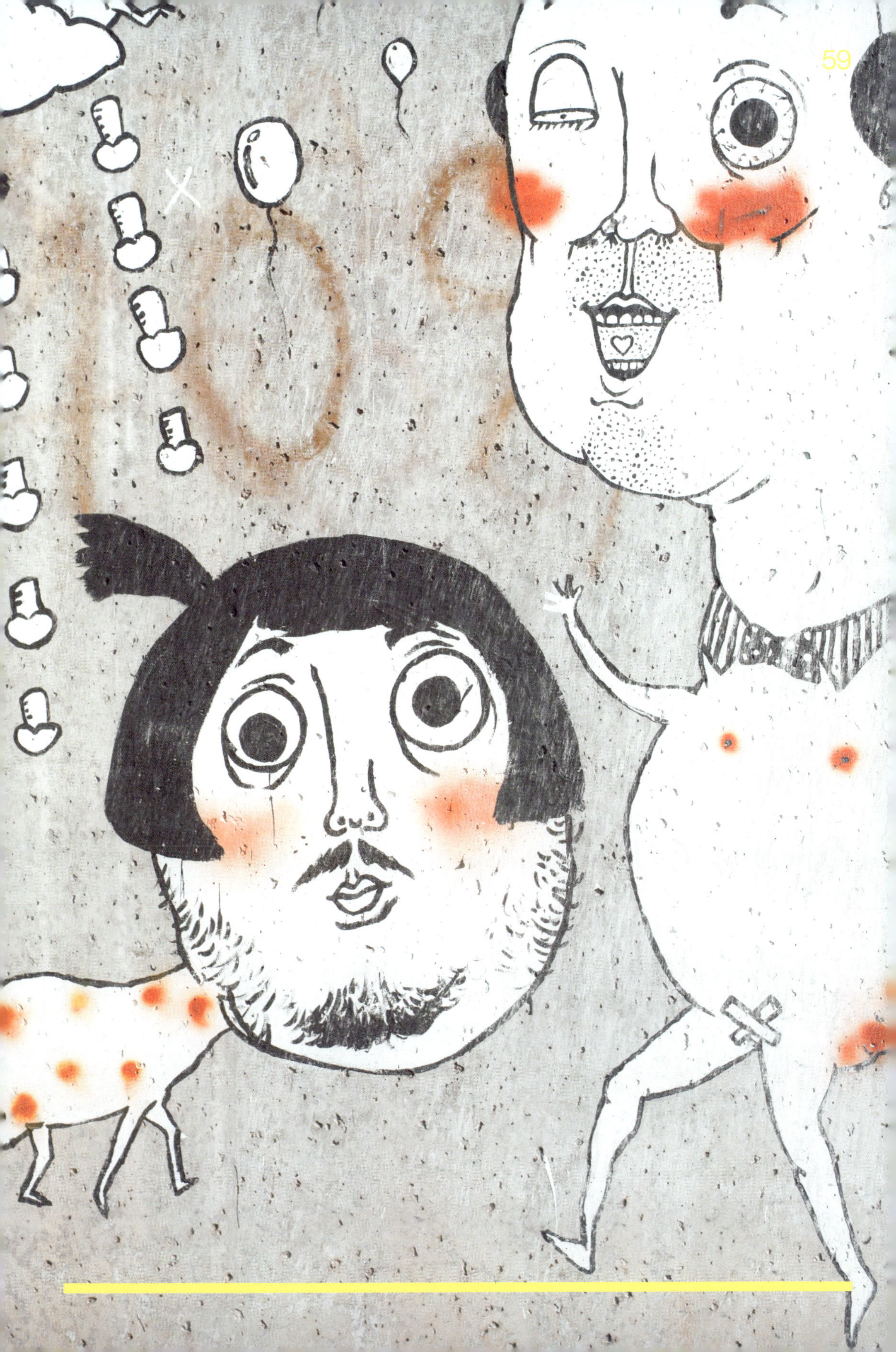

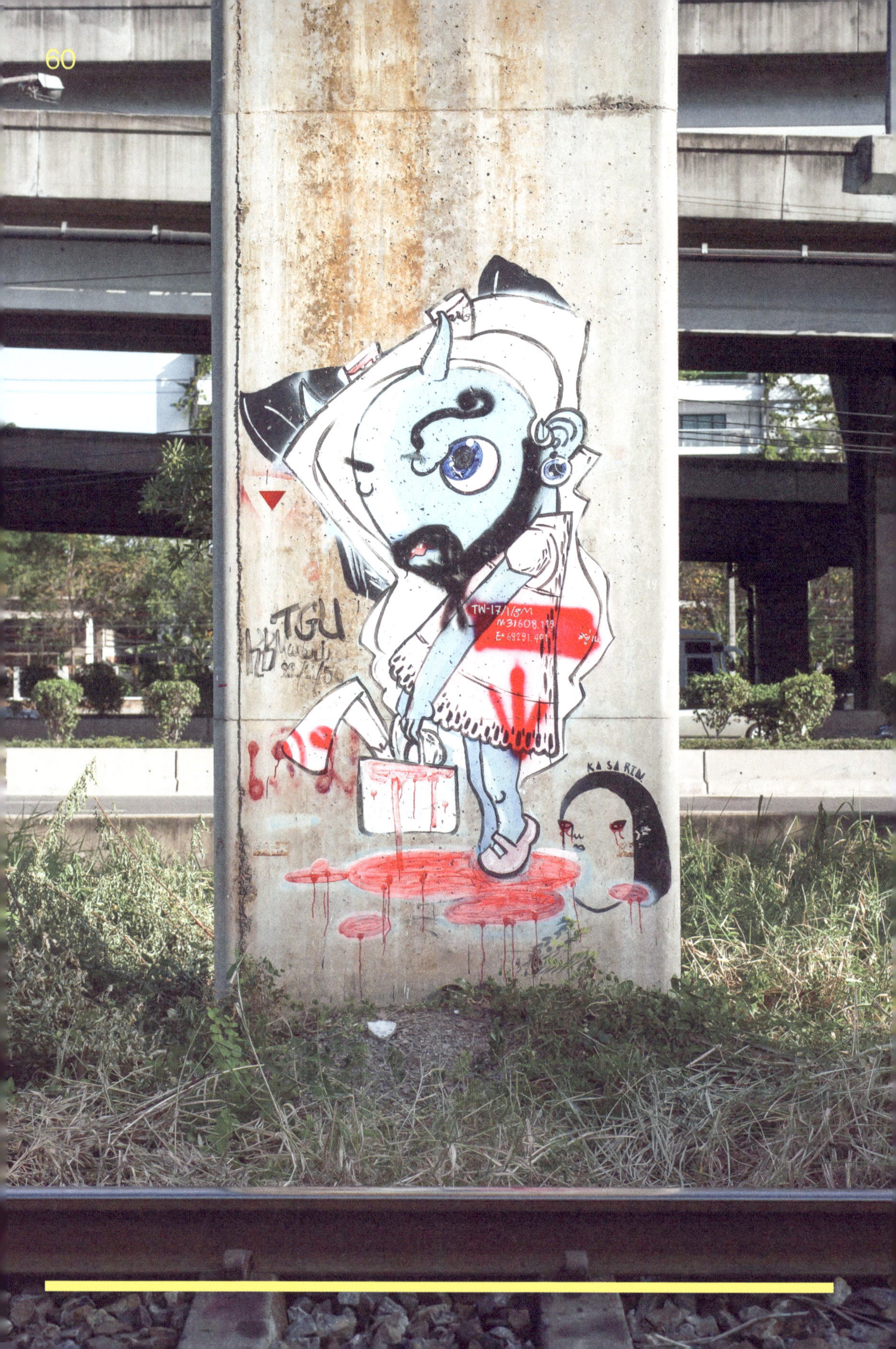
TGU
TW-17/1/5M
N=31608.119
E=69291.401
KASARIN

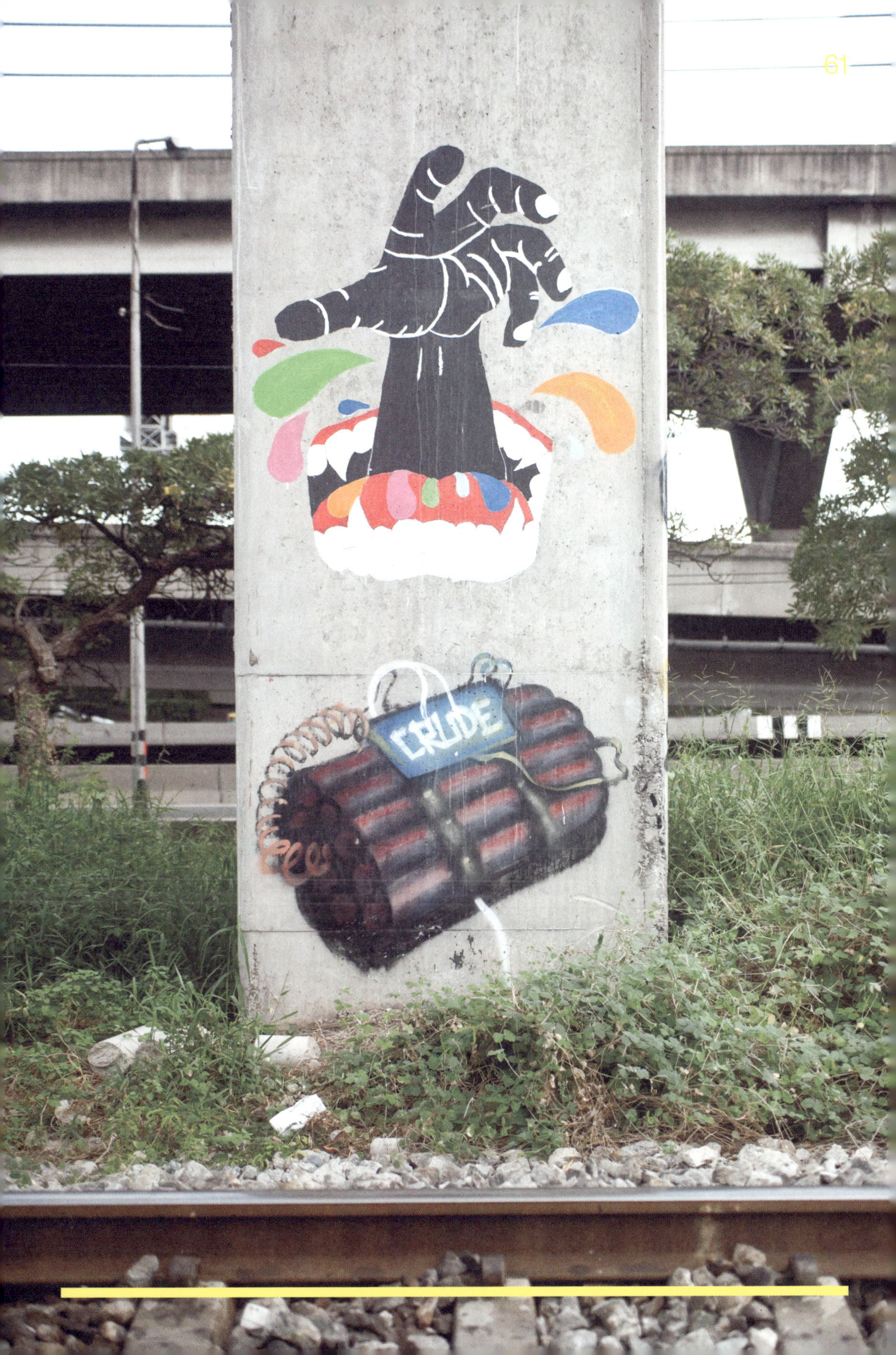
CRUDE

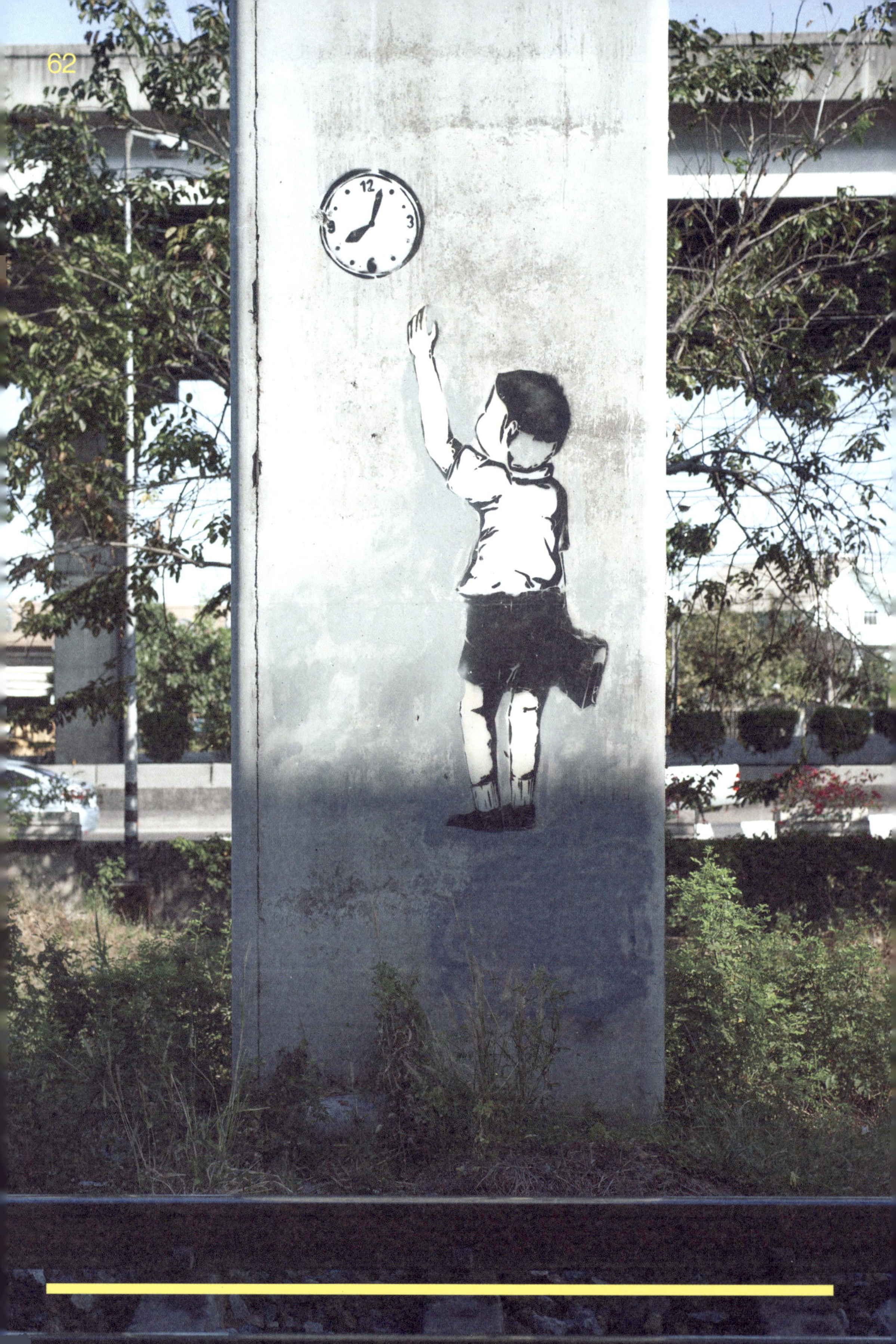

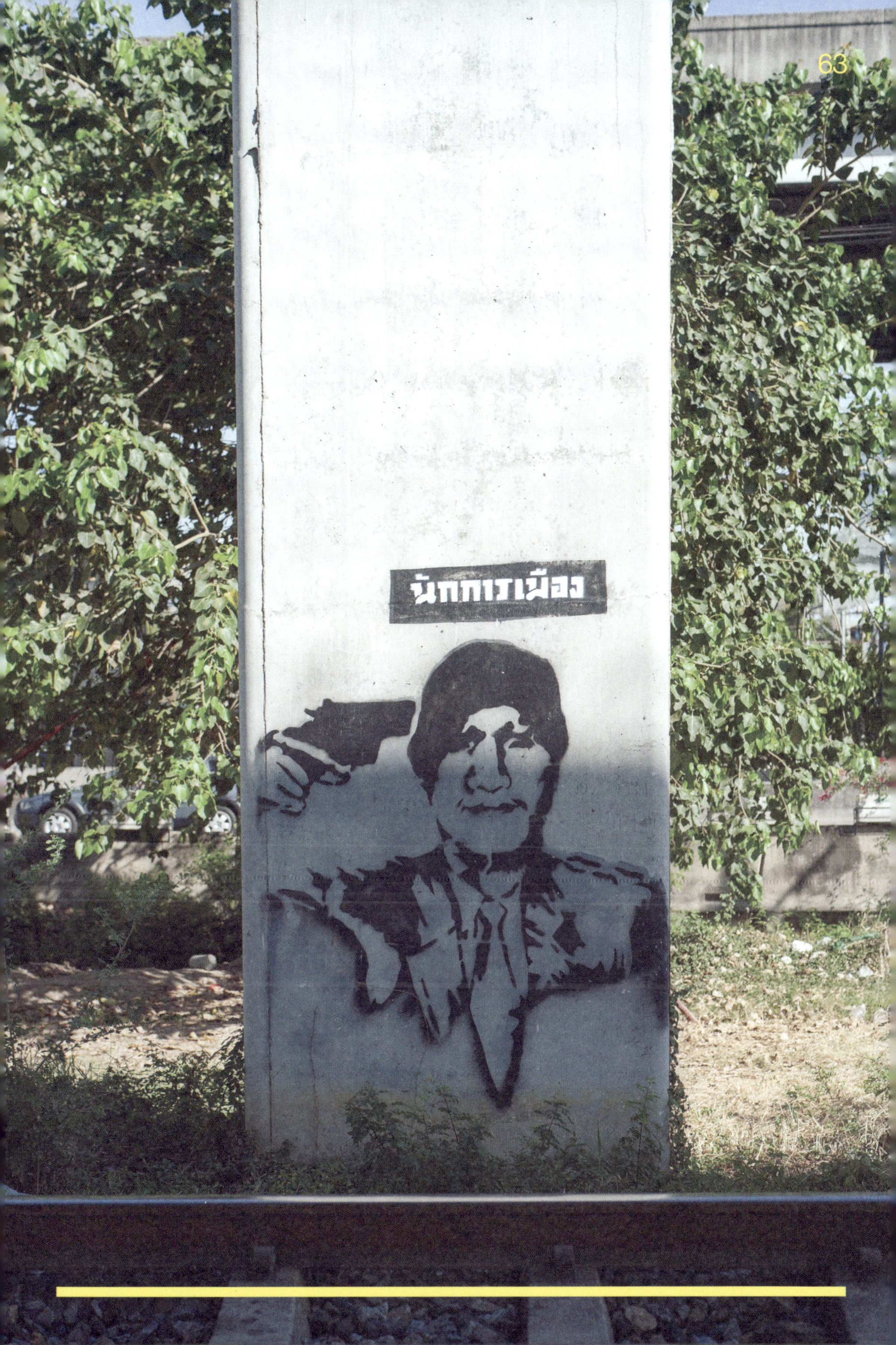
นักการเมือง

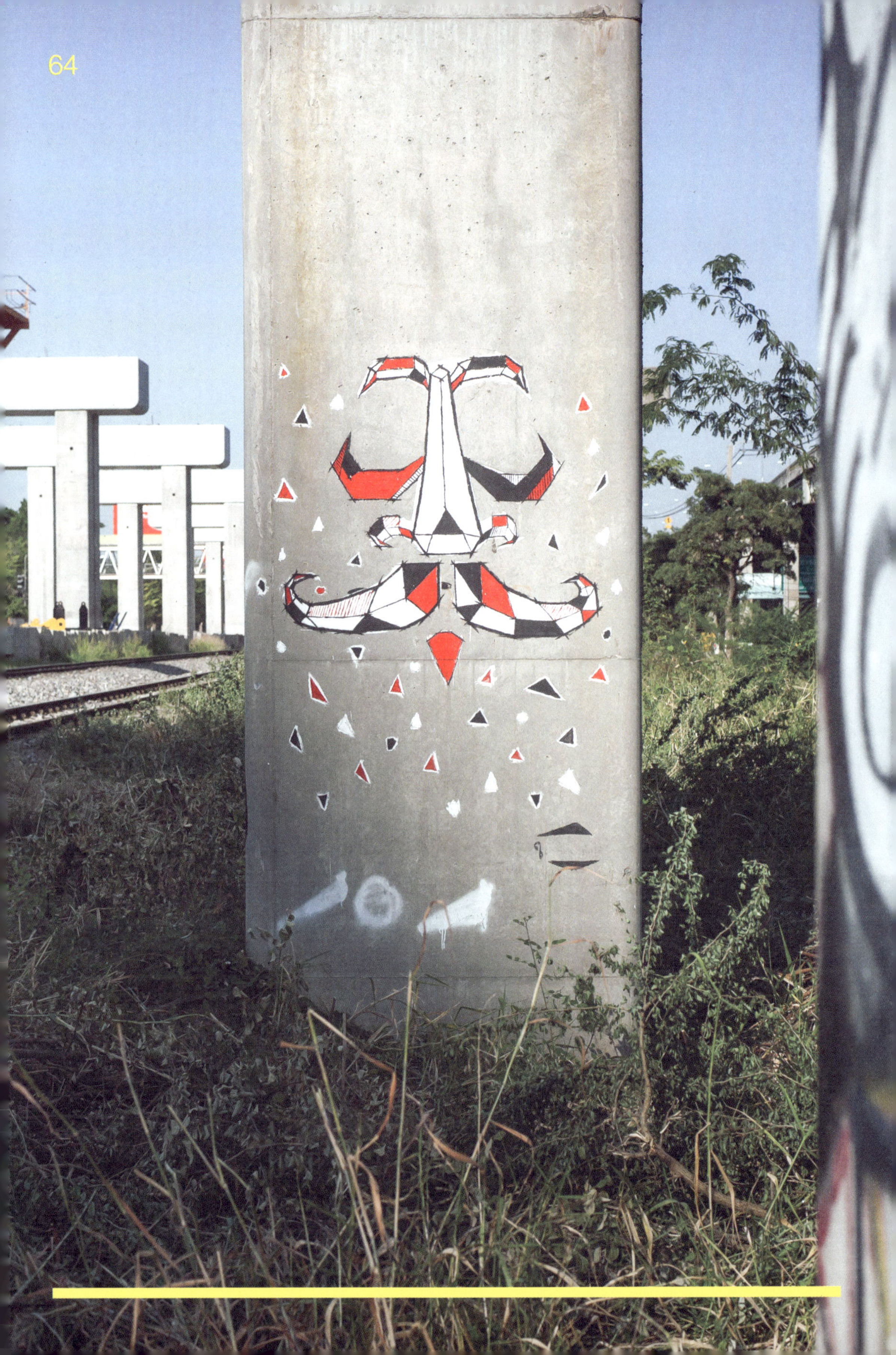

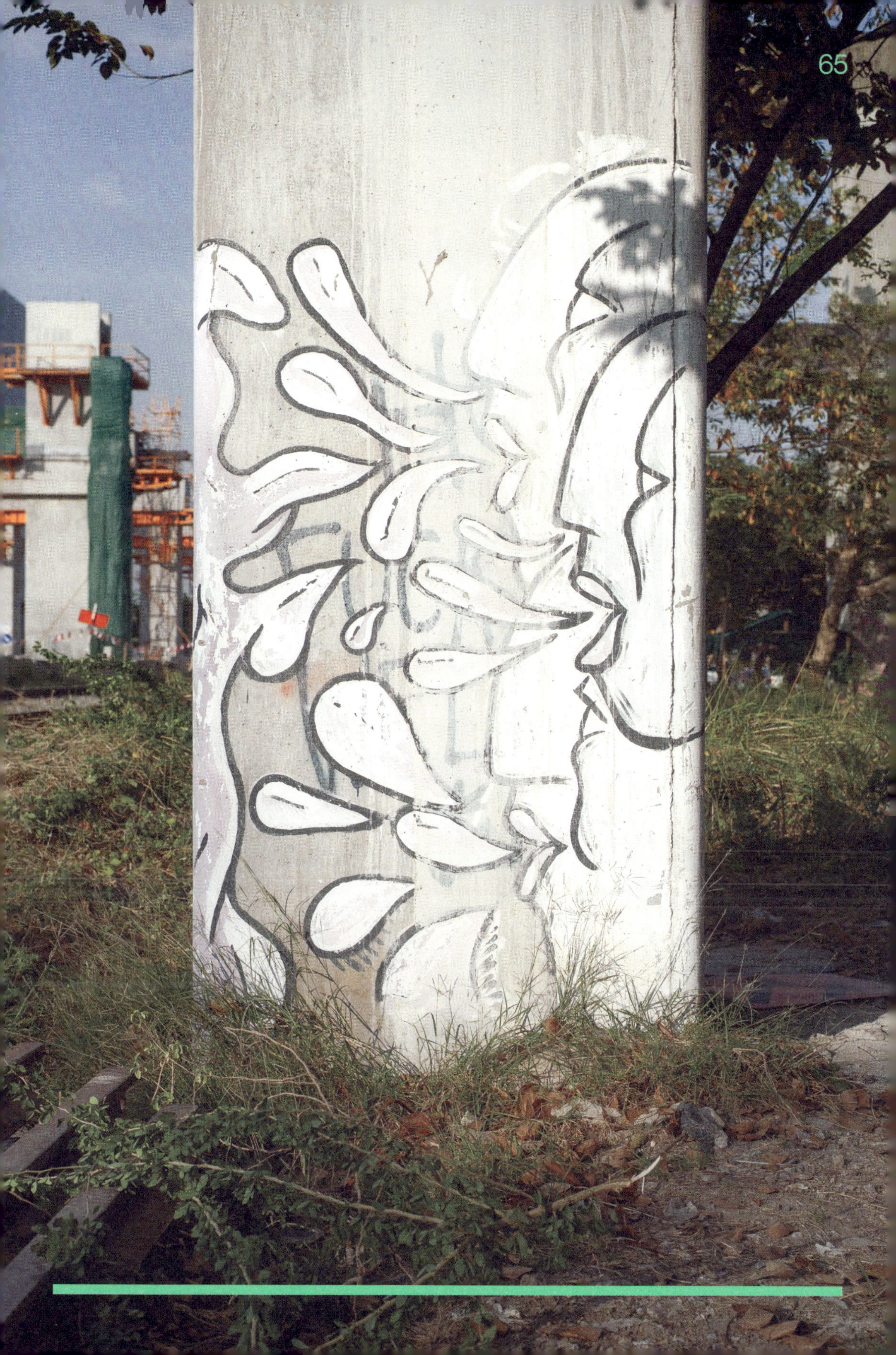

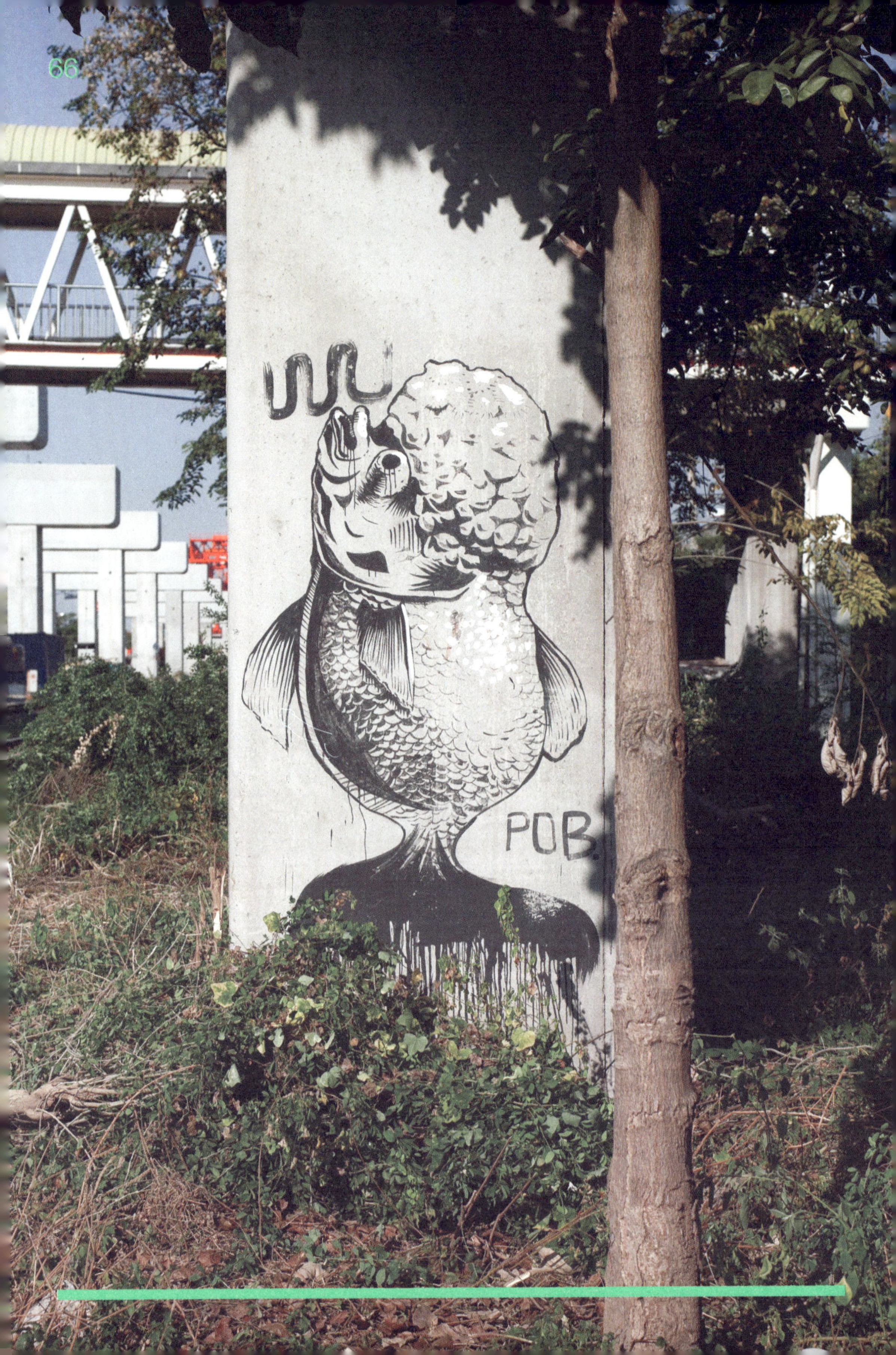
POB.

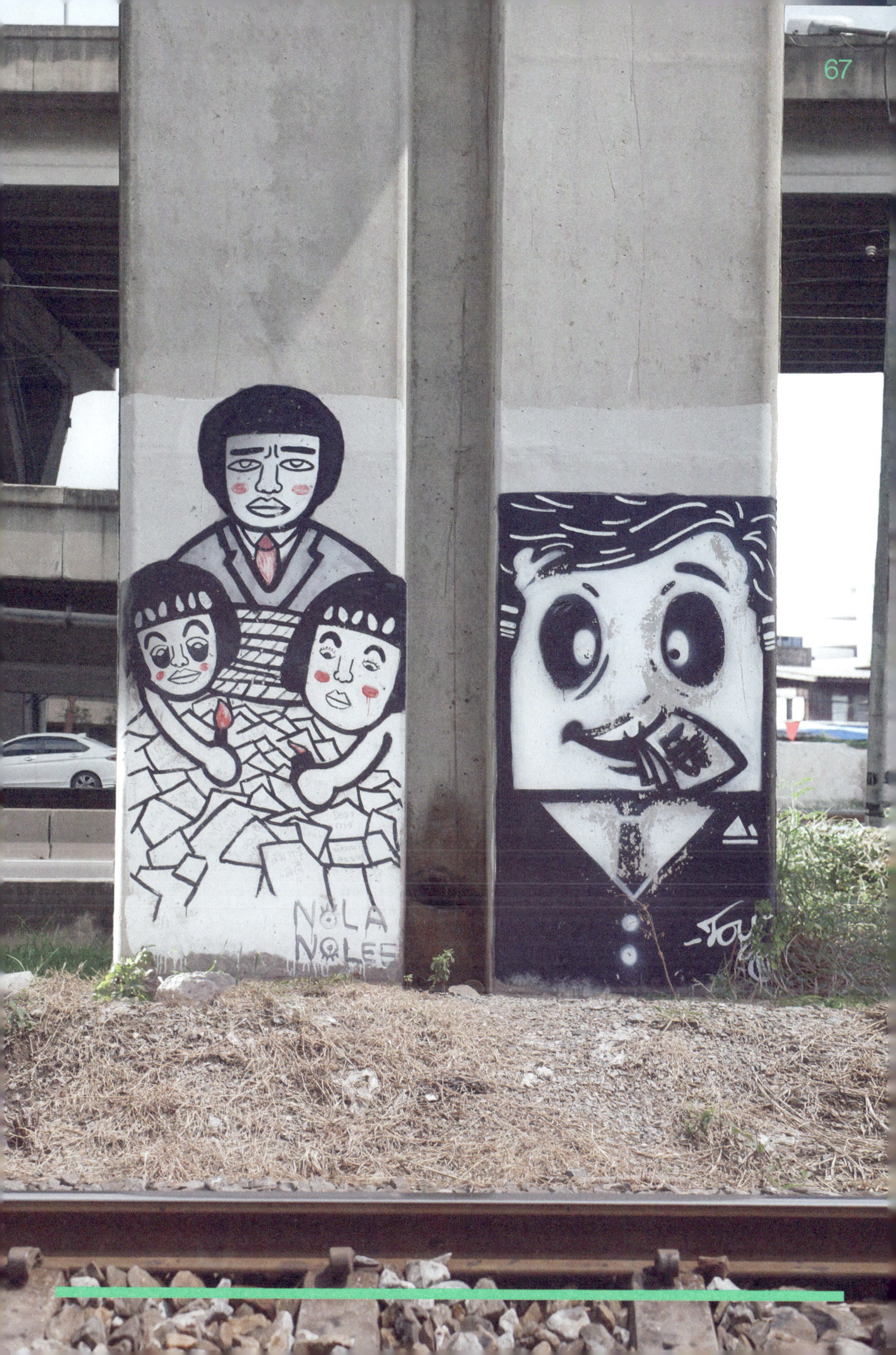
NOLA
NOLEE

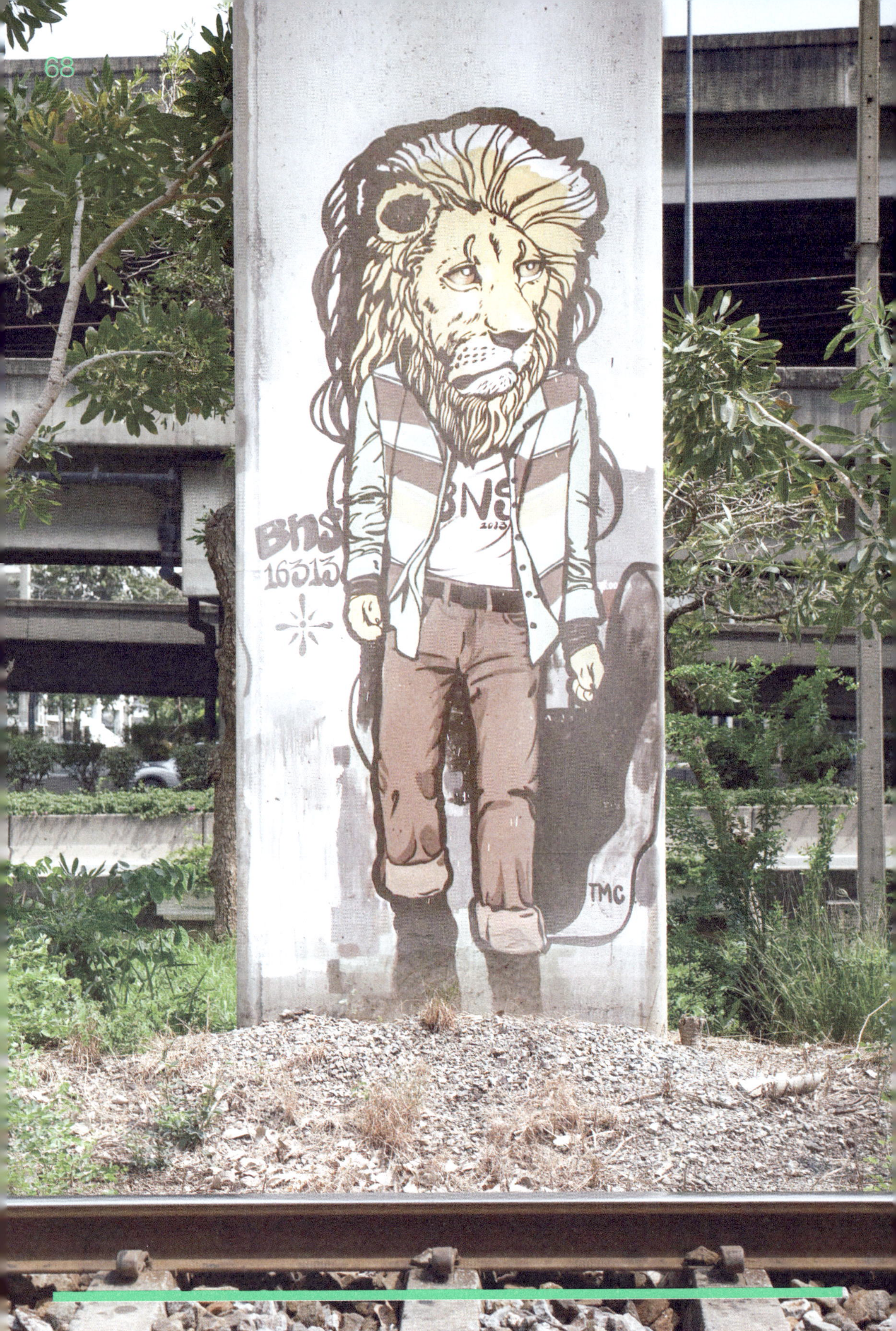
Bns
16313
BNS
TMC

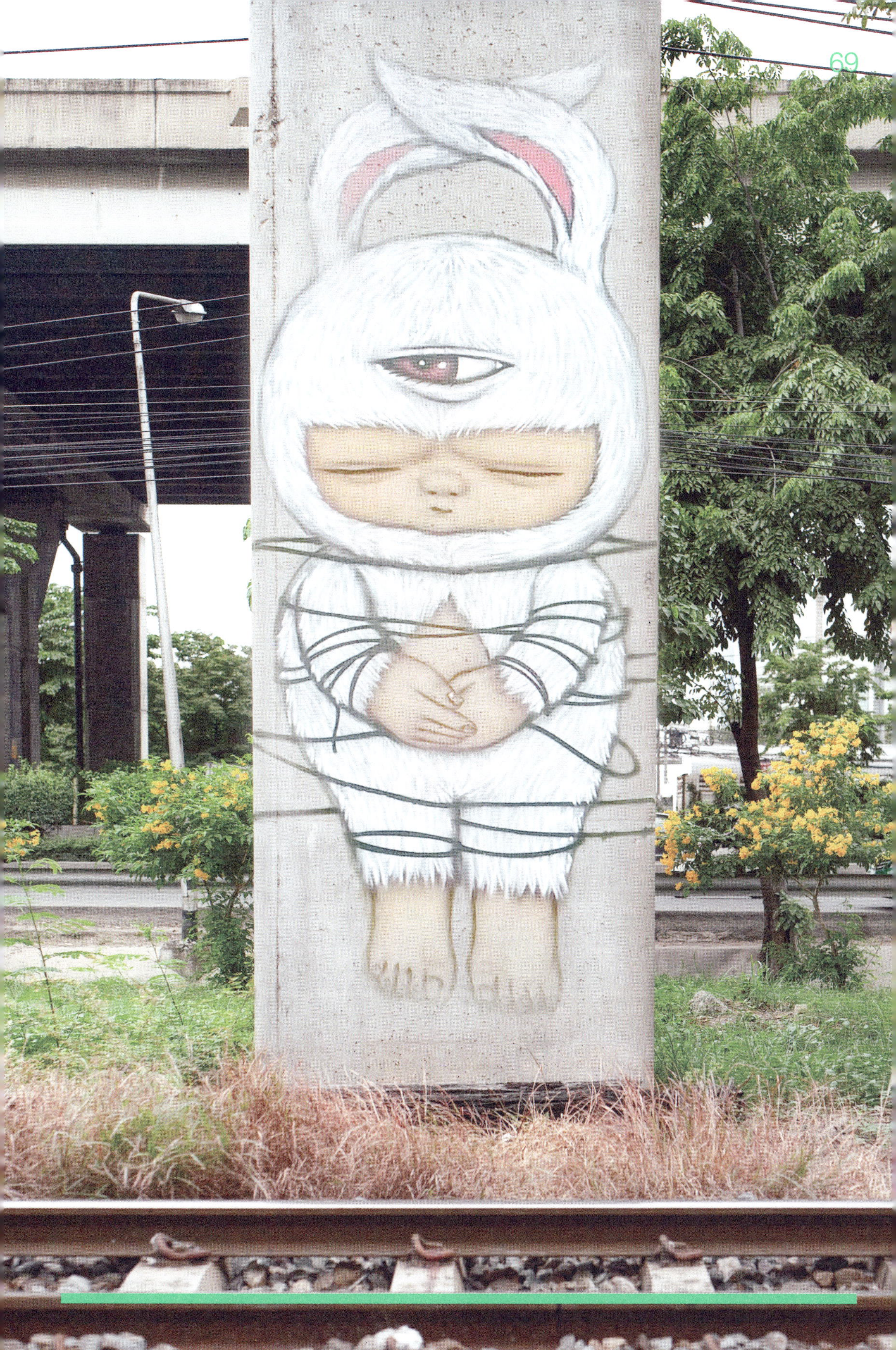

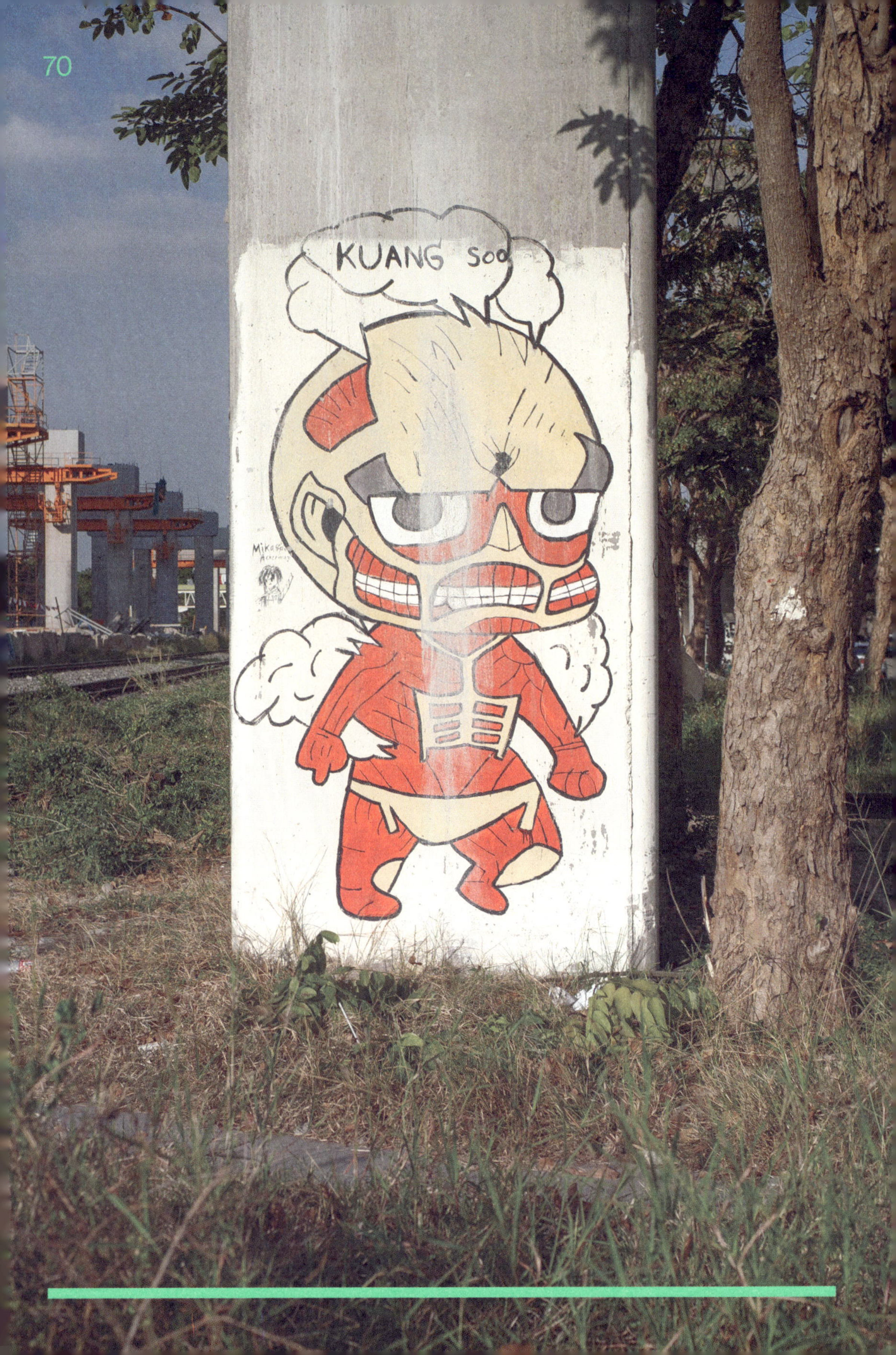
KUANG SOO

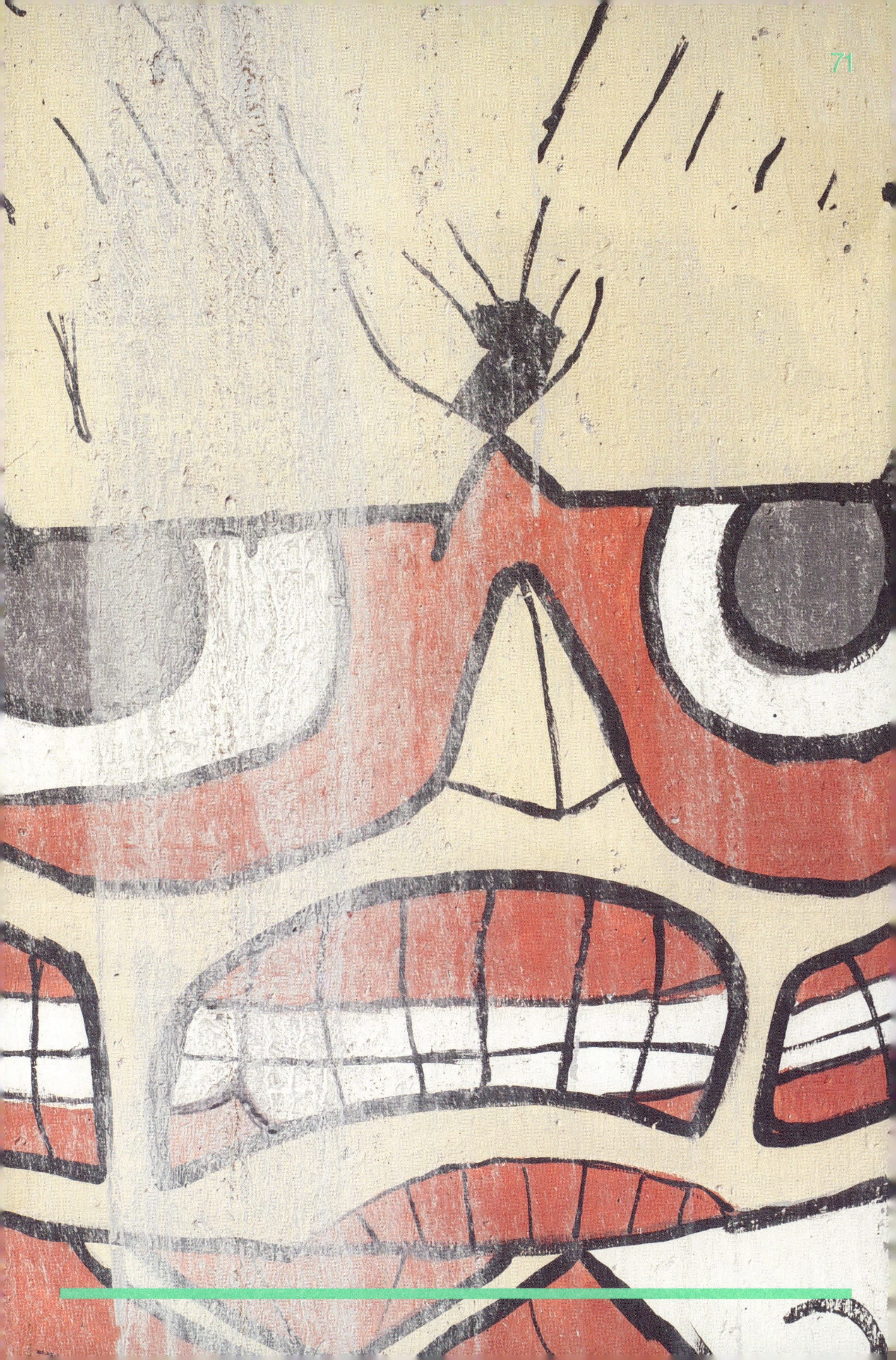

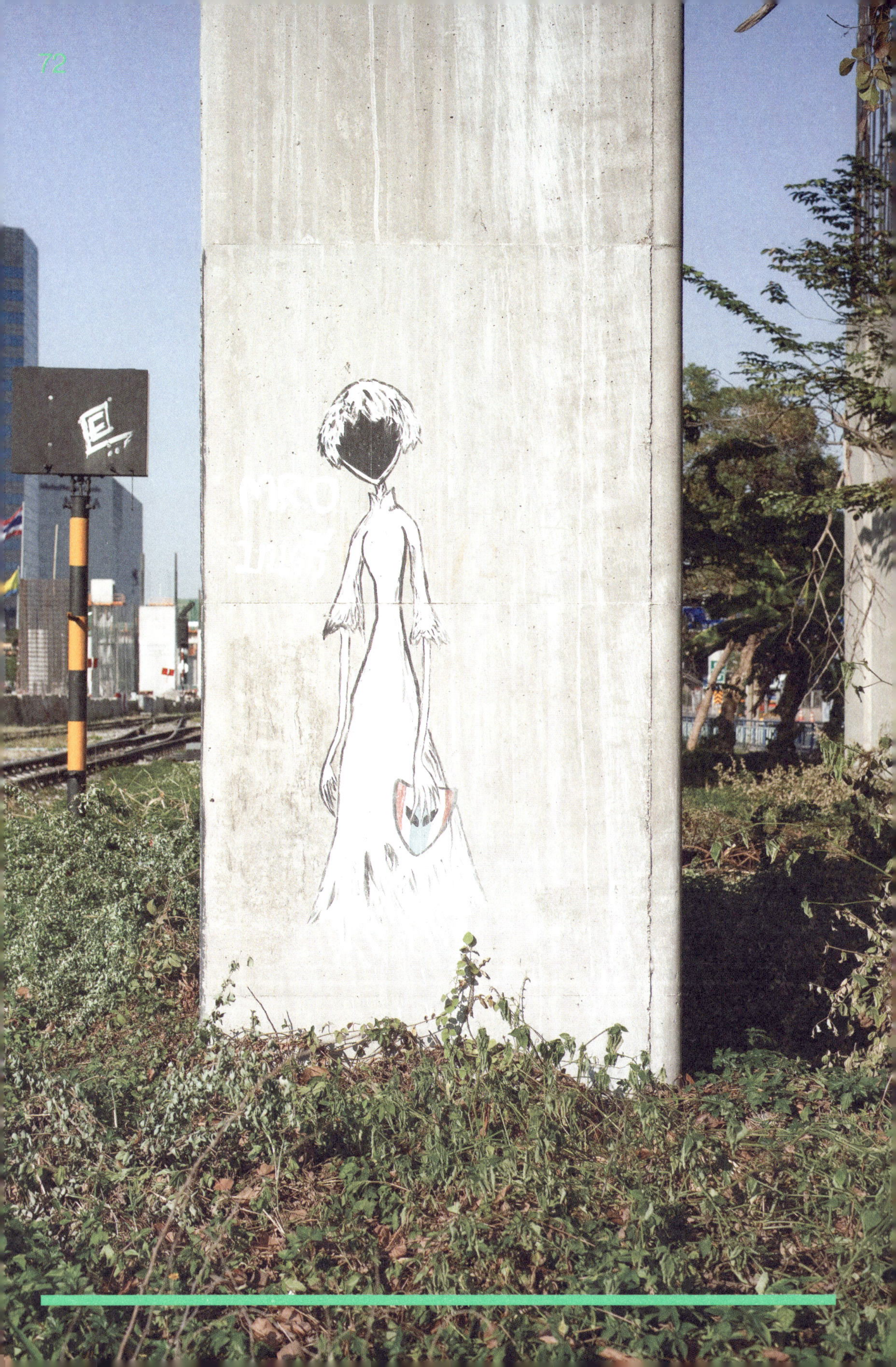

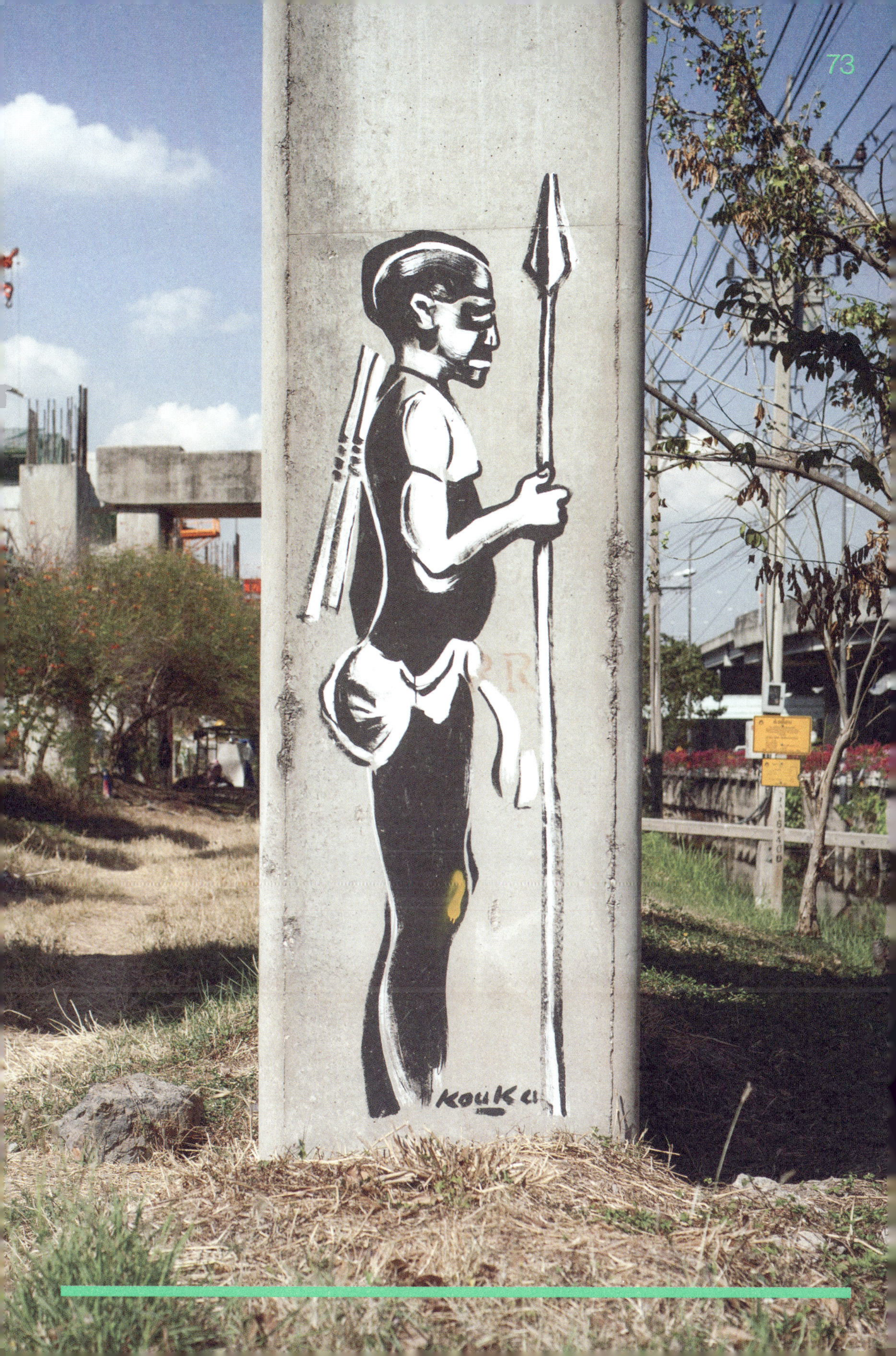
KouKa

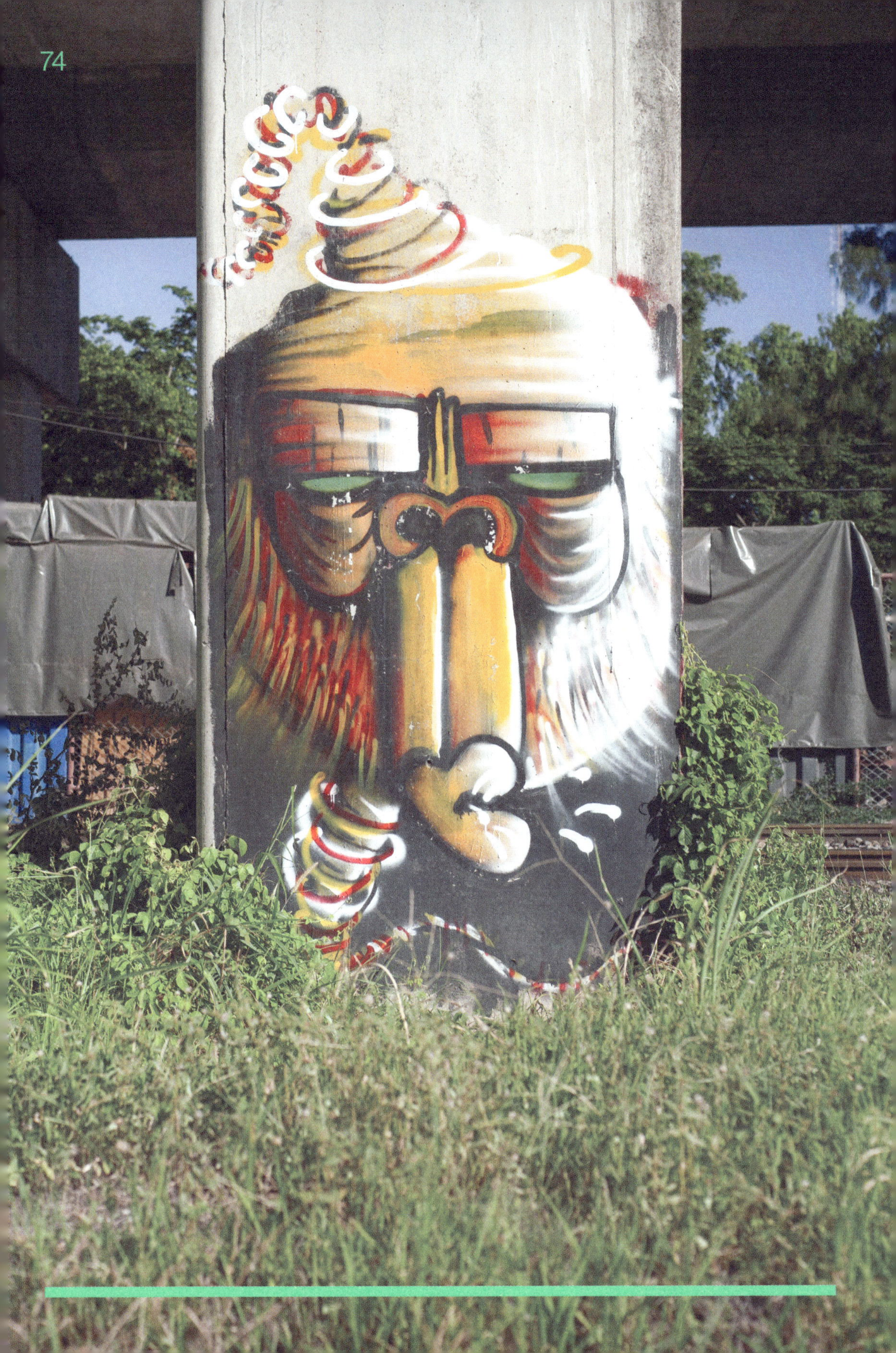

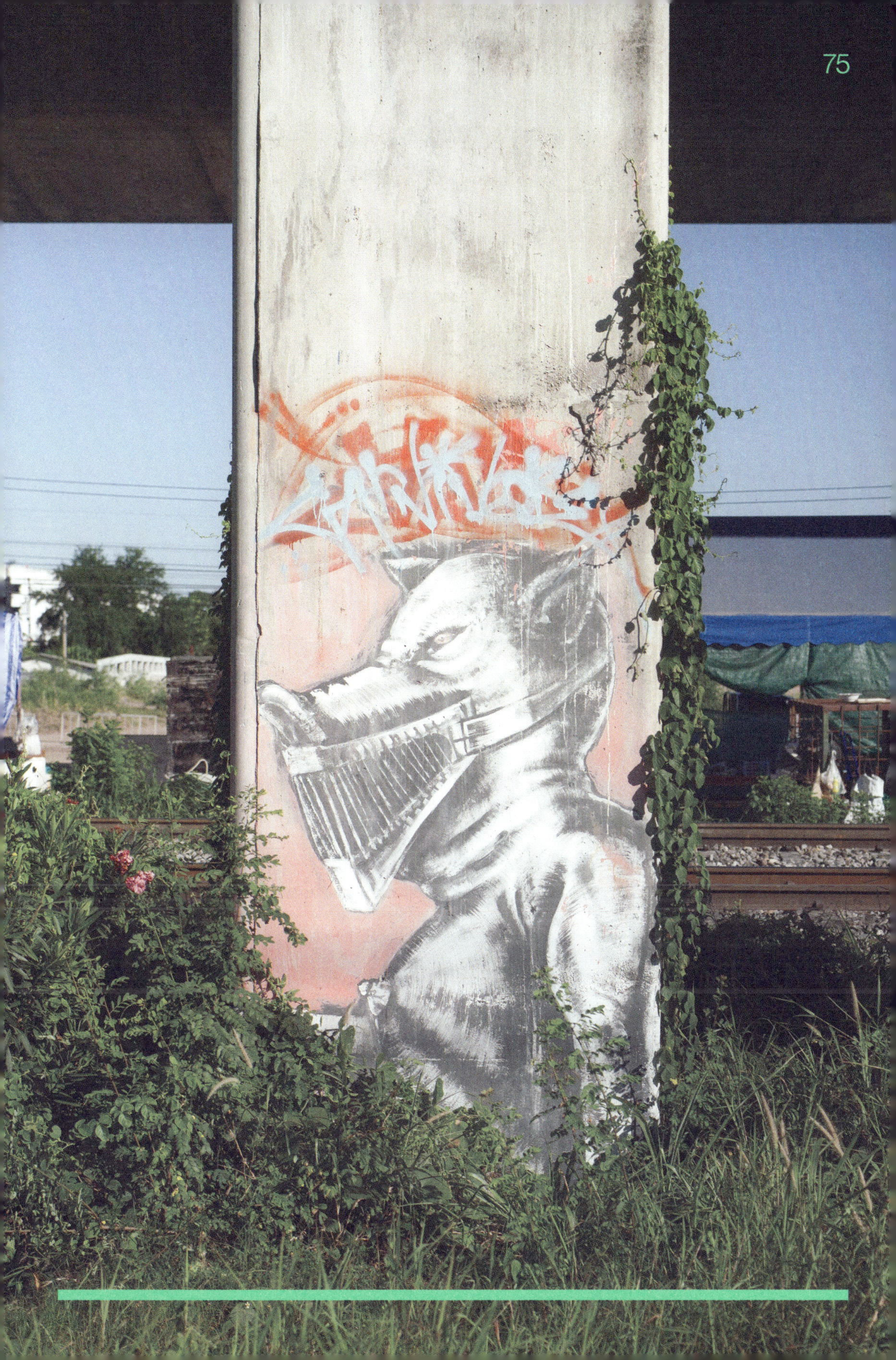

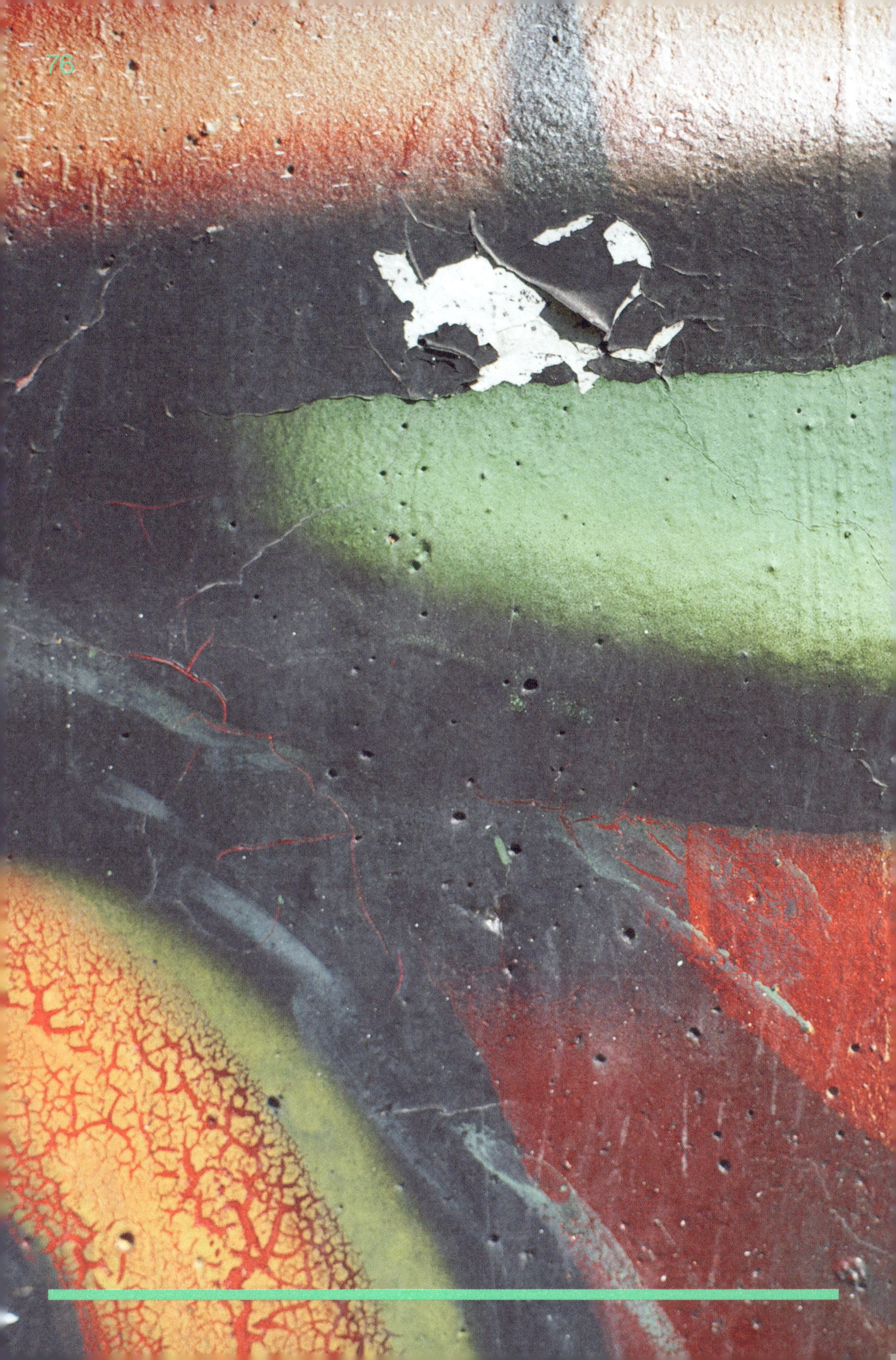

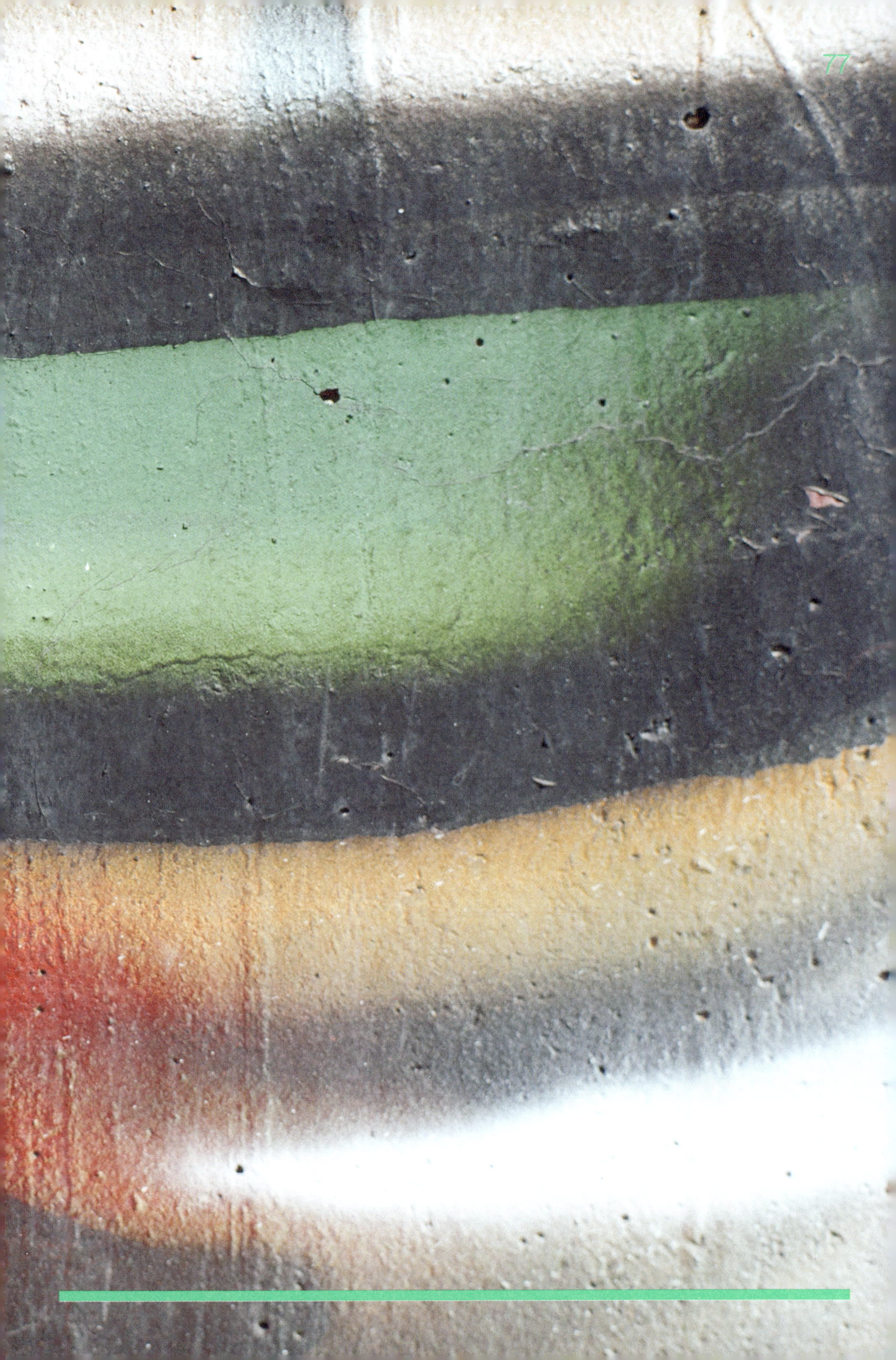

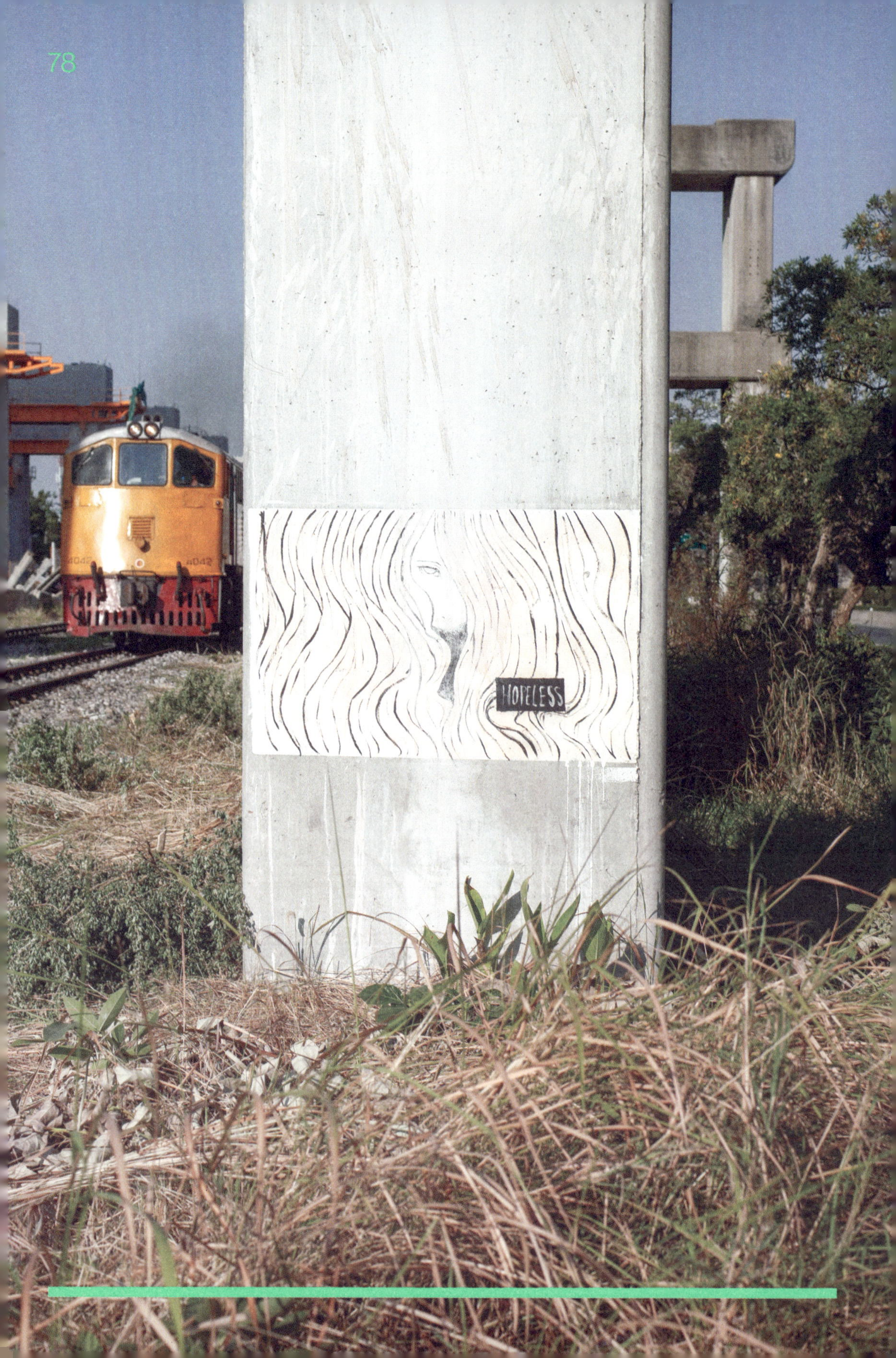
HOPELESS

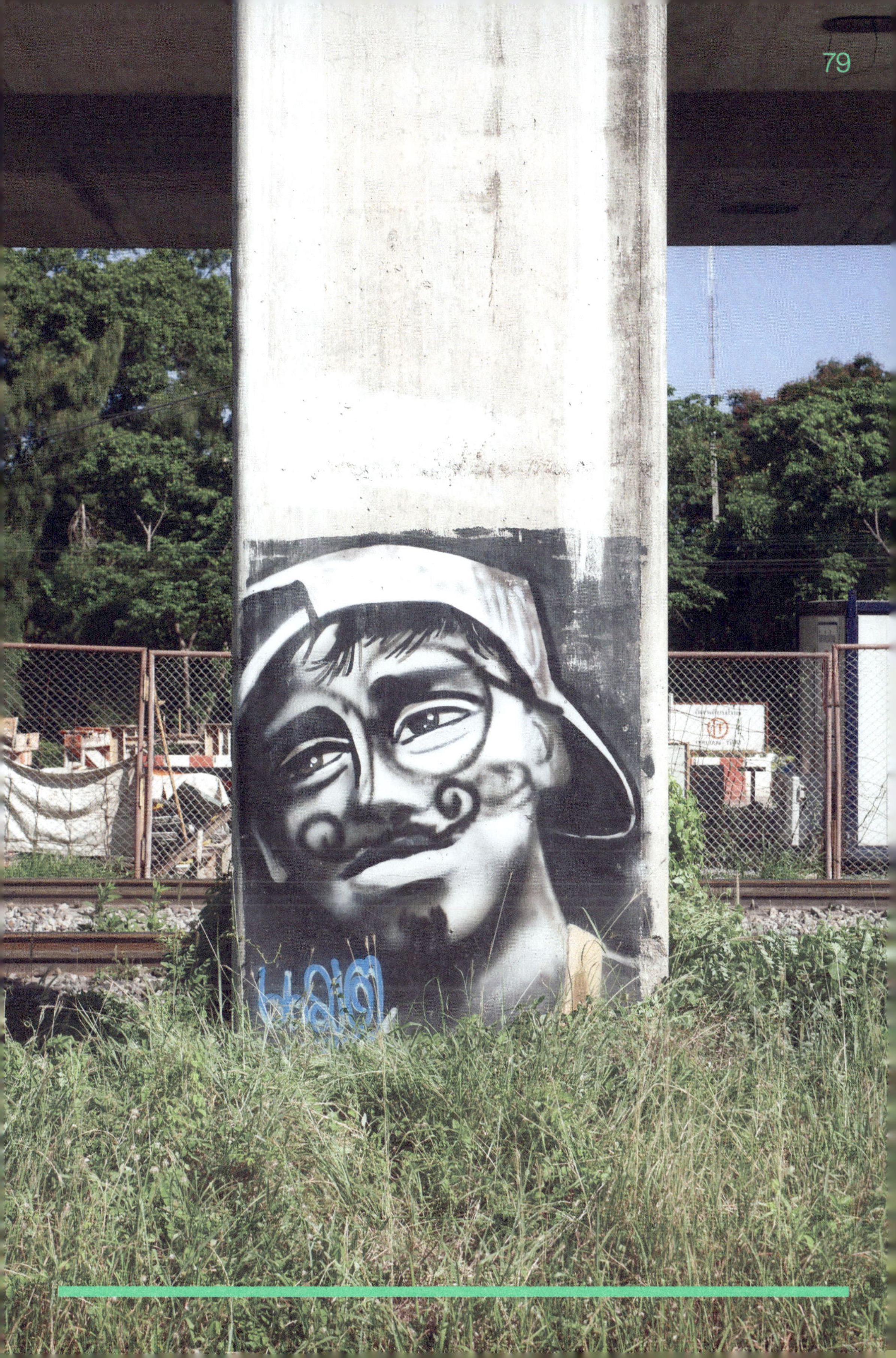

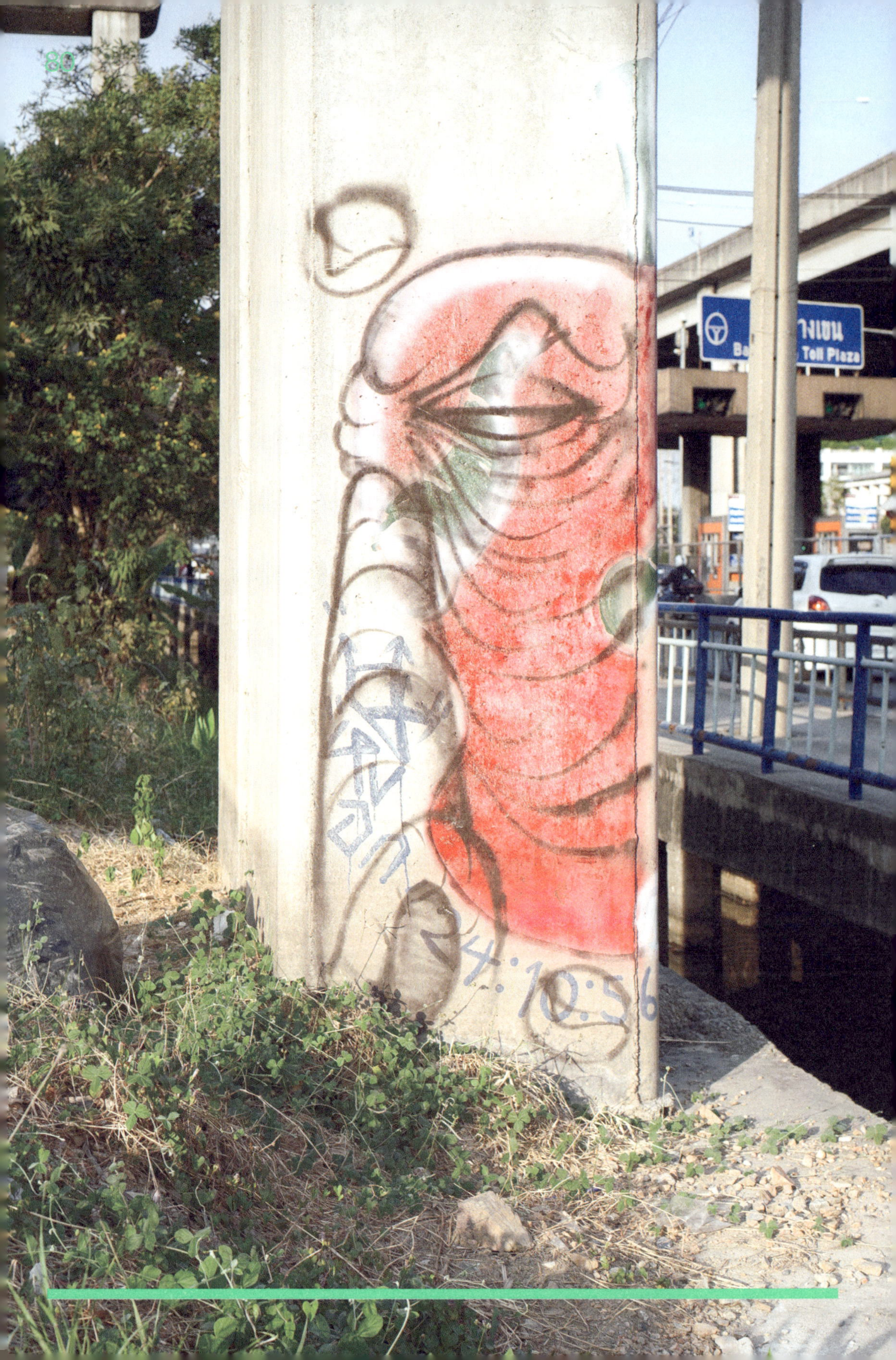
Toll Plaza

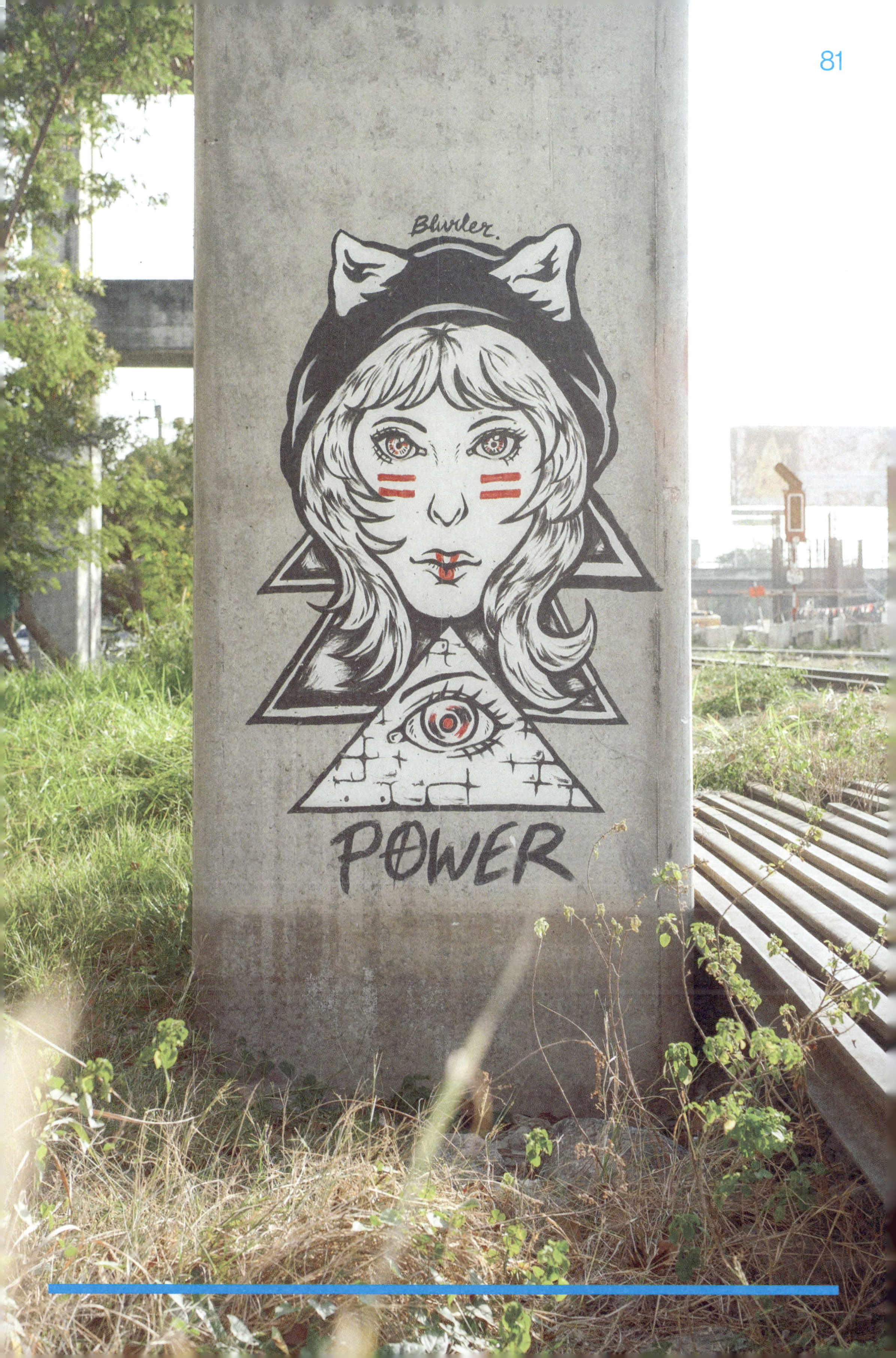
Blurler.
POWER

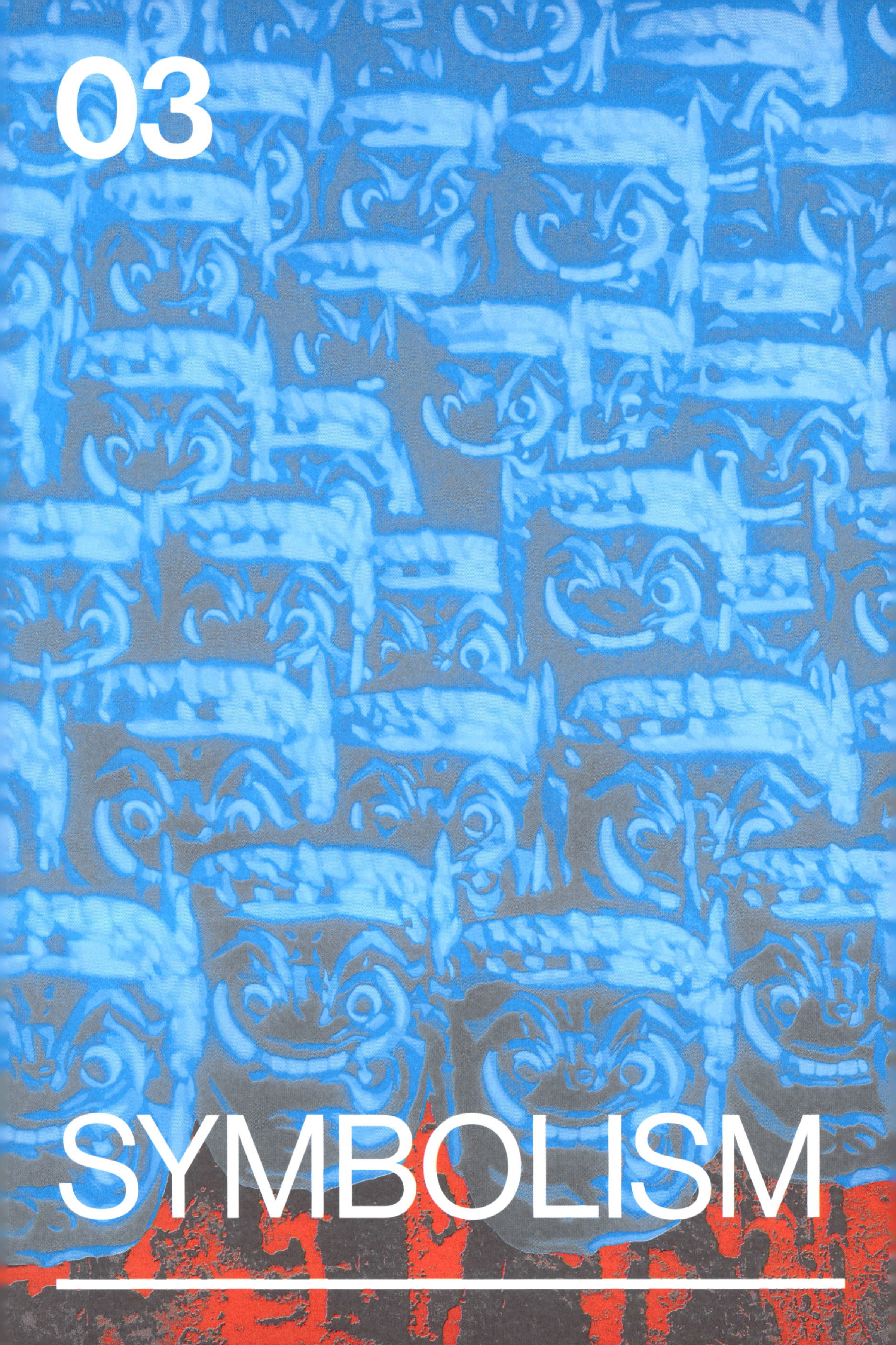
03
SYMBOLISM

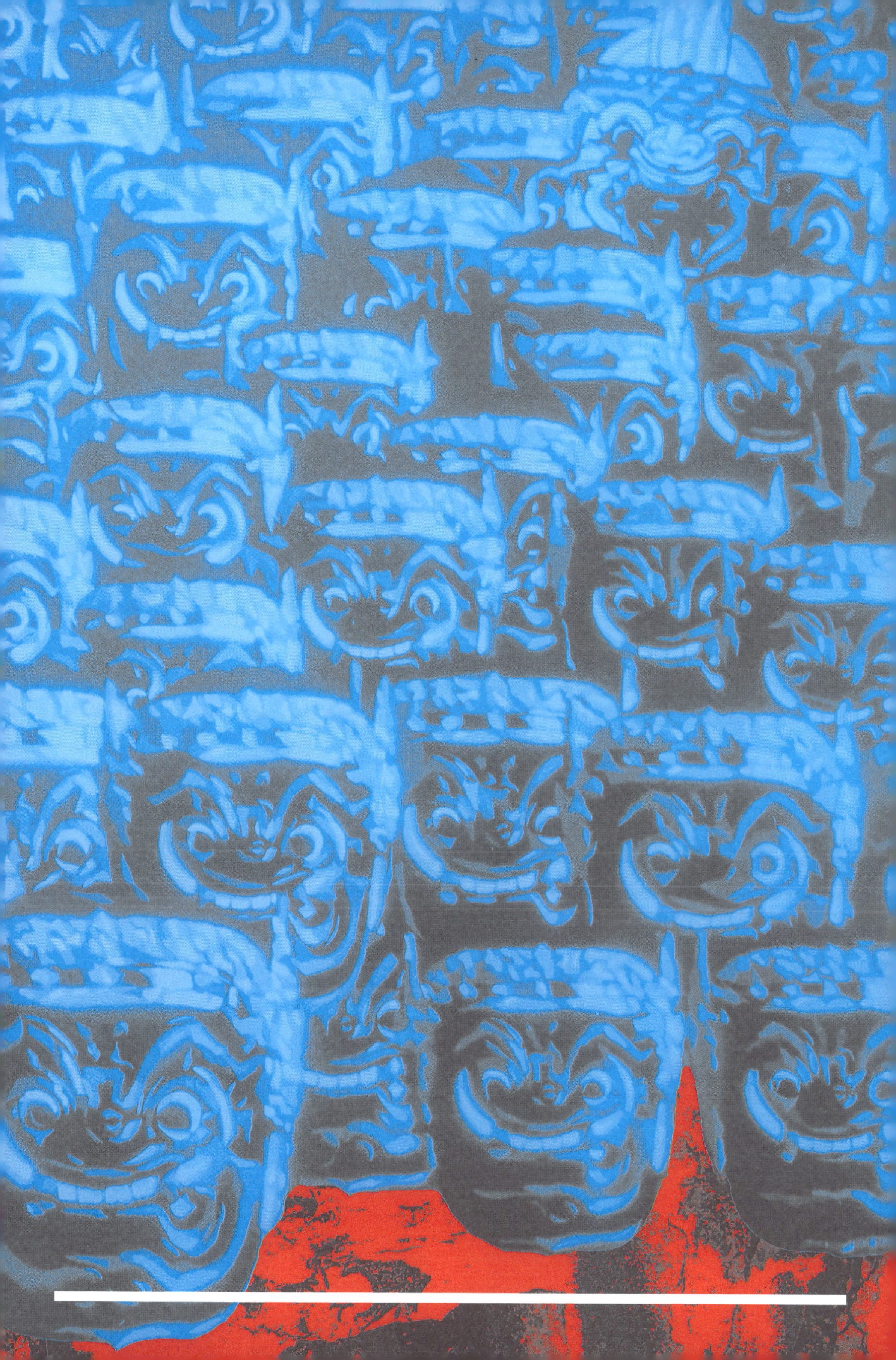

Since being cancelled in 1998, a large area of the Hopewell project's cement decking had been left half-finished near Wat Samian Nari. Concrete beams rested on temporary steel supports. Permanent columns were to be installed but never arrived. One morning in March 2012, the supports gave way and hundreds of tonnes of cement plummeted to the ground. The impact was so great, monks in the nearby prayer halls felt waves of energy surging beneath them as they sat in morning prayer. People on their way to work, trapped in traffic jams on the Vibhavadi Rangsit Road, saw a billowing plume of concrete dust roll out from the railway line. People walking along the line itself fled shards of metal and fragments of cement that flew across the ground. Having stood abandoned for more than a decade, and now collapsing, the Hopewell project had arrived back in the public's eye. Its symbolism, which would inspire the street artists who came to work there, was renewed.

For Bangkok's residents, the life-threatening collapse of this relic, at a time when the city desperately needed better public transportation, triggered indignation. That day, and in the following days, the talkback radio stations were alive with condemnation. The kingdom's ever-increasing Facebook presence was filled with chatter and the newspapers ran features about corruption and government failure. Many tried to trace how Hopewell had gone so wrong. People asked, not for the first time: Why didn't the project ever get finished? What happened to all the taxes spent on it? What happened to the officials who approved and then botched the works? What of the rumoured kickbacks to government ministers?

·MUEBON·

"Hopewell is a Hall of Shame for politicians and a Memorial of Corruption. Every new generation has questions about this place – What the heck!? Like, what the heck is that!? What are they doing here? When will it be completed? That's my money, isn't it? That's my parents' money. Yes, it's people's taxes that pay these stupid people to run the country and build stupid things."

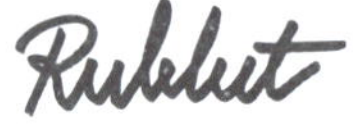

"Hopewell represents how rotten Thai politics is."

None of these questions were new in a city where corruption and development walked hand in hand. Nor was Hopewell the only large project that had been abandoned over the years. But somehow, within an atmosphere where failure and nepotism (see opposite) were being used as potent political tools, the Hopewell project became a charged symbol of government ineptitude and how it had robbed Bangkok of a future that was, literally, crumbling.

Despite their efforts, the authorities struggled to shift blame for the collapse. The official line was that the structure was safe, but scrap thieves had removed pieces of the support frames. People didn't buy the story. So, with news that the new Dark Red Line would be constructed in their place, the government announced a few months later in January 2013, that the Hopewell columns would be removed. This was their beginning as a part of Bangkok's street art history.

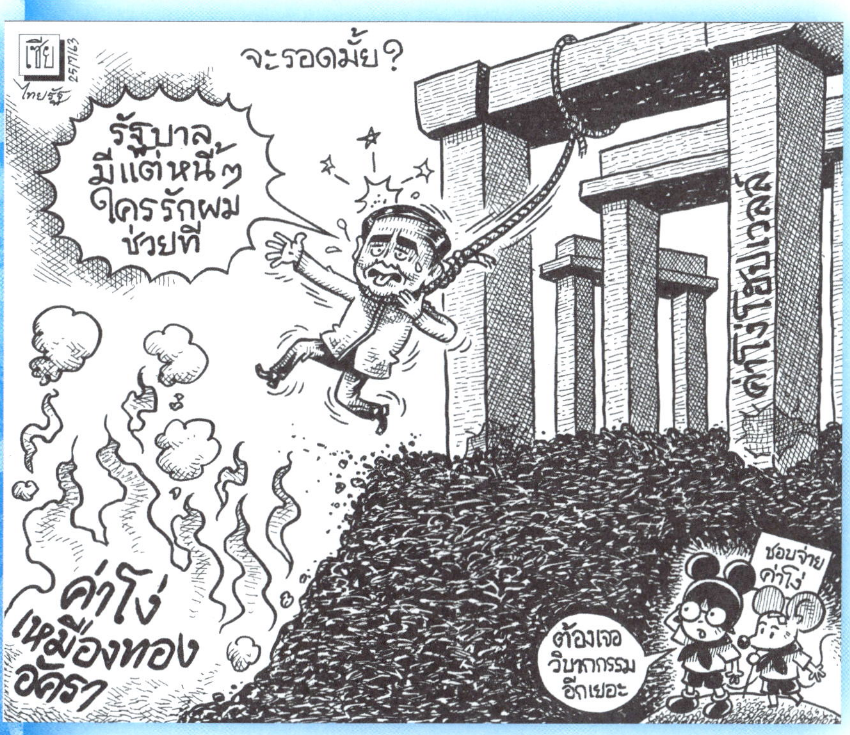

Cartoon by Sia Thairath. For translation, see page 252

NOLA-NO-LEE

"Usually it's hard to find a space to work in Bangkok. Usually, a wall is owned by someone so it's illegal to work there. Hopewell was different. It was built by corruption, so we didn't feel guilty about working there."

Rukkit

"Hopewell is a vast wasteland, as far as the eye can see. It's attractive for street artists."

• • •

The causes of the Hopewell project's failure lay at its beginning. Having run headlong into the project – to take advantage of the Asian region's financial boom of the late 1980s and '90s – there was a rumoured lack of cooperation between Hopewell Holdings and the State Railway of Thailand (SRT). By 1992, their relationship had become publicly fractious – each side blamed the other for causing delays. The project was suspended and the SRT accused Hopewell Chairman, Gordon Wu of not meeting his contractual obligations. Wu retaliated that the authority was under-resourced and had failed to acquire necessary land along the route. Wu's accusations rang true for many Thais who knew the pain of dealing with bureaucracy. In 1997, the baht was devalued and years of tenuous deals caused the inflated Thai property market to collapse. The resulting Tom Yam Kung financial crisis dried the rivers of cash flowing through the region. In 1998, the new government of Chuan Leekpai cancelled Hopewell's contract with just ten percent of construction completed. Over the following years, successive governments attempted various revival plans. In 2001, Thaksin Shinawatra's party won power and formally put an end to any hope that the project would be completed.

Thaksin remained leader of Thailand until 2006 when soldiers staged a coup and took control. For another decade, the columns waited, all lined up with nothing to support. The capital was disrupted by extended protests – Thaksin's supporters, the Red Shirts, against his detractors, the Yellow Shirts. An old divide opened again, between the urbanites (*khon muang*), who saw themselves as civilised, and the rural farmers (*khon ban nok*), perceived as uneducated. A series of leaders, came and went until an election was held in 2011. Thaksin's sister, Yingluck Shinawatra was voted in as Prime Minister. Like Thaksin before her, she was constantly dogged by allegations of corruption that culminated in yet more protests. Months of open unrest, brought parts of the capital to a halt. Yingluck stepped down and attempted to call fresh elections for 2014. During this period, the issue of government corruption was a key political weapon deployed to discredit Thaksin and Yingluck. It was a sharp tool in a country where many people suffered its effects each day. It's no secret that vast sums of Thailand's collective wealth has been squandered by these unruly forces. It was in this political climate that the Hopewell columns became a street art site.

ANONYMOUS

"The money spent on one column could benefit society in so many ways. It must have cost a lot. That could have been spent on building accommodation for the homeless. And then these columns were gone. Gone without any real use or benefit. I thought it was a shame that such a big budget was wasted on something unused and unfinished. Hopewell is a landmark. Every time I passed that area, it's like a set of statues that raise questions in people's minds like, 'What is that and why is it there?'"

At Hopewell, the real-world failure was now being adorned with real-world criticism in the form of street art, at the moment those issues were live. This heady mix of form, meaning and public anger, charged the art that appeared here. It captured, provoked and extended the symbolism and political potency of the site. As more and more street art appeared on the columns, the Hopewell site became more visible. With its form and fame, Hopewell became a cenotaph. The columns commemorated an alternative history of the city. In contrast to Bangkok's official monuments, this was a pile dedicated to hopelessness. Its inscriptions were not in brass and stone, guarded by those in power. This was a botched construction site with epitaphs in aerosol paint, offered by those whose hopes had been squandered – they would speak without sanction. Unlike symbols such as the Victory and Democracy monuments, this place would be torn down to conceal its meaning soon after dedication.

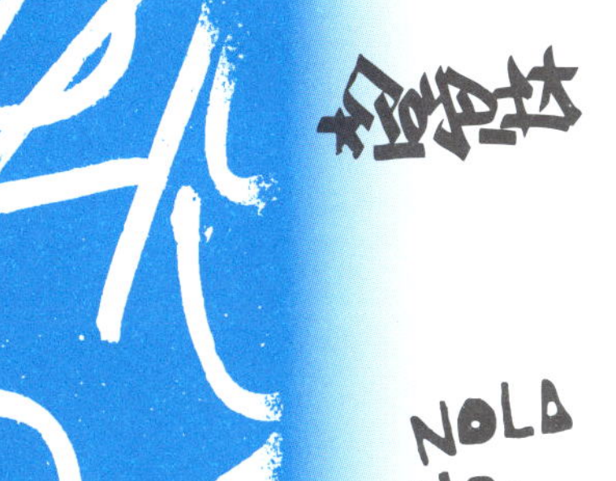

"Hopewell is a corruption monument. The level of corruption was so much, the project couldn't continue. So, it just stayed there. I kind of got used to it, because I have seen it every day since I was a child."

NOLA -NO- LEE

"When I think of Hopewell I feel sad. It's our money. We know everything, but we can't do anything. And that's depressing. Also, it's a huge place. The columns are big, but were all useless."

"It had been there for many years, but Thai people hadn't taken any action about it. Maybe this represents Thainess. It's symbolic of the way Thai people ignore things. They don't want to do anything about it. Hopewell is too bad, there was nothing good about it. There was only corruption."

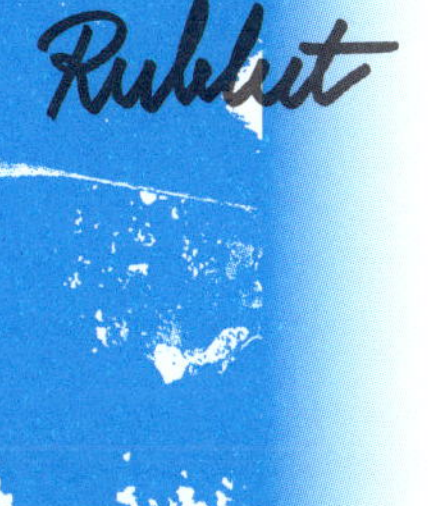

"When I saw a project like Hopewell it made me feel sad. If Hopewell was finished, it would have improved lives. There were much better ways to spend that money. There are a lot of loopholes and cracks in Thai politics. And these loopholes and cracks allow people to show their true colours. This makes me feel bad about Thai politics. This makes me feel bad about paying taxes for these useless columns."

There are very few places where street art is sprayed directly onto the actual manifestations of state power or policy that are the target of its critique. Perhaps the west side of the Berlin Wall in the last years of its life, Israel's West Bank Barrier Wall in Bethlehem and the Arc de Triomphe in Paris after the gilets jaunes protests in 2018. The combination is rare because charged political symbols are often protected by the state to ensure their potency is not hijacked.

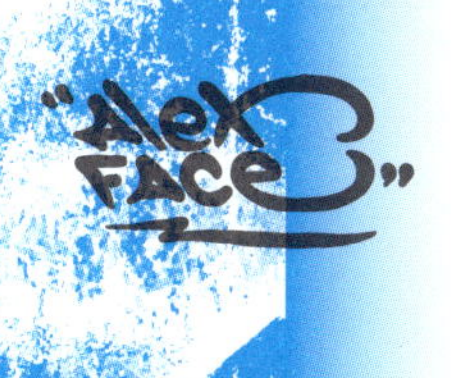

"Street art can be a tool to represent something that's going on. For instance, at Hopewell, why did people have to paint street art there? If people saw a lot of paintings at Hopewell. What's going on? I think it made

people see that place more. Some people will say, 'Oh, cool, you should paint on that, it's shit.' It means the Hopewell site can say something. It makes the place more relevant."

Many aborted projects in Bangkok are forgotten over time. They come and go without becoming a symbol in the way Hopewell did. Perhaps the columns' strange ceremonial air beside the highway was too eye-catching for people to forget. Perhaps it was because the Hopewell project, as the country's first major attempt at relieving traffic congestion through mass transit, had so much hope attached.

Because the Vibhavadi Rangsit Road was, for many years, the main connection to the city's international airport, the columns also became a conspicuous example of national failure. Most international visitors would not understand the historic and political reasons for the project's abortion but local people came to believe that visitors perceived it as evidence of Thai ineptitude, generally. Rather than being symbolic only of government shortcomings, the columns also came to represent, in the minds of Thai people, how international visitors saw the country. A taxi driver, speaking to *Khao Sod* newspaper in 2013 said, "Just get rid of them already! It's like our country's hall of shame to foreigners and to our next generations."

• • •

For street artists, the Hopewell site was unlike any other site in Thailand. Its open-air location, endless parade of columns, its peri-urban, industrial setting and visibility beside major transport routes, made it an ideal place for street art. It was the serendipitous combination of neglected infrastructure – perfect as a canvas – the blossoming of Bangkok's street-art scene and a topical political symbolism that allowed for a moment of heightened creativity and meaning. It was organic and earnest place making, without the usual affectation that accompanies the idea.

The railway easement, a stretch of unused land beside the functioning inter-city railway line out to Ayutthaya, was where the columns sat. This was a shady green strip of nature contrasting with the exposed railway line it abutted. Mature trees, clusters of grasses and shrubs grew plentifully. Birds sang and squirrels darted about in the branches. In areas, a small creek flowed. Dogs made homes there and snakes wove through the grass. Even elephants and their handlers would camp amongst the columns at night, before heading into the city to beg. People from nearby residential and industrial neighbourhoods walked back and forth across the tracks and amongst the columns. This was a gritty, mechanical setting, typical of Bangkok's outer back lots.

The Hopewell columns were brutally functional, a battery of heavy-set supports. These concrete invaders were accepted by the surrounding greenery of the easement which draped over them and provided a soft green cushion at their bases. Stark, aborted urbanism was cradled by nature. Some columns were connected to their neighbour by a thick crossbeam, upon which the elevated rail line would have sat. These formed gateways that aligned ceremonially – something like Japanese *Torii* or, as the columns would become known, Bangkok Stonehenge (see below). Ordinarily, such columns would be holding up one of Bangkok's many shopping mall floors. At Hopewell, they sat in the middle of nowhere, surrounded by grass, holding up nothing at all. This combination of grassy meadows and half-broken cement columns was a premonition of the death that awaits all cities.

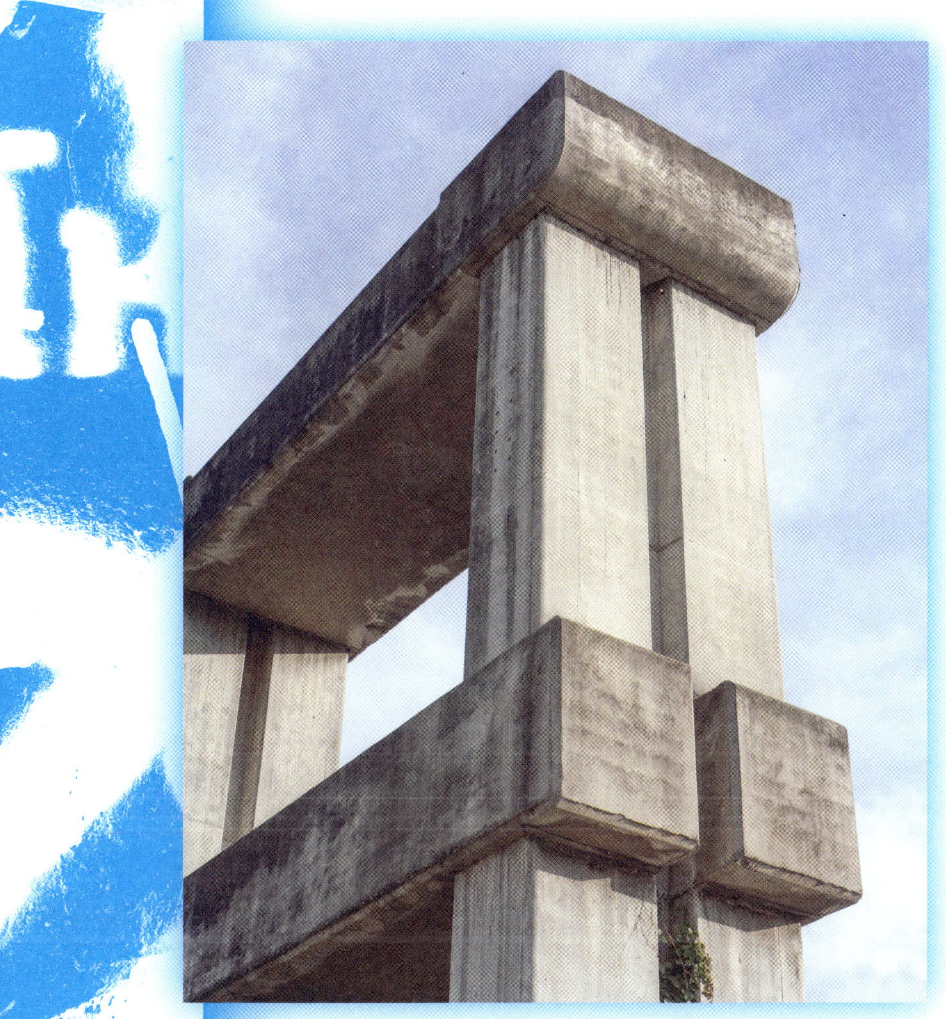

In this way, the street art was also framed by greenery. Strange faces peered out from behind foliage. Some pieces were positioned to be obscured by bushes in harmony with their setting. Like most contemporary graffiti and street art, that found at Hopewell grew out of a tradition begun in the US by teenage pioneers who painted train carriages in New York and Philadelphia. Here at Hopewell, every once in a while, a shock of carriages would fly past. In the sudden maelstrom that followed, the bushes and trees would mark the train's passing by frantically waving their branches back and forth. And Hopewell's menagerie of aerosol sprites would salute their distant common ancestor (see below).

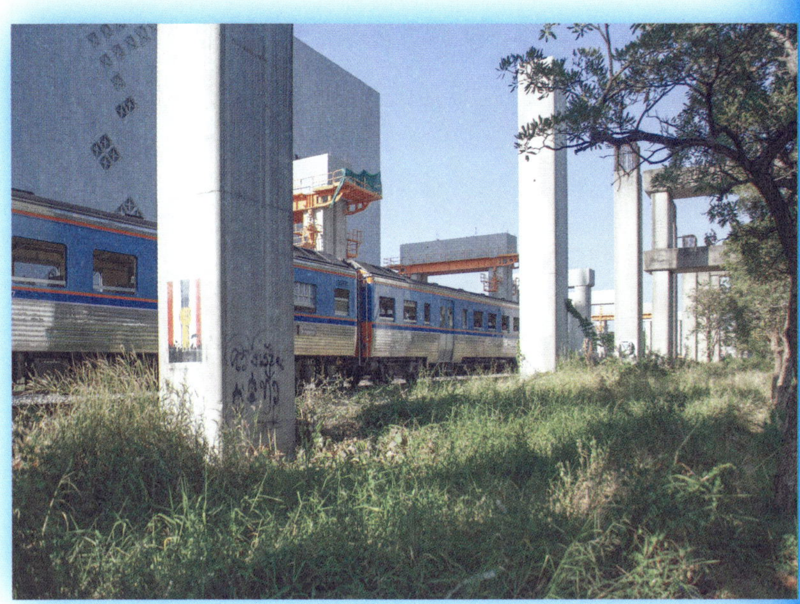

Usually, street art sites are formed of many layers of art. Over the years, each piece buries the previous work under another skin of paint, itself subsequently buried. There is competition for space and the more skilled artists dominate. At Hopewell, this wasn't the case. Every artist had the same amount of space to work with, and there was no buffing. The ordinarily stratified layers of art were separated out at Hopewell and placed beside each other. Beginners from the local art colleges stood next to established artists like Bonus TMC, Mamacup711, Bigdel, CRUDE and ALEX FACE.

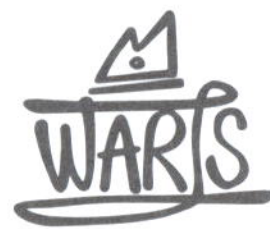

"Finding a physical space is one of the most important things in creating street art. There's always this sense of finding a space. It can be a war. Hopewell was different, there's a lot of space for everyone. It was like a Hall of Fame, to me. A space like this is rare in Bangkok."

Hopewell provided a huge number of blank canvasses in the form of incomplete columns, a paintable area roughly 1.2 metres wide and 2 metres high, repeated hundreds of times up and down the railway line. This art wasn't behind glass in a gallery, it could be found and touched. A population of apparitions, born of the imagination of Bangkok's street artists, began to cohabit here. The proportions of the available canvases resulted in many full-height, roughly life-size figures. This human scale made the art approachable. Wandering around, it felt as if you were in their presence. Standing eye-to-eye with the art, combined with its monumental setting, gave Hopewell spirit.

Thai artists could also freely walk through an open-air gallery of their peers' work. They could bite (draw inspiration from or copy other people's work) endlessly, and bite offline. By 2013, the typographic graffiti styles in Bangkok had become less prevalent, the balance had shifted towards street art and its character-based styles. The Hopewell art sat right at the centre of that change and was an important testing ground for the artists to develop.

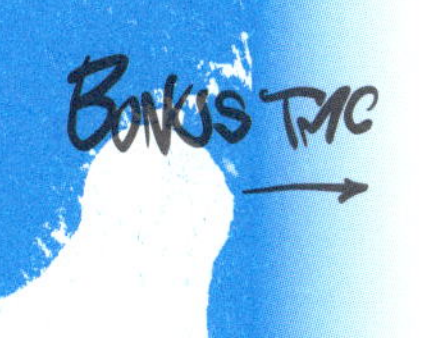

"Hopewell is really important for the development of Thai street art because it was a free canvas where people could go and practice. Also, it was a place that people passed every day, so it was easily seen by the public."

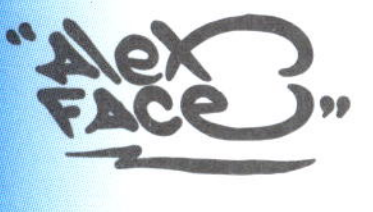

"Hopewell was important as a place that made people start to paint. There were so many columns, you didn't have to paint over each other. There I saw guys who were painting the first day, they said, 'Oh, Alex, hello, this is my first piece.'
'Yeah, cool man.'
It was more natural there. Sometimes, if you're at a place that is really organised, it's all set. But at Hopewell, it's like a beginning, it's more random, more cool."

It's not clear where they came from, but many people who worked at Hopewell mention a series of mysterious, official-looking stencils that appeared on the columns around Bang Khen Station in 2012 or 2013.

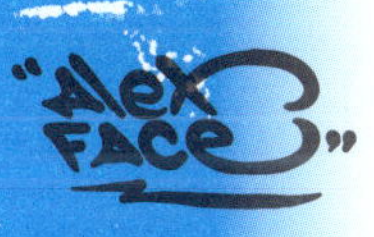

"Do you know why we went to paint? We saw a sign on the Hopewell columns that said, 'This column has been here for 20 years for nothing. So, if you are an artist, please come and paint it.' And I was like, 'What!?' I don't know who put it there. But, okay, let's go and paint."

With the early 2013 announcement that the columns would be removed, a new wave of artists rushed to paint at Hopewell. In March 2013, the street-culture magazine, *Go Play*, did a group bombing (many works done at the same time by different artists) of the Hopewell site around Wat Samian Nari. Although not the first to paint there, this event made the site famous. Limo, Leo, Jimmy, Cece and Bonus TMC, all participated. In October 2013, *ArtVenture* did another group bombing of the area around Bang Khen Station. This involved work by Mister Bows, ALEX FACE, CRUDE, Bigdel and Goh-M, and opened up a new area of the

Hopewell columns. Along with local artists, others from Japan, Brazil, the United States and the Netherlands also worked there.

During the following four years, there was a brief opportunity when the columns existed between being financially valued private property and rubble. This hall of shame became a Hall of Fame. The artists painted many things, but throughout the body of art that emerged, the theme of government corruption and failure would be visited many times.

Rukkit

"It was the right place for street artists because of all the columns and also its background story. There were plenty of areas to work. Free, unused columns that were the fruit of corruption. This made Hopewell attractive to experienced and amateur artists alike. And so the work was a mixture of those that tell political stories and those that aren't related to politics."

NOLA -NO- LEE

"Since Hopewell is symbolic of political corruption in Thailand at that time, street artists believed it would be a good combination, a good place to represent their own political thoughts. That's why we went there to paint something political."

Bonus TMC

"Hopewell symbolised government failure to complete the project. Later, it was completed artistically by a group of artists."

The word, 'hope' became a riff that would appear again and again. 'Hope-less', 'hopeful', 'no hope', 'hope well', 'fuck hope', all dissected the meaning of the site and what it represented (see opposite). The irony in the place's name was clear – Bangkok's people had hoped the project might help lift them out of an urban nightmare in the late 1980s. They then watched in despair as their hard-earned taxes were poured into useless cement columns. The artists expressed the frustration and humour of a people who believed they were effectively powerless to stop such forces.

MALKA

"Hopewell's charm came from its name. If the project was finished, maybe it would be a route of hope. But when it was abandoned, it became a huge free canvas for artists. Finding a physical space is always hard in Bangkok. To have that much free space to work was hopeful. For me, the word 'hope' made artists who lived far away from that area feel enthusiastic to go work there. The project name,

'Hopewell', made people have hope and expectation. When the project fell apart, it was like a paradise had collapsed. Then, artists went out there to create meanings and make sense of it. The Hopewell project should have turned out well, but it didn't. The artists criticised the things that caused their paradise to collapse. This was political criticism which, of course, revolved around corruption. The feeling people had for the word 'Hopewell' and the desire to criticize the failure of the project, made them go there to work."

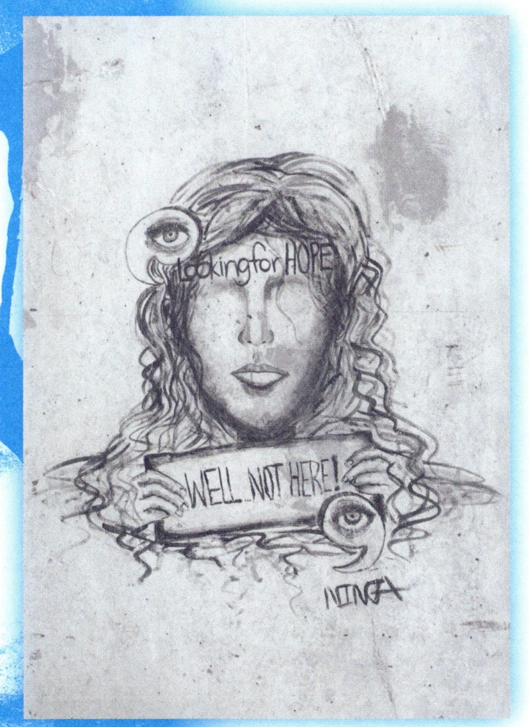

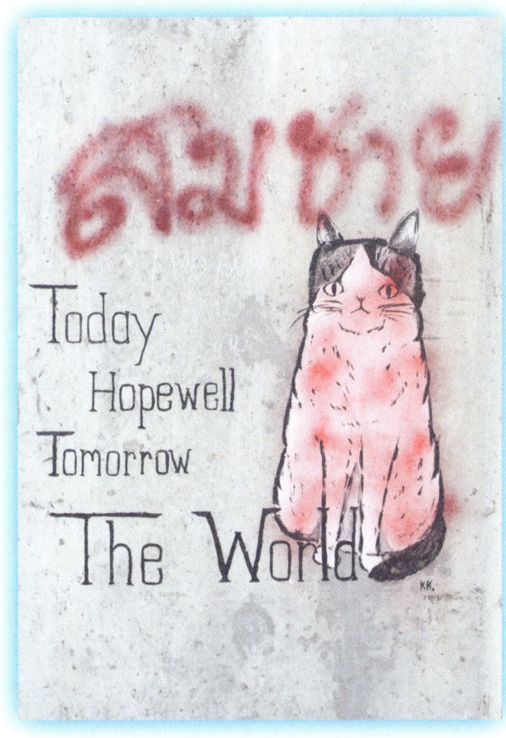

Toy depicted a suited man, his mouth full of cash, in reference to the greed of those with power (see page 67). A piece by Nola Nolee shows a similar politician tied to one of the columns above a pile of government contracts, she represents herself as two figures, about to burn the politician alive (see page 67). In each of these pieces, the necktie is a symbol of government and the corporation.

NOLA -NO- LEE

"It's about how the government wants to collect money from Thai people. The papers are budget papers of the government. I intended to show politicians tied to the Hopewell columns and then burning them at the stake, burn them alive with their budget papers."

KANS created a trompe l'oeil cavern on one of the columns, with twisted internal rebar and cement fragments forming a menacing, skull-like face (see page 108). From the cavern pours a stream of gold beside the English words, "Your tax inside". Another anonymous artist painted a man holding a gun to his own head with the Thai *nak kan muang* (politician) above (see page 63). ALEX FACE depicted his Mardi figure – a little, three-eyed girl – tied to one of the columns with a forlorn expression, a thought bubble rising from her head with the word 'Hope' inside. In another, Mardi is shown tied to one of the columns as if sacrificed (see page 69).

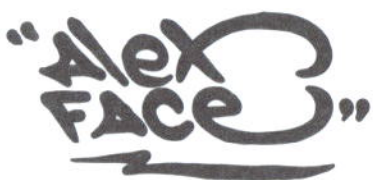

"I wanted to send a message like, this girl was stuck here for 20 years, this thing is not a victory."

Mamacup711's piece shows the faces of Thailand's poor weeping over the wasted money that went into the project (see page 40).

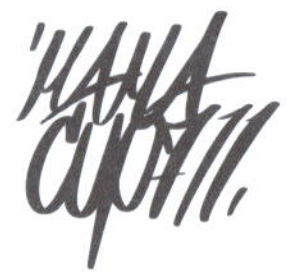

"My work at Hopewell is about tears and sorrow. It was what I felt at the time. I had seen the Hopewell pillars for a long time but never really knew what they were. They were there, but had no function. Then, all of a sudden, they were demolished. My art depicts the displaced, homeless and poor people. We could have done so many things for them with the cost of that project. Their situation was like a bird that could have flown to freedom but is stuck."

Hopewell was also a site where other political issues were addressed, such as environmental concerns around the damming of rivers like the Xayaburi Dam in Laos, which in 2012 became the first mainstream dam on the lower Mekong, and the proposed dam in Thailand's Mae Wong National Park. TEAS depicted a plump bird perched on barbed wire holding a placard reading "No Dam" (see page 41). ALEX FACE's Mardi is depicted as a mounted head of a stag holding a similar sign. Goh-M painted a sinister looking creature holding a "No Dam" placard and wearing a T-Shirt saying "Stop EHIA", a reference to the machinations going on around the Mae Wong Dam and attempts to avoid undertaking an Environmental Health Impact Assessment.

For many street artists this was just an interesting place to work, a laboratory where the endless supply of columns allowed them to hone their skills, or step into street art for the first, and perhaps last, time.

"Personally, I didn't care where these columns came from."

"For this project, we didn't think about trying to make a political statement by working there. These columns had been standing there for 15 to 20 years, so there's no hope there. Nobody cared about Hopewell for so many years. So I think when we did something nice in that area, and people drove by, they started to care more about that place. It gives some smiles to people in their cars, in the traffic jam."

• • •

At Hopewell, many of the street artists were reminding those who would listen, that these, soon-to-be demolished pillars, were bought with the hard-earned baht of average Thai people. If you ask those people whether they think the misuse of public money will be eradicated in Thailand, their answer may well be, 'Hopeless'.

·MUEBON·

"Corruption is everywhere in Thailand. The nation's structure creates inequality. It drives human greed and makes people want to be rich. Because, if you are rich in this country, you can live like a king. You can buy the cops, the law, you can buy everything. You can even buy someone's ideology or humanity. If you are poor, you have to work hard just so you can pay for your next meal. You will be exploited from every part of society. Government officials will intimidate you. You will be extorted at every opportunity. If you are born into a poor family, the system will keep you all poor – from your grandfather's generation to your father's and then to yours and your child's. No matter how much effort you make and how hard you work, your chance of advancement is 0.001%. The system was built to oppress the people. So, the poor will do whatever it takes to get themselves out of poverty. And sometimes it doesn't matter if that requires being corrupt. Corruption has become a common practice. It's always been like that in Thailand. This is one thing you cannot change. Because to change it means dismantling the old system. But, even if the chance of success is 0.001%, we have to hope that we can change it. We have to live with hope. Because, if we don't do anything, the chance for success would be 0.000%."

CIDER

"Corruption happens everywhere in the world, you know. So Hopewell has become iconic, all over Bangkok. Now, when you get pulled over by the cops, you have to pay 500 baht. Nine out of ten Thai citizens experience the same thing. When I was younger, to get a seat in a fancy

restaurant you had to give the waiter extra money to get your seat right away. Or when you go get your ID card done, you have to pay them extra money, to be up there first. So, money talks. I think that money pushes things around to make things happen."

In 2013, while the artists worked at Hopewell, a 21.2 billion baht contract was signed between the SRT and Italian-Thai Development to build the Dark Red Line from Bang Sue to Rangsit. And, in a final indignity, it was found that none of the Hopewell columns could be reused as part of this project; they were too small. The construction of this Dark Red Line is what drove the eventual removal of many of the Hopewell columns and the buffing of their street art during 2015 and 2016. As the new Bang Khen Station took shape, the surviving street art in the area was painted over.

The elections called for by Yingluck Shinawatra in 2014 never happened. Instead, the Royal Thai Armed Forces staged a coup. Soon, General Prayut Chan-o-cha took power as a caretaker leader. The constitution was suspended and the country again fell under military rule. Two years later, in 2016, King Bhumibol died and the man who had brought the monarchy back to the core of power and politics in Thailand, was gone.

During its first years in power, Prayut's government suppressed dissent and opposition. The new leaders called themselves the National Council for Peace and Order. One of Prayut's key promises was to combat the kind of abuses epitomised by the Hopewell project. Now approaching a decade in power, many Thais see that, more than ever, those in power can prosecute their political enemies' corruption while ignoring that of their allies. The legitimacy of the 2019 elections were widely questioned. Electoral boundaries were redrawn, the Electoral Commission was criticised for not being impartial and voting irregularities emerged. Despite not standing in the elections, Prayut was voted in as Prime Minister by the National Assembly, one-third of which is military-appointed. In the years after Hopewell disappeared, street art would be increasingly used to convey political messages. This was a result of the changing political climate, the proliferation of social media and the popularity of the art form.

As for the Hopewell project itself, in the end, as the new Dark Red Line neared completion in April 2019, the Thai Supreme Administrative Court ordered the State Railway of Thailand and the Transport Ministry to pay 25 billion baht (then about US$787.5 million) in compensation to Hopewell Holdings. Adding the columns' removal cost of about 200 million baht (about US$6.3 million), the total bill, as of 2019, came to 25.2 billion baht (US$794 million). On top of this, the public would also pay for the Hopewell line's entirely new replacement; as of 2020 around 88 billion baht (US$2.8 billion).

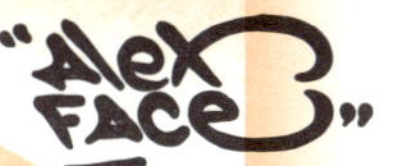

"People had questions when they saw that place – the long, long stretch of big columns beside Vibhavadi Road. I don't know how much money it was for each column, and you had to spend a lot of money to cut them out. Yeah, only the art came. But I don't know if it was worth the cost! We talked about it when we were there, 'This is like the most expensive wall we have ever done!' I'm so proud of that."

The Thai government had spent the Thai people's wealth on a project that would become symbolic of the ineptitude that caused its failure – effectively, what the thieves built with the wealth they stole advertised their crime to the very people they had stolen it from. Bangkok's street artists were there to do what they could to make sure this wasn't forgotten.

Rukkit

"Doing street art there put a spotlight onto Hopewell again. If there wasn't street art there, people would have forgotten about it. When street art appeared there, then people thought about it again."

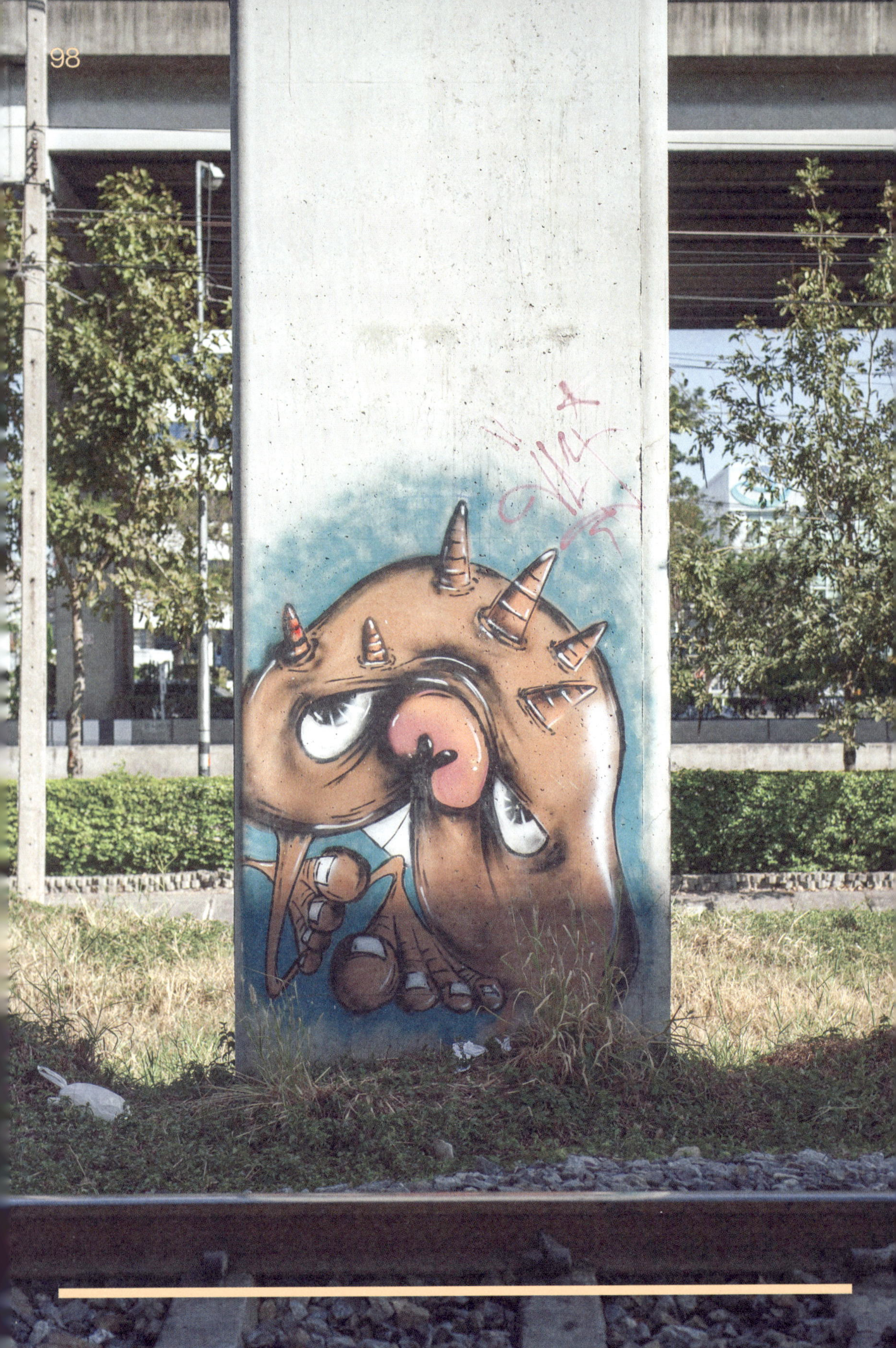

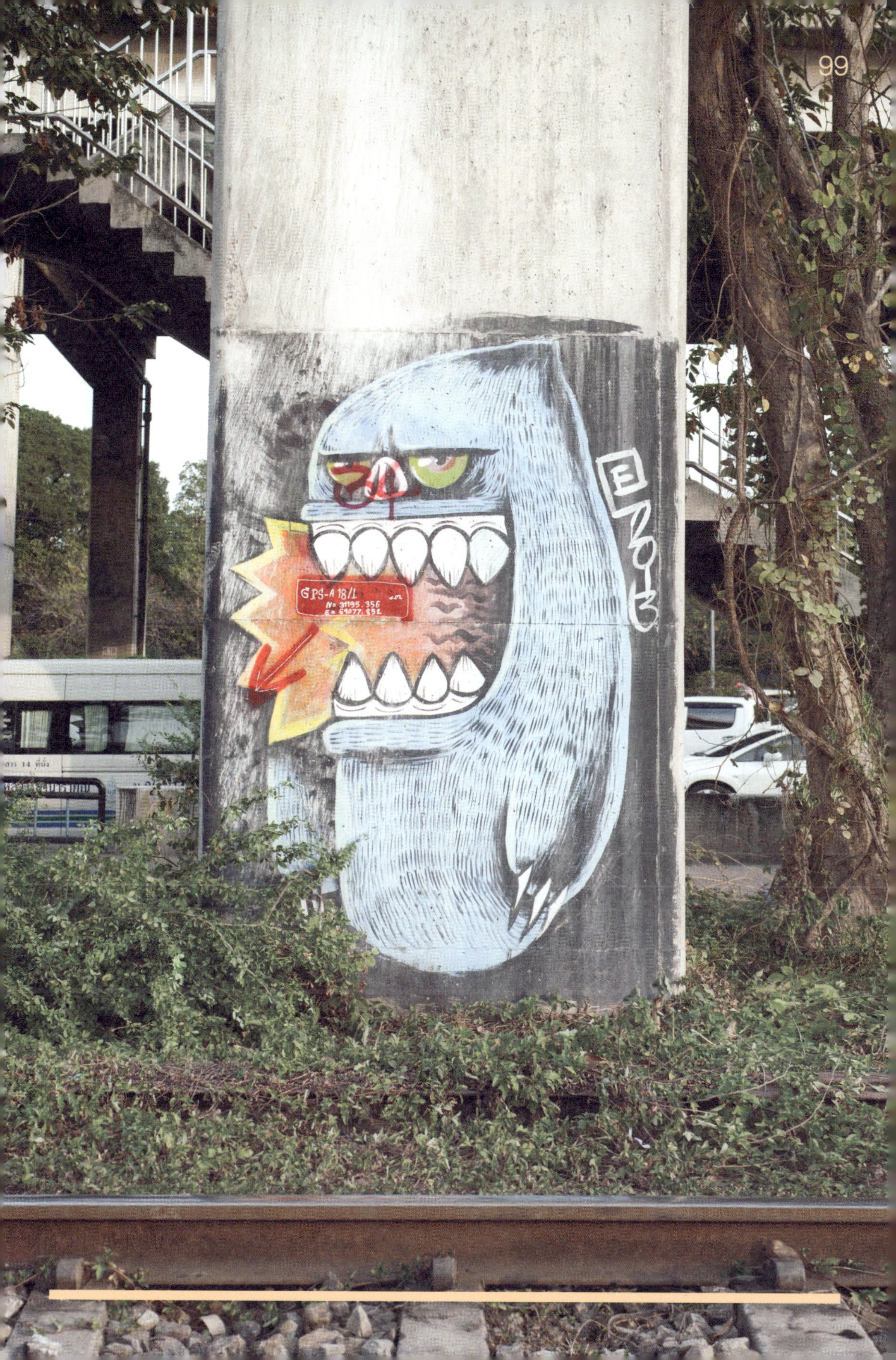
GPS-A 18/1

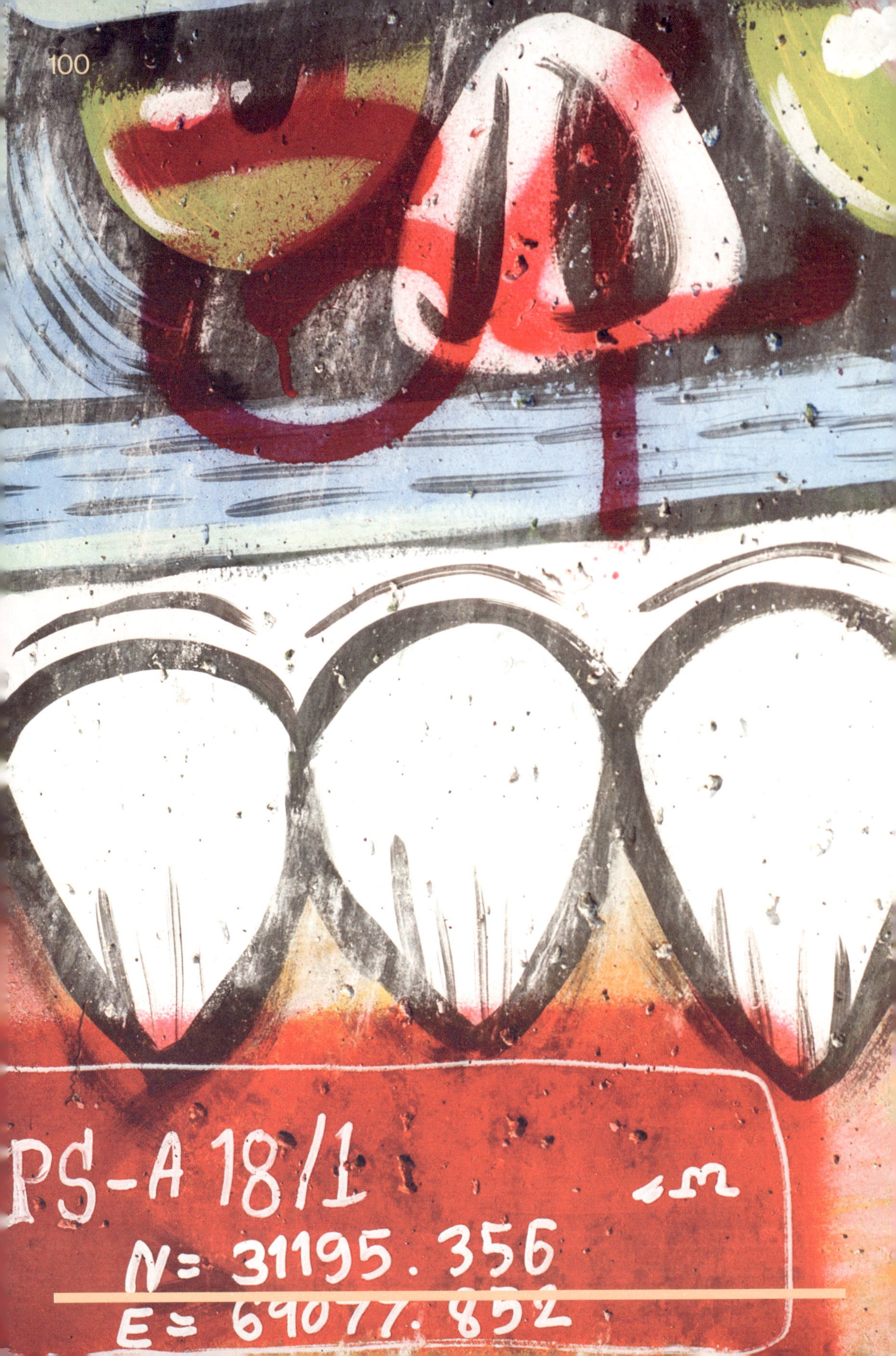
PS-A 18/1
N= 31195. 356
E= 69077. 852

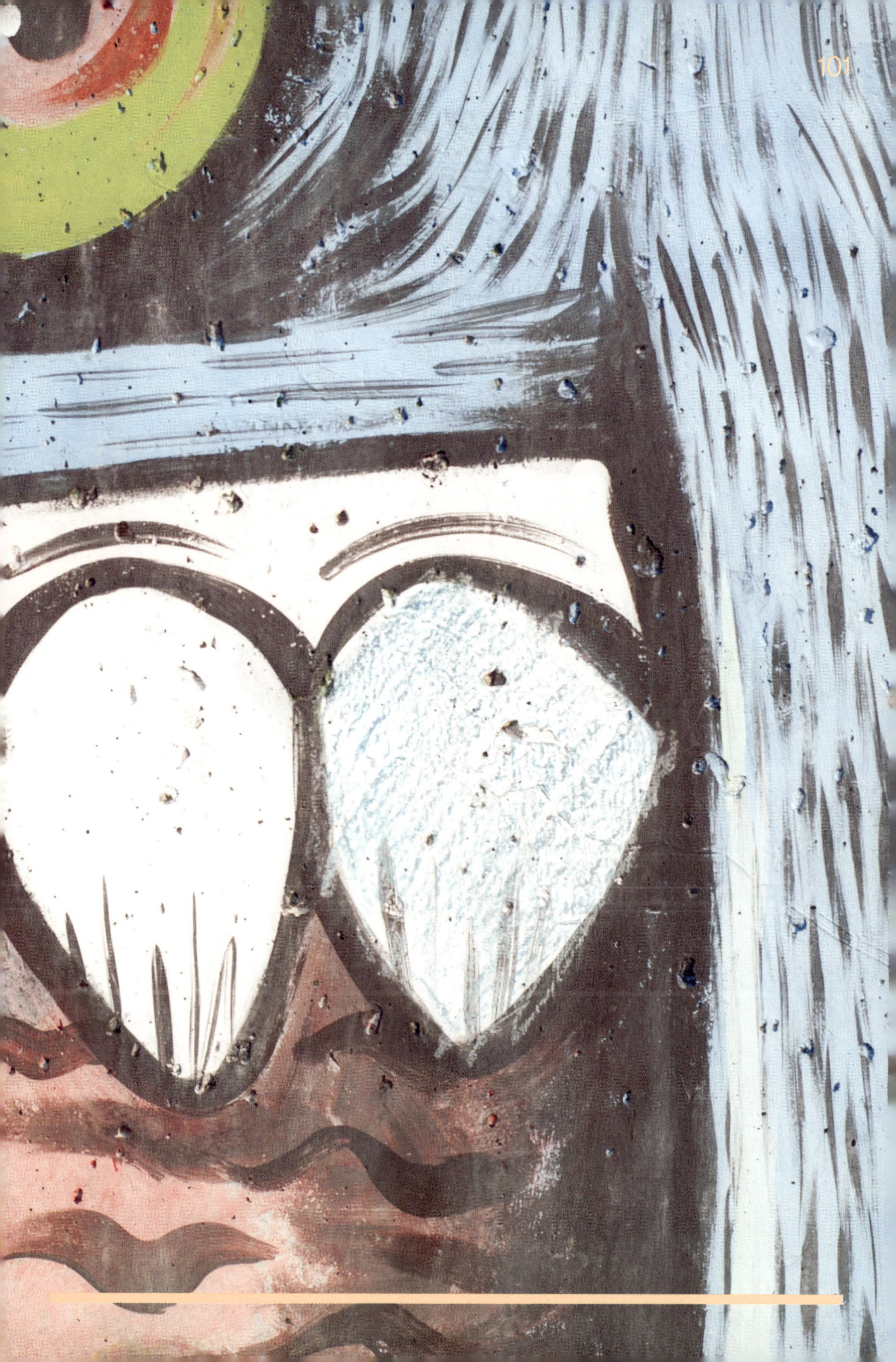

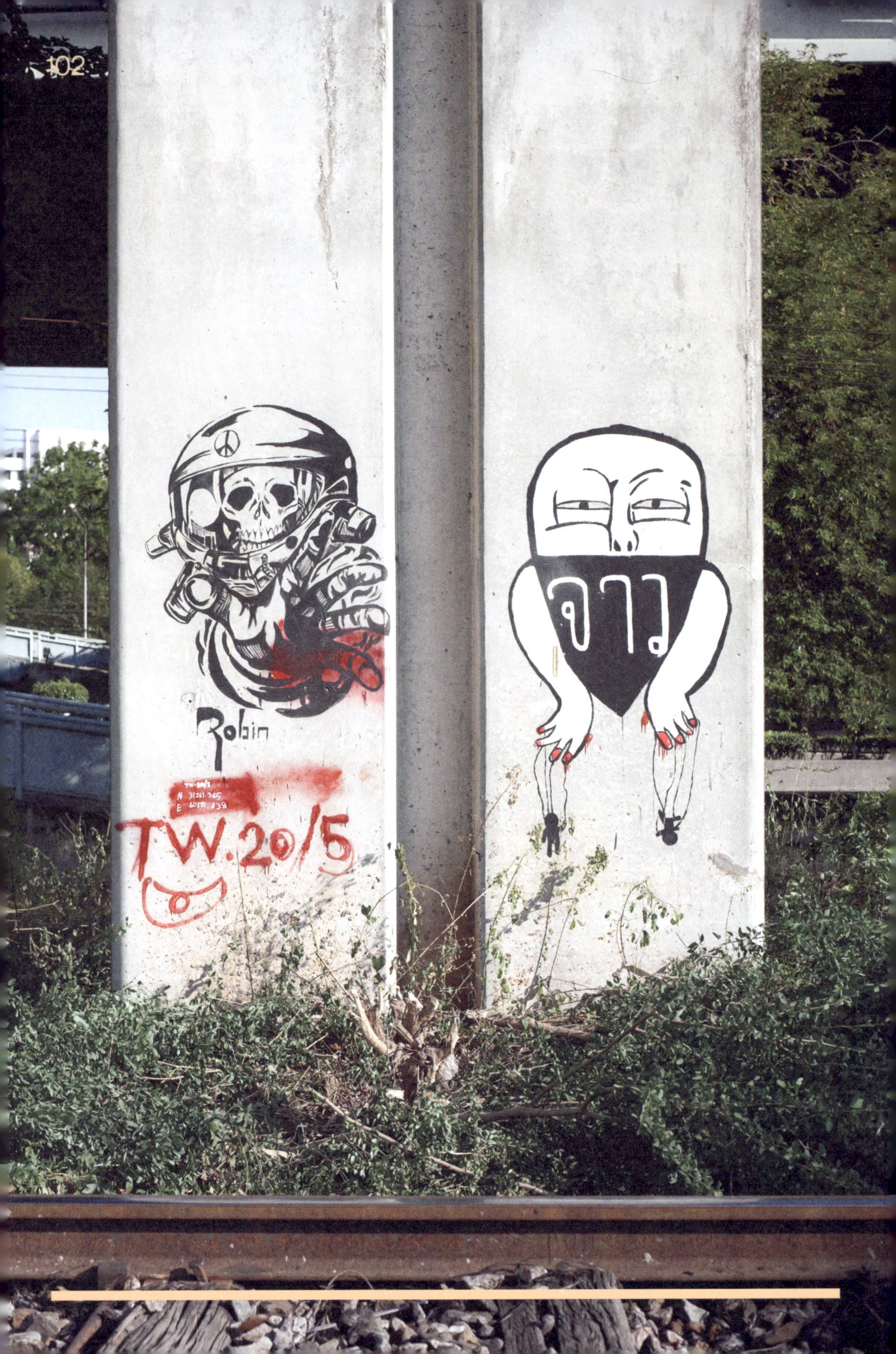
Robin
TW.20/5
จาว

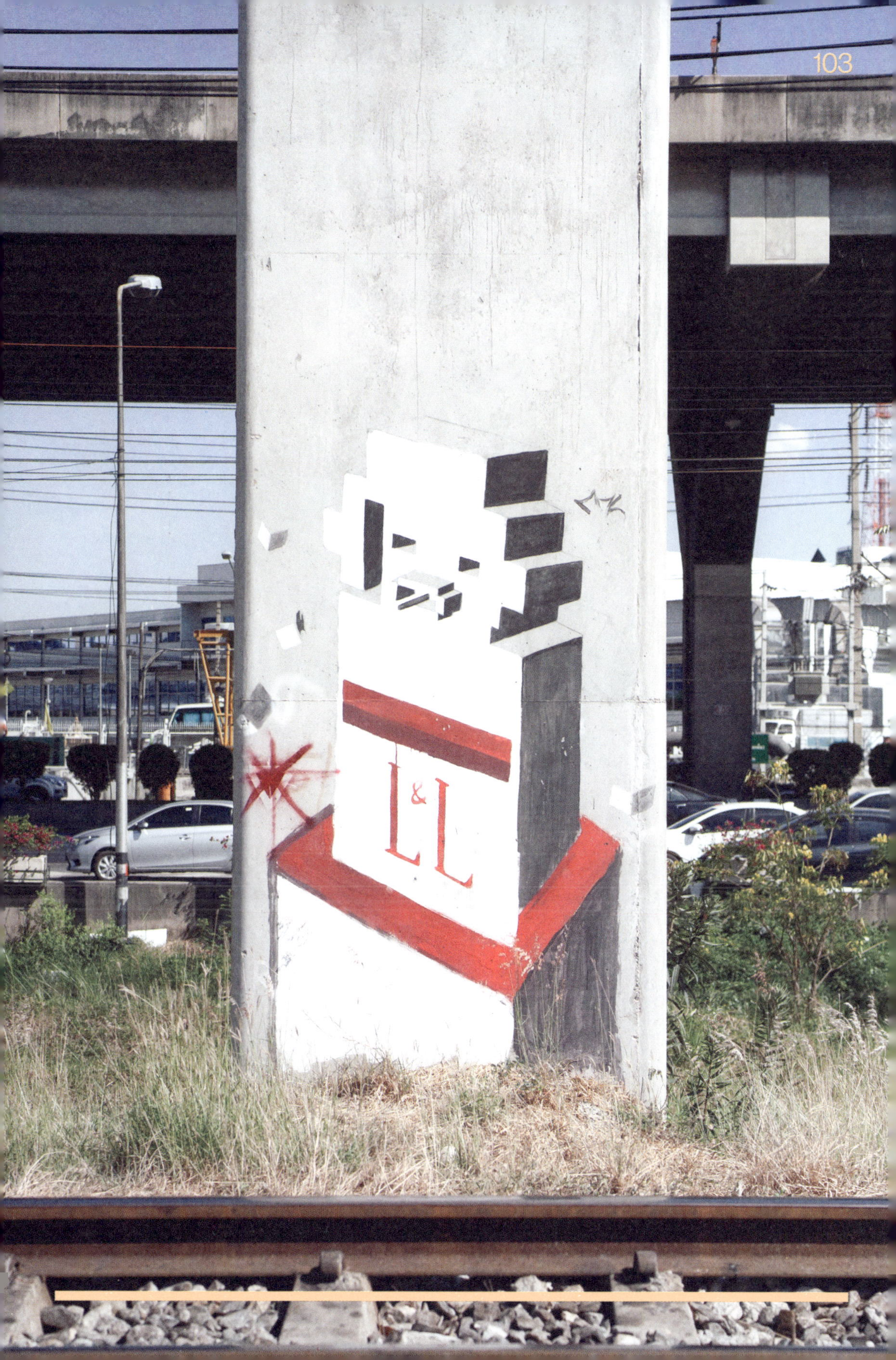
L&L

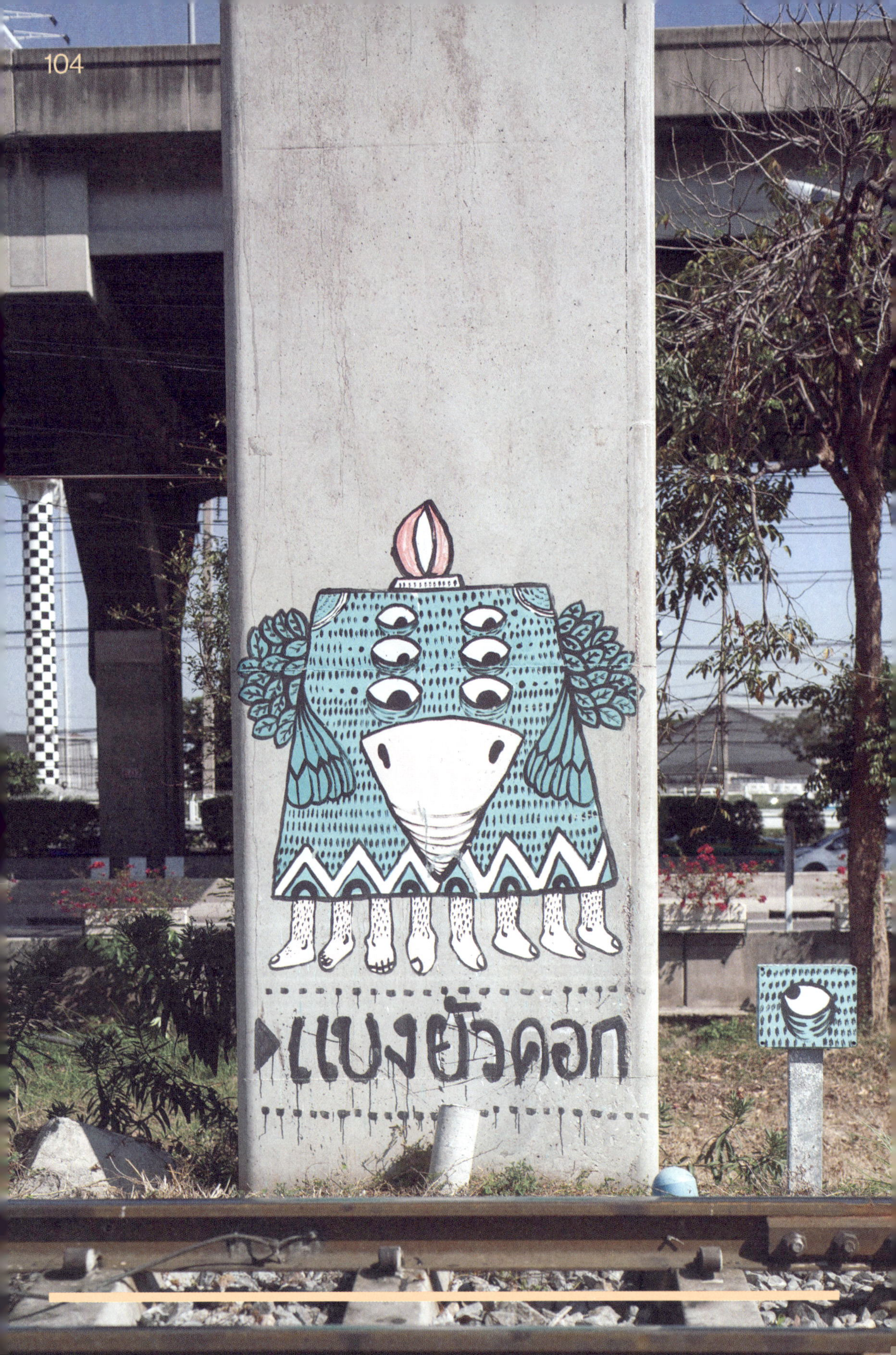
แบงยัวดอก

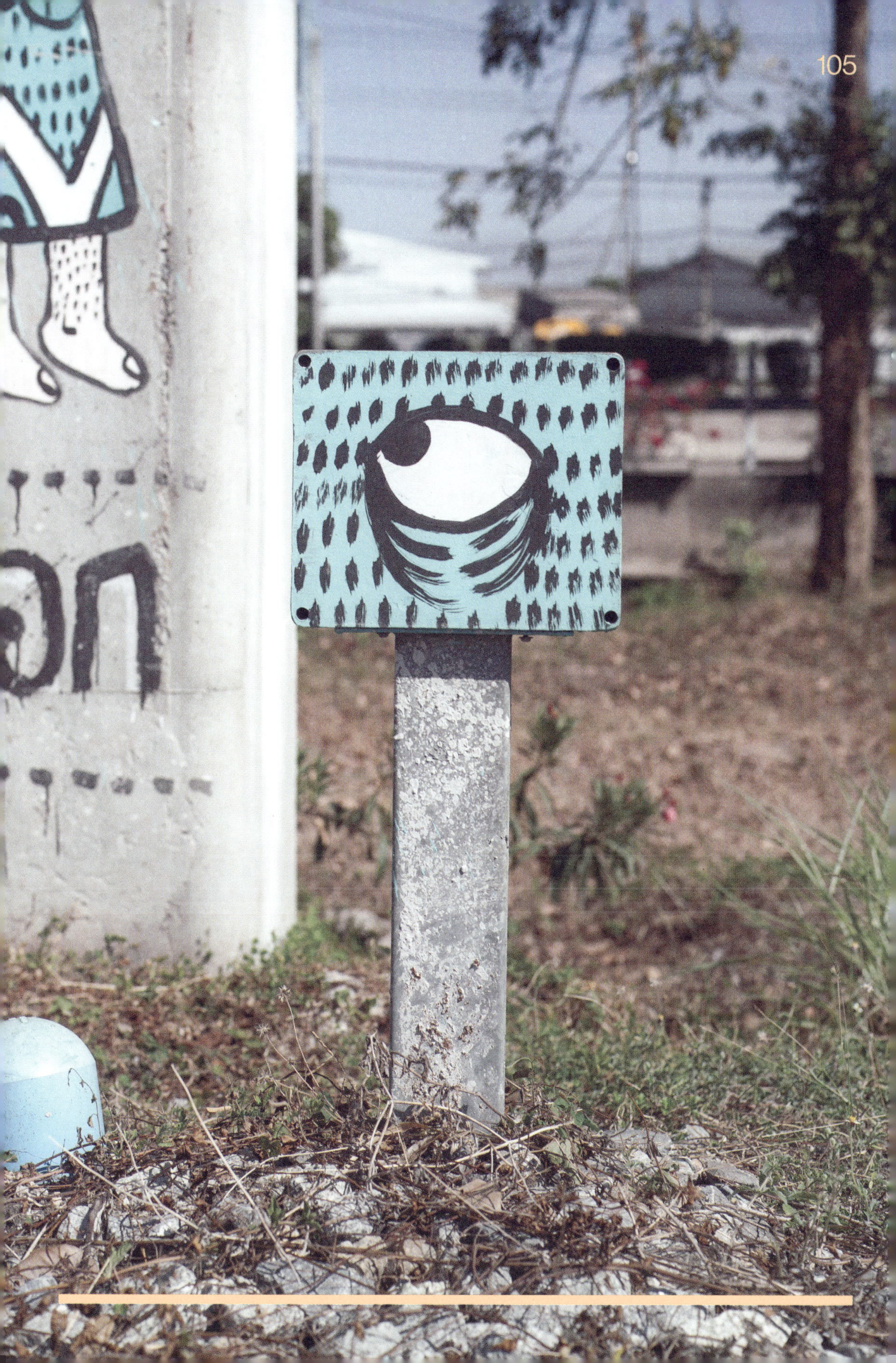

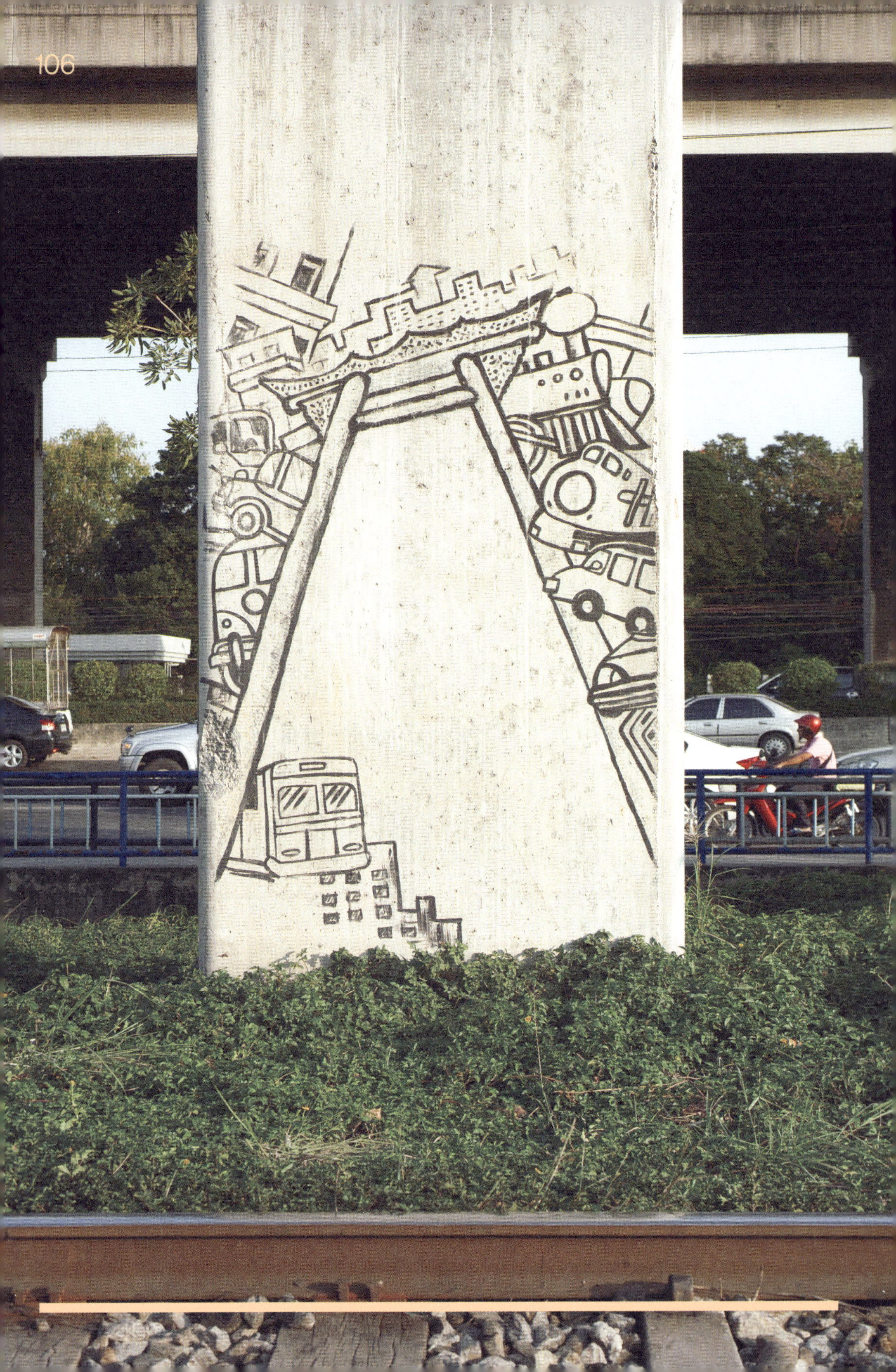

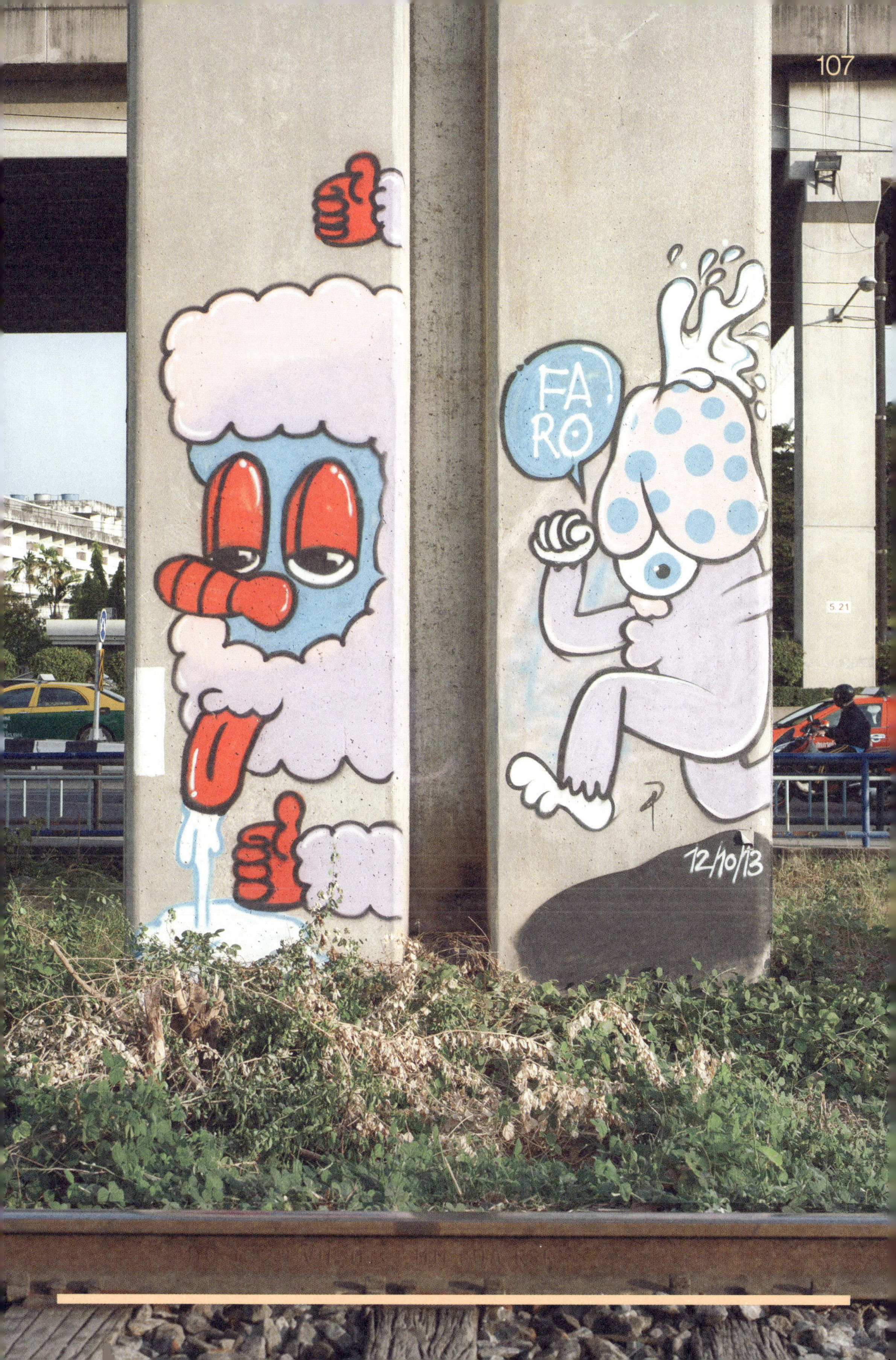
FA
RO
12/10/13

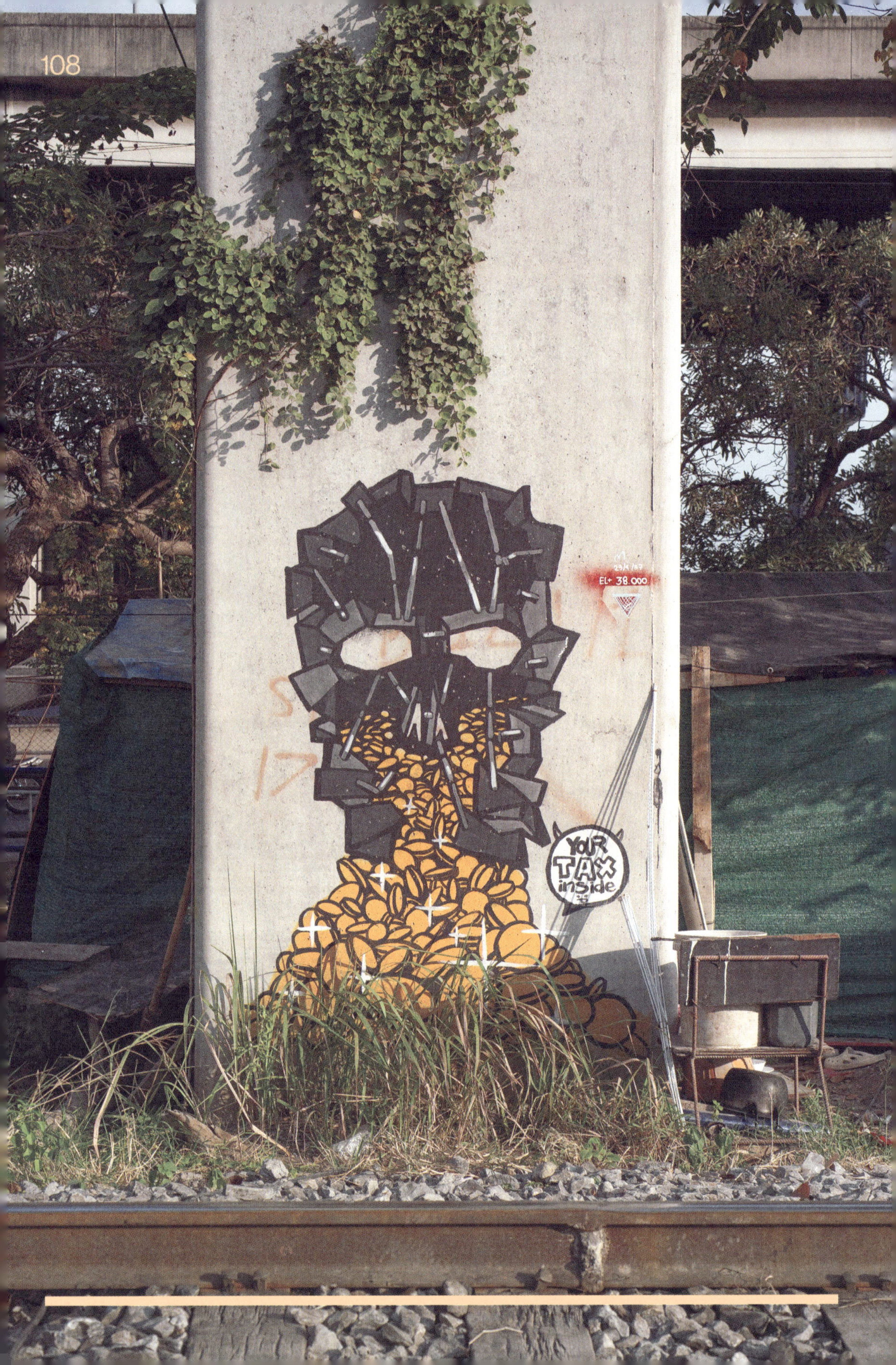
EL+ 38 000
YOUR TAX inside

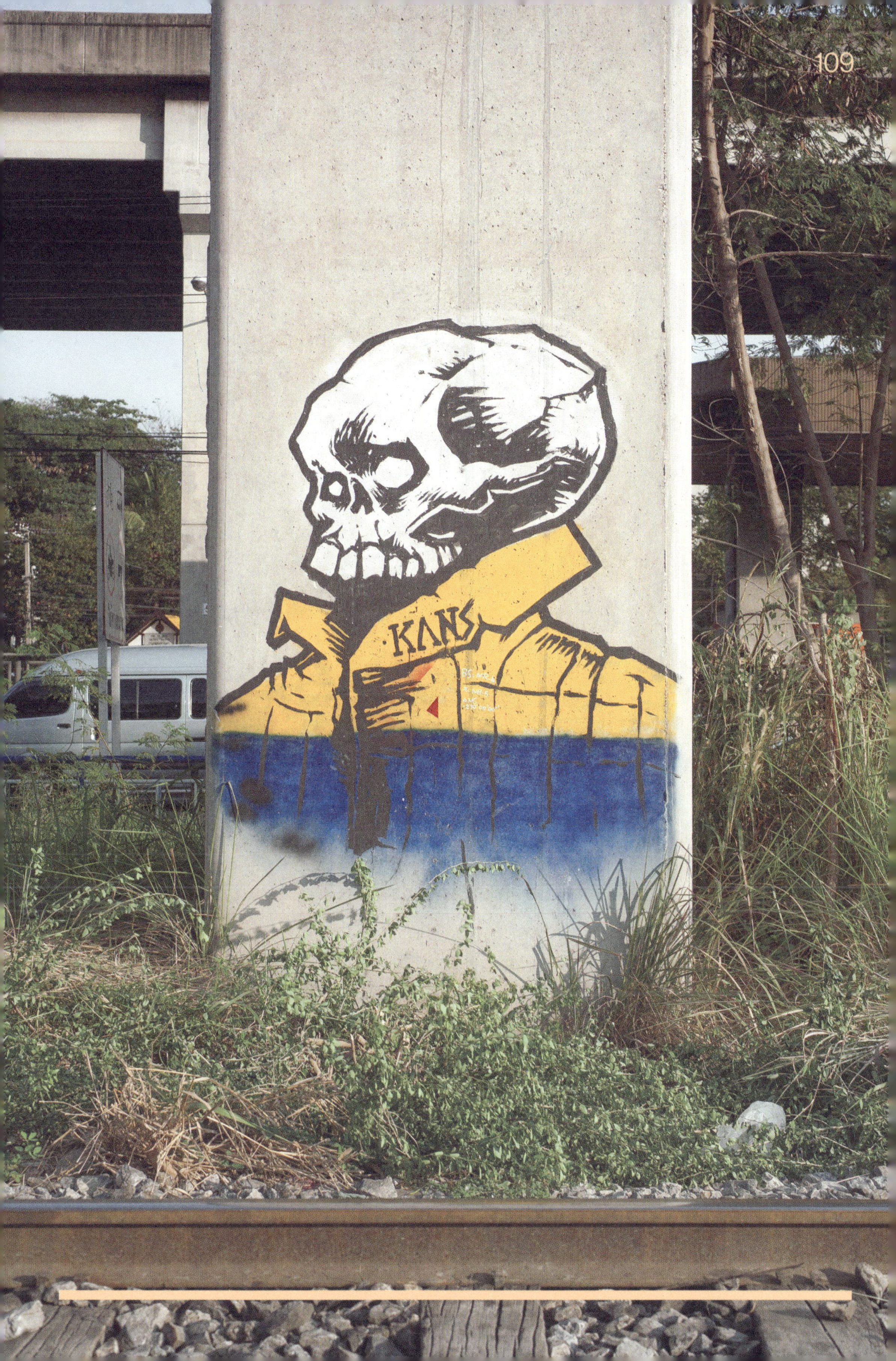
KANS

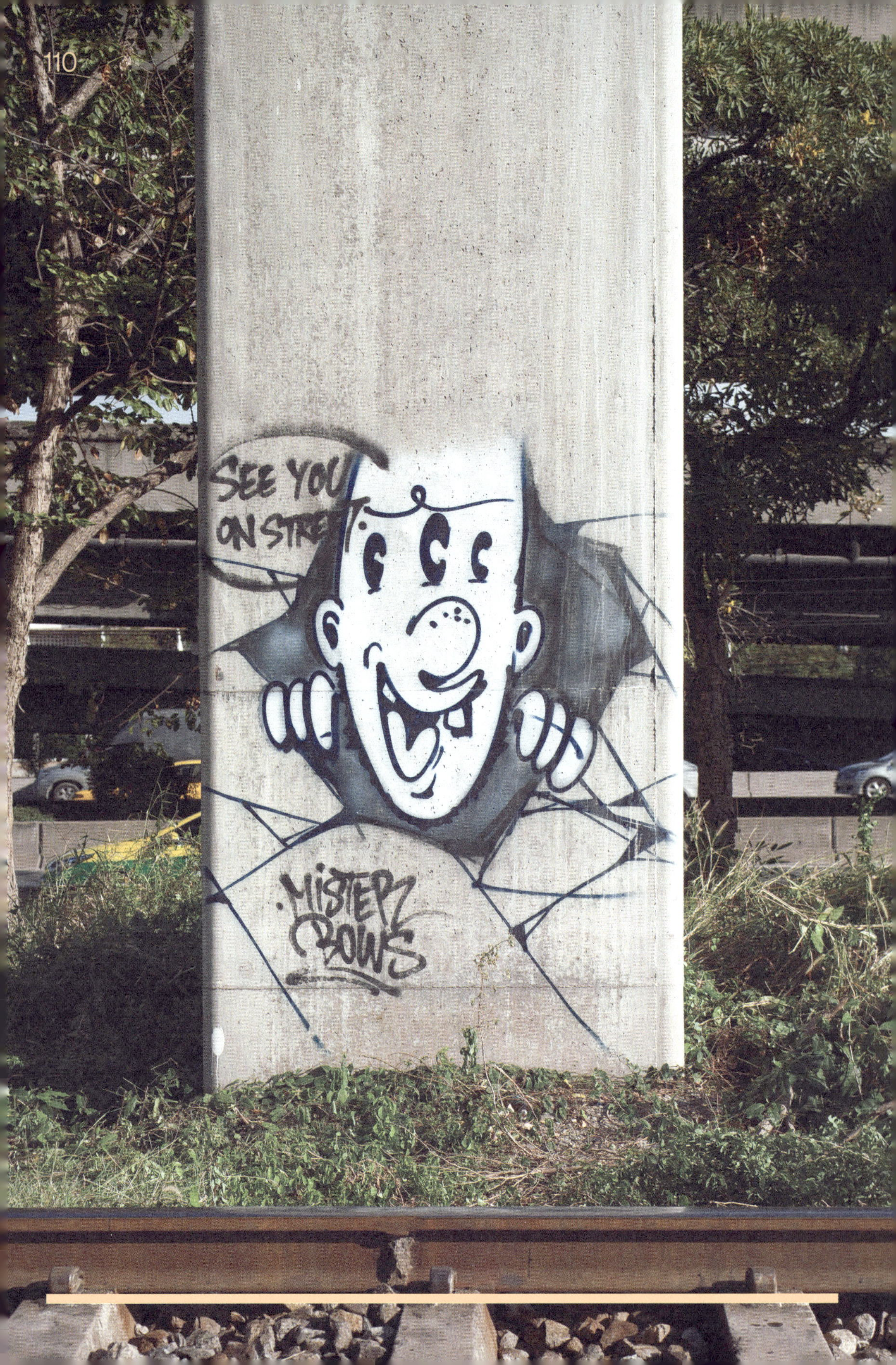
SEE YOU ON STREET.
MISTER BOWS

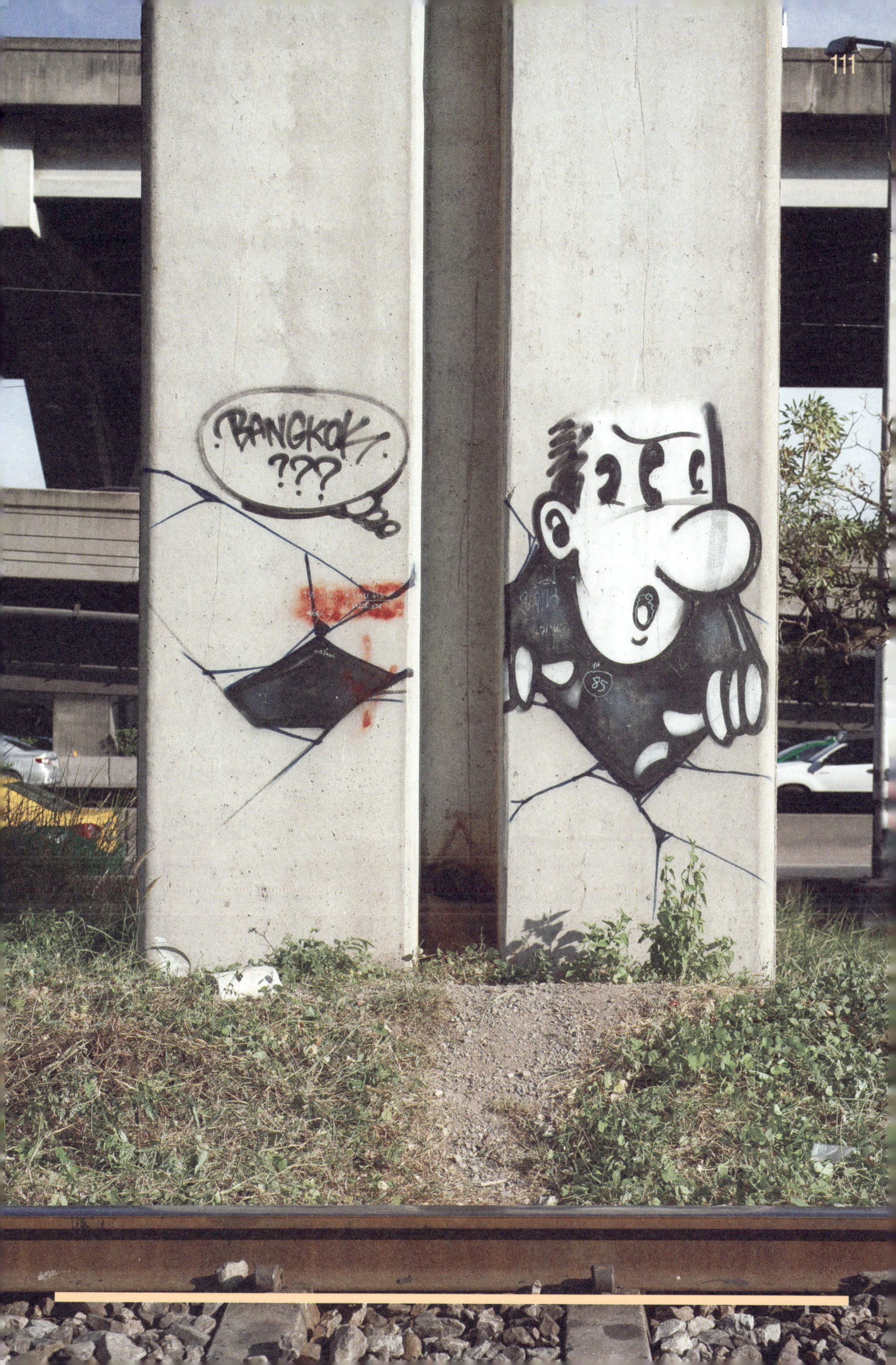
BANGKOK
???

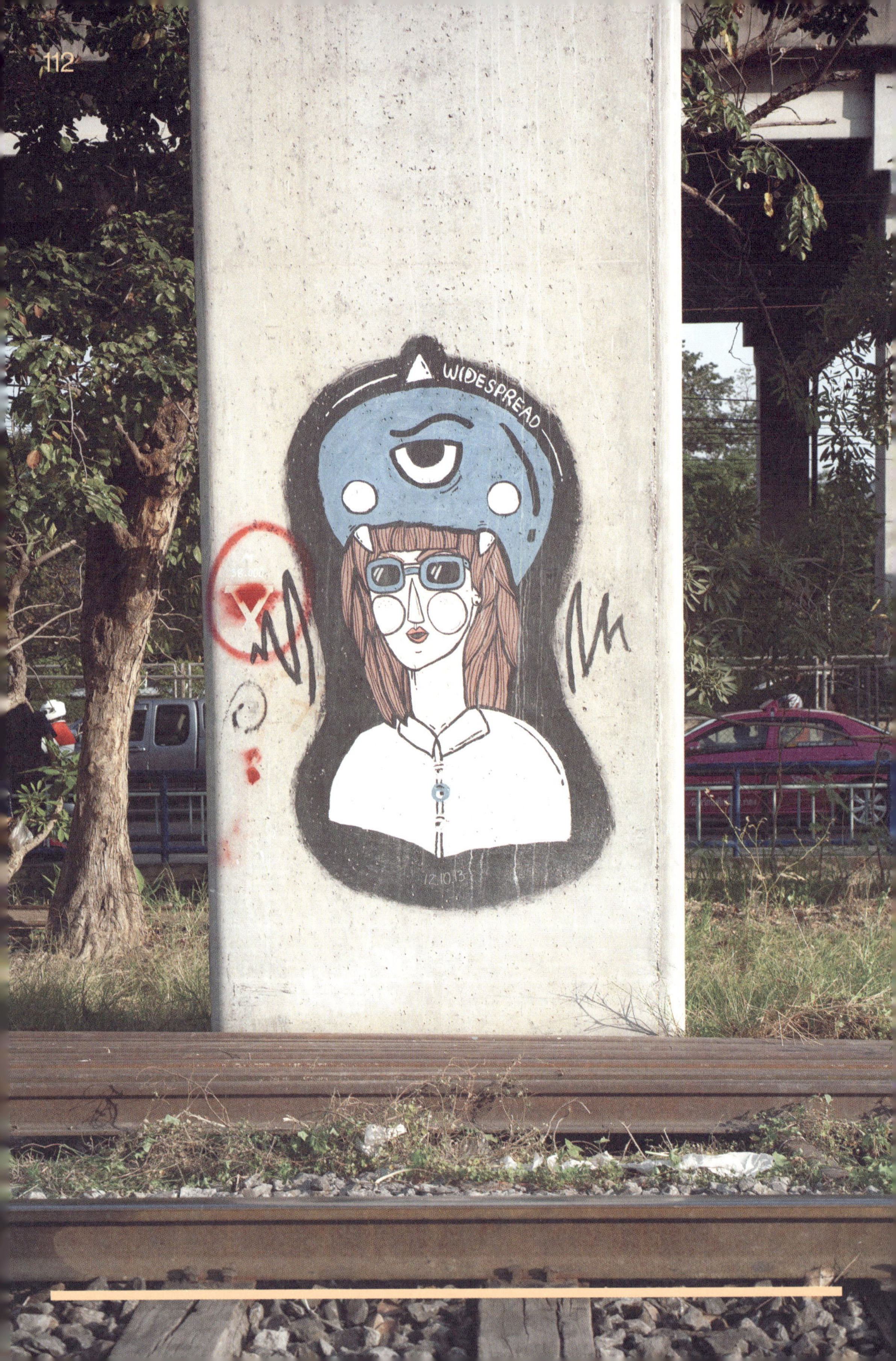
WIDESPREAD
12.10.13

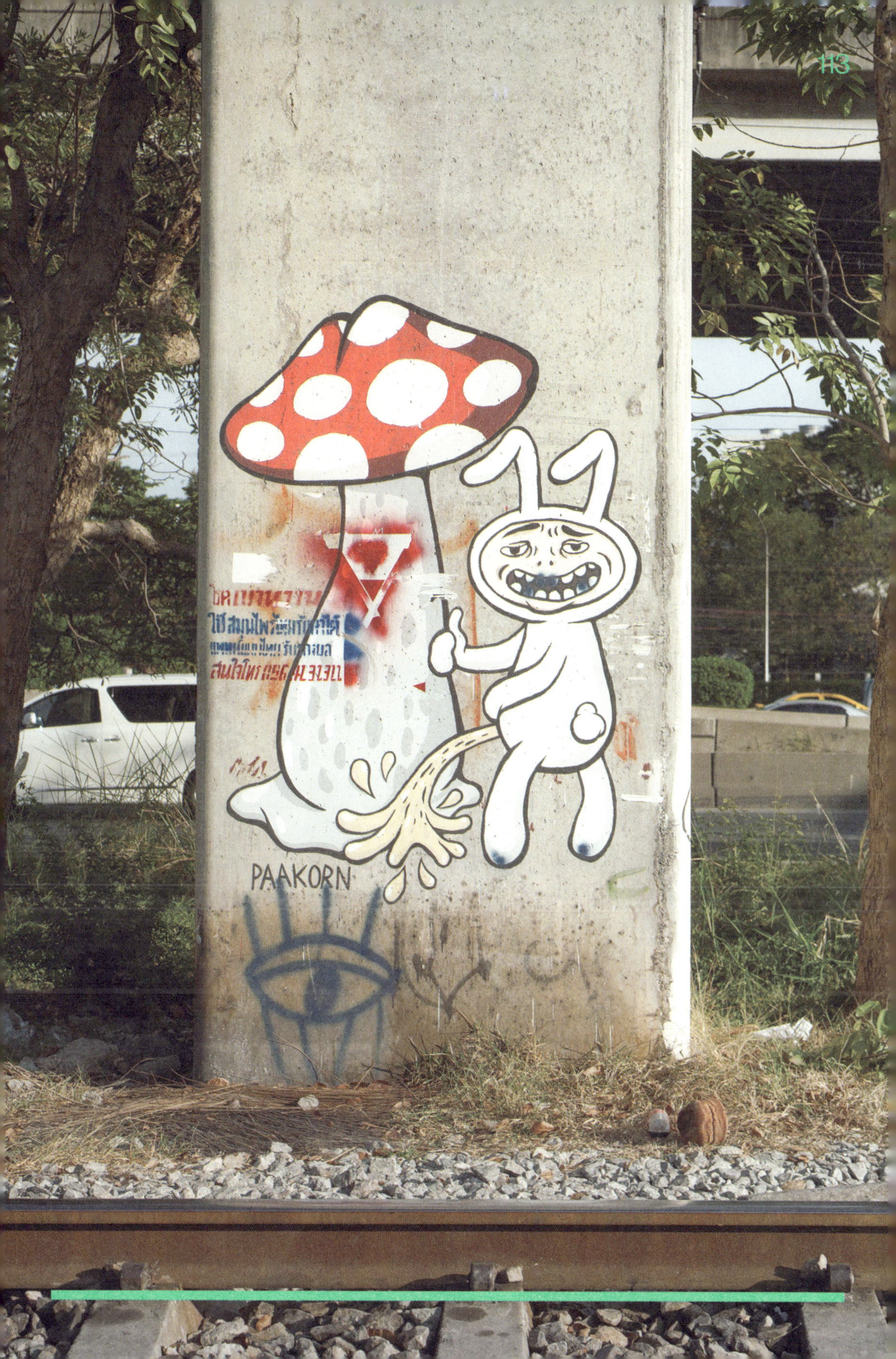
PAAKORN

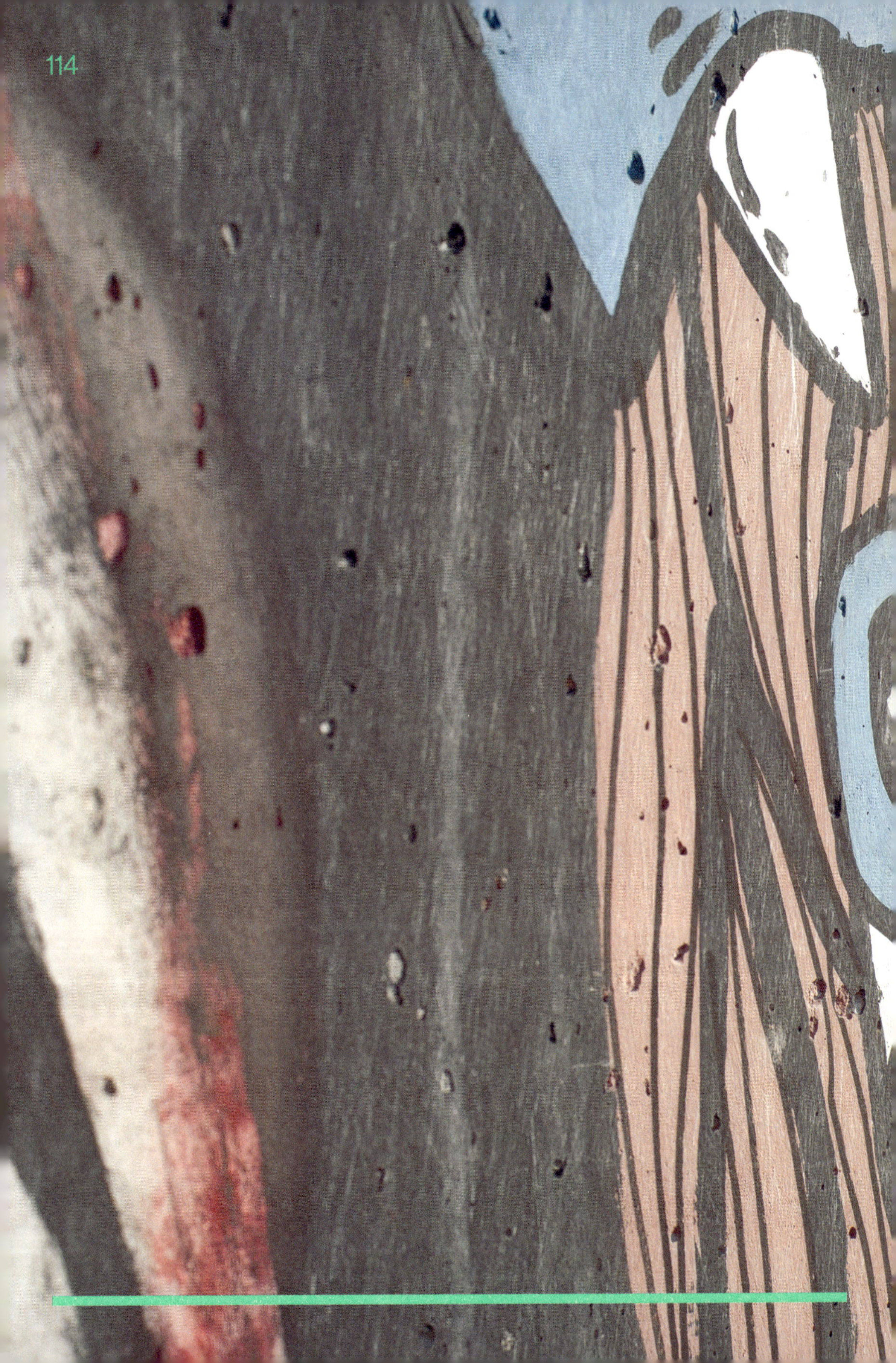

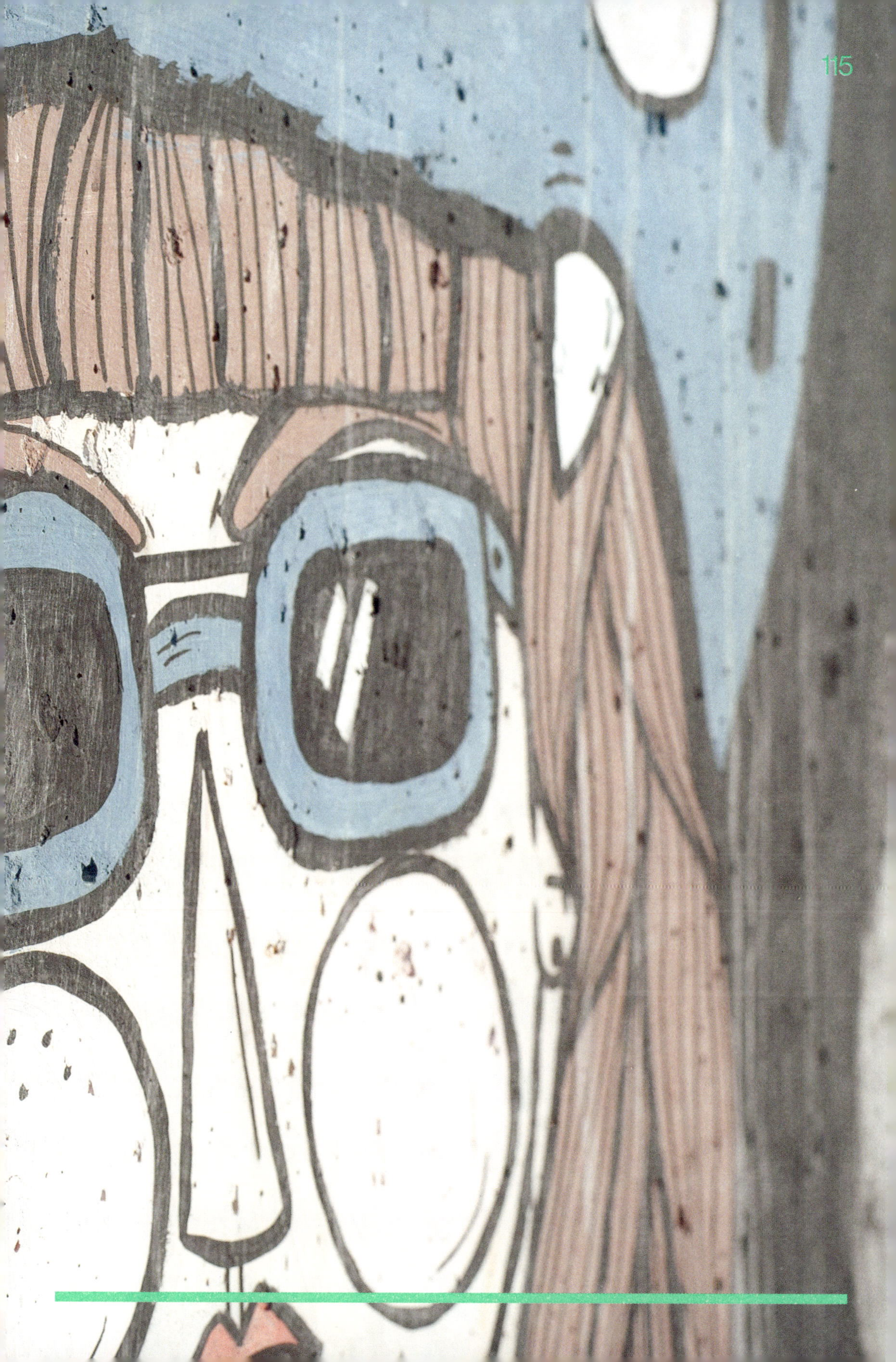

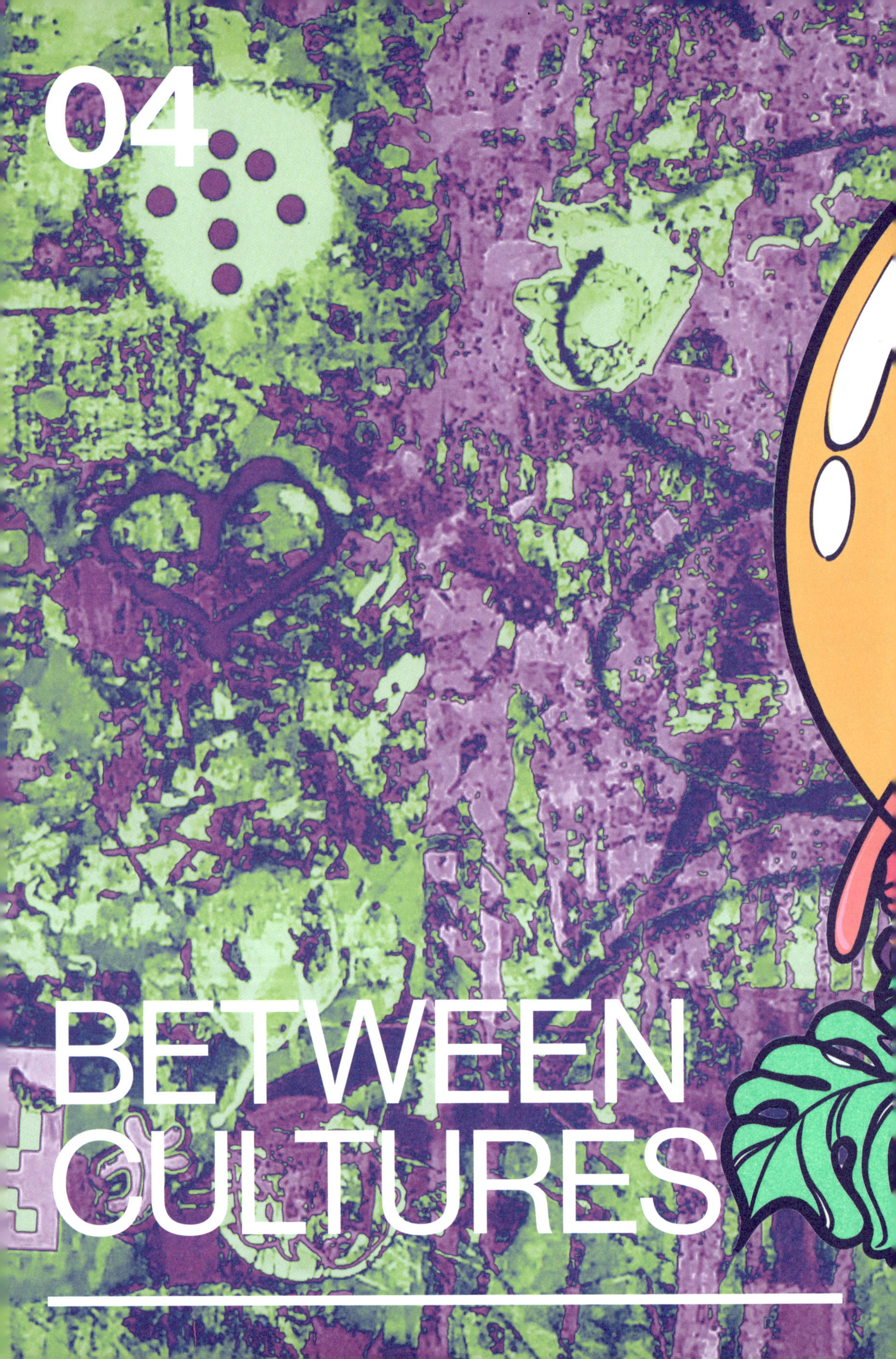

04

BETWEEN CULTURES

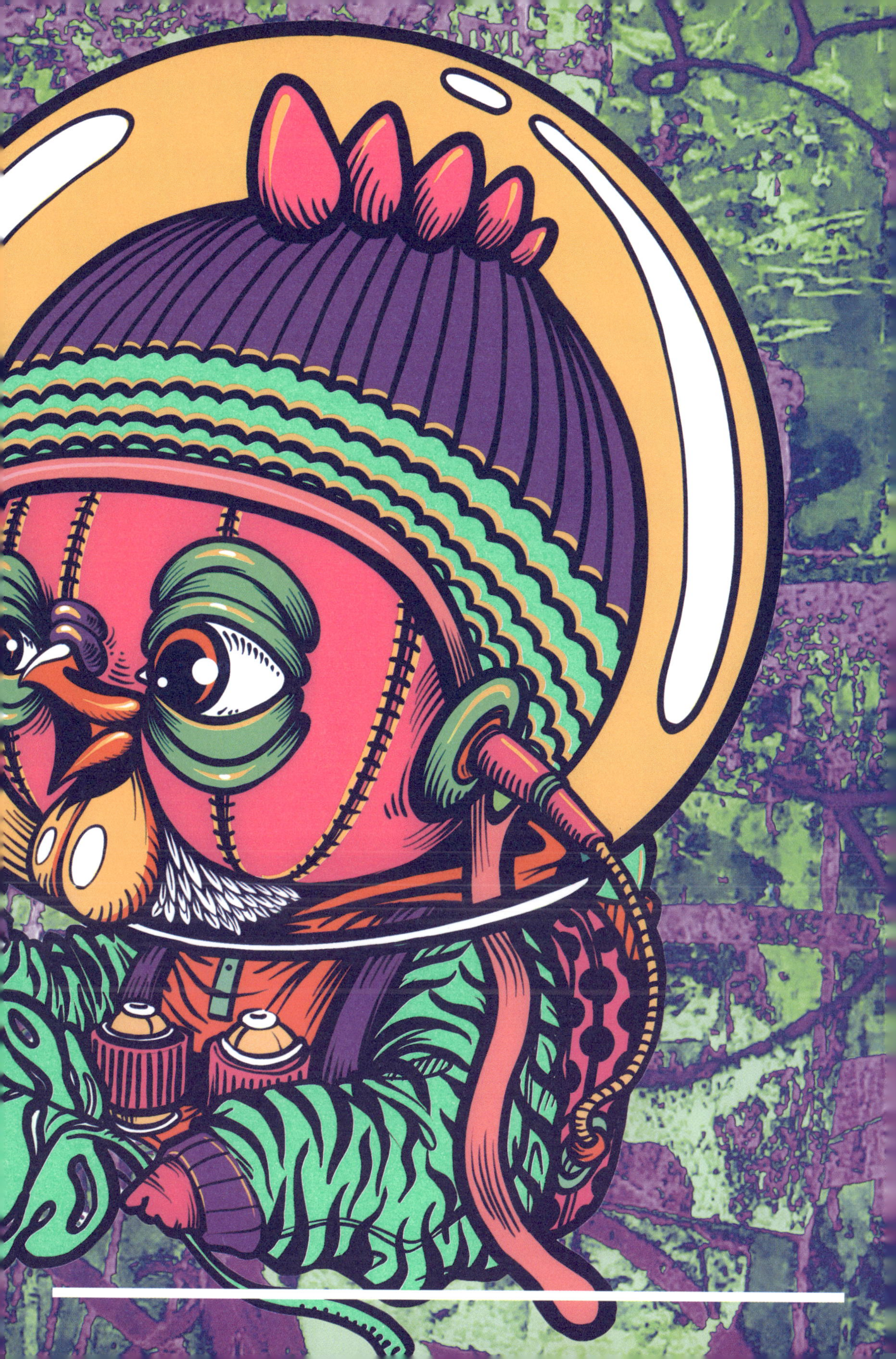

Graffiti has burned itself into the identity of many cities. New York, Berlin, Tokyo, Moscow, London, Melbourne and Rio have become famous for their graffiti and street art. In Bangkok, ALEX FACE's Mardi figure, SHEET's cryptographic maps, Rukkit's geometry, the wildstyle of CIDER, Poyd1 and others are today a part of the city's character. These are familiar faces and styles that pop up here and there, adding whimsy to harsh urban environments. The development boom that tore through Bangkok from the 1960s onwards, created a homogenous cementscape. Bangkok's embrace of American-style malls, high-rise towers and unplanned development led to a largely mono-tone urban form that gave current generations of street artists and graffiti writers their three-dimensional canvas. These incorrigibles rescue control of the city's identity from overwhelming commercialism.

·MUEBON·

"Part of the reason I do street art is because I feel that in so many public places, business takes everything with their advertising. But that's a place for everyone. Public spaces should actually be used to benefit people, physically and mentally. But it has become a space for capitalist exploitation, authorized by officials."

SHEET has drawn intricate sets of lines, symbols and scenes across Bangkok's footpaths for years (see below). He is prolific. Once noticed, his works begin to appear everywhere.

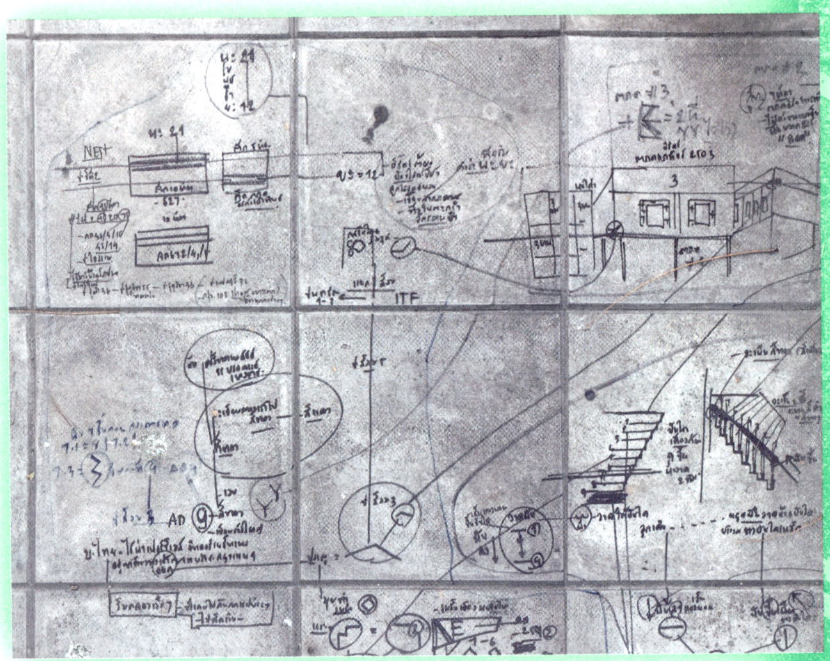

Piece by SHEET

SHEET

"What I do is a combination of a map and nature. When I draw the maps, I draw them everywhere in the city. I want to draw the whole city. I consider myself the handler of this case. I have made a promise to find evidence. How do I work? I walk everywhere so I get a sense of the city. If we were high up like a satellite or were a bird looking down, we would see everything. But humans are not satellites and birds can't draw for us. So, I have to walk everywhere, which takes a long time. I have to keep going. Once I reach a destination, I draw. Right after that, I move on to the next place."

Operating beyond the graffiti and street art tribes, SHEET is an outsider. Wholly dedicated to his work – perhaps more than any other artist in this book – he never stops, writing all day. So, if spending time on developing your style and furthering a message beyond personal fame is criteria for being a good creator (see Chapter 5), SHEET is well qualified. He lives true to the spirit of street art – a desire to communicate directly without the interference of an editor, publisher, censor, financier or authority. His work is simple, pure and he believes its message is critical.

SHEET

"I promised myself that I would find those who poisoned and murdered my family. My mum, my uncle, little brother and everyone was poisoned. While I was writing, I received some intelligence, evidence against a country leader. But it's locked high up in a tower, so I decided to write a map. When I have that proof, I want to tell people what happened to my family. This was a promise I made to myself. Before, I was a soldier and then I was discharged. I never had a successful career after that. So I decided to walk and collect stuff from the garbage and I found evidence that suggested my family really was poisoned."

Today, the boundary between private and public space is blurred, especially in the forecourts of major shopping centres. These places are exclusive, but not in the way they spruik. They are accessible and welcoming, but only if you have enough money in your pocket. For everyone else, including SHEET, they are unfriendly. Commercial places like this are removed from the organic life of the city.

·MUEBON·

"Years ago, they only had a few places for rich people. Now they're everywhere. I do projects with fancy department stores. Once, when I went to talk to the owner of a department store, security tried to stop me from walking into the plaza area, just because I didn't dress the way they expected customers of this mall to dress.

And I said to the security guard, 'But I go to talk to your boss, man. Why don't you let me in? You're poor, the same as me! Why you judge me that I'll come and steal something. No man! I'm an artist. I came to do something cool in your department store, man, and your boss pays me... A lot!' And this money I get from robbing capitalism, I burn it on making street art and other non-profit projects. I do this to spread other ways of thinking and enhance the taste of people who usually don't have access to art. And I have fun doing it."

Street artists and graffiti writers navigate paths between Bangkok's private, discarded and shared spaces. They search for spots where people will see their work but which are also hidden enough to allow undetected creation. The areas development forgot – canals, empty blocks, half-finished apartment towers. Places like Hopewell, that are beside major transport routes, become targets. Along with other remnants of the Tom Yam Kung financial crisis, like the Sathorn and Muang Thong Thani ghost towers, they provided street art and graffiti nurseries. Inevitably, they later became execution chambers, as the city consumed itself. Graffiti and street art ride the wake of urban decay then disappear beneath the next wave of development. The destruction and reconstruction of the city allows street art and graffiti to exist. Once the city had been reformed with cement and steel, the harshness of that aesthetic produced a natural corollary – the desire amongst some of its inhabitants to aestheticise it; to make these buildings, and the wholly globalised architectural order they represent, somehow connect to the people they cracked. This desire was heightened once that first set of late mid-century modern architecture lost its cleanliness and became aged and mould-stained. With the patina of twenty or so monsoons, much of Bangkok had become drab and repetitive.

Today, there are many places graffiti and street art can be found in Bangkok. Tucked away down allies or quiet stretches of road, paste-ups, tags, pieces and murals cling to walls across the city. And everywhere, woven in amongst it all, is the relatively ancient, Thai polytechnical student tagging. In some places artists and writers converge – these become Halls of Fame.

Chaloem La Park just off Phaya Thai Road in Ratchathewi district is an area of open space surrounded by the walls of neighbouring, half-demolished buildings. Once-private interior walls are now exposed to the neighbourhood. They display urban decay – steel rebar curling out of severed cement slabs, flights of stairs going nowhere, bricked-up windows and collapsed floors – a characterful 3D canvas (see page 152-159). Over the years, many local and international artists worked here creating generations of street art and graffiti, a constantly changing gallery. Chaloem La Park evolved from a demolition site and informal street-art space to a Hall of Fame after becoming a focus of the first Bukruk street-art festival in 2013. Today, it's a public park and one of the most instagrammable sites in Bangkok. Locals and visitors pose amongst the art hoping to absorb some of its potent vogue and to display the pilgrimage online (see opposite).

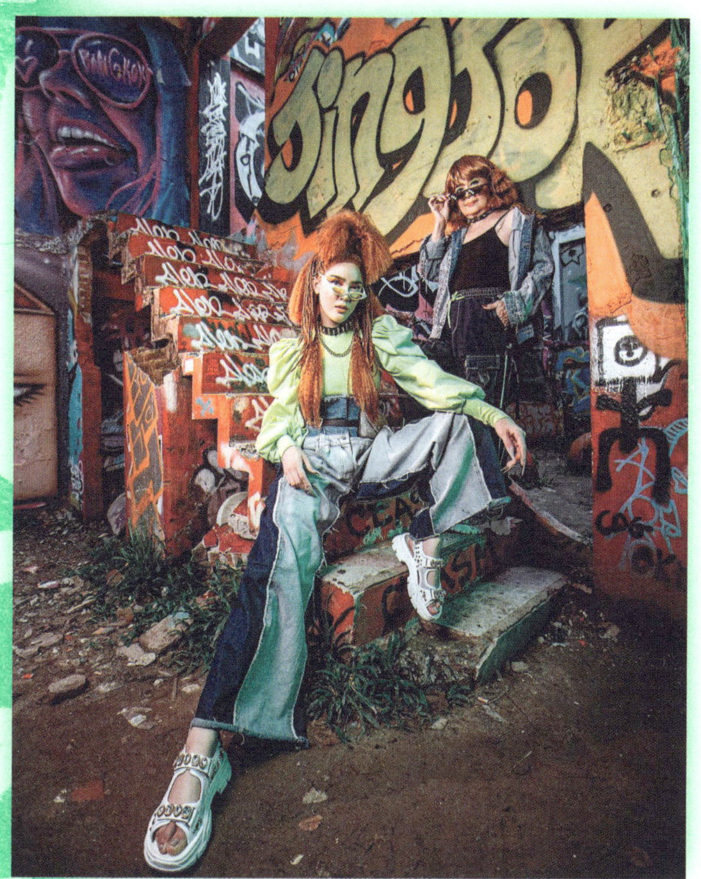

IG: Nisamanee.nutt

Many large murals line the Saen Saep Canal and its towpaths. The ferries that tear up and down the waterway carry thousands of people who see this art each day. The murals parade, one after another along the back fences and walls lining the canal, a gallery of pieces intended to be seen in motion. The low height and extended breadth provided by the form of the available wall space means the works tend to be large, elaborate, graffiti pieces (see pages 188-191). A family of graffiti typographies and forms dominates here – wildstyle and bubble letters. Because of this, they echo the early graffiti of New York and Philadelphia that was constrained to similar dimensions by the railway carriages they adorned. These predecessors of Bangkok's street art scene were also designed to be seen in motion, as the train carriages flew past stationary observers. At Saen Saep Canal, the art is stationary and viewers fly past in water ferries.

Out along the canal and down the Chao Phraya River, just off Charoen Krung Road is the Sathorn Unique Tower (see pages 216, 218, 228-233). Begun in 1990 and abandoned, as Hopewell was, during the Tom Yam Kung financial crisis of 1997, it was never occupied. Its absurd mass rises out of a neighbourhood still containing late 19th and early 20th century shop houses – rare survivors. Layers of mock-classical balconies cascade down the 49-storey tower like a wedding cake.

Over-sized Corinthian columns and key-stoned arches soar above the three-to-four storey buildings beneath. When a wind picks up, dust and rubbish breathe out of its wall-less sides and rain down on the buildings huddled below. Not far from the Hopewell site, in Muang Thong Thani, is another tower – also a half-finished and abandoned, set of apartment blocks (see pages 212, 214, 220-227). It is a newer Hall of Fame where many artists and writers worked during COVID-19. Unlike Saen Saep Canal and Chaloem La Park, these towers are interior worlds of street art and graffiti. Their art is hidden within what were to be hundreds of apartments. The endless supply of unfinished kitchen walls and dining-room ceilings are adorned with pieces – an aborted domestic dream subverted into a playground of alternative culture. These interior layouts are repeated hundreds of times, forming a maze. Once, the more famous Sathorn Unique Tower's instagrammability attracted backpackers seeking selfies atop its graffiti-crowned rooftop. In recent years, it has become guarded and signs now threaten prosecution of trespassers. Street artists and graffiti writers still break in to do pieces at its famed summit – mostly international visitors. Unlike at other street-art sites in Bangkok, the remotest work in these towers may only be seen by an audience of other street artists, or never at all.

By reeving across the borderlands of private property in Thailand, street art and graffiti challenge concepts of ownership. Because of this, they have potency that other sanctioned art forms don't. They communicate directly with the viewer. There is no filter between the creator and the passer-by. There is no curator that artists and writers have to go through to have their work up on a wall. They might form crews with like-minded people who share stylistic protocols, but there isn't anyone to dilute the sovereign creativity of their work, except themselves. And because that art is so publicly visible, street artists and graffiti writers have large audiences of fellow urban travellers. They ignore the law and get their message up. But this freedom often comes at a price.

SHEET

"I have been trying to explain to the authorities that my pen is not the same type used to vandalise the city. I have been using it for decades, I know it well. When it rains the ink washes away. It's not permanent. They always have it in for me and I always tell them nicely what I am doing. But it doesn't matter. Sometimes, they held me down, handcuffed me and hit me. The police and the army hurt me many times. I asked the authorities, 'Why do you arrest me and not people who ride motorbikes on the footpath?' Maybe because they see I'm old and I'm all by myself. but they come in a group. I told them that it's not illegal. It's about finding evidence that shows people with influence hide all the evidence when they break the laws. I tried to talk and explain, but they didn't care. Once, they caught me, and took me to Somdet Chaopraya Institute of Psychiatry and Srithanya Hospital. But I'm not insane! They poisoned me. You know, there are lots of people who died or went missing from the asylum. I was their

target. I survived many times. Once they woke me up from my sleep to stab me. Luckily, I didn't become blind but almost did and almost died. Last time it happened was four to five months ago. Now all the people know about the ordeal I'm going through, so a lot of them offer to buy pens for me."

Adorning places where ownership has dissolved, work may burn for years and be seen by millions, especially if it's up beside a rail line or highway. Hopewell's strange faces peered out of their cement forest at hundreds of thousands of people passing on the nearby Vibhavadi Rangsit Road. The colour and evocative forms of street art and graffiti makes them accessible. Their public placement makes them unavoidable for people who would never walk into an art gallery.

NOLA NO LEE

"Because street art can be communicated through just one picture on one wall, it can be seen by lots of people. Compared to other contemporary arts where you have to go to an art gallery to watch and interpret, it's not the way that street art and graffiti are used. They are vivid, lively and fun, and easy to understand, which suits Thai people."

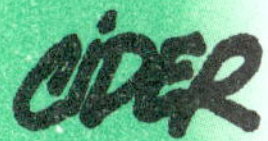

"The coloured pieces along the canal, I look at those like therapy for people to see free art, to understand the colours, and be like, 'I like this' or 'I don't like that'. Regular Thai people don't collect art. It's seen as a luxury purchase. They are not used to seeing urban art. They are only used to temple art. And to see the pieces on the canal changing all the time kind of gives them creativity. I think I'm beautifying the city."

MUEBON

"Street art has its own charm. It's like a stairway to other forms of art. And some people, who before, were not interested in art, when they see and understand street art, they become more interested and ask more. And this can make them interested in seeing other types of art, in galleries or museums, that are more profound and reflective. Art is a peaceful weapon. It's like a tool to inspire people to think or understand something. I believe that an artist is like a mirror that reflects society. And art is a record of society's history."

• • •

By using spray paint to mark walls, Thai street artists and graffiti writers are continuing perhaps the world's oldest visual art form. Cave sites in Australia's Kimberley (up to c. 30,000 years old), the Sulawesi caves in Indonesia (c. 38,000 years old) and the Cueva de las Manos in Argentina (c. 12,000 years old) all contain hand stencils (see below). These impressions were made by holding up one hand against a cave wall and blowing ochre paint over it with the artist's breath. The hand's negative impression was left on the wall. Modern street artists utilise the same principles; a pressurised can instead of lungs and acrylic paint instead of ochre.

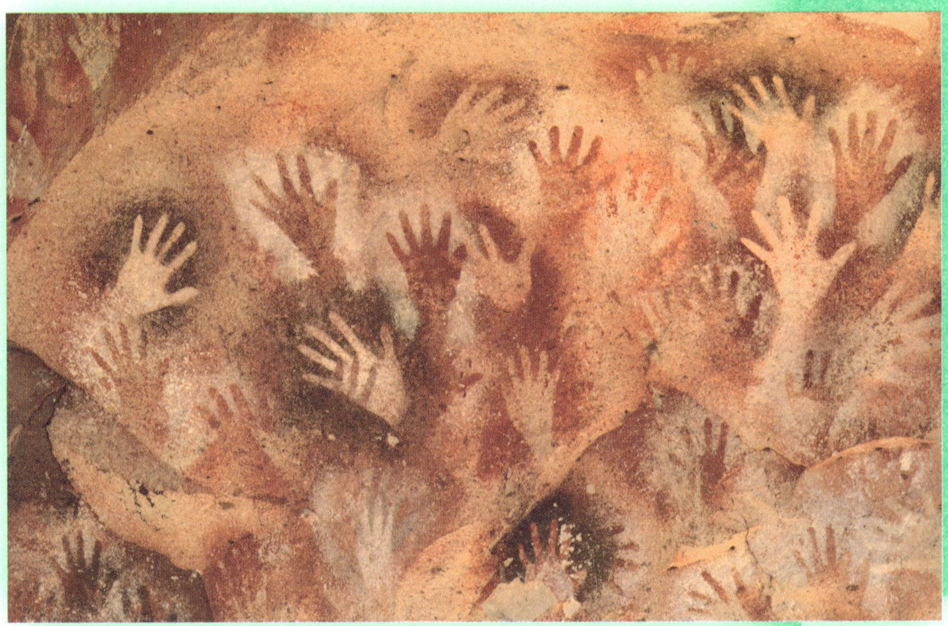

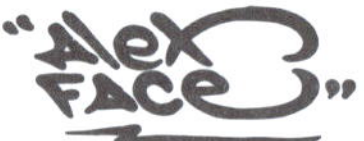

"If we are talking about humans. I think we need to paint on something. We painted in the caves in ancient times. Human beings need to write. If we cannot write, we cannot build things. First, we have to write it down and plan it. That's our nature."

From these early beginnings of human culture, people began to build permanent dwellings and link them with shared spaces and paths. A new habitat was born – the city. Since then, public unsolicited art has gone hand in hand with every urban culture. That art has ranged from idiotic through commercial advertisements to momentous declarations. In the last 200 years, the changes brought by technology resulted in cities that became higher and denser than ever before. People were removed from the village settings of their ancestors. This trend arrived more recently in many parts of the Asian region where, within living memory, the kind of metropolis Bangkok is today was unimaginable. After World War II, it become a global trend to build vertical cities that necessitated apartment living. 2008 was the first time in history when the balance of humanity shifted to live in cities.

Despite enormous numbers of people living closely together in modern cities, many feel separated in ways that previous generations didn't. Paradoxically, the modern globalised city disconnects people.

In the Asian region, over the last 50 years, rural people moved into cities and those cities dissolved their rural ways of living. The old neighbourhoods that characterised Bangkok before the 1960s became fractured. The variety that went before was homogenised. The isolation these new cities encouraged led many to look for lost community. With disconnection, especially amongst the young, came its inevitable companion – a yearning to belong. As in other cities, Bangkok's teenagers created their own communities through gangs. They picked up spray cans, too.

Earlier generations of graffiti writers were not people who considered themselves artists. People like Josef Kyselak, who travelled the Austrian Empire during the 19th century wrote his name on public walls until the Holy Roman Emperor asked him to stop. In the US, late 19th and early 20th century hobo graffiti was a subcultural language. They would leave markings along the ever-expanding railway network as a way of talking with fellow travellers and as evidence of their existence. Beginning in the 1930s, Arthur Stace wrote the word "Eternity" hundreds of times across the footpaths of Sydney, Australia.

The street art and graffiti seen around Bangkok today, grew out of styles that began in the dense urban centres of the northeast United States around 1965-1967. The modern spray can had been around for roughly 20 years by then. Gérard Zlotykamien, Harald Naegeli and others were early pioneers in Europe. Peter-Ernst Eiffe scrawled graffiti across Hamburg beginning in the 1960s, after a breakdown and would later be treated in psychiatric institutions. Perhaps the first in the US was Cornbread and other kids and teenagers in Philadelphia – COOL EARL, Kool Klepto Kidd, CHEWY, Joe Kool, Karate and others. Also perhaps the first in the US was Julio 204 and TAKI 183 in New York, where teenagers wrote their street number with their tags – PHIL T GREEK, JOE 182, BABY FACE 86, CAY 161, PAPO 184, JUNIOR 161, STITCH 1, BARBARA 62, EVA 62 and others. In these first days of the modern graffiti movement, where the art was almost completely typographic, the practice of tagging spread from city to city. They tried to, "Get their name up." As Norman Mailer wrote in *The Faith of Graffiti* in 1974, "You hit [paint] your name [tag] and maybe something in the whole scheme of the system gives a death rattle. For now your name is over their name, over the subway manufacturer, the Transit Authority, the city administration. Your presence is on their presence, your alias hangs over their scene." They were often African American, Hispanic and immigrant-descended teenagers from poor communities (see next page). As most do at that age, they felt disconnected from their parents, teachers and the cities they lived in. These kids were sometimes in trouble with the law. Cornbread had spent time in youth correctional centres where he and gangs painted their symbols across the walls. He later took the graffiti of the incarcerated into the street, and so modern graffiti was not only born in the streets but also in prisons and institutions.

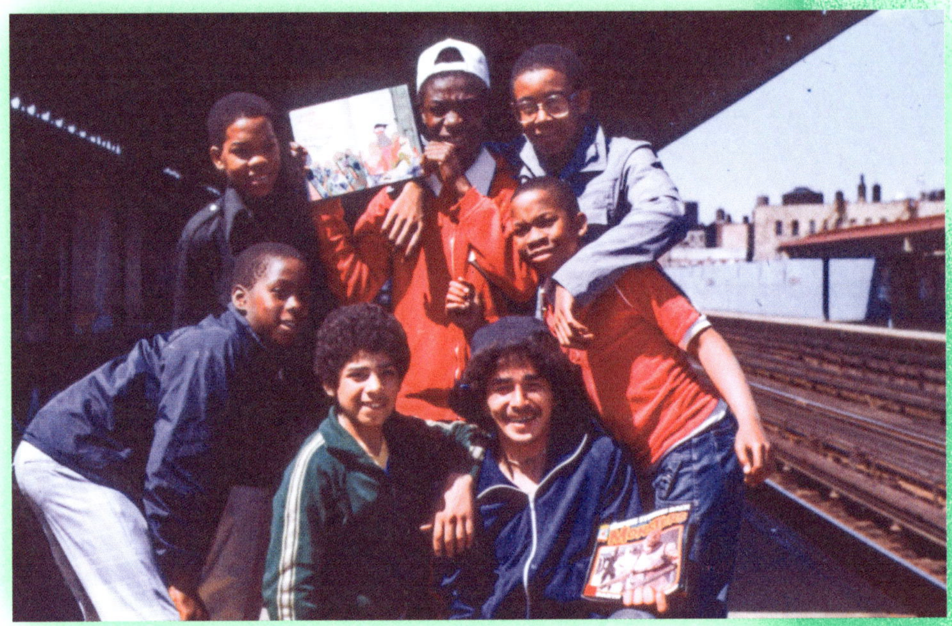

Smily, Ebony Dukes, BS110, Pod and Others. Intervale Station on the 2s and 5s, The Bronx. 1979 by Henry Chalfant.

These first US writers, born a decade or so after the great war their parents' generation endured, were navigating a new world amidst some of the swiftest change seen in human history. Like many industrial-age cities by then, New York and Philadelphia teetered on the edge of bankruptcy as populations moved and tax revenue fell. By the 1970s and '80s, these cities had high crime rates. Their glory was broken (see opposite), and post-war experiments in modern planning and housing had soured. Like the cities they lived in, the graffiti writers searched for a new identity. And so, modern graffiti and its resulting street-art traditions were fathered by teenage outsiders amidst the decline – and subsequent rebirth – of great American cities. This makes modern graffiti and street art perhaps the only art movements to have been created by teenagers and children. CIDER is one of the few graffiti writers working in Bangkok today who learned directly from this US tradition.

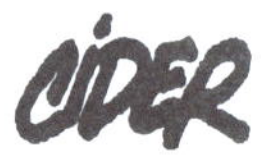

"I'm from Thailand, but I didn't grow up here too much. I grew up in America. Nowadays, I do a lot of the traditional style graffiti. At the same time, I'm also inspired by the graffiti crews I'm down with, Los Angeles' Mad Society Kings, South Korea's Life For Knowledge, Germany's Stick-Up-Kids, San Francisco's The Harsh Reality and CCLB. To me, once you master the traditional foundation letterings, you can do anything. It wasn't that these graffiti kids in America were poor, it has nothing to do with poverty. Kids do that shit because sometimes, when you're in school, you're already against what the school teachers are saying. What the schools are

teaching in America is sometimes unreal. For example, we were taught that Christopher Columbus shook hands with the American Indians, when in reality they mass murdered and took the land away from the Native American Indians. There's a lot of bullshit inside the school system. Colour and race, sometimes you get bullied in school because you are a different colour. So that's when gangs started happening, kids get together. The graffiti kids and the gang thing are something totally different. Both did graffiti but were somewhat different in their motives when it comes to spray painting. Living in the bay area, I grew up seeing my friends in gangs. When I first moved out there, I was 16 or 17. My first best friend in America got shot in a car. He was involved with a Chinese gang, they called a shooter on him from New York. Shit like that happens around America, for some reason. In Thailand, graffiti writers don't have to deal with that kind of violence. The kids in the US do graffiti because they feel like all these things are intense. The only thing that sets them free is art. They go out and put their name up. It's like when people say, 'Graffiti saved my life.' You know, if I wasn't doing graffiti, I'd be doing all that bullshit stuff with my friends. They were stealing car rims and all that shit. I come from a comfortable family, but I went to America, and I got to witness all these things, which was kind of like an education for me. You don't have to be poor, you don't have to be a minority to do graffiti. You can be of any race, because you are beautifying the city."

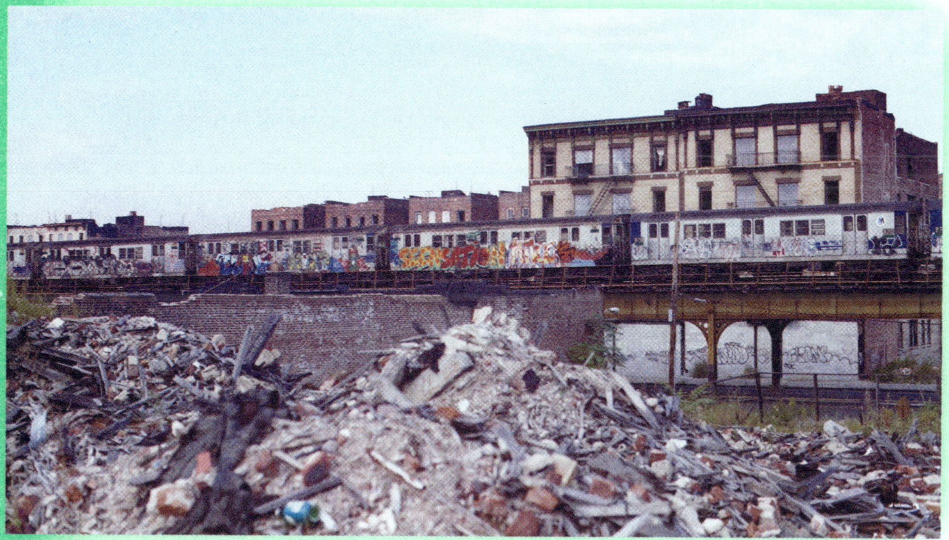

Destroyed and Abandoned Buildings along Hoe Ave and the IRT Line in the Bronx. 1982 by Henry Chalfant.

Into the 1970s, early US writers developed the simple tags they had started with. The graffiti styles became more and more ornate. Lines, arrows, crowns, bubbles and stars were added. Graffiti mingled with teenage gangs like the Savage Nomads, Hallafied Sisters, Young Galaxies, Nomadic Hunters, Savage Skulls, Jolly Stompers, Tomahawks and Black Spades. For some of the graffiti kids, these pre-existing gangs provided a family and protection they didn't have elsewhere. Some would become entwined with violence, turf, drugs and tribalism. At the same time, many writers rejected the gang culture and built groups of friends who would go out working together – in this mix, the first graffiti crews emerged.

As the '70s moved towards the '80s, writers like Futura 2000, who pushed abstraction and fine line work, PHASE 2, JESTER and COMET who developed the bubble letters, Dondi who developed characters and intricate lettering, RIFF 170, TRACY 168 and many others, found new territory. The variety of colours and forms exploded, and a distinctly new art style was born. The simple tags of the first writers had evolved into a stylistic language that would become a globally identifiable art movement. The urban cultures that graffiti was contemporary with, grew at the same time. DJing, rapping, breakdancing and their associated regalia – albums and their cover art, clothing, and a strong cross-over into skate culture – would become the vehicles that spread graffiti around the world in the days before the Internet.

The legendary 1983 documentary, *Style Wars*, helped to package this new culture and allowed many of that early generation to speak about their motivations. Skeme, then a young graffiti writer, and still working today, explained to his bemused mother, "It's not a matter of so they know who I am. It's a matter of bombing, knowing that I can do it, you know. Every time I get in a train, almost every day, I see my name. I say, 'You know it!', 'I was there!', 'I bombed it!' It's for me. It's not for nobody else to see. I don't care about nobody else seeing it, or the fact if they can read it or not. It's for me and other graffiti writers, that we can read it. All these other people who don't write, they're excluded. I don't care about them. They don't matter to me. It's for us." They wanted recognition from a small sub-group of the many people who would see their art in public – friends and fellow writers. Others, such as Iz the Wiz wanted to be remembered across time: "A lot of trains. A lot of fun. A lot of art. Art that's going to be a part of New York City's history forever." These were young men with little power over the city they lived in trying to be known as *something*. They were having fun, rolling with their friends and escaping home lives and a school system they had little interest in. They broke the city up into fiefdoms defying the daylight world of state control and spoke to each other in a secret language in plain sight. A brotherhood was created amongst teenage misfits, as it was in Thailand amongst Polytechnical students.

Begun with simple marker tags, then crowned with decoration and colour, filtered through gangs and into crews – by the '80s, graffiti had become part of something celebrated and marketable, hip-hop culture. Exhibitions were held, photographs were taken and books were written. Hollywood got in on the act with *Wild Style* (1983), *Beat Street* (1984) and *Turk 182* (1985), films that promoted partially true versions of the scene. While some would embrace this commercialisation when aerosol first hit canvas, many early writers put their cans down as they grew older. Having satisfied their teenage desires, they became mechanics, shopkeepers and train drivers. Interviewed in the 2016 documentary *Wall Writers*, TAKI 183 said, "By 1972, I had stopped writing… there was nothing else to do. I was a writer of convenience. It was never important to compete. You know, I didn't want to start hanging off bridges and going into train yards. Just like I never considered myself an artist."

It's unknown exactly when these styles came to the Asian region. In their book, *Graffiti Asia*, Suridh Hassan and Ryo Sanada suggest that modern graffiti art arrived via Japan. Writers like Very, Graver, CIDER, Poids, Dabs1 and the Oops Crew did early work in the region. Some of these writers had direct experience with the graffiti and hip-hop scenes in the US and elsewhere, acting as bearers of a tradition and teaching techniques and behaviours. By the 1990s, with many of Asia's economies having grown dramatically over the previous years, modernity was increasingly defined by consumption of international fashions. Around this time, and in some cases earlier, hip-hop scenes emerged in the Philippines, Japan, Malaysia, Taiwan, Korea and Thailand. In these days before the Internet, album covers, magazines and clothing were vehicles that brought graffiti culture and styles into the region. This, combined with returning nationals or visiting internationals, created a steady influx of graffiti so that by the mid-90s there were street scenes popping up across the Asian region.

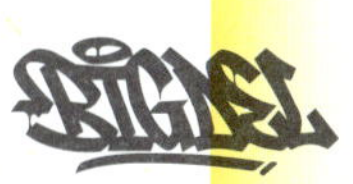

"At that time, there were hardly any bookstores with imported books in Bangkok. There was only Tower Records, and the books, the new arrivals, were monthly. So it took time to study. There was me, CIDER and Ctru. We didn't have computers back then, because they were quite expensive. We had to go to the university library. We browsed the Internet and checked out the new posts. Back then, the first website was graffiti.org. When I opened the skateboard magazines, I saw some graffiti in the back-ground of the skate park photos. I looked at that and learned from that. I was also learning from the design of T-shirts I saw. Now, with smartphones, everything is quick."

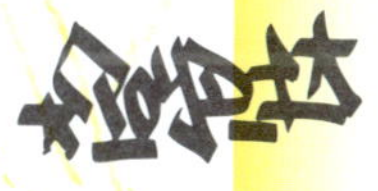

"I started in 1995, in Chiang Mai. Around the first time I tried skateboarding. I saw some videos, and in the back-ground, there was a lot of graffiti."

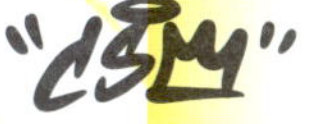

"I think it started from hip-hop, album covers, Limp Biz-kit, Linkin Park. Teenagers saw it there and they didn't know what it was but they wanted to paint that kind of thing. Skateboarding culture, also. One of the first crews I heard about was 13Crowns from Pattaya."

While the styles of the US graffiti scene were being copied from magazines, its culture doesn't appear to have been adopted in Bangkok before the late '90s. CIDER and Bigdel, two graffiti writers working in Bangkok in the late '90s, assert that these early days were defined by people working on legal walls, doing commercial murals for bars and restaurants with permission. The criminal aspect (illegally painting on private property) and the crews needed for back-up, weren't a strong part of the Thai scene's first years.

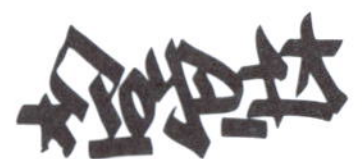

"I can't say who began doing graffiti in Thailand. Actually, each region in Thailand had its own graffiti crew, and they began at the same time. Bangkok, Chiang Mai and Isaan. Each group worked in their own region. Then sometimes, they came to meet and work with each other. That was at the beginning."

While the first Thai graffiti writers to adopt US styles were largely working legally, their Thai progenitors, the polytechnical student tagging tradition, was steeped in territorialism and violence. The severity of that violence would make many US contemporaries drop their cans in horror.

• • •

Members of polytechnical colleges, mostly teenage boys, had been warring for decades in Bangkok. Four schools constantly clashed and were known as The Four Kings: Kanok Technology School, Burapanol Technical School, Prachachuen Technology School and Intara School. Still alive today, this culture involves marking out territory and celebrating school foundation days using large stencils displaying the school's name, emblem and colours (see page 132 and 134). Like the first US taggers, they use spray cans because they are quick and portable. Groups of students converge to paint walls that fall within their unclearly defined territory, and to mark out new claims.

"Back then, Thai graffiti was all about polytechnical schools. Right before the founding anniversary day, they would go spraying or stencilling. With just one spray can in hand, they are ready to go. The technique is the same as graffiti's. Various schools and gangs would fight. They would mark their territory. Looks like the story of graffiti in the US. But in Thailand, the school fighting came first."

When students from a rival college are seen to be transgressing these boundaries, brawls, bashings, stabbings and shootings ensue. The violence is public and often results in students maiming each other in broad daylight as dismayed adults look on – most recently between Pathumwan Institute of Technology and the Rajamangala University of Technology in the city's commercial centre.

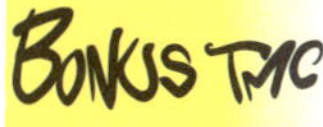

"When I was young, I was really interested in how the student gangs painted their work and buffed each other. That graffiti actually communicated with the public. At that time, there were no serious graffiti artists as it would be today, it was just gang graffiti. They got influenced by American hip-hop culture and they tried to experiment with new styles."

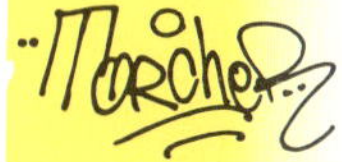

"These rivalries started a long time ago, since the 1980s. Fights between Polytechnical students take place close to a foundation date anniversary or just before the admission period to discredit rival schools in the eyes of prospective students. Invitations to fight revolve around territorialisation. Each school will create stencils around. If a rival school sees the stencil they might delete or tag over it. The school that marked it originally would then go and investigate who tagged over or deleted theirs. Now, sometimes it might be a third school that wanted to conspire to create a fight. It is part of the battle and the rivalry. It's another strategy. The stencil work was very well organised. Students would be divided into three teams. Each team had a different task. First team helped watch out for rivals or police and they would roam around with their motorbikes to ensure that. Second team is the one carrying the block and doing the stencil. The third is the one that has your back. The third team will stand around the second team in a circle to protect them from a rival school. If there is a clash, then the third team would fight first to ensure that the second team can finish their work – observation team, operation team and protection team. And then, after a while, students would go and delete the stencil by themselves with white paint to prevent other schools from deleting it. Stencils could be used to mock as well. For example; Rajamangala University's symbol is a hammer and a rival school mocked it by changing the hammer into a penis."

The students have structured hierarchies and systems of initiation. Younger students are put through physical and psychological trials before they are allowed to enter the gang. Senior members are identifiable by their '90s hairstyles – longer and dishevelled – and their baggy trousers and shirts. The gang violence became so common that attempts were made to standardise school uniforms so students can't identify their rivals. Dedicated gang members ignore this rule and continue to proudly display their school symbols.

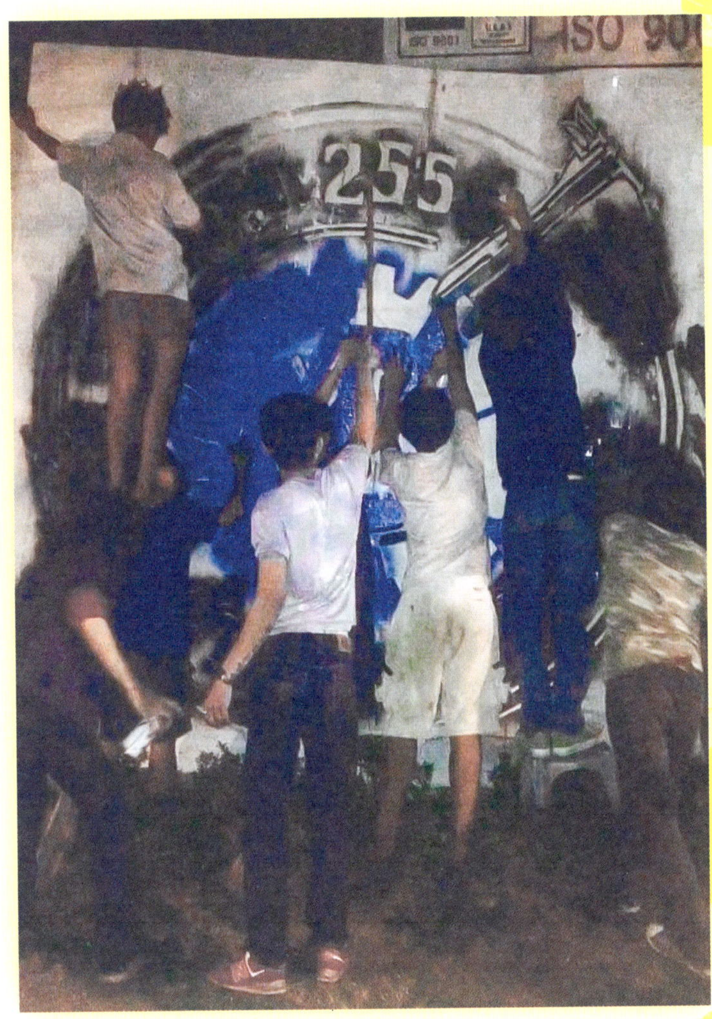

Thai polytechnical students working on their school stencil

"The culture is based on the SOTUS system – Seniority, Order, Tradition, Unity and Spirit – which exists in many colleges, schools and universities. This is a system that creates violence, that's true. But there are some good things in it too, there's brotherhood. We even had a kitty when we did the stencils to bail people out in case anyone was arrested, or for when we organised a drinking party. Everyone has to contribute, it's like a fund or a tax. When you enter into a workplace or

when you want to find work, later in life, these people are there to help you. For instance, just yesterday, one of us was facing a problem, and the rest in the SOTUS system were so willing to help. This means that people who graduated from the same school do not leave anyone behind. It's very rare that the students would not feel united and help each other in terms of work."

This tradition may go back as long as the schools themselves, some almost 100 years old now. It's taken so seriously that organised assassinations are carried out. In 2018, a young man was shot four times by a student from a rival school as payback for a previous murder, and there have been many others. The young victim was targeted because he looked like the boy who was being avenged and because he was from the enemy school. The motives for this violence appear to be as much about protecting brotherhood as about destroying enemies.

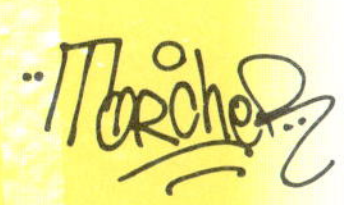

"I can't fully say it's a good system, but it's not too bad. So this practice continues. And part of it involves marking out a school's territory, or grabbing a bus, and going a long distance, just to pick fights with other schools. It's part of being young, reckless and wild. It also has become a circle. Somehow the system would result in a love-bond between the students. When we get older, we will tell the younger generation to not do it anymore. But they don't listen to us. It must be because example speaks louder than words. I am wondering if traditions of graffiti gangsters abroad are similar to ours in any way?"

This culture does parallel the teenagers who brought the modern street-art movement to life in the US. The systems of hierarchy, trials, rituals, uniforms, territory, blood-sworn oaths of protection, defence and support are common to the Thai student gangs and the US teenage gangs. In this way, the birth of polytechnical student graffiti in Thailand may have predated or emerged in parallel with that of the US. Either way, that same tumultuous adolescent drive to compete and belong that led to the first graffiti crews in the US was also the art form's crucible in Thailand. The first US writers marked out the neighbourhood they lived in; the first Thai writers marked out the area their college claimed. This is a foundation stone of Bangkok's graffiti and street-art history – utterly violent, territorial, fuelled by adolescent rage, tribalism, fierce loyalty, and love.

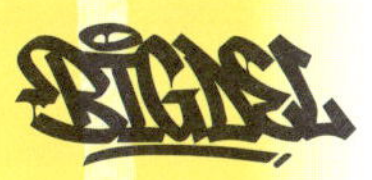

"They have the same idea, just to go out and paint on everything, to tell who they are: *I'm the king of this school and this neighbourhood.*"

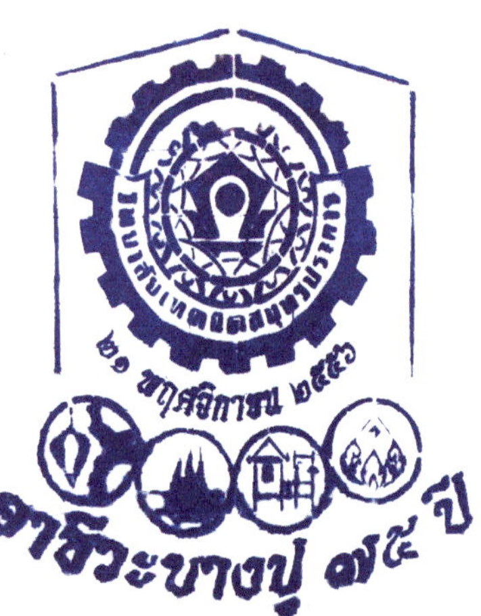
อาชีวะบางปู ๗๕ ปี

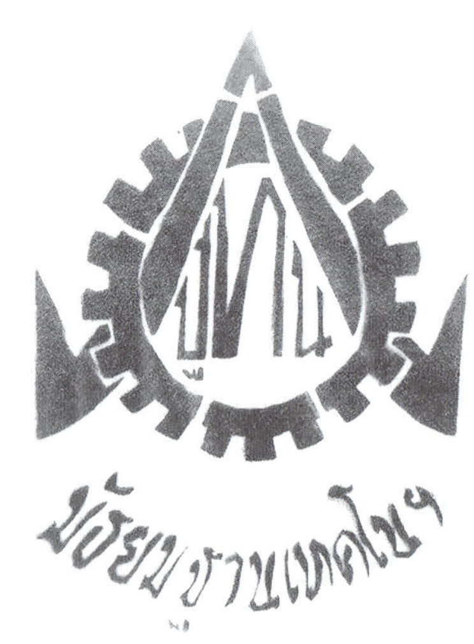
มัธยมช่างเทคโนฯ

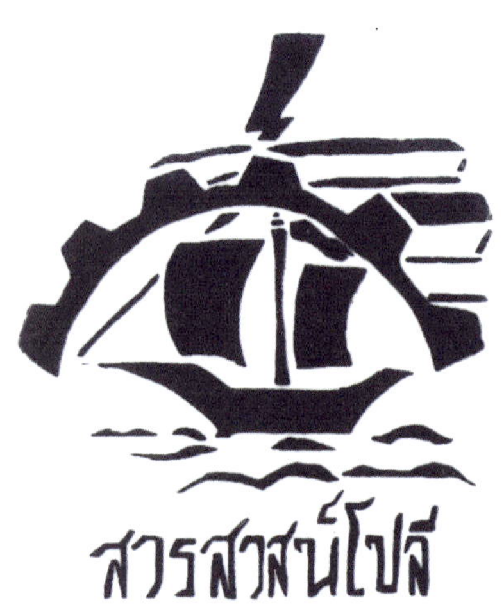
สารสาสน์โปลี

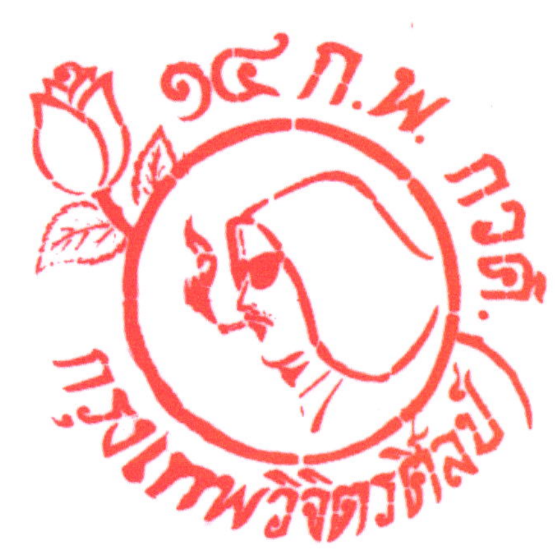
๑๔ ก.พ. กวศ.
กรุงเทพวิจิตรศิลป์

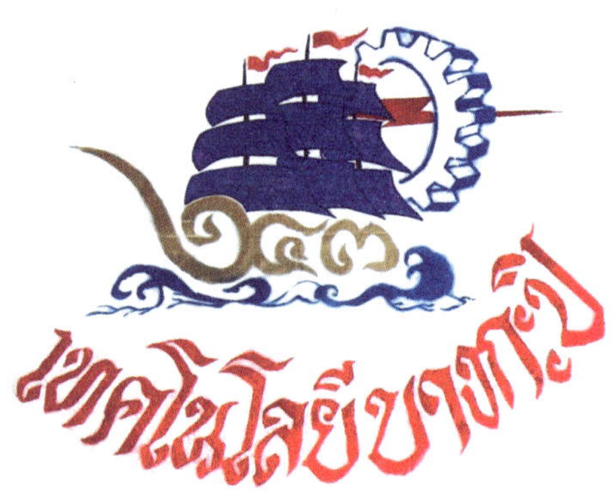
๑๔๓
เทคโนโลยีบางกะปิ

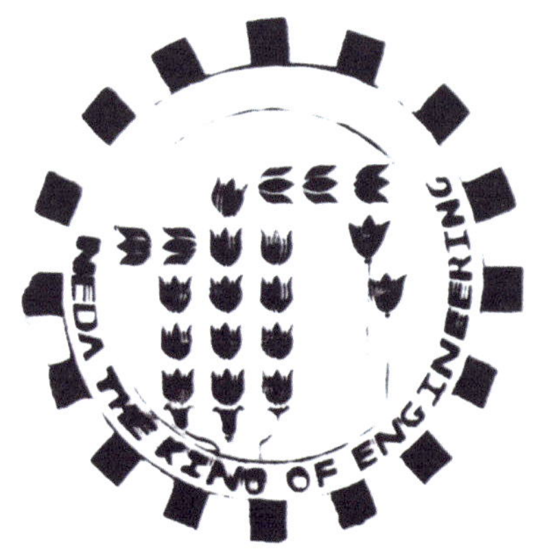
NEDA THE KING OF ENGINEERING

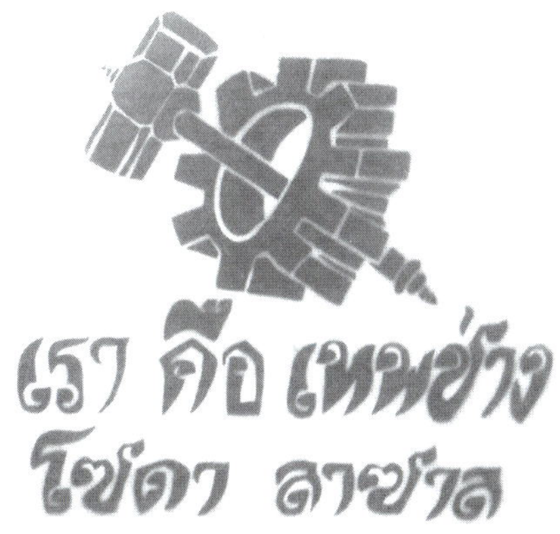
เรา คือ เทพช่าง

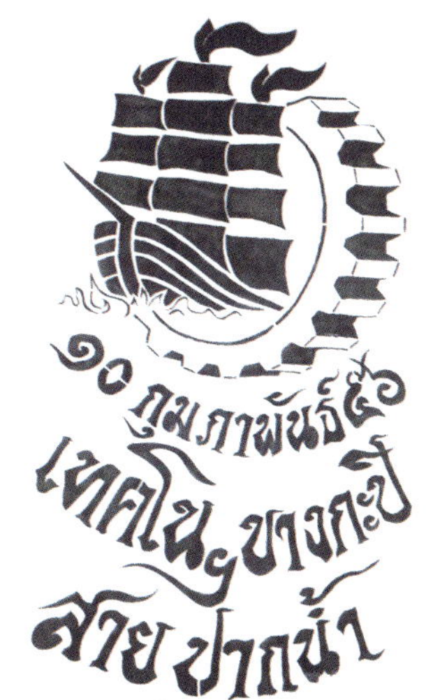
๑๐ กุมภาพันธ์ ๕๐
เทคโนฯ บางกะปิ
สาย ปากน้ำ

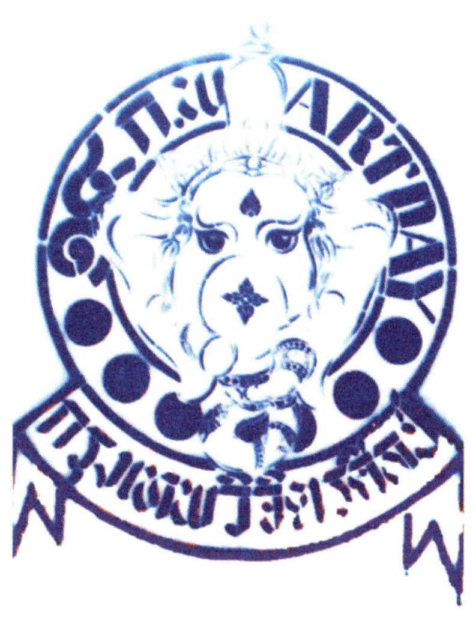
ARTDAY

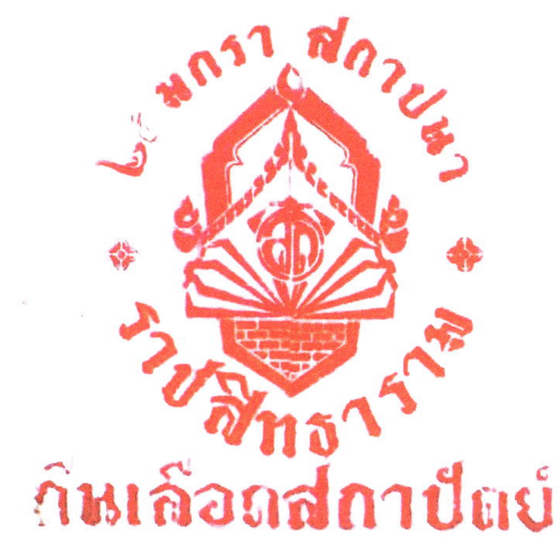
มกรา สถาปนา
ราชสิทธาราม
กินเลือดสถาปัตย์

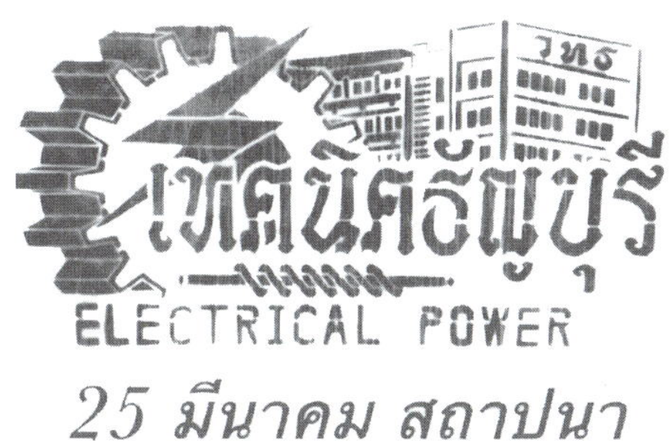
วทธ
เทคนิคธัญบุรี
ELECTRICAL POWER
25 มีนาคม สถาปนา

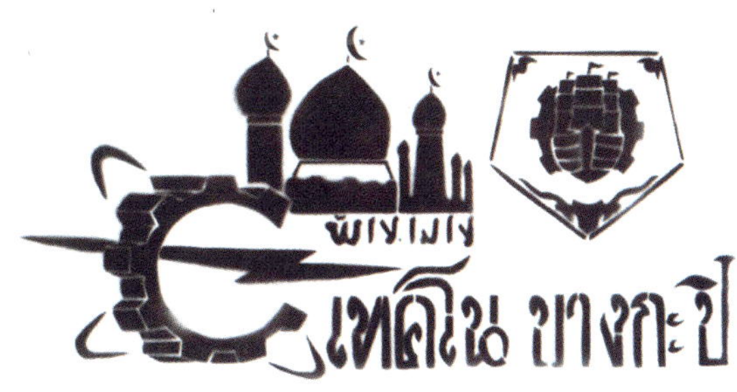
เทคโน บางกะปิ

While polytechnical student tagging pre-dated the arrival of US graffiti styles in Thailand, the modern graffiti and street art styles seen today did not come directly from student tagging. These two spheres of public aerosol art developed in parallel, largely separate from each other. There are some street artists who started out as polytechnic student taggers, but very few. Street artists have also tried to teach student taggers new skills and styles, but they were never really interested. They have their traditions, and want to keep them.

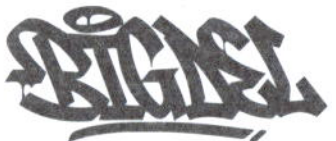

"Polytechnic student tagging and graffiti never crossed, they are parallel. But they never bomb [paint over] each other. We give each other respect, I think. Some polytechnical students develop their own style and become street artists or graffiti writers."

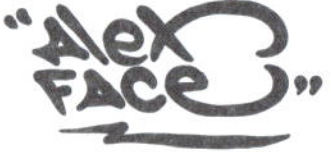

"I think they just look for empty walls, white walls to paint their school name, that's it. The students don't paint on graffiti because it's not going to pop out, it's not going to be clear. If it's not a white wall, they don't want it. We've been talking for a while about finding some of those guys, maybe bringing polytechnic students to study the skills of street art and make their work better. But they don't care. They don't need the skill, they just paint."

Despite their different modern styles, student tagging grew from the same Thai cultural soil as graffiti and street art, with the same shared urban and national history – the same place and people. And because it pre-dated the arrival of the US-derived graffiti in Thailand, student tagging is regarded with admiration and respect by modern graffiti writers and street artists.

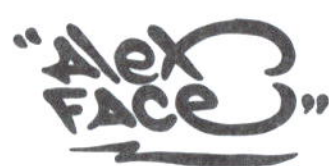

"It's the real Thai-style graffiti."

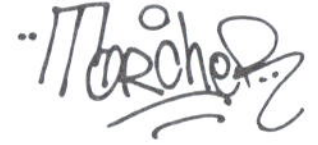

"Perhaps we can call student tagging Thai-style graffiti because it came from using fonts just like US-derived graffiti. However, after some years, polytechnical students started using logos and cogs and plumb bobs in their designs. They combined these elements with the school name. Whether this is graffiti? I would say so. But it's more Thai than international."

• • •

The first roughly 15 years of the modern graffiti and street-art scene in Bangkok, between the mid-1990s and around 2008, was not widely recognised locally or internationally. The art form wasn't visible. There were few public sites, although some Halls of Fame existed, like the current site of the Bangkok Art and Culture Centre (BACC) which was then an empty plot. This early work was mostly typographic wildstyle and bubble letters in English – US-derived graffiti. For the average person, this was unapproachable and impossible to read. The graffiti writers working before 2000 – Poyd1, CIDER, Bigdel, Pakorn BNA, NEV3R, Ctru, Lans, Zids, Coad, Dea1, Golf Land; and the crews, 13Crowns, DBK, CSA and others – were largely doing it for each other. There was little interest from the contemporary art scene, as there is for modern Thai street art today. CIDER, who was among the first to bring the US graffiti culture to Bangkok, asserts that he and the crew, BAI (Bangkok Artists Independent), helped ignite the contemporary street-art scene in Thailand around 1998. CIDER had returned from the US where he had picked up the New York foundational styles and, although he wasn't the first to do graffiti in Thailand, he is one of the early figures who transferred the scene's associated culture.

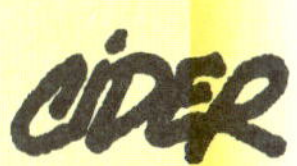

"When I came back in 1998, the only graffiti here was like murals in clubs. They were done by a group called DBK [Down Brown King]. And there's this other group called 13Crowns out of Pattaya. Then there's these Chiang Mai guys called CSA, [Chiang Mai Street Artist]. So graffiti was popping a little bit, here and there. But a lot of them were on peoples' buildings with permission. The idea of going out and getting your name up was not happening yet. They didn't have that part, so they were just doing hip-hop murals. Hip-hop characters, hip-hop letters, you know, hip-hop sprays and everything. A lot of what the kids are saying these days is like, 'I'm first, it was me!' Fuck that. Down Brown King were the first people I saw doing murals back in '98, '99. Then there was us, PMT BAI crew. We took the Thai graffiti scene and went next level and put THAILAND on the international graffiti map."

·MUEBON·

"When hip-hop culture first came to Thailand, it was before the Internet. Music videos with rapping, DJs and b-boys sometimes showed graffiti in the background. That is one of the main elements of hip-hop culture. Thai youngsters liked and followed this culture because it was something new to Thai society and the world, also. But with Thailand's inequality, only the elite or those from well-to-do families could afford to have access to this knowledge. Like those who gained experience from traveling or studying abroad and seeing things. When they returned to Thailand, they claimed they were the first to do graffiti in Thailand. Actually, many youngsters

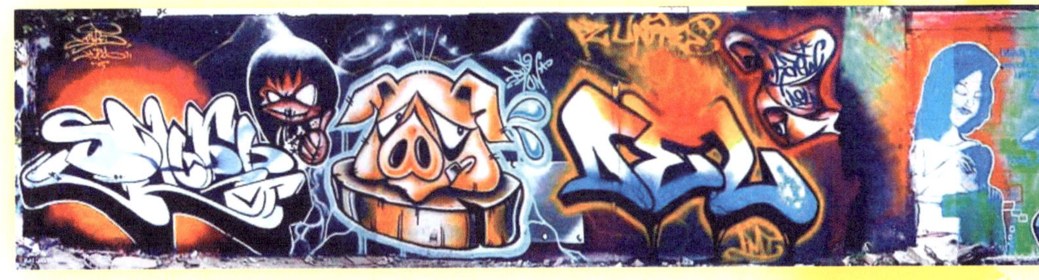

Pieces from 2002 by ESA Crew (GOH-M, PUK, BIGDEL), BAI Crew (POYD1), DSG Crew (GUMDIK, MONSTER, JUNE, ACID, SUCK1, COLE)

and teenagers scattered across the country did graffiti, as well. But they were unknown and outside the center of progress in Bangkok, without access to information and media."

The BAI*PMT crew helped move Thai graffiti into the street and to create a street culture. They brought many US graffiti behaviours and traditions into Thailand. To paint in the street meant challenging laws and perceptions of property ownership. This new generation of Thai crews – in the tradition of US crews – had hierarchies based on experience and an apprenticeship-like culture of proving yourself through mastery of typography. They also dedicated themselves to working on the street and finding visible places to paint illegally.

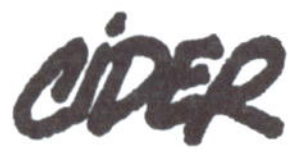

"There was no graffiti on the streets in 1998. There was nobody. So I formed a group of friends who were interested in the culture. I started teaching them and telling them what it's all about. And then, eventually, formed a crew called PMT – it stands for Por Mueng Tai. It means, 'Your father is dead.' It's like 'Motherfucker', you know. It's a 'Fuck you' type situation. BAI, Bangkok Artists Independent, was the stepping stone before PMT. We made a lot of noise. People were excited because we were changing the look of a lot of abandoned spots. It was a bad time, where businesses went abandoned quick because of the Tom Yam Kung financial crisis. People got interested in it. We got paid for it. People started seeing it. We were on a lot of TV programmes, a lot of bullshit. We were the first people up on *a day* magazine, they did a whole issue about hip-hop with Joey Boy and all these people. Kids started coming out and following us when we went out painting. They were like, 'Yo, can we get down with your crew.' We started what these kids are doing today. The world did not know Bangkok then. There would be no graffiti here without me. I basically put Bangkok and Thailand graffiti on the map."

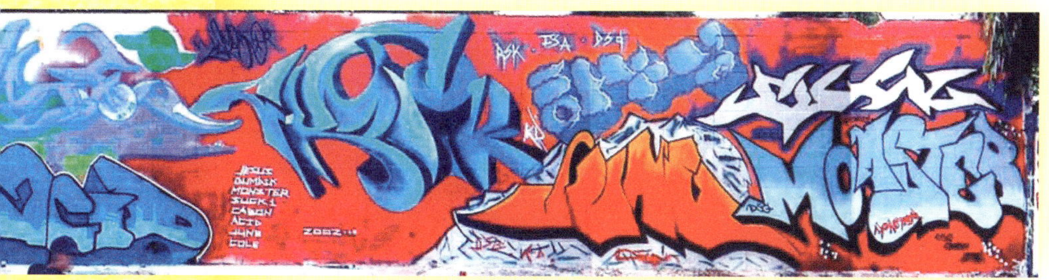

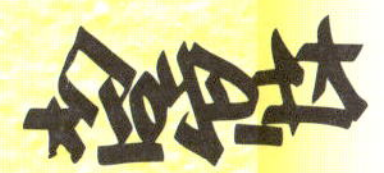

"I met a friend from L.A., and he came back and taught me about tagging and piecing. Then I moved to Bangkok in 1998 and I met CIDER, and we started a crew, PMT, in 1999, until now. I had worked before I met CIDER. So we teamed up to make a crew."

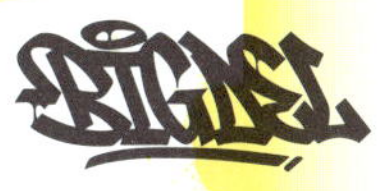

"We don't know who exactly brought American wildstyle here, because there was no Internet at that time, not even graffiti books or magazines. There were also people in Pattaya and Chiang Mai. I was part of the PMT crew, and I think we might be the first crew interviewed in a magazine at that time."

As this early graffiti moved into the street more intensely in the early 2000s, artists like Poyd1, Bigdel, CIDER, NEV3R, Pakorn BNA, Lans, Kimes, Kper, the TC Crew, along with BAI*PMT and others all wrote their work around the city in increasingly varied bubble and wildstyle letter forms (see above, next page and page 186). The typographic styles continued to dominate in Bangkok. These artists worked more and more in the open – abandoned lots, high-up places, private walls – and referenced the spaces their art occupied. During these years, many graffiti writers were painting both figures and lettering. This was common to other Asian scenes at the time, like those in Hanoi, Taipei, Hong Kong, Tokyo, Seoul, Kuala Lumpur, Manila and Wuhan. As early as 2002, artists like Finger and Kool did works that were purely figure-based murals. Crews like BAI*PMT and particularly DOB (Death of Bland) included b-boy figures and other characters in their lettering. ZIDS worked with animals like roosters and bulls, CIDER used a blue-haired guy peering out from amongst his wildstyle. Poyd1 worked with figures derived from US hip-hop and skate culture like capped b-boys and skull faces. These works, combining letters and characters represent a bridge between the scene's graffiti beginnings and the character-based forms that would, by 2008, dominate in Bangkok and remain popular today. By painting characters amongst their lettering, graffiti writers laid a foundation for the Thai street art styles.

By around 2012, the character-based styles had become popular in Bangkok. This newer set of styles involved large murals, figures, characters and scenes, and was colourful, patterned and rarely included type. In Thailand, this is often referred

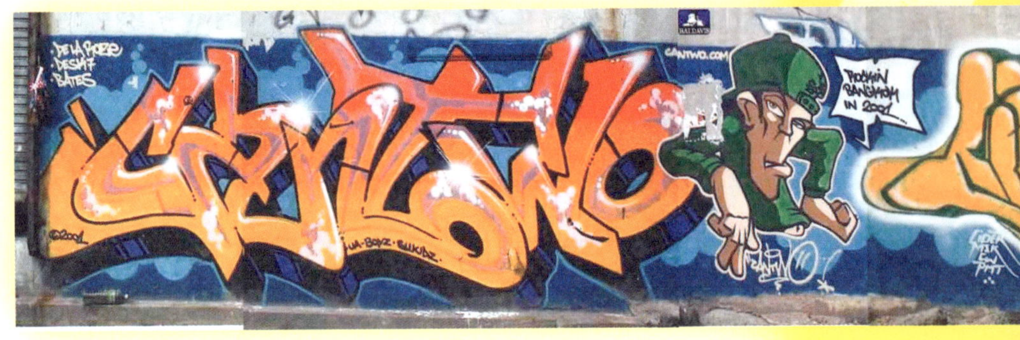

Pieces from 2001 by CANTWO, CIDER, CO2

to as 'street art', as opposed to the older 'graffiti' – both used as English borrow words in Thai. Mamafaka was a pioneer of street art in Bangkok and showed the engaging diversity that could be achieved by focussing on an iconic figure with his MR.HELLYEAH! Through the B.O.R.E.D design collective, he helped to bring street art to a wide audience by splicing its styles into the commercial product and graphic design industries. Similar developments were going on around the world as stencil art became well known and fashionable. ALEX FACE was another early proponent of character-based street art. His Mardi figure was one of the first consistent uses of a character in Bangkok, and can be seen everywhere today.

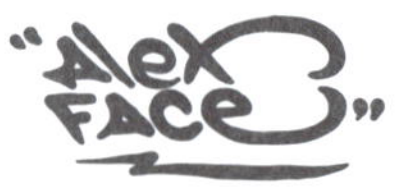

"I started painting my name around. But not long after, I felt like it wasn't my nature, I wanted to paint pictures. I studied fine art. So I think with a picture it's easier to recognise what it is. Painting my name, it's more abstract, people are not going to recognise it easily. For me, when I'm painting my name again and again and again, it's really boring, so I draw pictures instead. It's more fun for me. That's my personal style."

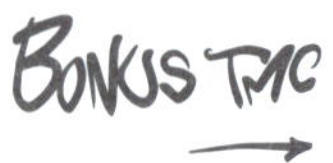

"I feel like character styles can expand. So I started doing characters in the year 2000. Back then, I was friends with Alex Face. So I started tagging along with him and did characters. I wanted to create characters that could communicate with people."

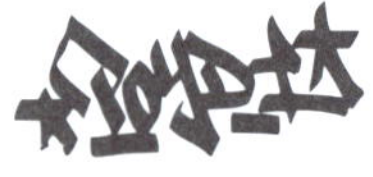

"Polytechnical students were working for more than 30 years. I think street art started in the year 2000. In that year, I gave an interview for *a day* magazine. That was the first media about Thai graffiti. And there were some guys who created characters then. Also around that time, people started to know about Banksy, Shepard Fairey."

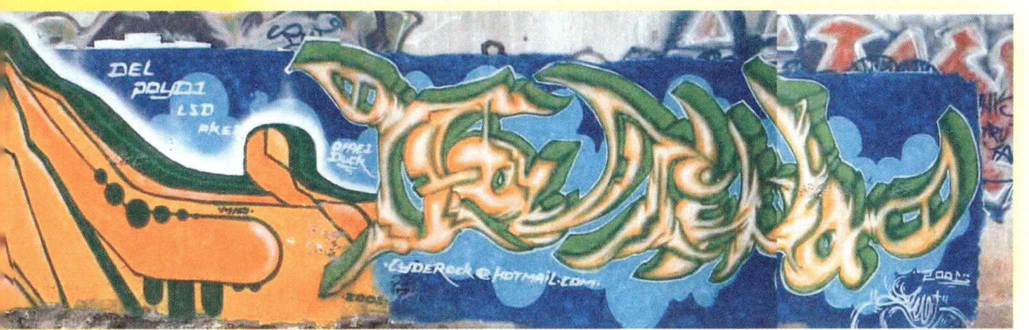

This transformation was driven by a new generation. They were influenced in their childhood and teenage years by the hip-hop culture that had become popular in Thailand during the late 1990s and early 2000s and by seeing glimpses of graffiti around Bangkok as kids. Many were also coming from art schools, with an education that was more formal than graffiti writers who learned through crews or were self-taught. The typographic dogma of the graffiti tradition was rejected by many of this new generation – either because it was too difficult and time-consuming to master, or didn't offer enough variety for their interests. For the graffiti writers, mastery of lettering was a pathway to acceptance as worthy; for the new street artists, it was a stylistic straight jacket.

ASINT

"People who like characters started to go their own separate ways and develop their own characters. In the last ten years some artists specialised in characters. ALEX FACE for example. They set a new example that it's possible to be a street artist and do characters. Many other artists saw that they, too, could draw characters, instead of sticking to fonts only. There are also artists like Rukkit whose background is in graphic design."

Rukkit

"I started as a graphic designer. Because I used a computer for work, when P7 asked me to join the big mural at BACC, my freehand was very bad. That's why I had to find a new method to work in. I first started by experimenting with stencils, because stencils don't require much spray technique and are easy to scale the work. I tried to use block stencils with restricted shapes, such as straight lines and curves to create an image. It's like playing with Lego toys. With this technique, my own style was invented."

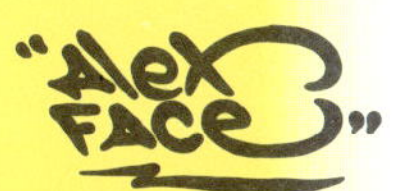

"It took a while but after a bit of time, people who were painting graffiti were more like arts students, people who studied art. That changed the styles a lot. They became

more characteristic, more like a cartoon, more like art. They did letter styles for a bit, but then some people did both, they did throw-ups [a larger and more complex tag usually with colour and intended to be created quickly] or letters and character style. Yeah, I think that's why. For me, I studied art. So personally, I love to paint a picture. I prefer more character style or cartoon style. I tried to do wildstyle before, but it was too hard for me, it's really difficult. Also, English is not my mother language, so I don't really understand the nature of English letters well."

Compared to the older generation of graffiti writers, this new generation of street artists wasn't so interested in communicating in a secret wildstyle language. They didn't identify as part of the graffiti culture that was a continuation of the US tradition with its illegal and gang-related creed. This new generation wanted to connect with as many people as they could through legible, engaging art. The complex, unreadable and English-based wildstyle letters – the proud heritage of the graffiti writers – would not achieve this. So, largely ushered in by young art and design students, the character-based street art tradition took hold in Bangkok.

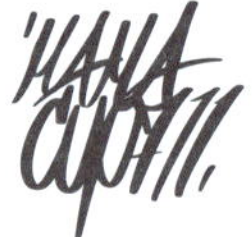

"Characters are more recognisable. You create one character and you can adapt and adjust it to fit any place. Characters are more memorable. Like ALEX FACE, Mamafaka, P7, Benzilla and AS!N's chicken. These characters represent the artists more than the typographic style. And they get more attention from people, and are easier to recognise than typographic wildstyle. There are so many people doing street art in Thailand. Characters help artists to stand out."

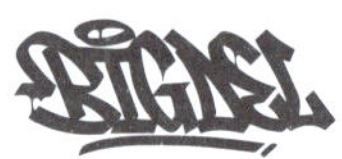

"The difference between the font and the character style: I think character is easier to understand for Thais – three-year-old kid to eighty-year-old grandma, 'Okay, it's cute' and then they come and take photos. But if you see the wildstyle, with all the arrows, nobody can read it. So people ask, 'What are you doing, what do you mean?' We got a lot of questions. I think this happens all around the world. Graffiti artists try to develop their own style, to make it more modern, but they also keep their own original style. Even now, I do a lot of character work but mix it with my graffiti style."

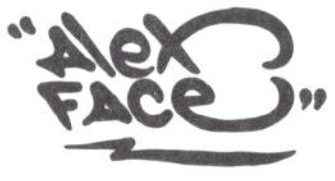

"I don't want to say that the letter style is not good, or this one's better than that one. I love everything, I love tagging, throw-ups. I do tagging. I do graffiti, but I think

character style, people can remember more easily than the letter style. It's easier to put your character up on the wall and people can recognise you. The arts scene – not only in Bangkok, but everywhere in the world – changes in the same way. Mural painting and character style, realistic painting, they turn the building into a big canvas, like a big piece of art."

Artists from around the world began to work in Bangkok as word spread – largely via the new conduit of the Internet – that a rich street-art scene was developing in Thailand. Jace brought his famous character Gouzou to Bangkok in 2007 (see below). Around the same time, Mr. A appeared, as did works by CANTWO from Germany, Space Invader and many others. Thai artists saw this work and were further influenced by what was going on in other countries.

Piece by JACE

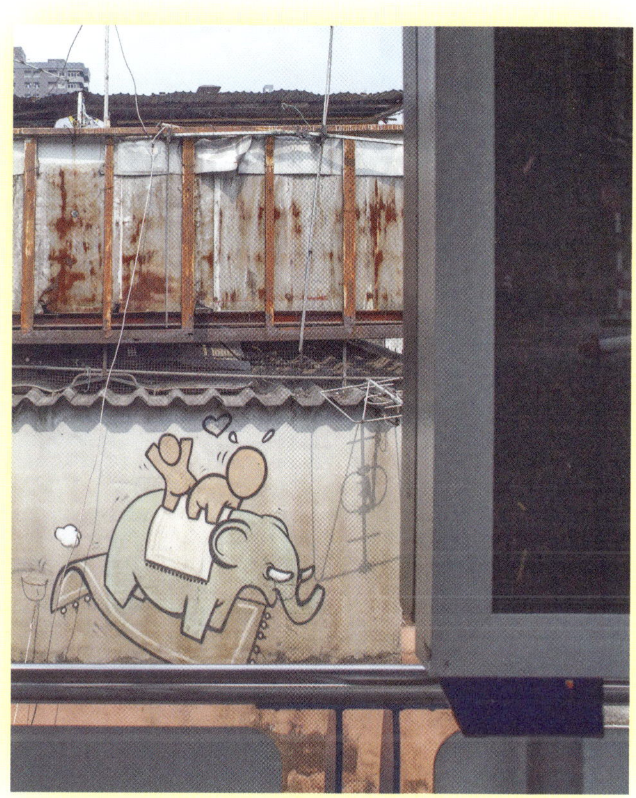

The emergence of character-based street art brought new techniques, styles and motives. The continuing presence of the graffiti tradition meant that inevitably, a contrast would emerge between the two approaches – one older, one newer. The two schools would come to define themselves and each other in different ways. Tribes emerged and Bangkok continued its role as a stage upon which the meaning of Thainess was performed. Student tagging, graffiti, street art were all part of this performance. The differences between these traditions were pushed to the forefront during 2013 when a conflict arrived in Thailand that revealed much about how the different groups viewed themselves, their scene and the country they live in.

• • •

As character-based street art became popular around 2013, the Bangkok graffiti and street art scene was visited by its first international beef. The roots of this conflict lay in a run-of-the-mill US graffiti dispute. In 2007, a duo of younger artists were arrested while writing in New York City. They accused another, older writer, of ratting on them to the police. The older writer denied this and shot back with volleys of abuse. The feud bubbled along for years, as many do. The younger duo had visited Bangkok during a journey through the region, so their works were visible in the city. In 2012, the older artist allegedly paid local Thai writers to tag over and buff the duo's work. He declared online that he had his "Killa dogs out in Bangkok dropping bombs." Local writers on one side would also buff pieces by local writers on the other side. Although the beef in itself is insignificant, it was a revealing moment in the development of Bangkok's street art and graffiti scene.

When the dust settled, perspective showed that some local artists had become swept up in a battle that had no direct relevance to Thailand's scene. Those Thai writers who had buffed other artists' work, had not stopped to consider whether this kind of beef, common in the US, fit the Bangkok scene. This was a heady time in the city's street art and graffiti history, Bangkok was on the cusp of being internationally recognised. There may have been an eagerness, on the part of some artists, to be part of the beef – Bangkok's first international street-art feud. Some writers may have felt proud that older US writers would call on them. For others, there was a lingering sense of unease – as if local writers had been appropriated in a feud that didn't concern them. Many questioned whether becoming a part of the international scene on these terms was worth it. Idealised notions of Thai people being peaceful, friendly and uninterested in conflict also played into the tensions and many artists, looking back on the feud today, reference how such conflict is un-Thai.

BONUS TMC →

"Maybe that buffing gang all moved to New York! Just joking. I don't know. Actually, after that, the artists who buffed around, were mostly banned by other artists from street art. Buffing is quite rare in Thailand because everyone knows each other quite well. We consider each other to be brothers and sisters. People in this scene know each other."

MAUKA

"That incident didn't have much impact on Thai artists. I don't think it is a typical Thai characteristic to like fighting or be confrontational. The Thai scene doesn't accept

this behaviour. We only want to have fun as brothers and sisters. We all know each other. In the end, It's not the scene that suffers, it's those who vandalise other people's work. I believe that we reap what we sow."

ANONYMOUS

"Thai people, in their hearts, don't like fighting. Thai culture has an element of respect: 'Thais are peaceful and loving' [from Thailand's national anthem]. Because graffiti culture came from abroad, Thai people don't pay much attention to following that culture. Also, there's a lot of space to work on. There's no need to compete. Except for the city centre. As for bombing and buffing, I don't think Thais like to do that unless they really despise one another. Why go bombing knowing that if we bomb someone they would bomb us back? Better to use the time to find an area for work."

Conflict, competition, buffing and bombing are still a part of the graffiti – and to a lesser extent – street-art scene in Bangkok. The genuinely ferocious violence and tribal culture that Thai polytechnical students live and die by is one of the foundations of the art form in Thailand. The gritty world of graffiti still has remnants of that culture of aggression. Rather than being an unwelcome import, conflict was here already. The 2013 beef, however, was foreign.

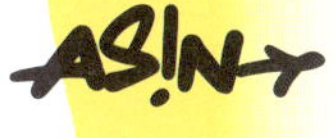

"It depends on what they have adopted. Those that are into street art will adopt street-art culture. Those into graffiti, will adopt graffiti culture which includes bombing. It's more like 50/50 with those who are into the confrontational western style of street art. There are those that only create their own work, those that bomb back if they get bombed, and those that only bomb without creating their own work. It depends what culture they have adopted as their own."

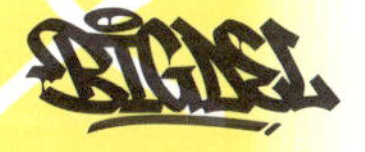

"Our graffiti culture is quite different here in Thailand. It's different from the United States. They have their own story, but here in Thailand, we have a different culture. I look for old walls that nobody cares about and I try to make them nicer. I try to paint as much as I can."

The 2013 beef continues to this day. Bangkok's involvement had no calming effect. But, for the city's street artists and graffiti writers, it was a juncture when what had been largely a local scene was forced to consider its identity in a global context. Because of the very different origins of the older graffiti writers and the newer street artists, they came to different viewpoints on what that conflict meant. The street artists regarded the episode with bemusement, while many graffiti writers saw it as part of the game.

ANONYMOUS

"I don't care about conflict, I don't care about the 2013 thing. Everyone talks about this story a lot. But for me, it's not important. If you are fighting and people can get something from it, that's good. But I don't focus on this story."

"Thai people in general weren't really into this fight because both parties were foreign. My friends and I were interested because we did graffiti. But street artists weren't interested because they developed their work and used Instagram as their platform. They didn't care about bombing or tagging. So for people who did graffiti we were interested in this fight. But for people who were into street art, they weren't interested."

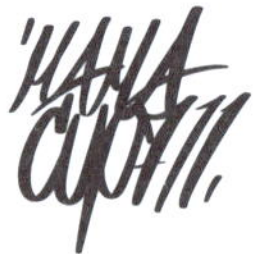

"Nowadays it's about the Internet and social media – people create work and show it on social media. So when these guys go buffing other people's works and don't publicise it, people forget that this tradition exists. Out of sight, out of mind. Bombing definitely still exists."

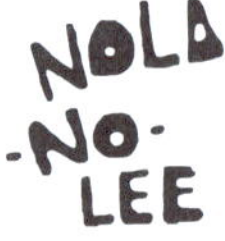

"I don't really care who fought with who. I just look at what they create."

The younger duo in this beef do work that is about fostering notoriety. The pieces they created in Bangkok were done primarily to advertise their presence, rather than to say something political or be visually appealing. The older writer is an old-school brawler and represents the cultural beginnings of the street-art movement. He was one of the teenagers who helped create modern street art and who had to fight their way up from marginalised and low-income communities. These attitudes and this culture were reflective of the economic, racial and social history of the US, but not of Thailand. While Thai street artists adopted many of the artistic styles coming out of the US by 2013, they were mutating the deeper cultural tropes that came along with them. As the scene became more internationally connected – as Bangkok had in the decades before – and as it branched into the two schools of street art and graffiti, these artists asked the same questions many of the previous generation's city-dwellers did: what is it that makes us Thai? How are we different to the rest of the world? This tension between wanting to be respected by the outside world, but not wanting to copy it, being influenced, but not subjugated, being modern and still somehow traditionally Thai, is as old as Bangkok itself. It was the arrival of this outside conflict that forced many in the local scene to consider which established norms they were willing to adopt in order to align with the rest of the graffiti and street-art world.

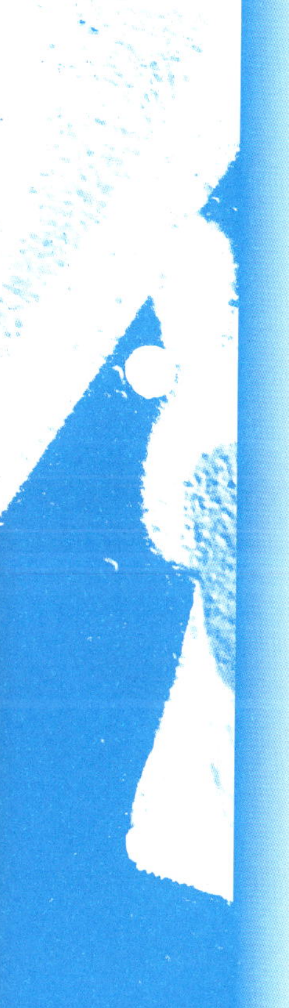

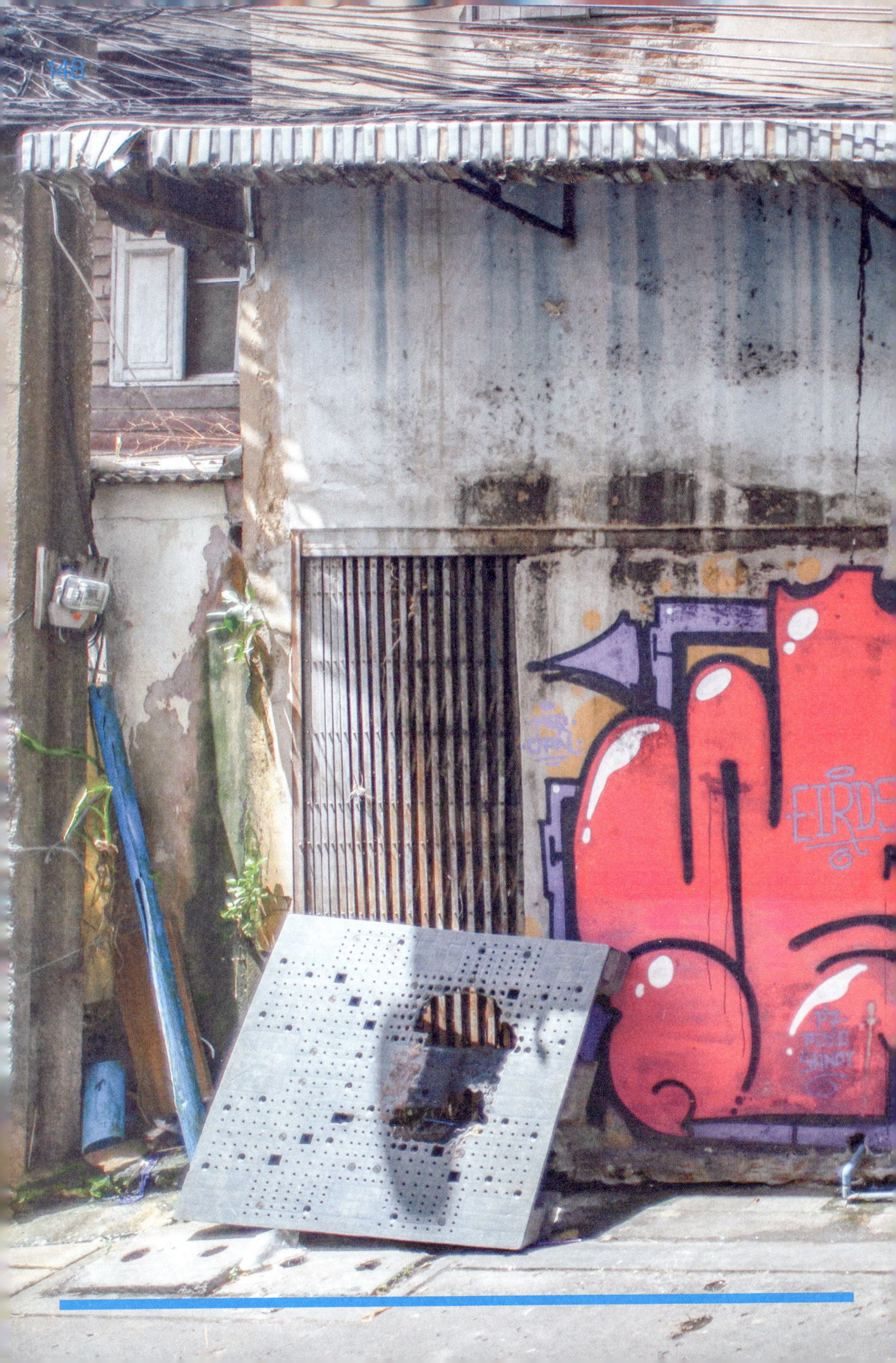

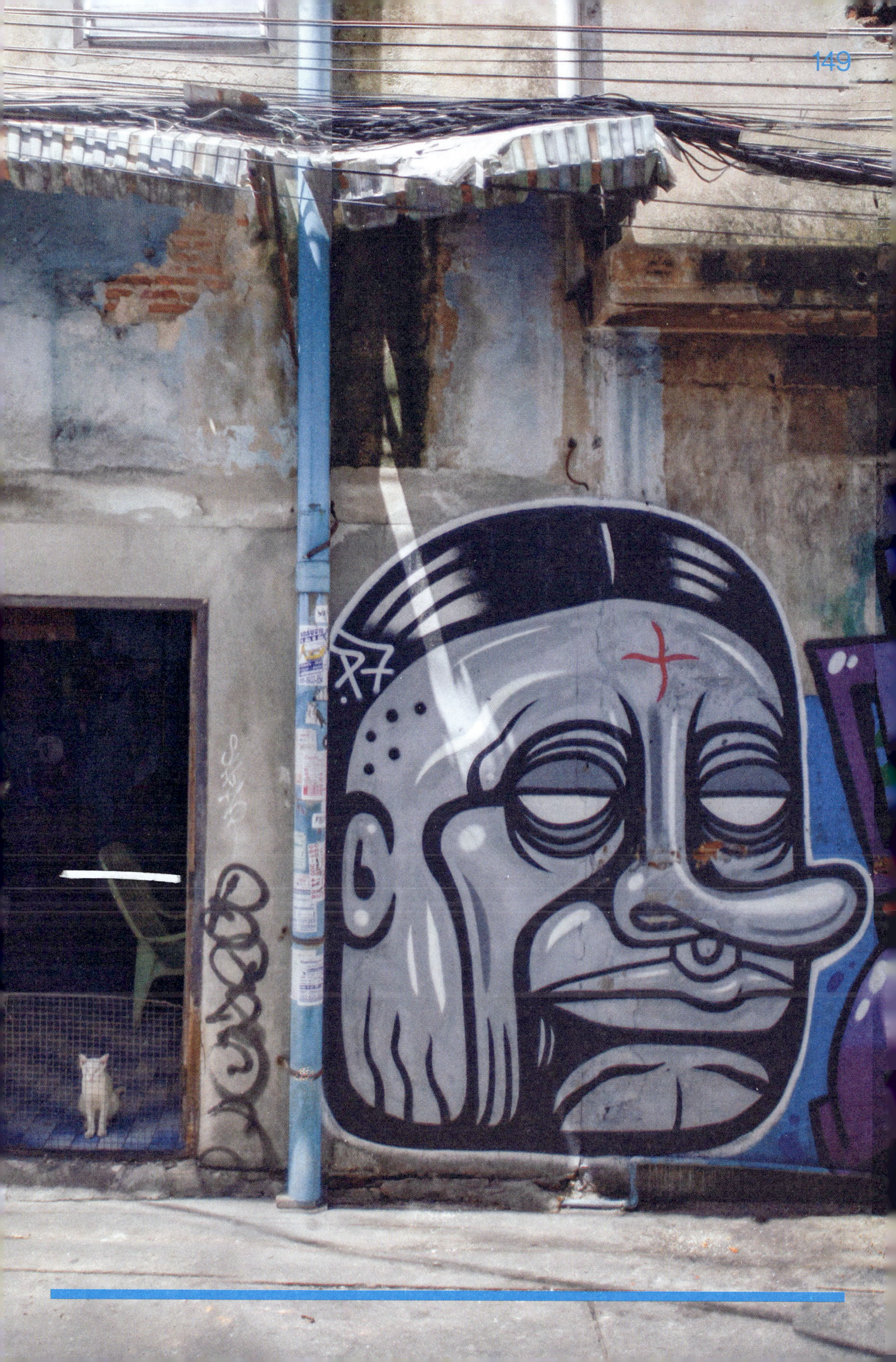

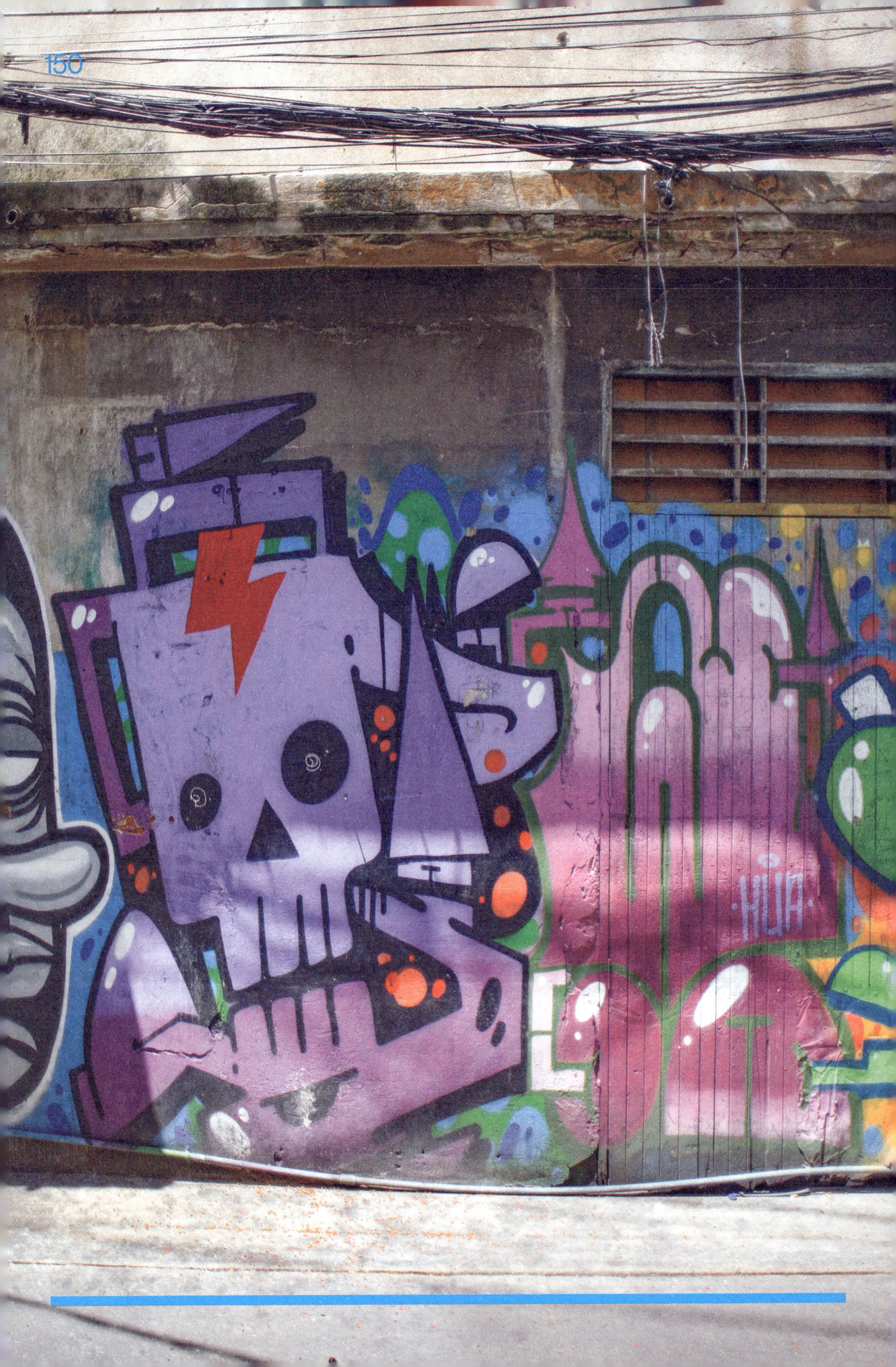
HUA

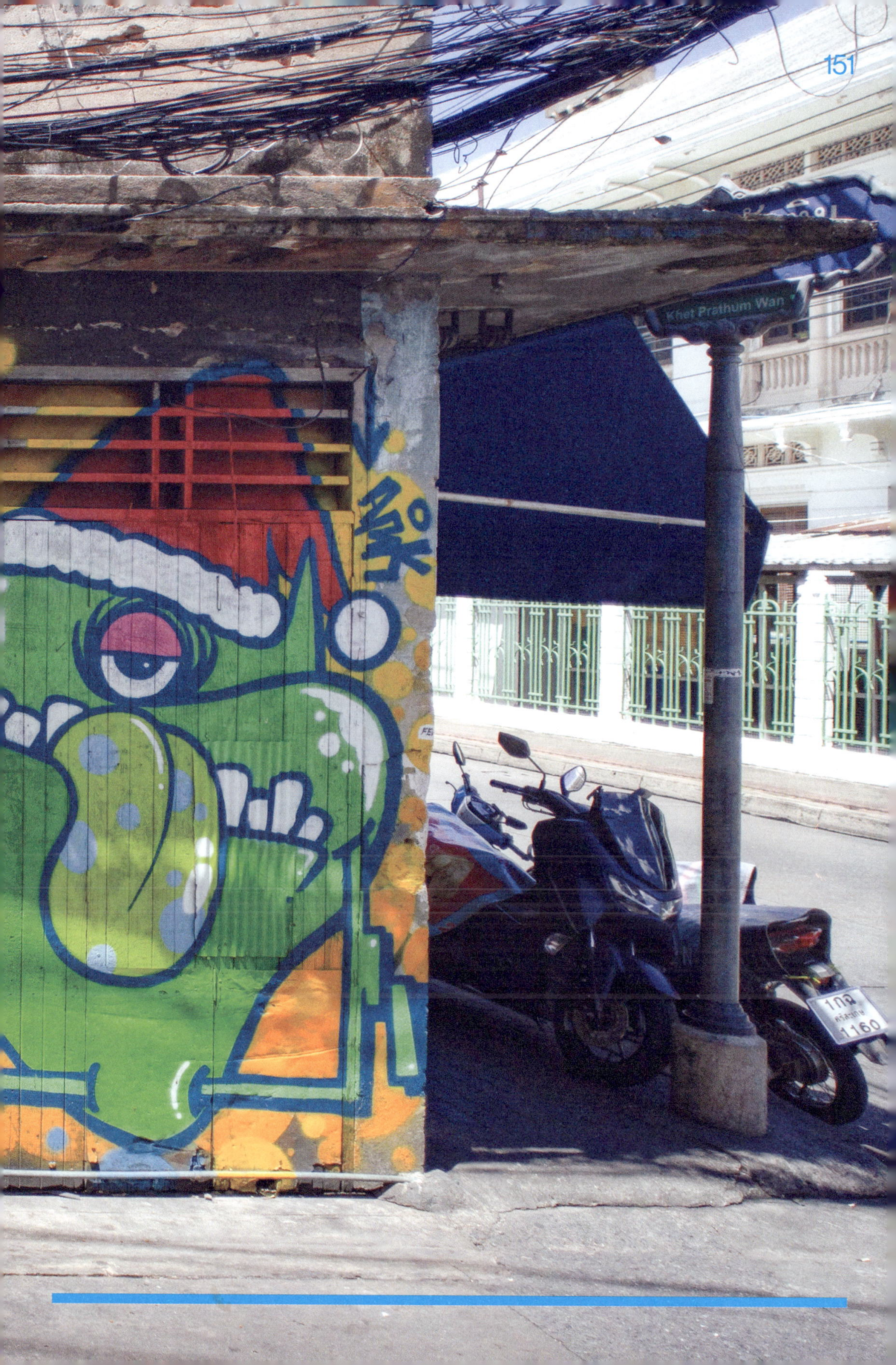
Khet Prathum Wan

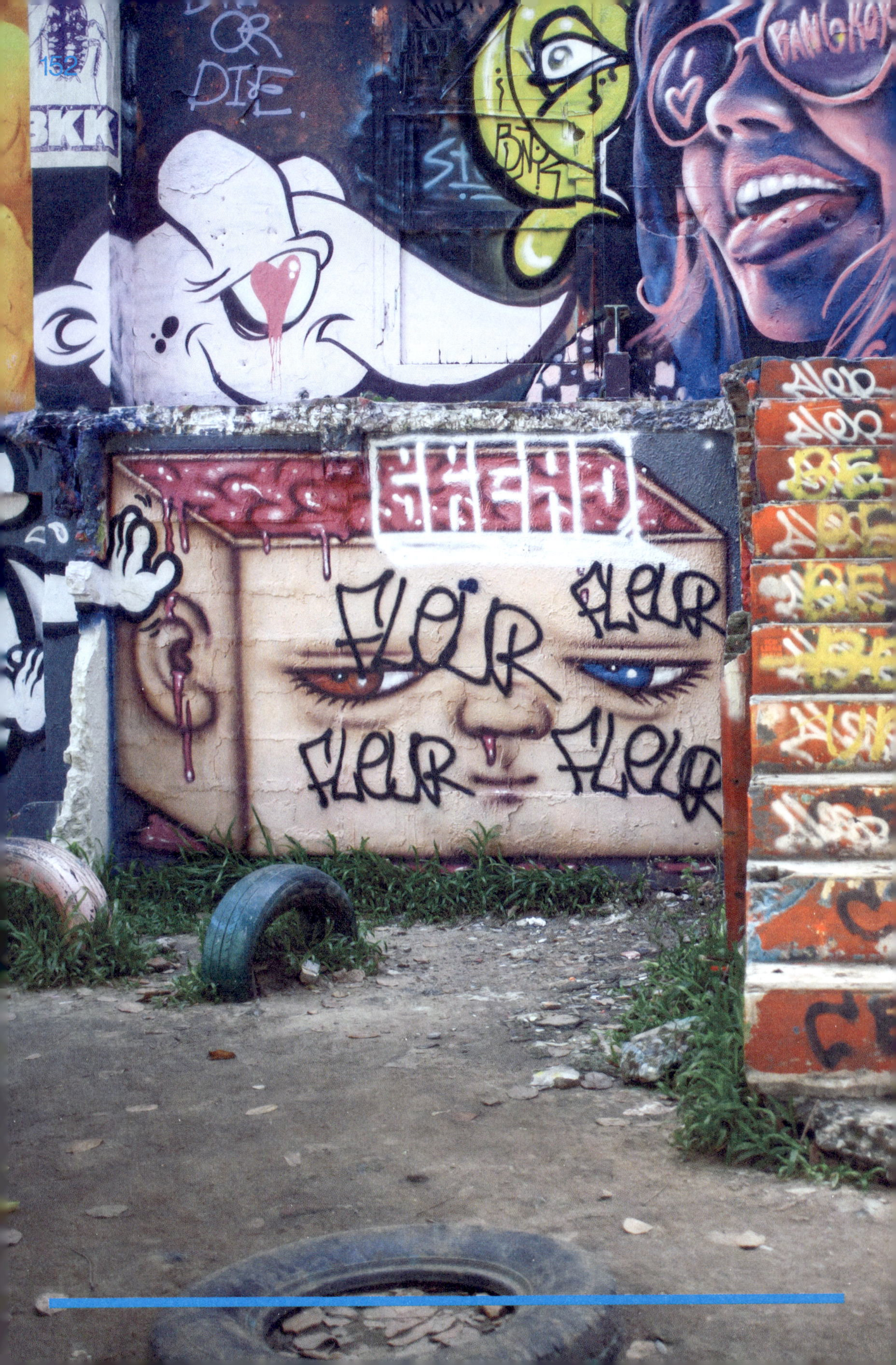
OR
DIE
BKK
FLEUR
FLEUR
FLEUR
FLEUR

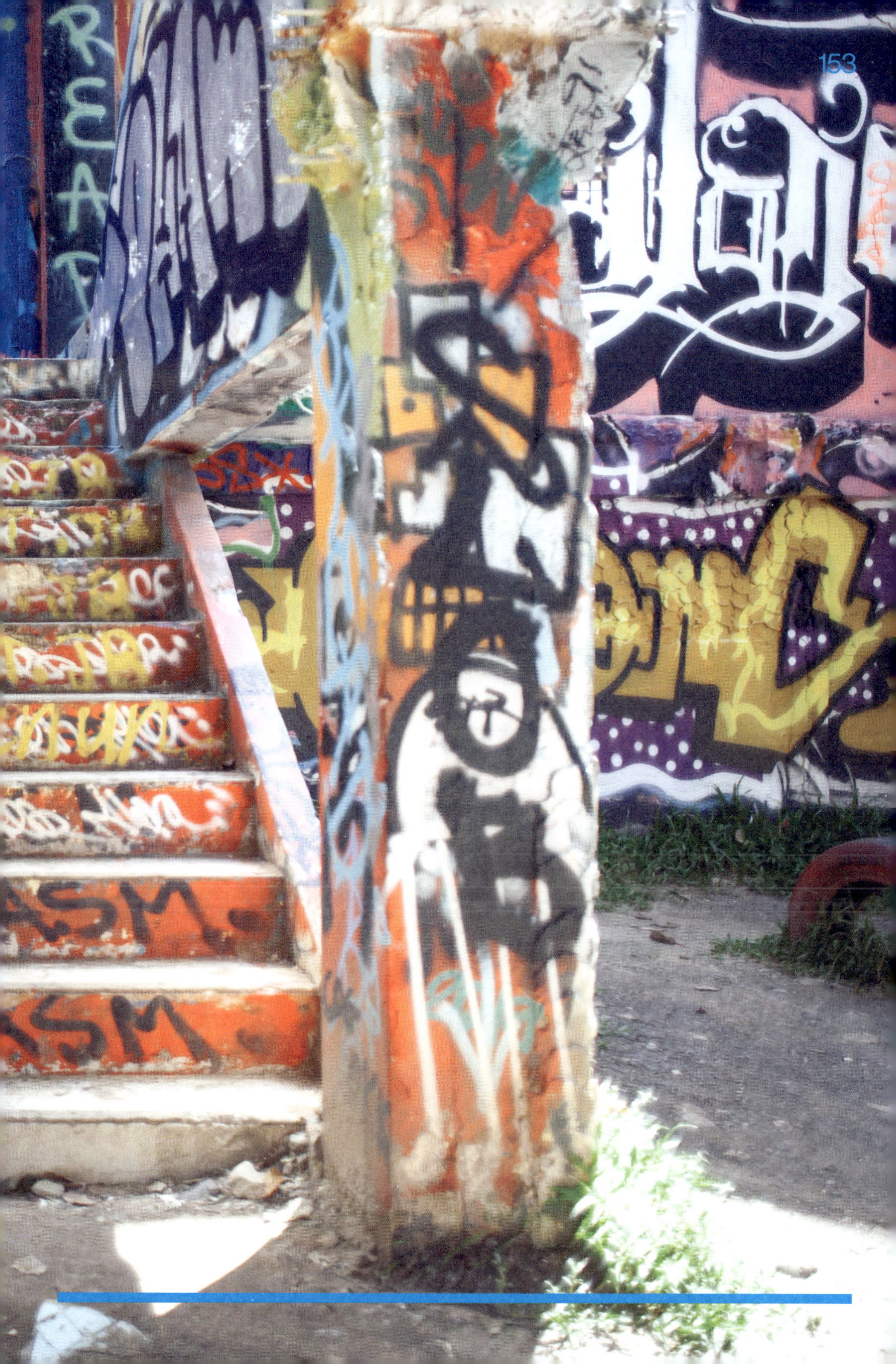
ASM
ASM

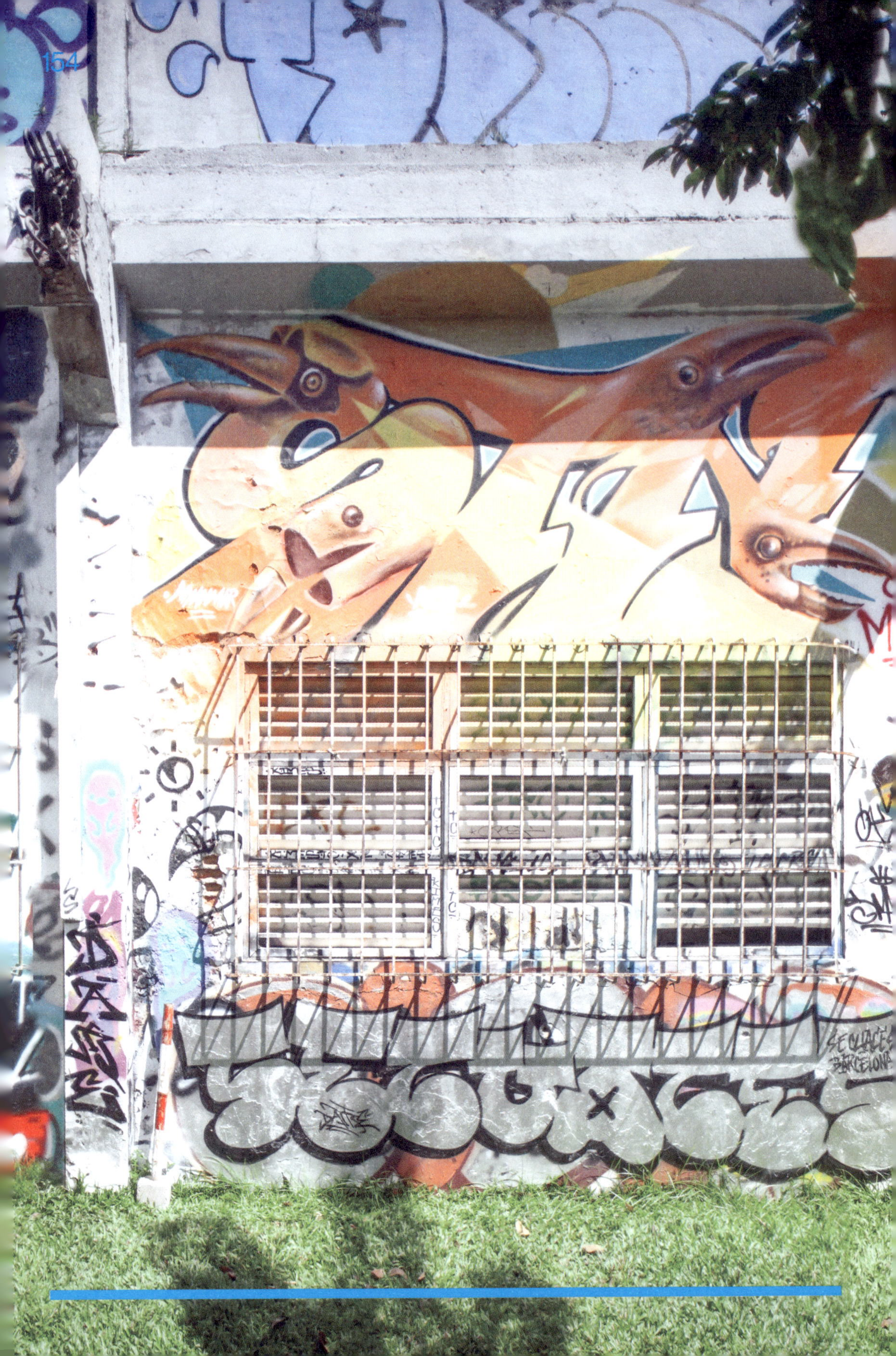
BARCELONA

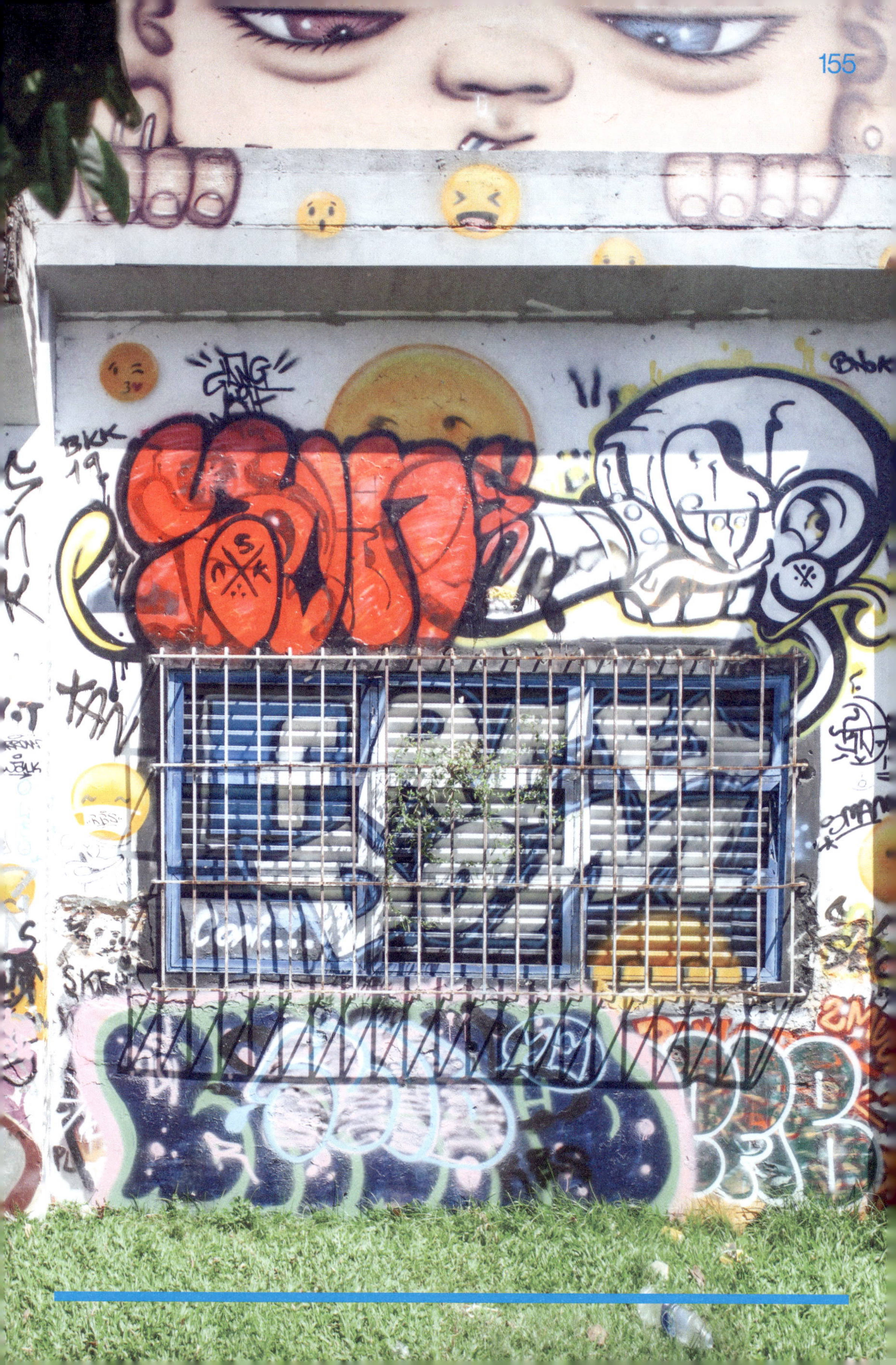

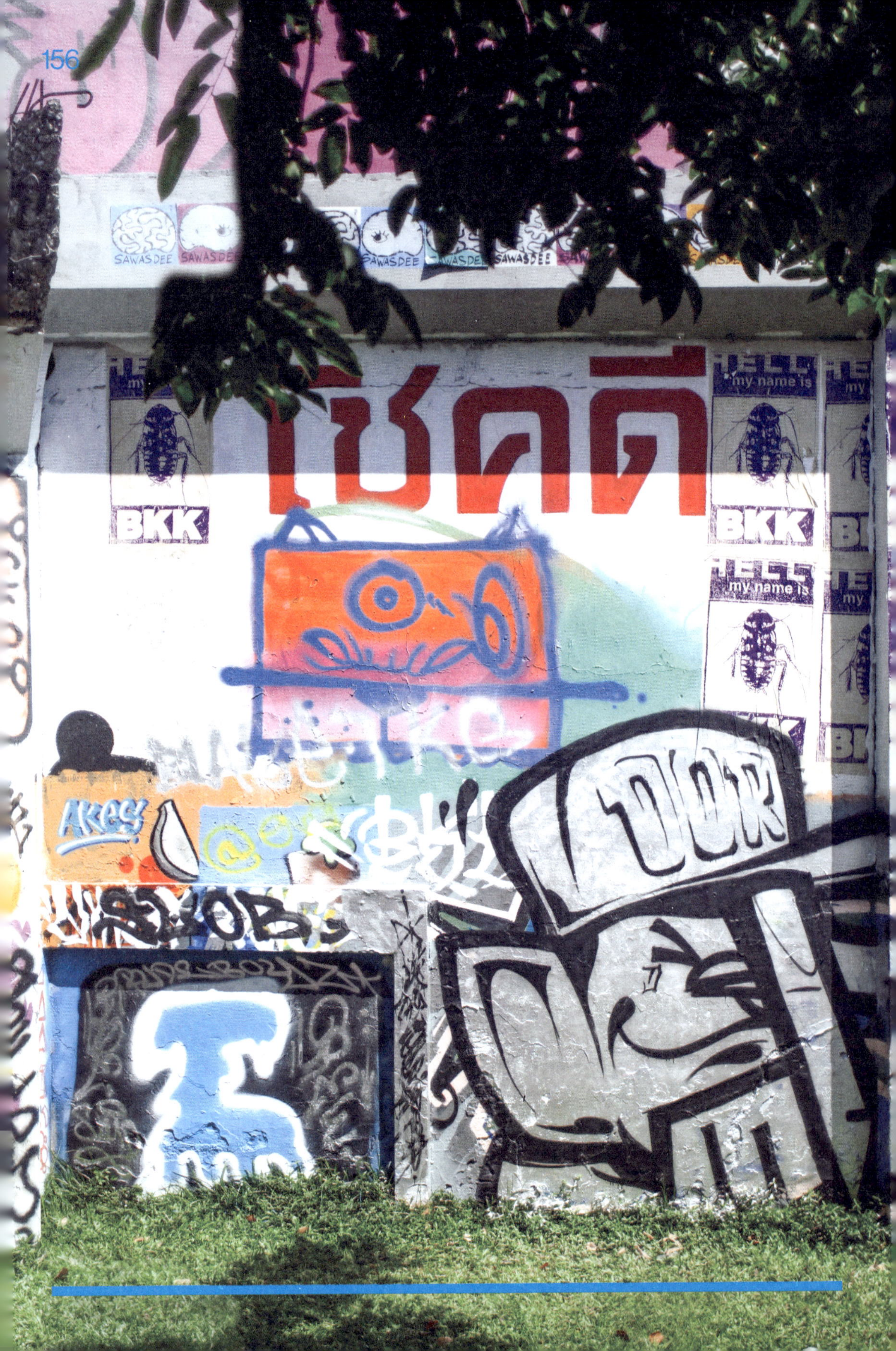
SAWASDEE
โชคดี
my name is
BKK
AKES

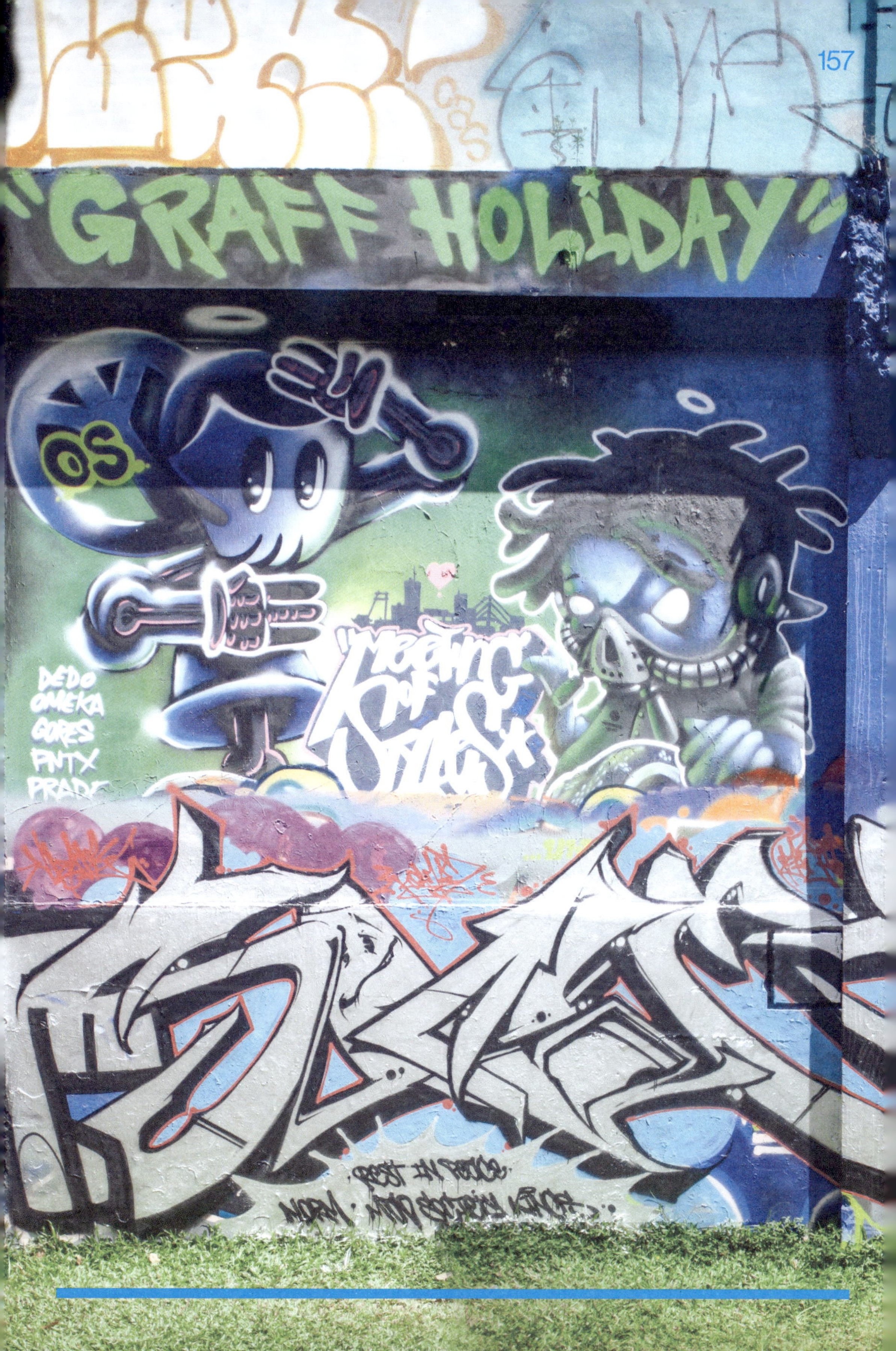
"GRAFF HOLIDAY"
OS
DEDO
OMEKA
GORES
PNTX
REST IN PEACE

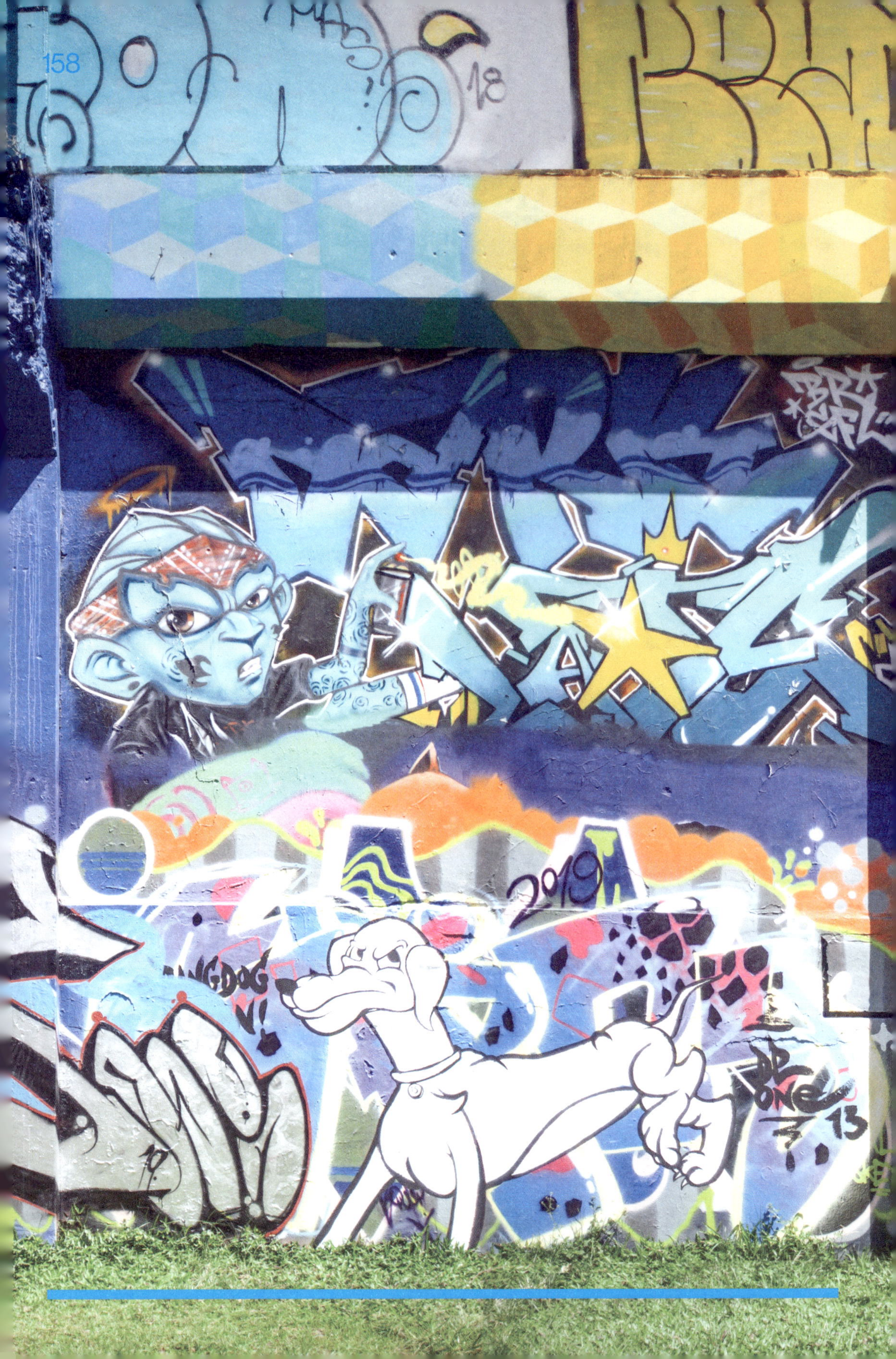
2019

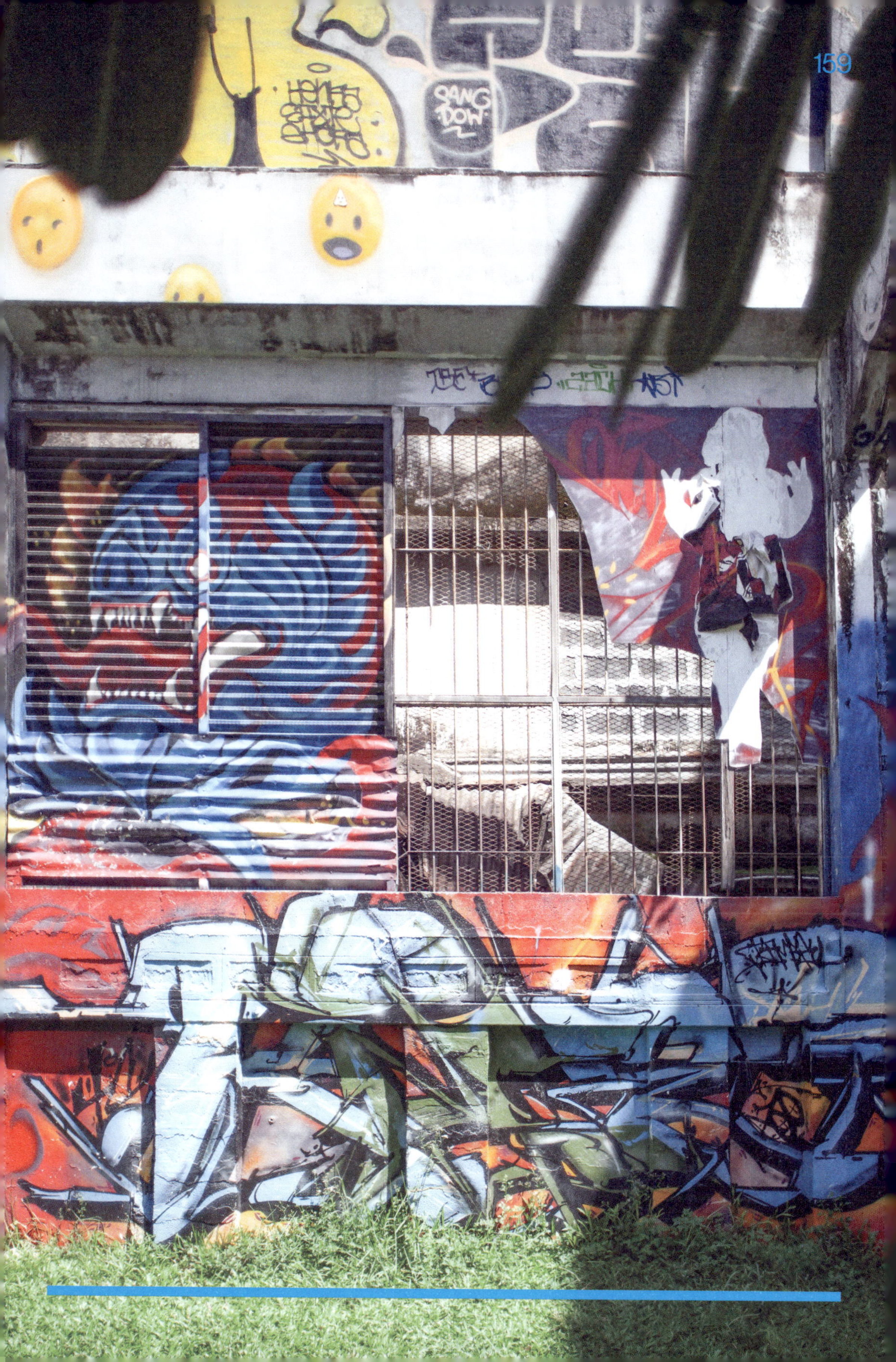

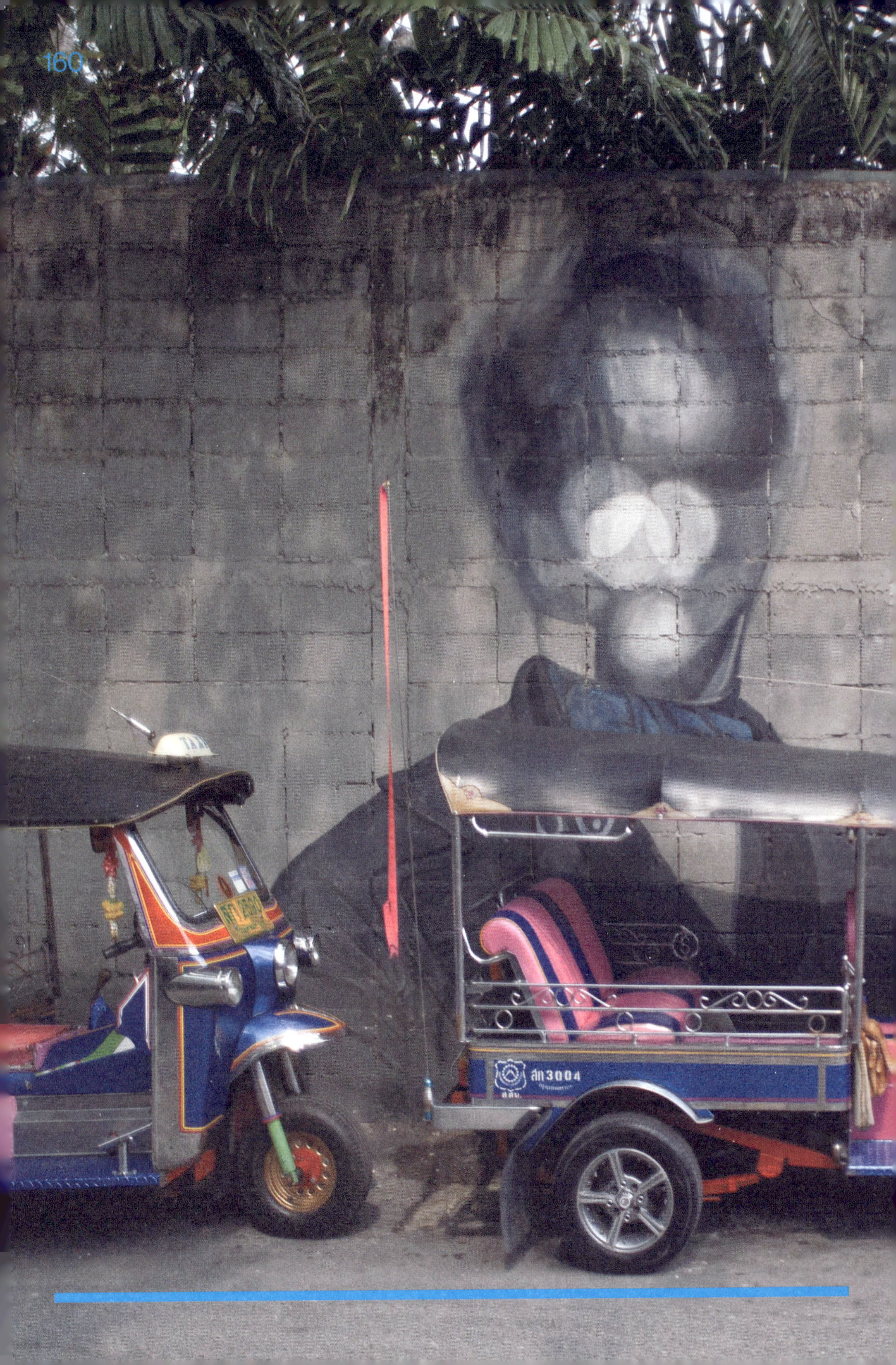

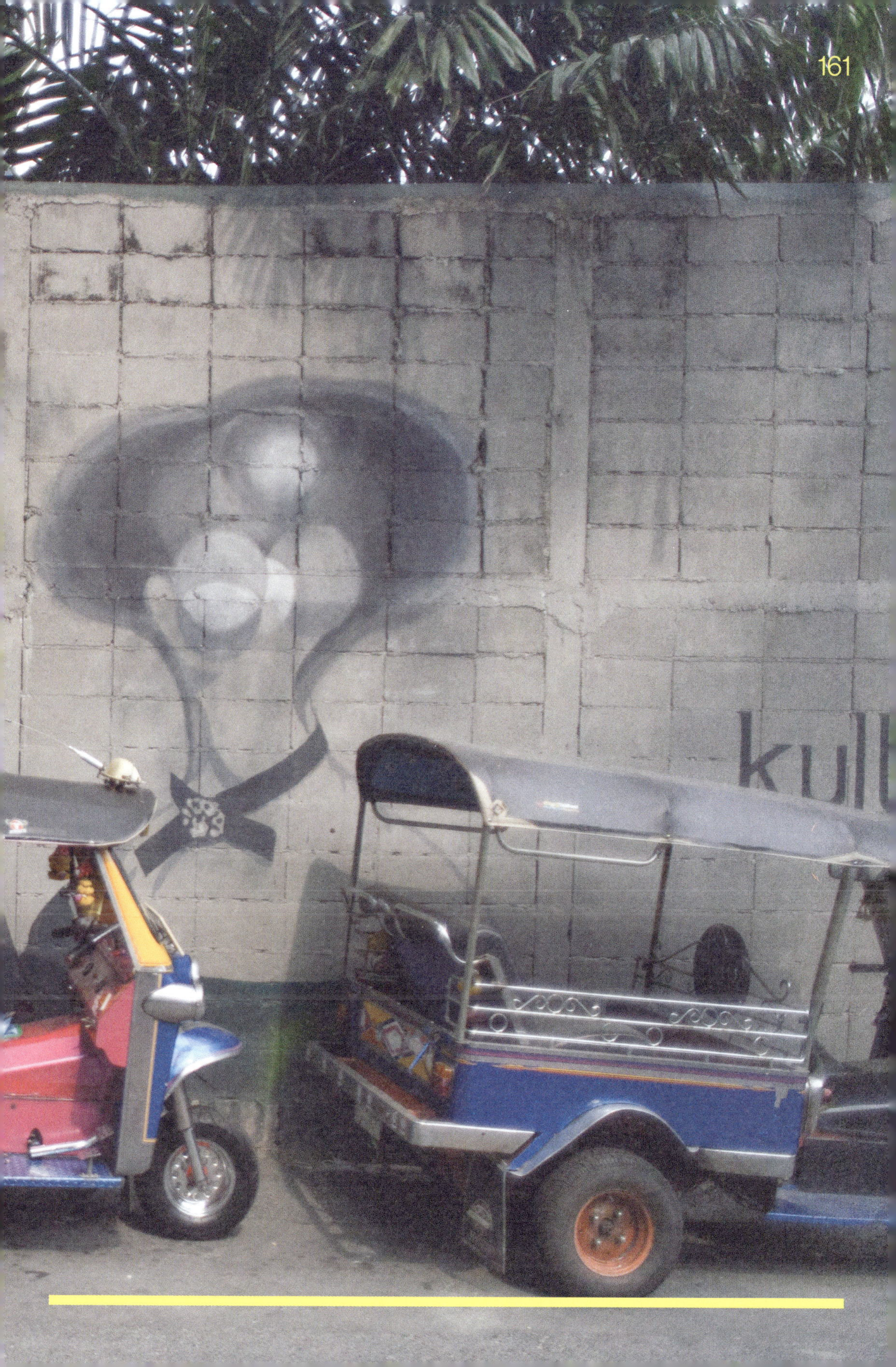
kult

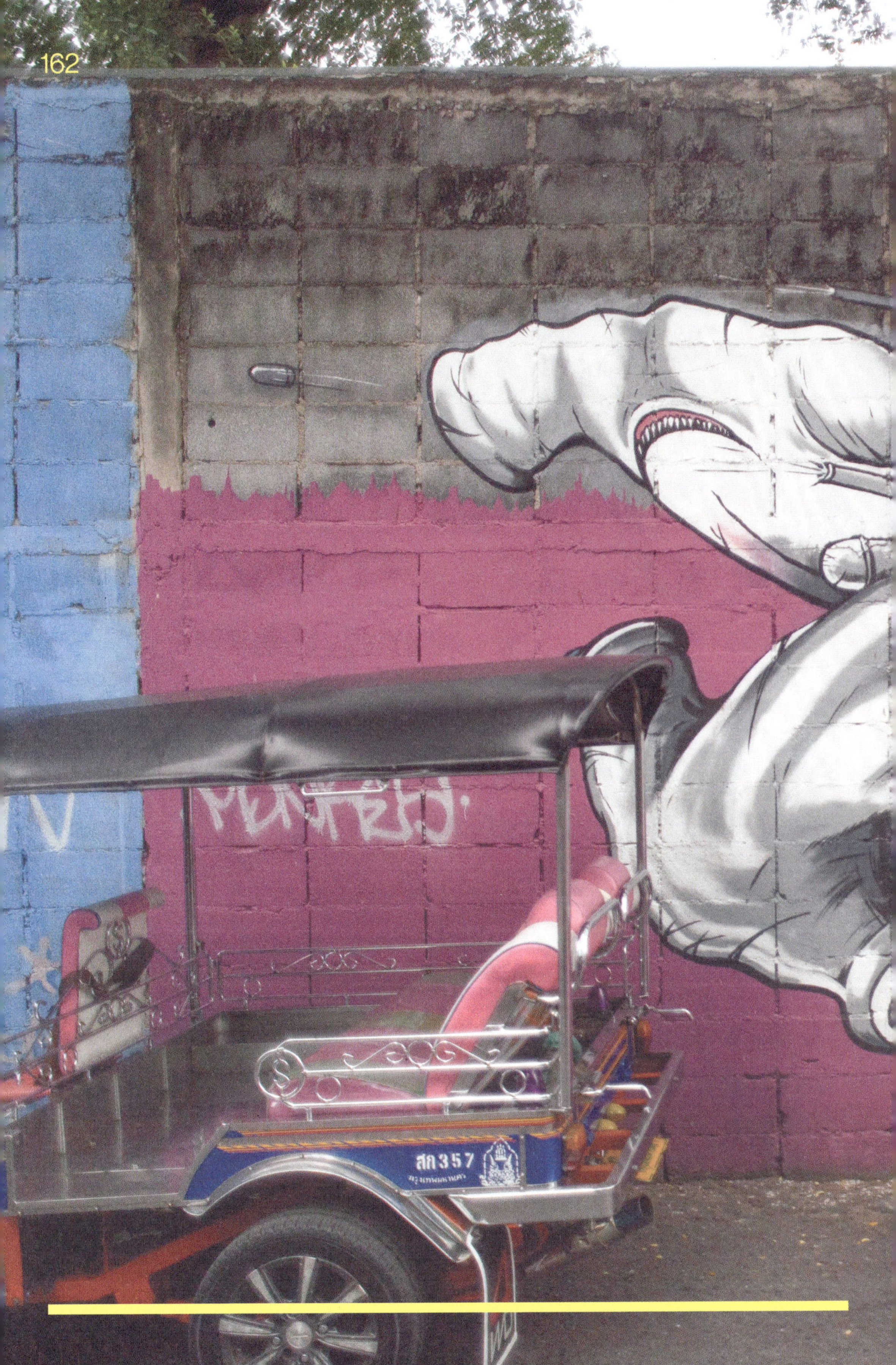
สก357

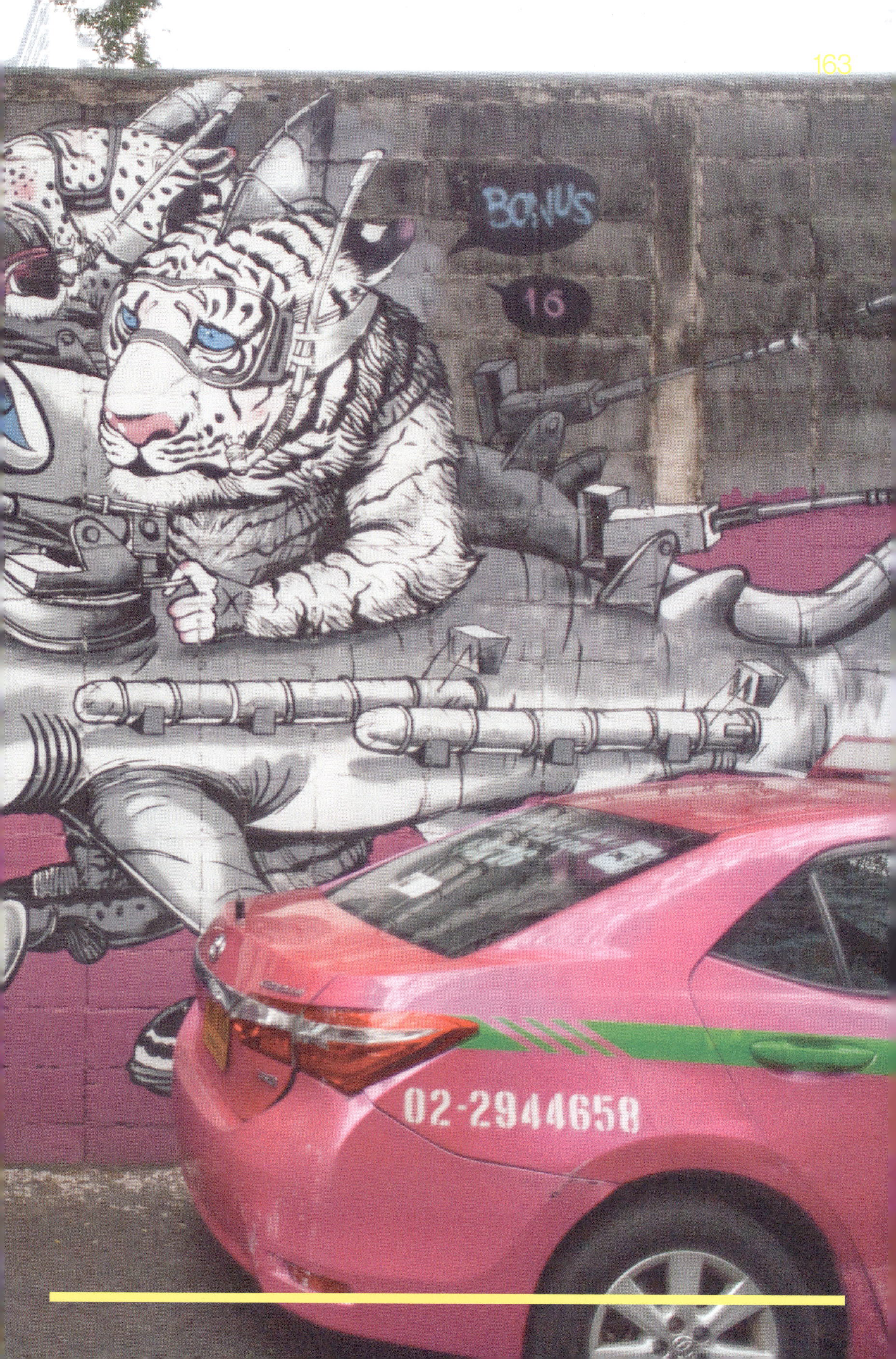
BONUS
16
02-2944658

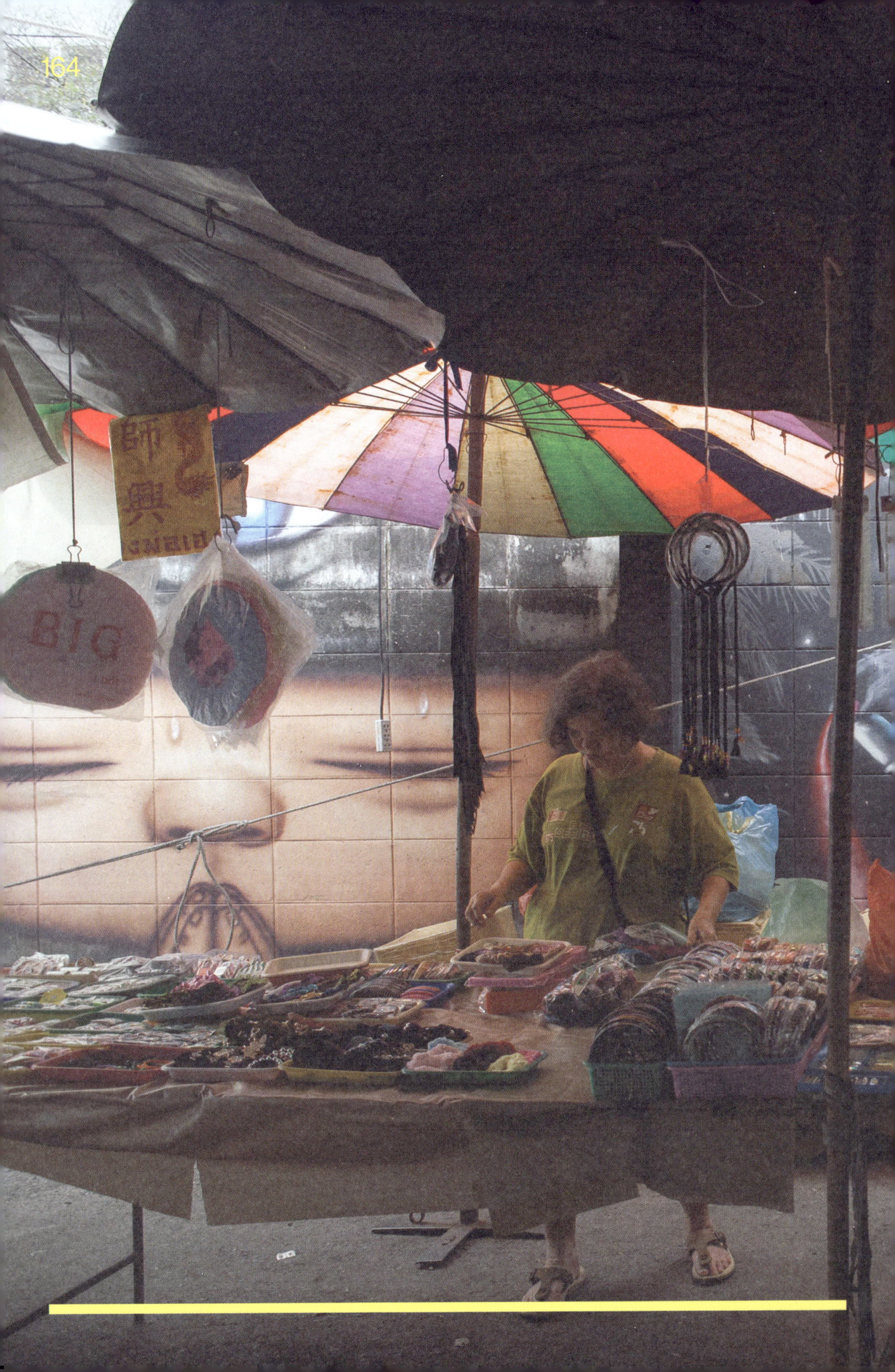
師
興
BIG

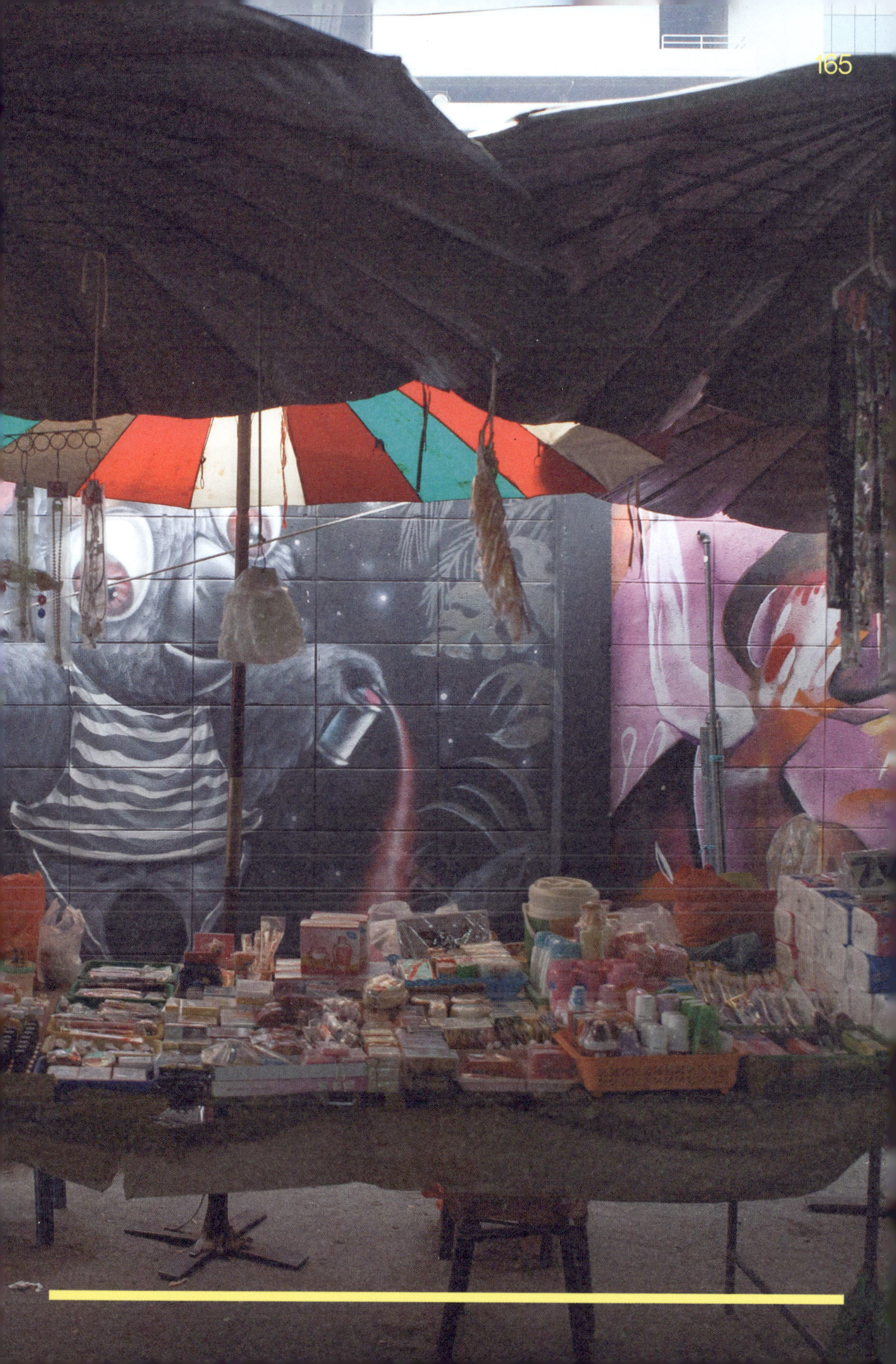

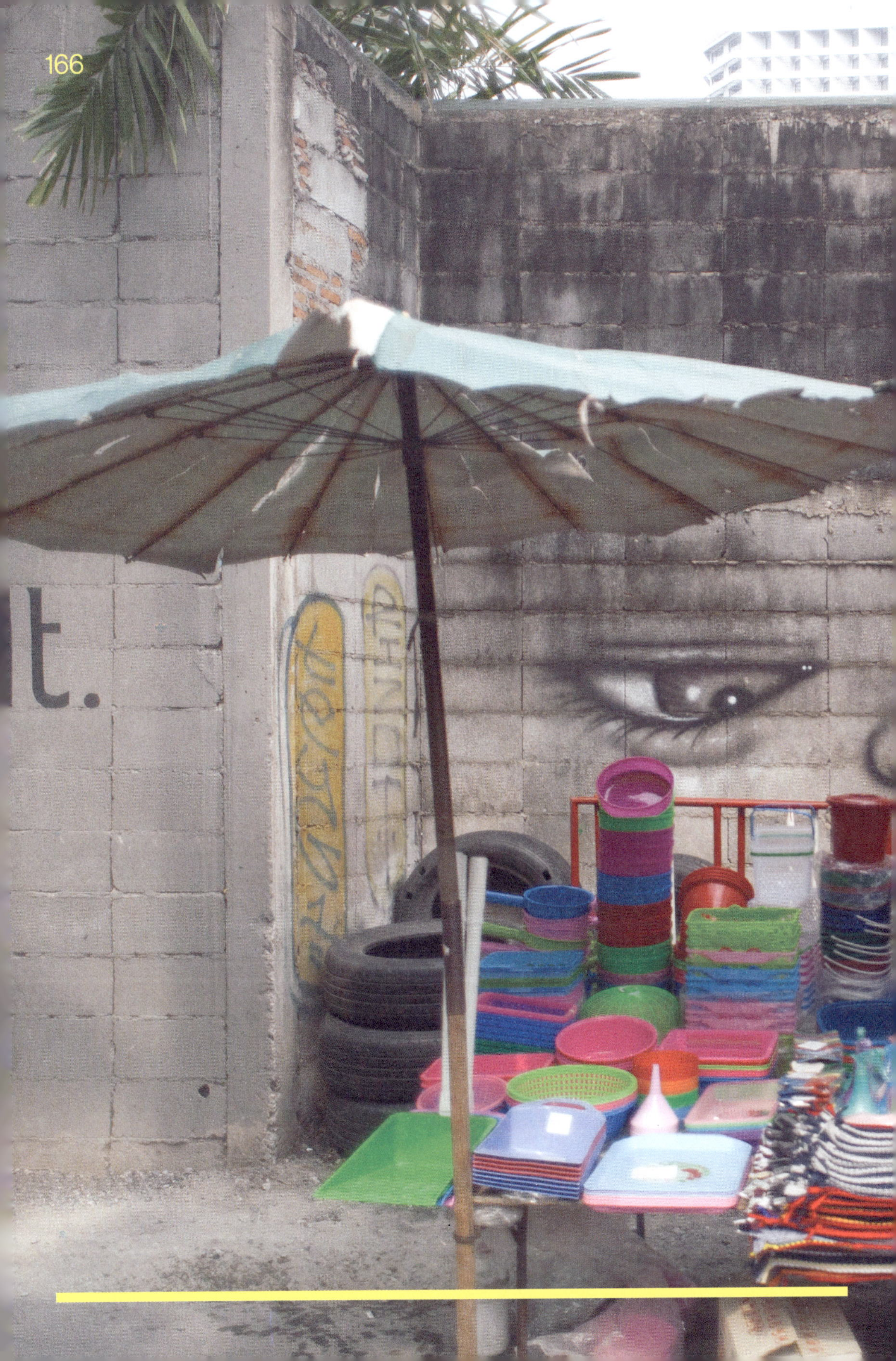

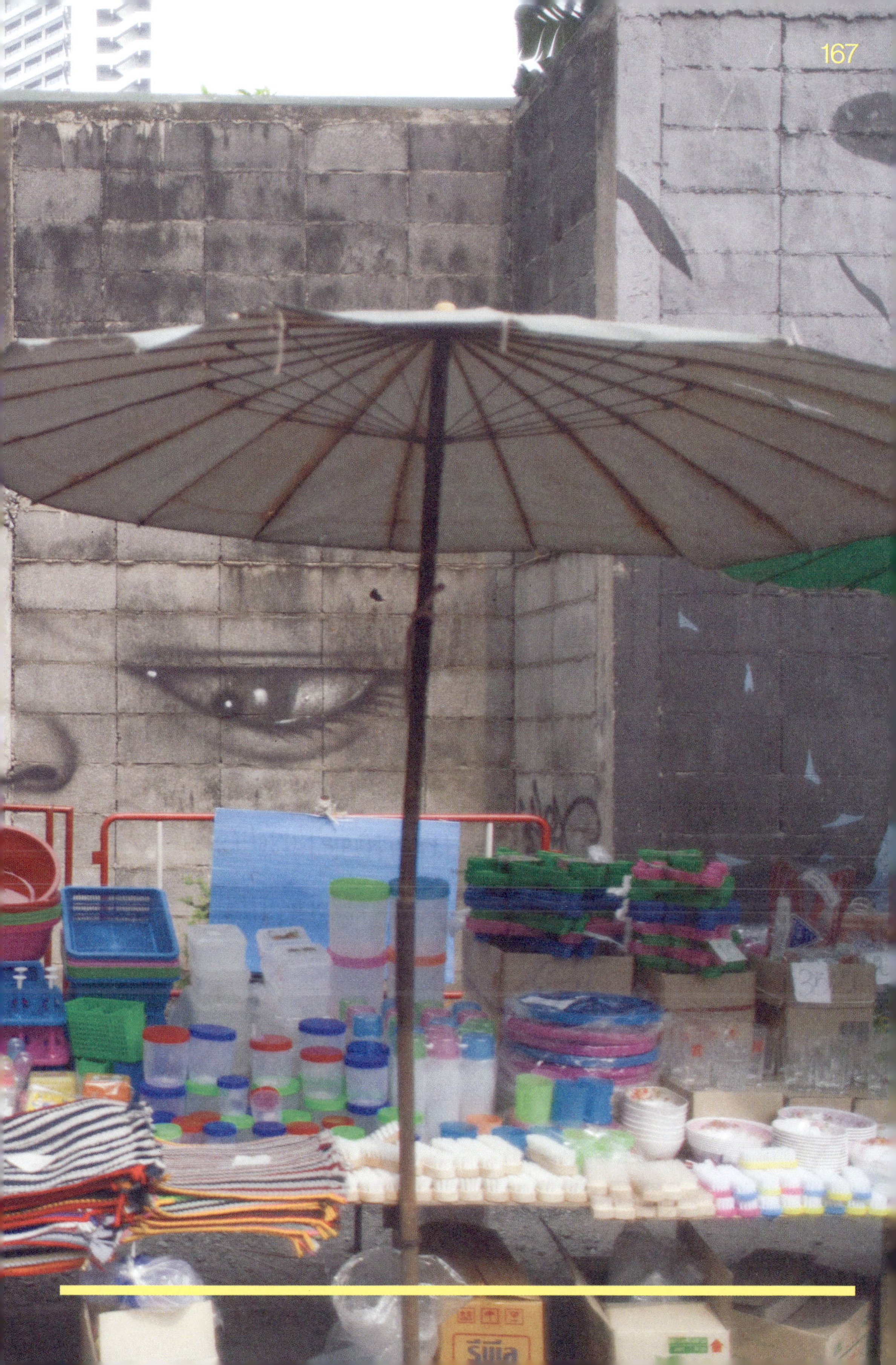

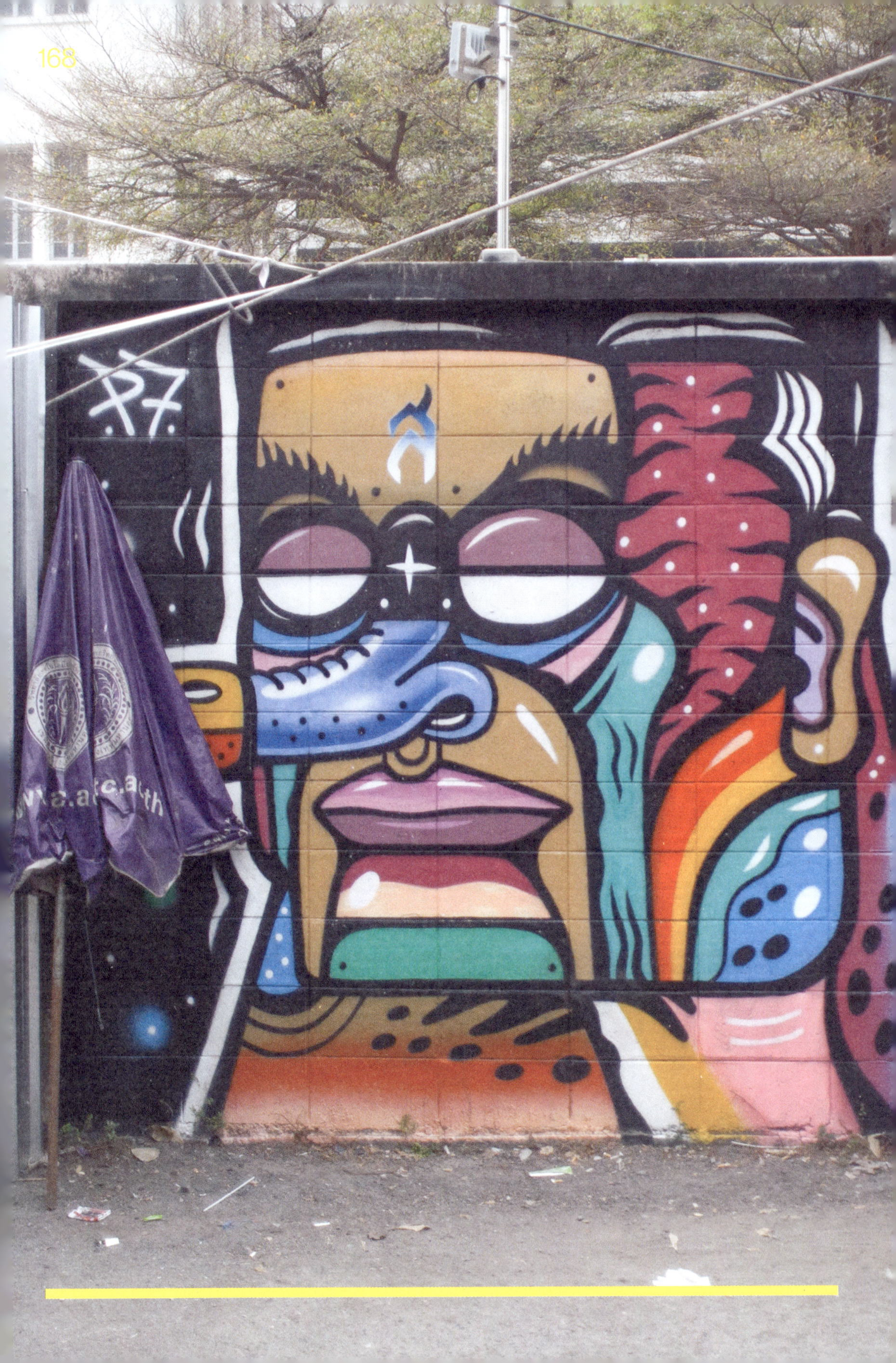

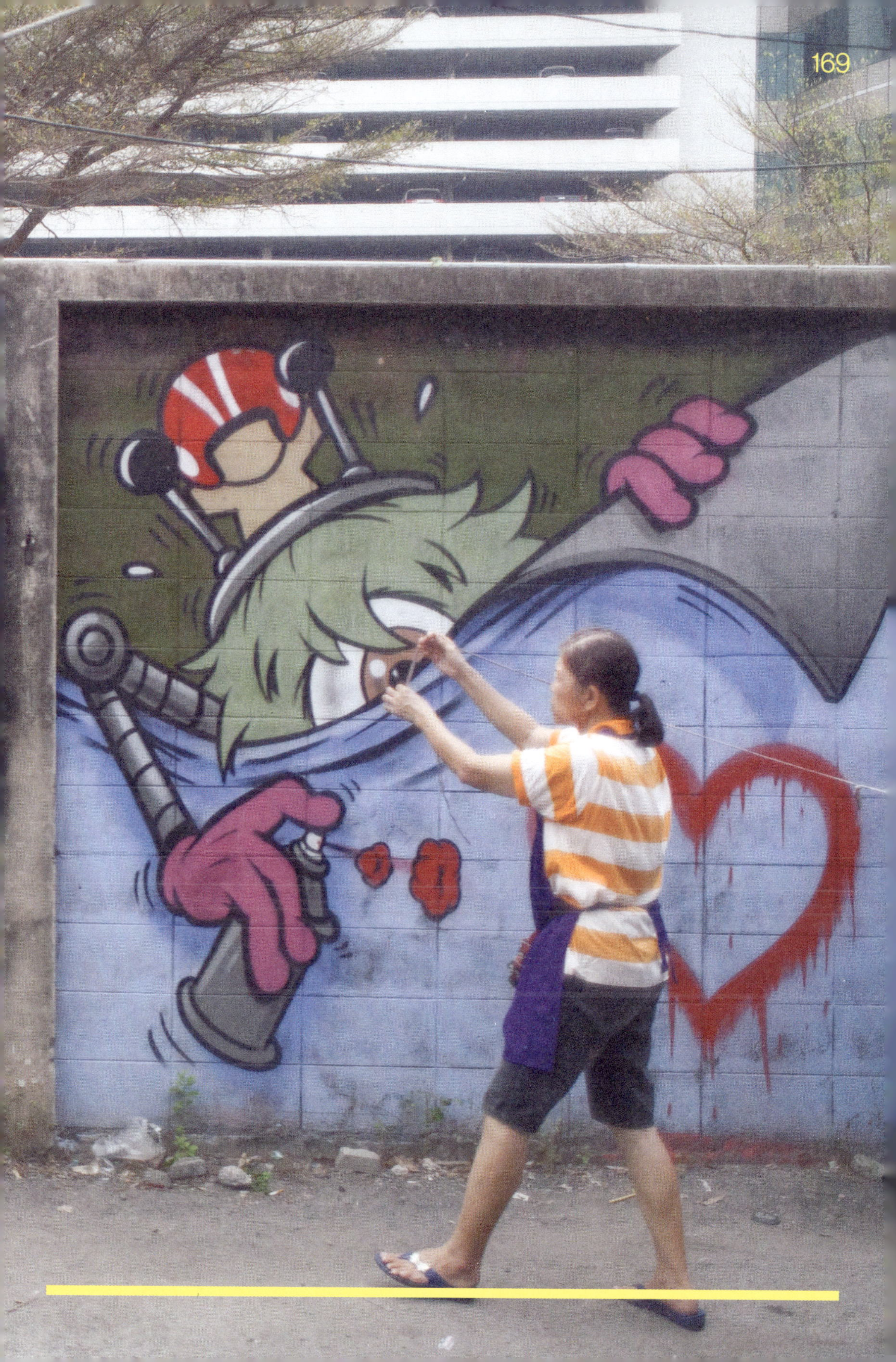

05

TRADITIONS

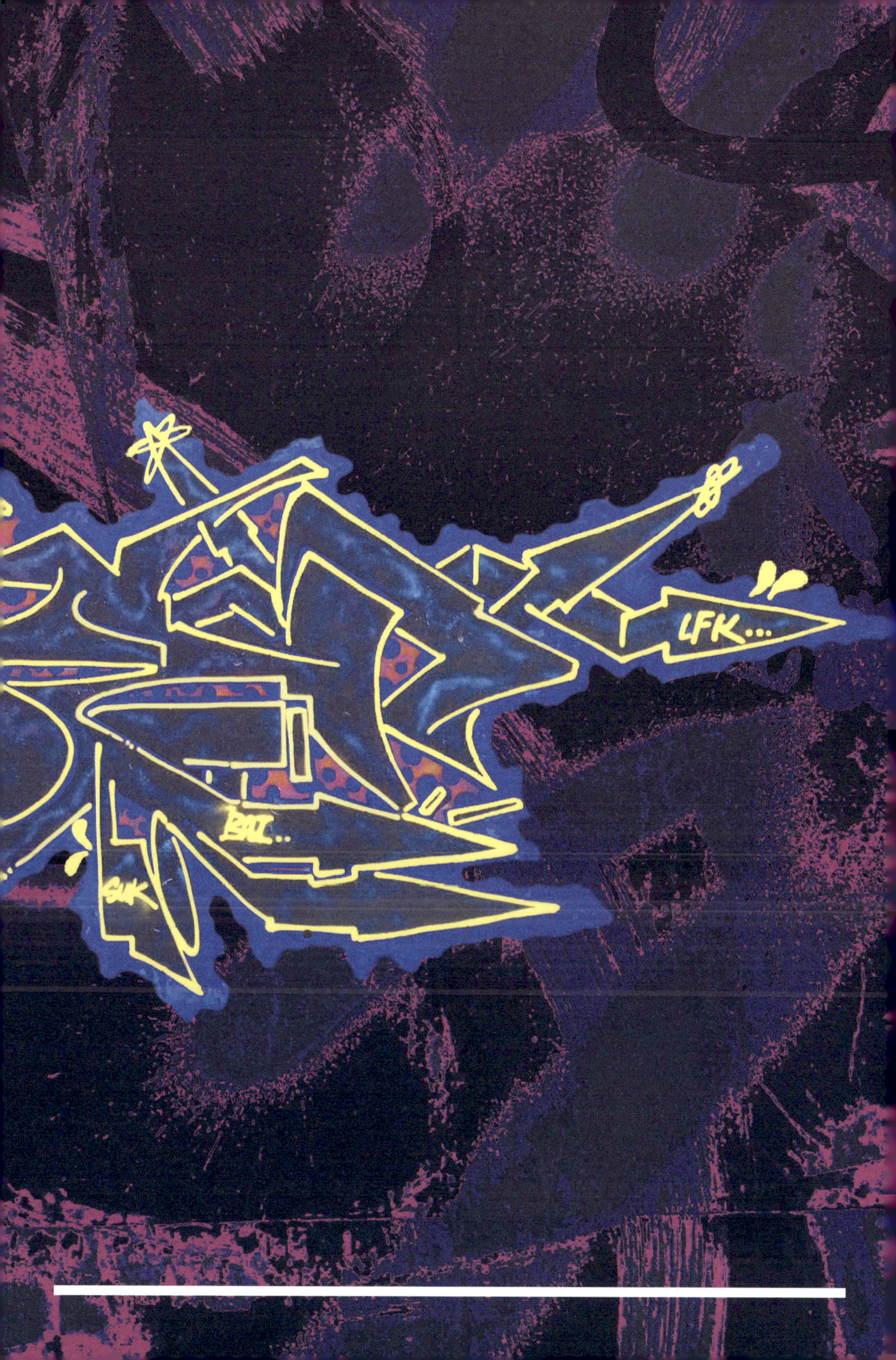
LFK...

By 2013, there were three distinct schools of public aerosol art in Bangkok: the newer, character-based street art, popular with a younger generation; the more traditional graffiti, still linked firmly with its US origins; and the long-standing polytechnical student stencil art and tagging, part of a much older Thai student gang culture. Today, murals and intricate pieces featuring recognisable figures and discernible narratives – street art – is popular. The old-school graffiti styles are also being adopted by a new generation of kids who marvel at their complex intricacy. This sprouting of street art from the trunk of graffiti mirrored a global movement towards character-based styles. But rather than a linear evolution in Thailand, from student tagging to graffiti and then to street art, there was a branching of these art forms – they exist together. How these tribes self-identify reveals much about their values, motives, influences and history.

The terminology is debated everywhere – 'street art' versus 'graffiti' – especially by those who are not street artists or graffiti writers, and is not really definable. The perceived differences between these two schools became important in Bangkok around 2013 – the time that Hopewell became a street art site. Many self-identify as belonging to one or the other group, but where they place themselves may not be where their fellow artists would. In Bangkok, these elements tend to be mixed – wildstyle writers do characters, both graffiti writers and street artists do political work, fame-seeking and fame-shy people exist in each camp as well as those who work illegally and those who don't. Some began in the graffiti tradition and moved into street art, some adhere firmly to the graffiti tradition today. Others reject it outright.

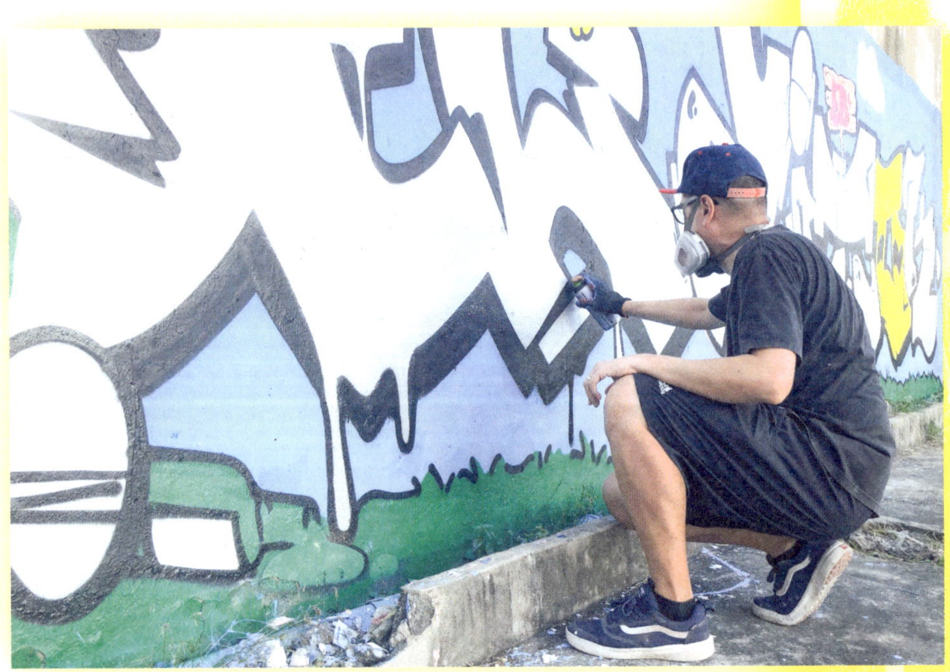

Bigdel working

Which group artists align themselves and others with is insightful. Not because it clarifies the definition of street art and graffiti – it doesn't – but because it reveals what these tribes value and detest. The divisions signify what it means to be genuine, proven, skilled, and defines good motives and bad ones, how skill should be taught and what the value of collaboration and rivalry is. It reveals a self-portrait of the ideal street artist or graffiti writer, as the case may be. By looking at these divisions, commonalities emerge. While many separate their style into these groups, they use common criteria to define a good and true creator's merits beyond the differences between street art and graffiti.

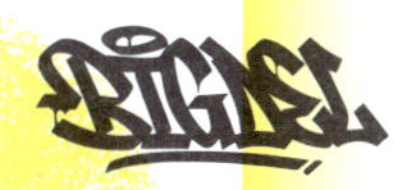

"I think the ones who bring up the difference between street art and graffiti are the fans, the ones who share it online. For me, we can go together. Sometimes there is a split between street art and graffiti in this culture, it depends on who you're asking."

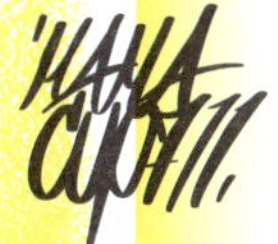

"For me, there is no difference between street art and graffiti. I grew up in the graffiti culture, but I also love street art because it has variety."

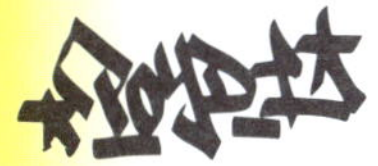

"The two groups, graffiti and street art are not that much different, because what they have in common is they use public space to create a piece."

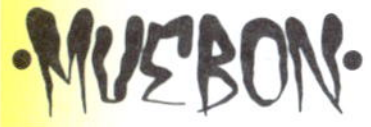

"We love the public places together, we love the walls together. But we have different styles and different approaches."

The graffiti writers came before the character-based, mural-creating street artists. This created a friction between the old and the young, between the originators, and those who move it beyond where it began. The young want to find new territory and shed the restrictions placed on them by previous generations. Those who came before, as bearers of knowledge and tradition, expect proper respect to be paid.

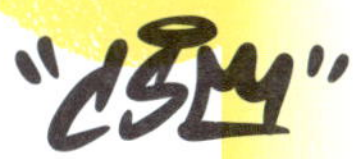

"In the early days there was a conflict between those who did graffiti for a long time, and those who wanted to make graffiti more accepted by people, and more beautiful. The artists who had done graffiti for a long time, they thought the newcomer artists are fake graffiti artists because they worked in the studio, and then suddenly they came out on the street and did their works and became famous. But

the graffiti artists had painted for a long time and were not as recognised. It was a big conflict at that time between old school and newcomer artists. The old school were a bit jealous also."

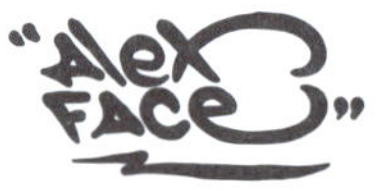

"If you do graffiti, those guys think street art is not real graffiti. 'Some kid from art school just painting the wall', that's what they say."

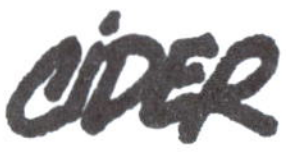

"Street art? Not really my thing. I have friends involved in the scene but there's also these street-art fuckers that would go around, take advantage of all the spots we painted in the city illegally. Some of these guys would paint over our work with their dumb wack murals on top. Come on now dude, there's a million walls in Bangkok. These fucking clowns will paint over us and would be like, 'This is better.' But when we go over their stuff, they will bitch on the Internet, 'These graffiti guys are gangsters trying to bully us'. They cry like hurt little bitches. If you are in this game, the graffiti game, you have to deal with the consequences. This ain't 'We Are The World' type bullshit."

Regardless of whether someone is a street artist, graffiti writer or mix of both, being dedicated to your style and true to your motives over time is a key virtue. CIDER, regarded as one of the earliest Thai graffiti writers, grew up in the US and upon his return to Thailand in 1998, continued his work. He established early Bangkok crews with graffiti writers like Ctru, Poyd1, and Bigdel. In the graffiti tradition, younger writers are expected to master the typographies, each letter of the alphabet, day by day, writing them thousands of times to get the correct stroke widths, lines, curves. They then develop can control over hundreds of hours.

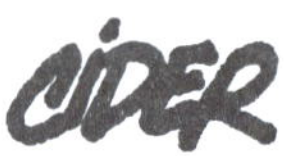

"You have to go through a certain number of years and experiences in order to be accepted by your peers. If you're in Thailand, you get accepted by the people who came before you. If you're in America, you get accepted by your crew and people within the culture. I've been painting since 1992, back in high school, in California. It wasn't easy back then. I've been involved in graffiti arrests before, picked up by them and all that type of bullshit growing up – part of the game. The graffiti crews I got put down with are, MSK [Mad Society Kings], THR [The Human Race/The Harsh Reality], S.U.K. [Stick-Up-Kids] and LFK from South Korea. In graffiti, when you get up, it's not about painting for only weeks

and months but you have to paint for years in order to excel. It's not that I paint for a week or a month and I will get into the gallery scene and sell paintings. It's not the flavour of the month type shit. It's not like Starbucks – 'This month we have the special Christmas, vanilla, eggnog'... Fucking 'Sour cream' bullshit. I'm not like that. You just have to put in work. So the difference between street-art people and graffiti people? We put in work. We do letters. Sometimes we do characters. We could be out there doing illegal graffiti, risking our lives. And the most important part of it is, we take risks putting our names up."

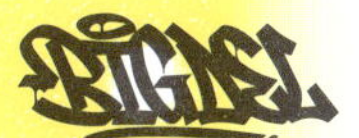

"A lot of kids today, they see the outcome, but they don't see the road you have to go through. A lot of them ask on Facebook, 'I want to be like you, how can I start graffiti?' But they can't be like me in a year. I've been doing this for twenty years. When I started, I was obsessed. I had my notebook and I wrote, A, B, C, D, E, F, G in different styles, every day. Then, after a year, I put more design on it and I developed and developed it. Kids also send me photos of their first pieces on Facebook and they ask me, 'Is this good?', 'Is this bad?' I never judge the beauty of something, but the intention. If I can see the kid has put in a lot of effort, I encourage them. You have to become who you are. You have to prove yourself. What matters is, after five years, are you still doing your work or not?"

With their beginnings in art schools, and lack of interest in typography, those not from the graffiti tradition don't go through this schooling. They use new forms and styles that are not part of the lexicon of graffiti writers (see next page).

"Because I didn't come from graffiti, I came from graphic design, so I used that style to solve the problem that my freehand wasn't good. I colour with freehand, but my outline is a modular system, a template. It's good for my style."

HEAD ACHE

"For me, I just do my art more and more and more. The graffiti writers, they always say, 'Oh, stencil art is easy to do. Anybody can do that.' So, if you follow my art, I do it every week. New pieces, new pieces. Harder and harder, until now. No way you can do this. This is the way to prove your art."

Student taggers are regarded as a tradition on their own, operating under separate rules built on rivalry and brotherhood. In this way, Thai graffiti writers and student taggers share a common cultural ancestry. They both came out of mostly male sub-cultures that formed gangs and used public aerosol art as a way of representing allegiance and territory in contravention of formal law. One amongst US teenagers, the other amongst those in Thailand. That focus on rivalry, getting your name up and representing your crew means the student taggers won respect from graffiti writers.

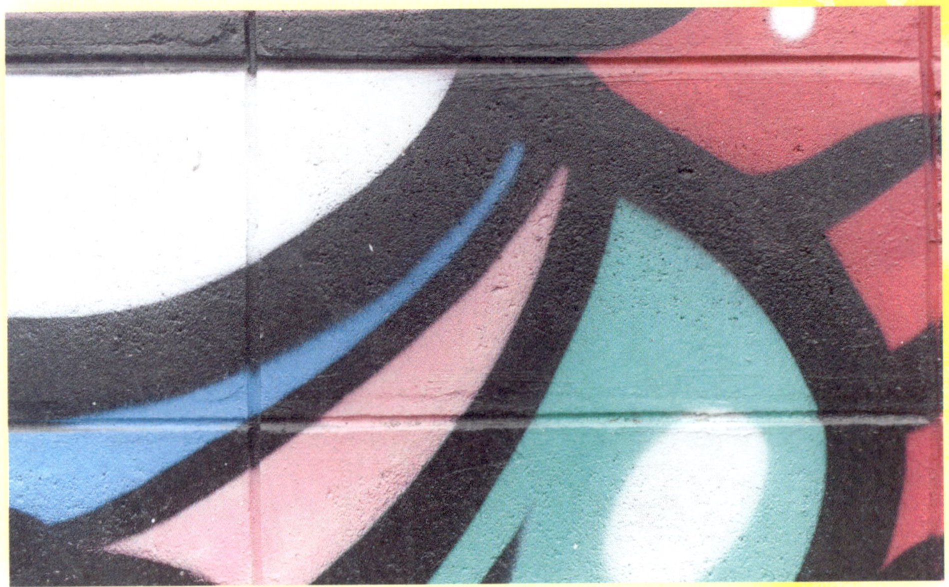

Street art detail by P7

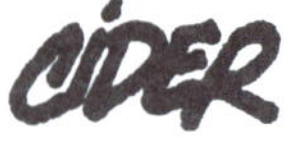

"Polytechnical student taggers have a great sense of pride in their school and they chose the spray can as a tool to represent who they are because you can work fast with a spray can and you can get away quick. It's cool. I like it. It looks really nice. Those guys, the technical school kids, have got more balls than these street-art kids. They are real rebels. They're more raw. They keep it real to themselves. Somehow they have this thing for their school, I respect that. They represent their own thing. I don't understand it, though. Shit can be violent. Handguns... It's like gang-banging. But street artist people, they are just soft and talk a lot of bullshit."

In Bangkok, doing your art for something bigger than yourself – for your crew, your style, your school – is one of the virtues of a legitimate graffiti writer. And in many ways, is shared by street artists who often use their work to draw attention to social and political issues they feel strongly about.

"It's not about doing graffiti or character style. It's about finding your own unique style, you've got to make people recognise that it's your style. If you don't have a signature style no one knows it's your work."

Almost all artists and writers take commercial work. There is recognition in the scene that people have to make a living, so those who can do it through their art are seen as fortunate.

ANONYMOUS

"I don't consider street art to be pure art. There's a lot of business involved. Popular artists are often hired to do commercial projects whereas us, graffiti artists walk around putting stickers on walls."

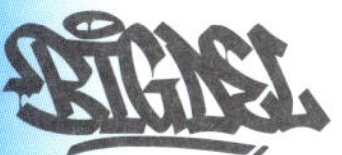

"As the scene became more popular, artists from various backgrounds, such as graphic designers, illustrators, or even painters, started to paint on walls. So it's no surprise that these works are more popular and accessible than text-based graffiti. This might make some graffiti writers, who pioneered working in public, feel like they are being taken advantage of by artists who come later. Personally, it doesn't matter what kind of work you do – graffiti or street art. If you're still out there looking for walls, come rain or shine, spend money on paint, and continue creating works that are unique to you, I think that's probably the most important thing."

The exception to this is artists who are seen as only doing commercial work without also going out and doing pieces that are true to their own style, crew or message.

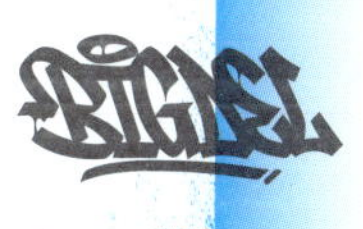

"I understand the artists who do commercial work. They do a commissioned job but the next week, they go out and do their own work. It's okay. We all have to find a way to support ourselves and a way to support our soul. It's very hard to make a living in Thailand. Now, it becomes a job. Okay. I can use what I like to earn money. Why not? And then, after doing that commercial work, I go and do my thing. So I have two worlds."

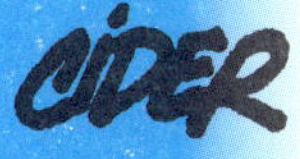

"Graffiti in Thailand is personal fame. Street art in Thailand is personal fame plus, 'I want to get paid quick and hop in galleries' – a get rich quick scheme. These street artists or legal wall painters are like, 'If I don't get paid,

I stay at home and watch Netflix' type people. I have nothing against getting paid, though. But these clowns go over our graffiti walls to get permission walls and avoid confrontations when asked why. But for people like us, if we have a commission, we'll think about it. If the commission makes sense, we'll do it. Every profession has to have integrity in what they do."

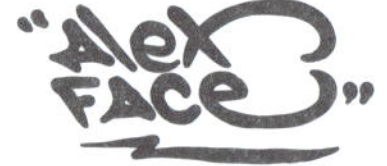

"I think when a kid who grows up in a subculture like graffiti and then becomes a man, he still likes graffiti. So he thinks 'I'm going to open my restaurant' or he becomes a fashion designer. It doesn't mean we don't do graffiti any more. Even now, I still do tagging, just for fun. Sometimes when I'm painting a mural, people expect something nice. Sometimes I want to do something fun – doesn't matter if it's good or bad, some abandoned building... I still do my old-school ALEX FACE tag. Before the baby, I used to paint a big face, that's why I call myself ALEX FACE. I still paint the face for fun, sometimes."

A more recent aspect of these differences, is whether political or wider social messages are depicted. Compared to graffiti, street art and stencil art more commonly contain political messages. However, even in the earliest days, graffiti artists did political work, as a piece by PMT from 2001 depicting Thaksin Shinawatra, his deputy Prime Minister, Chavalit Yongchaiyudh and other politicians, shows (see below). Street artists tend to be poetic with their messages. Coming from formal art training, as many street artists do, there is a value placed on being cryptic and symbolic. Street art delves into many social and political issues and the very nature of graffiti – born, as it was, out of rebellion – has politics for a spine.

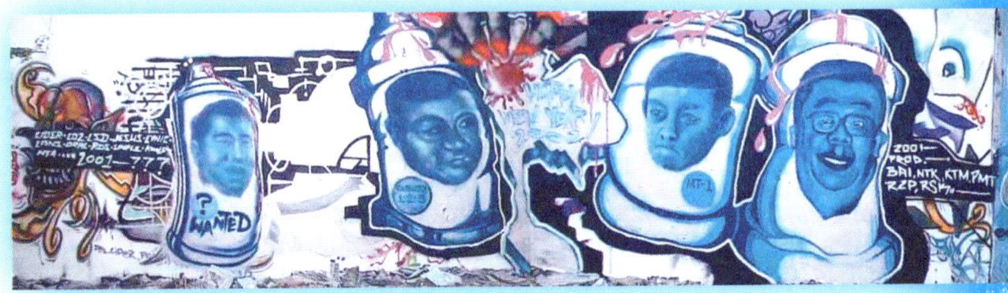

Piece by PMT Crew

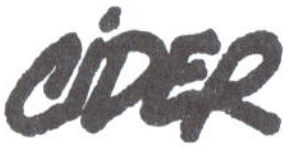

"Graffiti, we put work into it, we risk our lives at night. We rebel against the system, or certain political movements. Sometimes graffiti artists will go out there and write political messages. – they just want to voice their political statement."

Many graffiti writers shun the title 'artist' and prefer 'writer'. The pretence associated with the term goes against the graffiti grain. In turn, street artists often criticise graffiti writers for being egotistical and doing their work just to get their name up. Graffiti writers similarly criticise street artists for using political issues to get famous. For both these tribes, membership of a movement is important, membership of a club is shirked.

ANONYMOUS

"Some street artists just think of topics like, 'We feel sorry for the kids, let's do it for the slum people.' At the same time, they will be talking shit about rich people like, 'They are taking advantage of the poor,' this and that. But then, they are behind the scenes mingling with the richest, taking pictures, kissing asses, collaborating...etc. You need to have integrity in what you do. There's a big mural at Chaloem La Park of some kid, 'I want to go to school.' I want to see the painter give money for this kid to go to school. It's not much. You want to do something for a cause, DONATE."

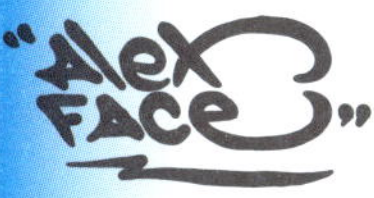

"Graffiti is about putting your name everywhere, putting your ego everywhere."

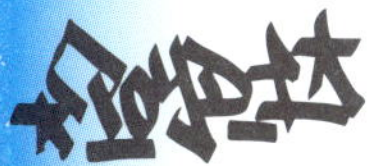

"Street art is a platform to communicate something to the public, but graffiti is more like a name, a tag. That's it."

•MUEBON•

"It's hard to give a short explanation about the difference between graffiti and street art. Because they are traditions that don't come from formal education. They come from the resistance and social evolution of the oppressed lower classes who fight against an unjust system. The people who are not seen or heard express themselves through street art. This continues to evolve today. The focus of these traditions is individuality. Formal education can't come up with a curriculum or formula to teach street art. Take graffiti, for example, each writer has their own goal. Some want only to bomb repeatedly, to have their names fill the city while not caring about the city's aesthetics. Some put effort into creating beautiful works that are well designed and meticulous. Some just want to shout a message to society about their social or political feelings and opinions, without aesthetic concerns. Some prefer working in studios and rarely come out on the street, even though they might have become famous as a street artist. So the art form doesn't have any rules. It supports the individuality of small people in society. Anyone can get up and do graffiti or street art in public."

HEAD ACHE

"For me, street art should make people think something. For me, graffiti can't do that. Graffiti is just something like a signature, or branding. But that's nothing for me. This is how I separate graffiti and street art in Thailand. If you use the word graffiti to describe me, I will not accept it. I feel super-bad that I have to use the same art form as they do. Because their art, for me, is shit. What the fuck? You call that art? You paint other people's houses with your name? Who wants that? If you're proud of your art, why are you afraid to show your face?"

This mutual criticism reveals a dividing line, not between what makes someone a street artist or a graffiti writer, but between what makes someone worthy or unworthy – whether they are interested in personal fame or representing something beyond themselves. When a street artist decries a graffiti writer as being concerned only about getting their name up, they are aligned with graffiti writers, who accuse street artists of selling out and using politics to get known. Attempting to get famous quickly, loses respect. Dedicating yourself over years with skill and consistency, gains respect – regardless of which style is chosen.

These divisions and commonalities within the scene are part of a constantly changing dance that has taken place in Bangkok since before graffiti and street art existed. It is performed for two exacting audiences, one applauds the old, the traditional, the 'Thai', and the other applauds the new, the modern, the international. Because Thai street art and graffiti have both local and international origins, deeper tensions around Thai identity are felt in the scene.

ANONYMOUS

"There is no Thai style. Everyone uses English. Because Thai is not international. Old school, Graffiti, wildstyle came from Europe and America. Our country is a small country. If we use a Thai style, no one will care. Even if someone starts doing a Thai style, I don't think people will support it, nor would it receive a big audience."

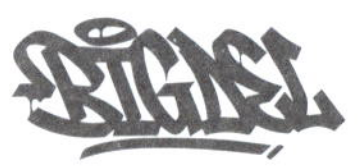

"Had the Internet and social media never existed in Thailand, and Thai people had developed graffiti in our own way. I don't think graffiti would have come this far or been accepted by society. Graffiti would have still been looked down on as work from the street and not considered an art form."

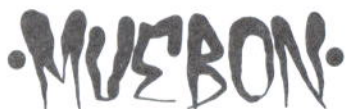

"First of all, what does it mean to be Thai? When we use what we think of as unique Thai patterns, they also have characteristics borrowed from Cambodia, India, China and other neighbouring countries. I think that Thainess is

a mixture of all of these. It's a distortion of history that makes us proud of being Thai. Inequality, corruption, coup d'etats, pretentiousness and the concepts of 'Good people' and 'Good Buddhists' are all tied to Thainess. They are rooted so deeply that we cannot distinguish between them. If I try or don't try to insert Thainess into my work, it will inevitably seep in. No matter how hard we try to be cool and create work as if we were New Yorkers, we will only ever be Thai artists who imitate New Yorkers."

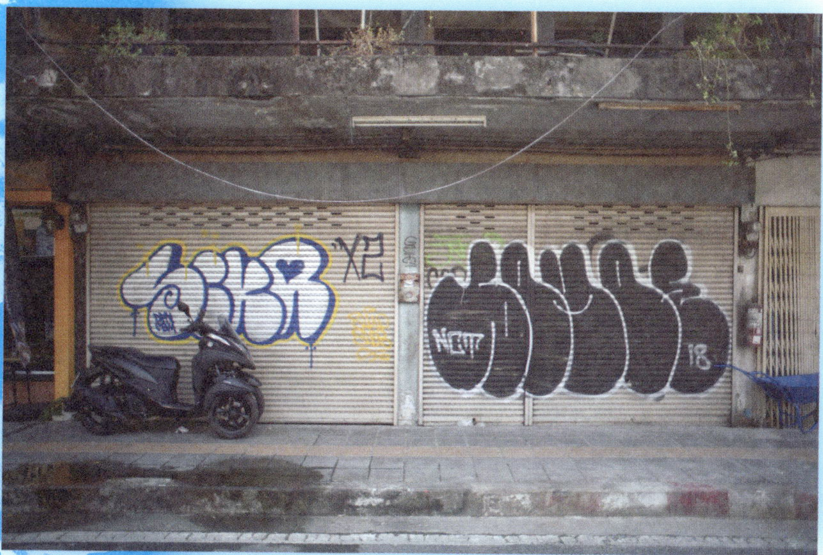

Graffiti by SIKA and DAYOE

• • •

Coinciding with the emergence of character-based street art around 2010, and Hopewell's use as a street-art site in 2012 and 2013, was an explosion of print and then digital social media focussed on street art in Bangkok. A feedback loop emerged where street artists began to record, communicate and publicise their work which was then consumed by an ever-expanding audience. Magazines, like *a day*, did early features on Thai graffiti art. In 2009, the Bangkok-based art, fashion and design magazine *GoPlay* was launched. It focussed on the Bangkok scene and helped spread appreciation for graffiti and street art. *GoPlay* featured many artists' work and interviewed them in their studios or while working in the street. Hip-hop culture was popular at this time. This meant street art and graffiti became an aspect of being on-point for aspiring alternatives amongst Bangkok's middle and upper income earners. Since 2012, the Thai-language YouTube channel and TV show *ArtVenture* also championed Bangkok's street culture. The show was produced by the artists Bigdel and Goh-M, with the tag line "Graffiti, Street Art, Street Lifestyle", signifying how a new generation viewed the gritty urbanism of Bangkok as a part of their identity. These years after 2012 saw many aspects of Thai street art and graffiti evolve from subculture to popular culture.

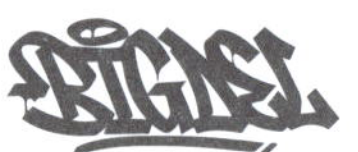

"I used to do a TV show called *ArtVenture* for people to see the process of doing graffiti. It's not like we grab a spray can and just go for it. We have more processes – thinking what we want to do, how to choose the wall, and how to do this and that. I made that program not for the graffiti writer, but for others to understand what we were doing."

By 2012, the international street art and contemporary-art community was also becoming aware of the Thai scene. Several local embassy funds and other sponsors supported the Bukruk street art festival in early 2013. This began the conversion of Chaloem La Park from an informal demolition site and Hall of Fame (see below) into a sanctioned, Instagram-ready park. Another of the festival's activities was the creation of large pieces on the Bangkok Art and Culture Centre (BACC) building. This broadcast a statement that street art had a place in modern Bangkok or, at least, a place in its commercial core. A new pride emerged amongst the street artists working at the time.

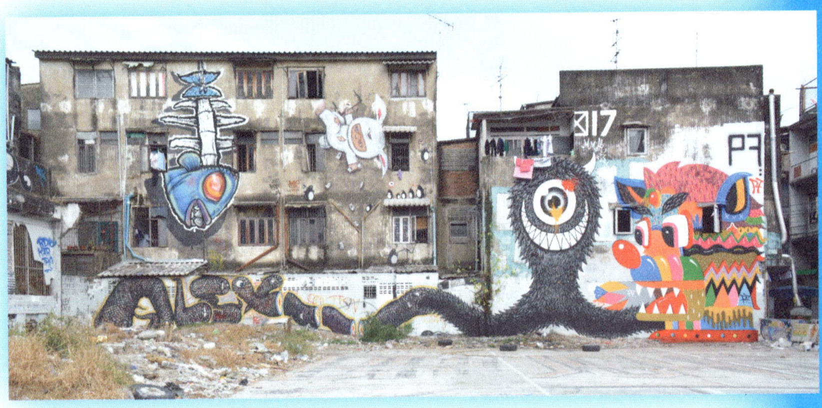

Chaloem La Park in 2013. By Vincent Lim

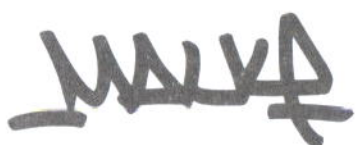

"Bukruk was really important because it helped make street art more visible, especially in the media. It made street art very popular at the time. A lot of people went there to take photos. The government also got to see what street art was. Most of the art at Bukruk was in the character style. So it was an event that had a huge influence for the character style of street art in Bangkok."

HEAD ACHE

"First, no street art, only graffiti. First, tagging, then bubble letters came, and then colour. After colour came, it looked better but it's still graffiti. After Bukruk, there's more street art coming. The Bukruk project was the first time we saw a big piece of graffiti or street art."

Six months later, in September 2013, Mamafaka, drowned tragically at Phuket. The death of this young artist was featured widely in the media. The general public became interested in him, his work and the exotic scene he was part of – introducing a wide range of new people to street art.

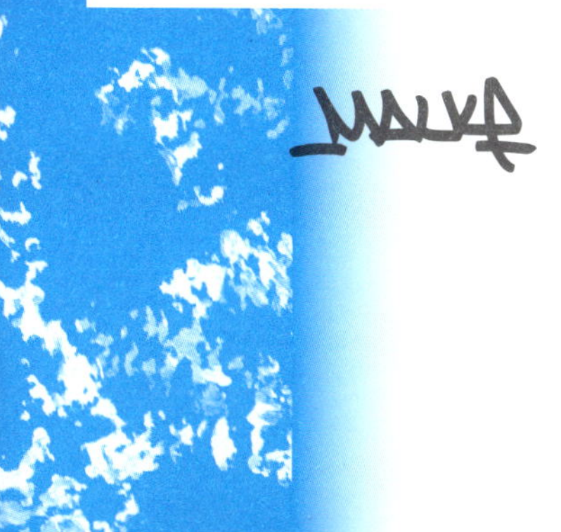

"By 2010, characters had already started to become more popular. ALEX FACE must have been the first who started doing characters. I am not sure, but I think the boom in characters started when Tum, aka Mamafaka, passed away. It made people curious about who he was. People wondered why his death became a news story. The younger generation started to look into characters because of this. So the character style influence was probably from both ALEX FACE and Mamafaka."

HEAD ACHE

"The guy that was important at that time was ALEX FACE, some people think Mamafaka. I know them both. For me, it's ALEX FACE and Rukkit."

Facebook and Instagram took off in Thailand between 2010 and 2014 as Internet access rose sharply. It's largely through these social-media platforms that street art is now shared and seen. This transformed the street art and graffiti scene. Suddenly artists could bite pieces from across the globe. Previously, while glimpses could be stolen from imported magazines, a plane trip was needed to really see international street art and graffiti. By 2012, artists could see anything from anywhere.

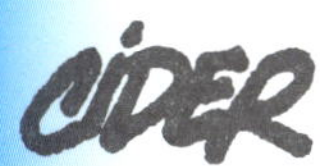

"The Internet is good. It gets people out there faster. It lets people see what's going on in the world, easier and faster. I'm not hating it, I'm on it all the time."

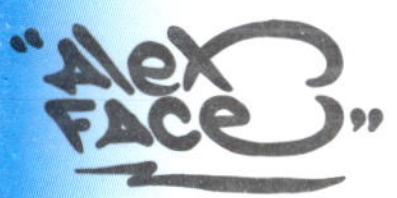

"The Internet helps to improve the local styles because you can see information from everywhere. For me, if I look on the Internet, I don't feel like I want to do something from this guy or that guy – I just see what's going on. I can see different art from everywhere."

Rukkit

"So, there are pros and cons of the Internet. It can be a source of inspiration but at the same time, imitation. The Internet helps you see other people's work which inspires you to create work. But it's not like you want to copy their work. You want to create something that has not been done before, that's in your own style."

The audiences also changed. Before the arrival of the Internet, people had to physically journey into the street and see a piece in its urban habitat – perhaps from afar, out of a train or bus window, or maybe standing in front of it. The art was experienced with all the noises, smells and complexity that it lived amongst. The form of its setting and the people who lived nearby were the art too. The place itself, like at Hopewell, was sometimes symbolic. Standing with the art meant being in the artist's mind. This was a unique aspect of the scene, now less common. Today, there is no need to go anywhere at all to see the works. It's no longer street art, but phone art. Created on a public street, experienced through a private screen.

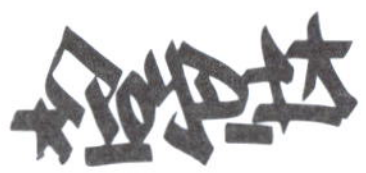

"Social media and Instagram helps artists to get more engagement from their audience. The artists can paint anywhere and then they post online and people can see their piece. Some artists have a fan base, so they can paint and post and get likes. That is different from the pre-Internet era because then, we had to find a wall that is big enough and visible enough to get people's attention."

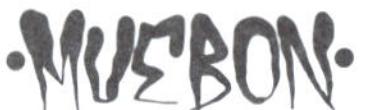

"Now, the world has changed, you can't get famous from work on the street. Now, you get famous from the Internet."

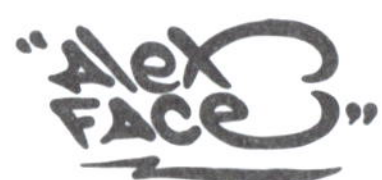

"Before, when we painted walls, we didn't know who would see it. You needed to go there to see it. Then, we didn't have anything to share online. If you didn't go there, you won't know I painted. In early 2002, it was fun, when people said, 'I saw your work.'
I said, 'Where?'
'Over there, in Phetchaburi Road.'
'Okay, I know where that is. You saw it?'
'Yeah!'
So I think that's more special, because he was there. But now it's different. We have social media and people look on the Internet and feel like they want to go and see the real thing too, it makes them want to follow us onto the street. Many times, they say, 'Why don't you put the address so we can go and see?' I think it's okay if they see it on the screen but they also want to see the real thing, so it makes them travel. Some people travel just to see street art, and they collect the pictures. They try to go as much as they can. I don't know... It's different."

The colour and beauty of graffiti and the identifiable, figures of the character-based styles make them a good fit for today's online swipe culture. As Instagram channels images through their phone screens, people glimpse these pieces for an instant.

Then they are gone, and onto the next thing. The way artists gain followers and likes on these platforms also makes many in the scene question the legitimacy of online fame. The criteria used to determine high-quality work is not as clear in the digital age.

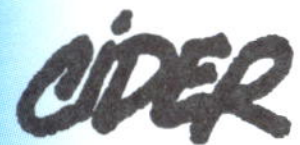

"They use the credit card now. What's up with all this bullshit graffiti that gets all these likes? Nobody knows them. Now you see a lot of global-clone graffiti or street art on Instagram with ten thousand followers. Like, what!? Now they're buying followers? Some crazy shit."

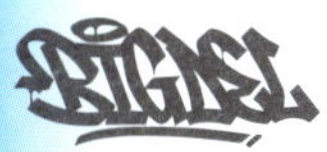

"The pro is you can find anything you want in one second. The con is, next minute, 'Oh, I don't want it anymore.' You can't even know if you like it or not."

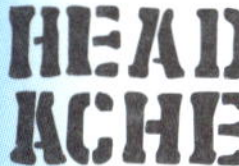

"I don't understand why it's hard for new kids to get their own style or their own signature. Now they have more things to study, but they have less skill. Today they like this, next day they like that. It's a kid thing. It's a problem of the teenagers."

And for the Thai people, whose homes and neighbourhoods are adorned with this art, they appear to view graffiti and street art as being below the traditional art forms they are more familiar with. The struggle amongst street artists – and less so graffiti writers – to be seen as something more than vandals is global. And that creates a dichotomy, the desire to be acknowledged but to remain an outsider – respected, but not accepted.

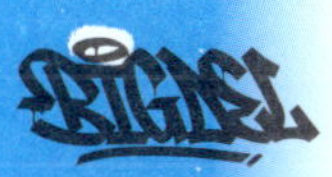

"Most Thais don't accept graffiti writers or street artists as artists. They consider us to be technicians, like a carpenter or something. They see us as technical, but not creative. If I go out painting with a paintbrush, people will say, 'Oh, an artist is working now.' But with spray cans, people will say, 'Vandalism'."

"Public acceptance of street art has increased. In the past, the public would associate this kind of scene with someone causing trouble – polytechnical students and vandalism."

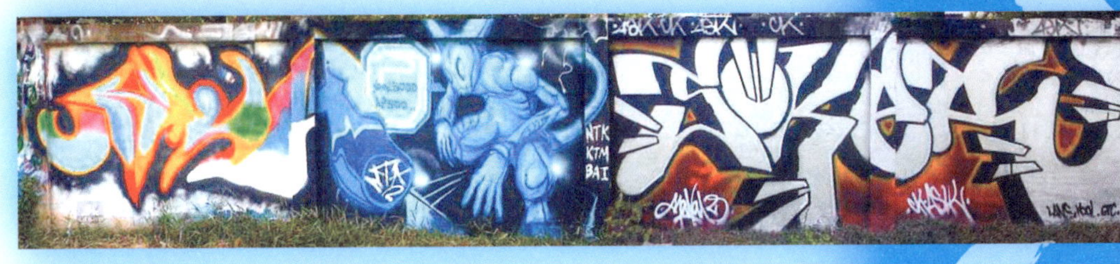

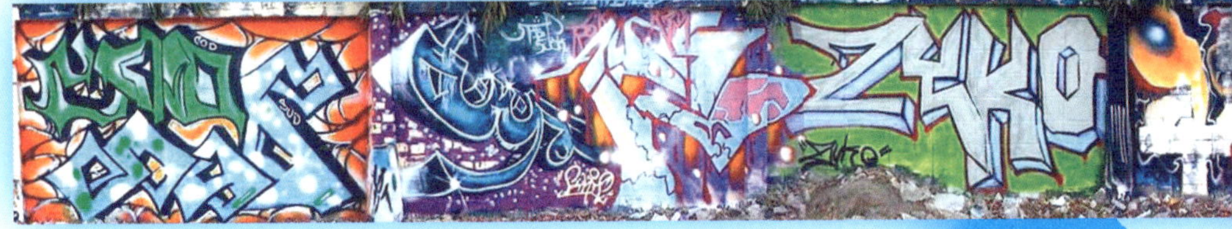

Above : Pieces from 2002 by NTA, CATMASK, SOKER, JIM, POYD1, LUXE
Below : Pieces from 2002 by COD, SUD, UNKNOWN, ZYKO, UNKNOWN, ZIDS, LANS, CATMASK

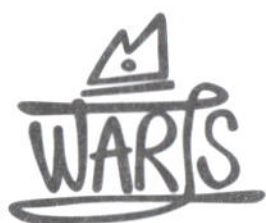

"In the past, graffiti wasn't accepted in the Thai art world. People would separate graffiti and street art from art. They wouldn't call us artists. But nowadays, we have shows. We have more of a place in society. People seem to be a little more open minded."

Graffiti and street art began as outsider traditions. For many street artists and especially graffiti writers, they retain this grit; for their work to be fully legitimised would be to betray the art form's potency and ability to challenge state control over who has the right to speak in public. The fiery subversive attitudes of those kids in New York and Philadelphia live on amongst parts of Bangkok's street art and graffiti scenes. And woven through those attitudes are older threads. The local originators of graffiti, the student taggers, were young men coming to the city from the country, as many still do today. They were born into slow, connected, communities and after just a train ride, found themselves in the heart of a modern city. Each of those young men, in their journey from village to city, was living the transformation that Bangkok experienced over half a century as it went from a series of hamlets to a metropolis – from the old Bangkok to the new. Having left home, their search for a new family was like Bangkok's search for itself having left the past – a tale of urban transformation that Thailand's first graffiti writers told.

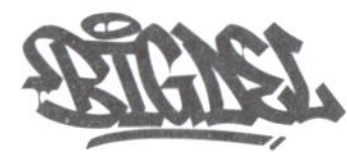

"We focus on ourselves more and more. I don't know why, because of the technology maybe. I prefer the previous time, before the Internet. There was a lot of beauty to it then. We love the Internet, so if the Internet can mix with the beauty of before, it would be great."

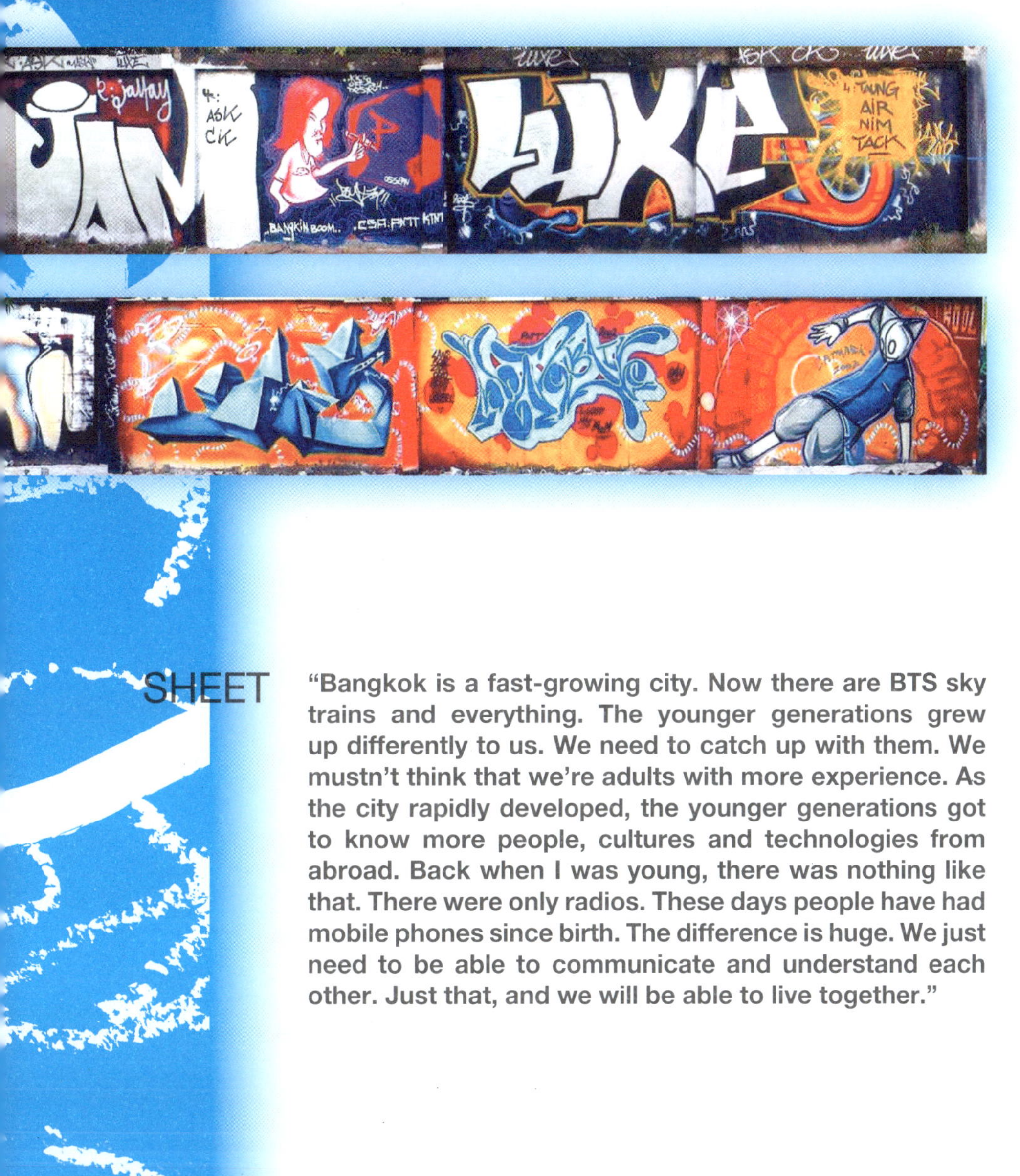

SHEET

"Bangkok is a fast-growing city. Now there are BTS sky trains and everything. The younger generations grew up differently to us. We need to catch up with them. We mustn't think that we're adults with more experience. As the city rapidly developed, the younger generations got to know more people, cultures and technologies from abroad. Back when I was young, there was nothing like that. There were only radios. These days people have had mobile phones since birth. The difference is huge. We just need to be able to communicate and understand each other. Just that, and we will be able to live together."

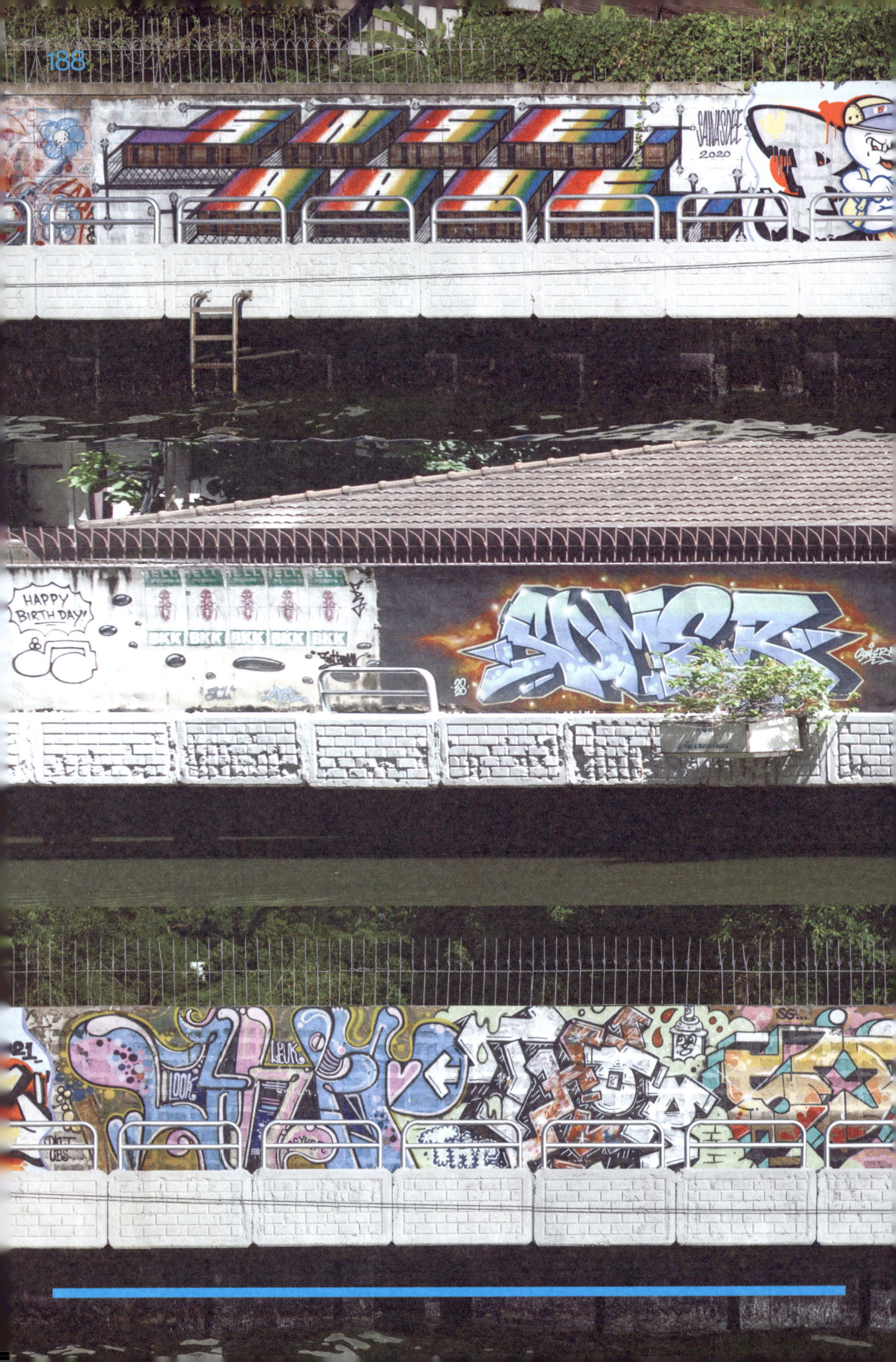
2020
HAPPY
BIRTH DAY!
BKK BKK BKK BKK BKK

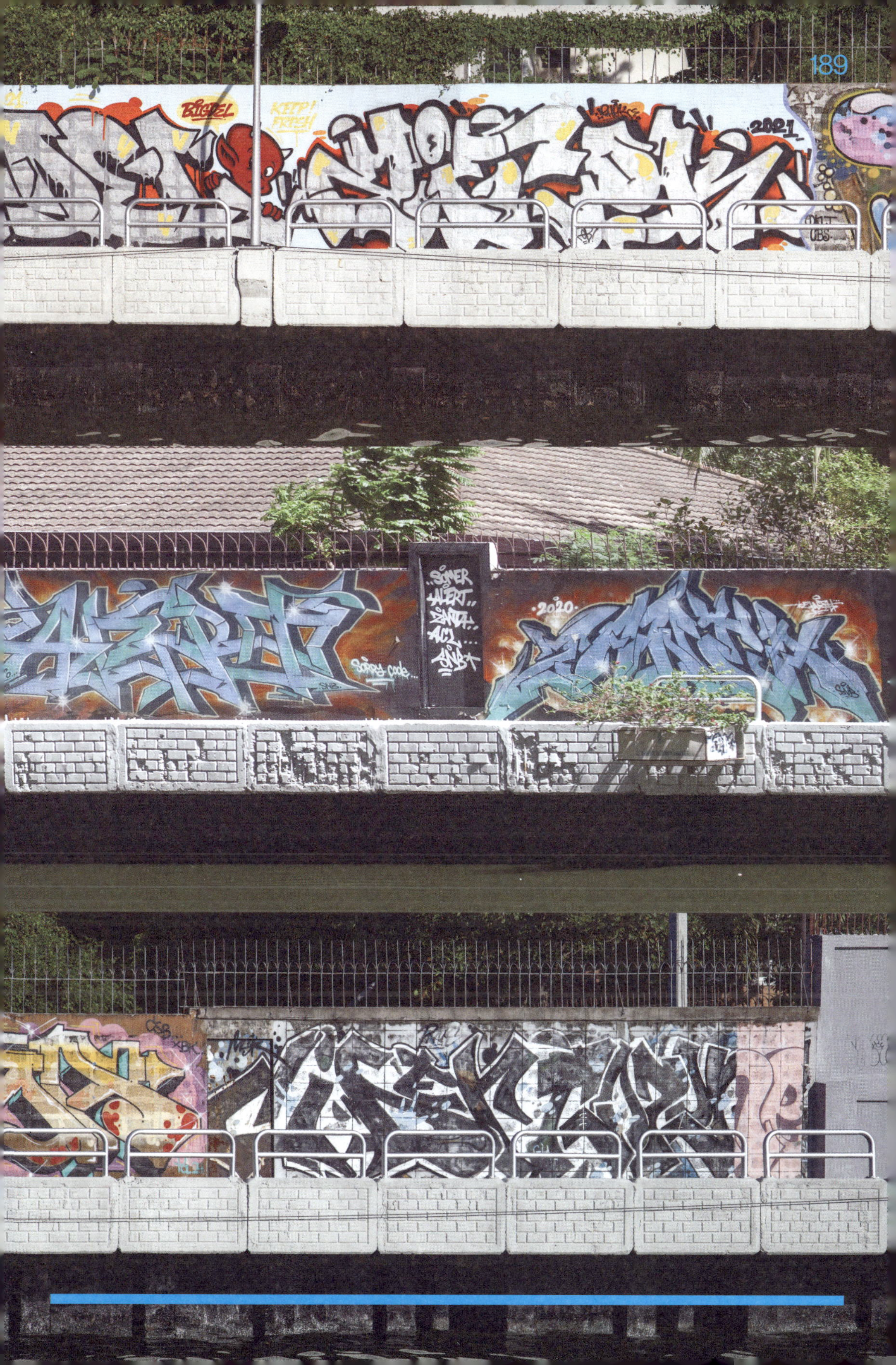

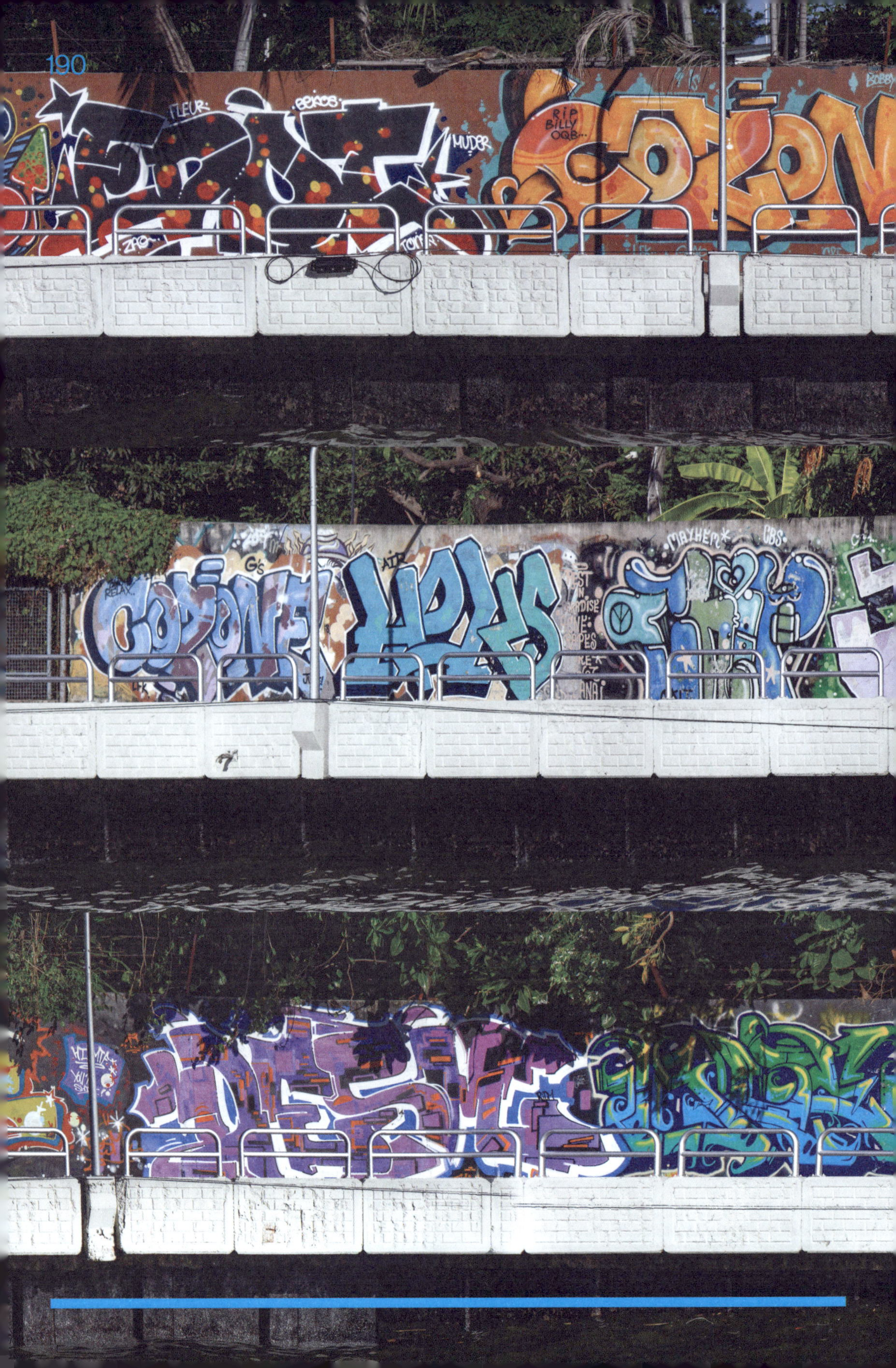
FLEUR
MUDER
RIP
BILLY
OQB...
AIR
MAYHEM
CBS

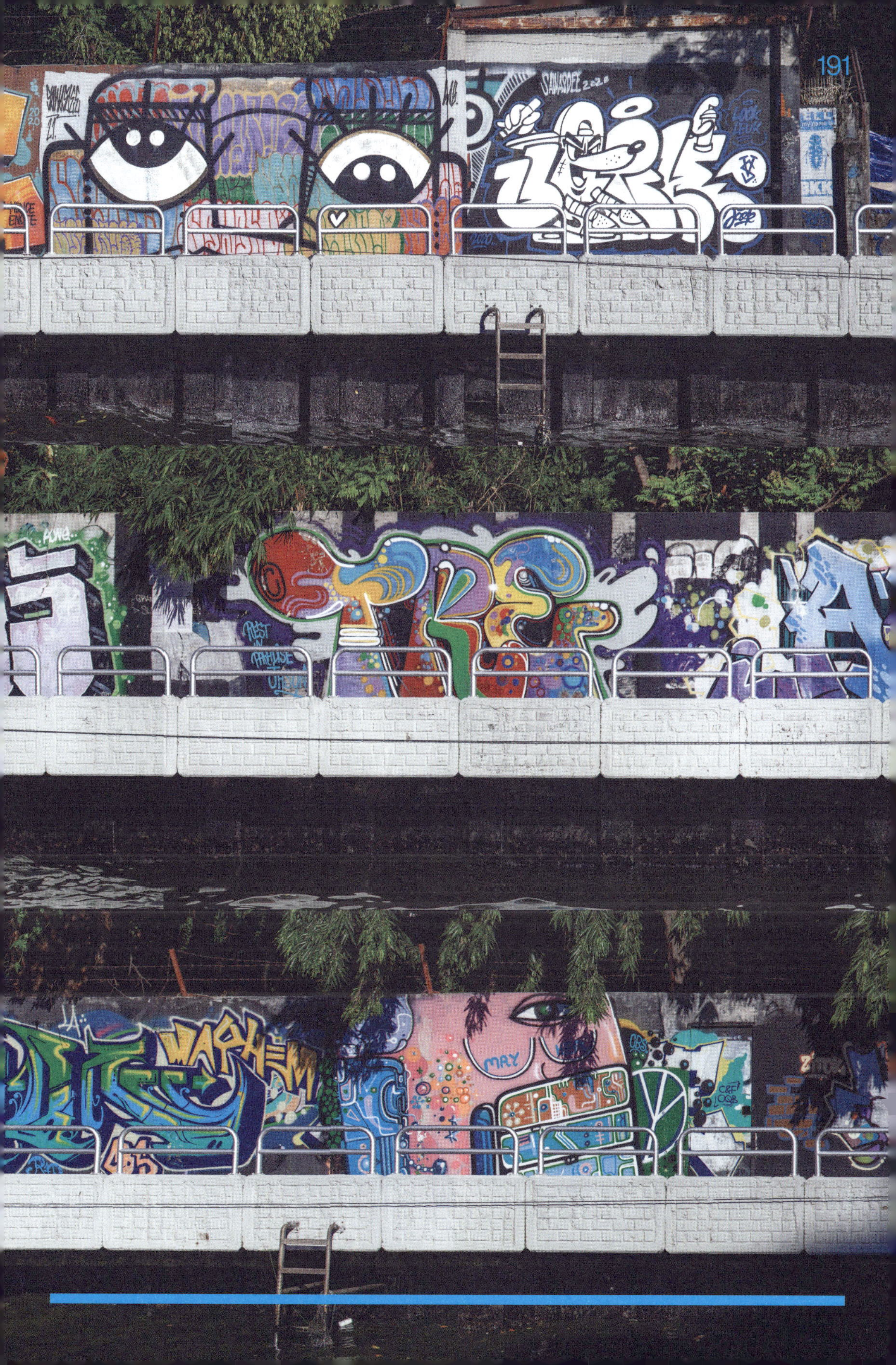
BKK
REST IN PARADISE
MAY

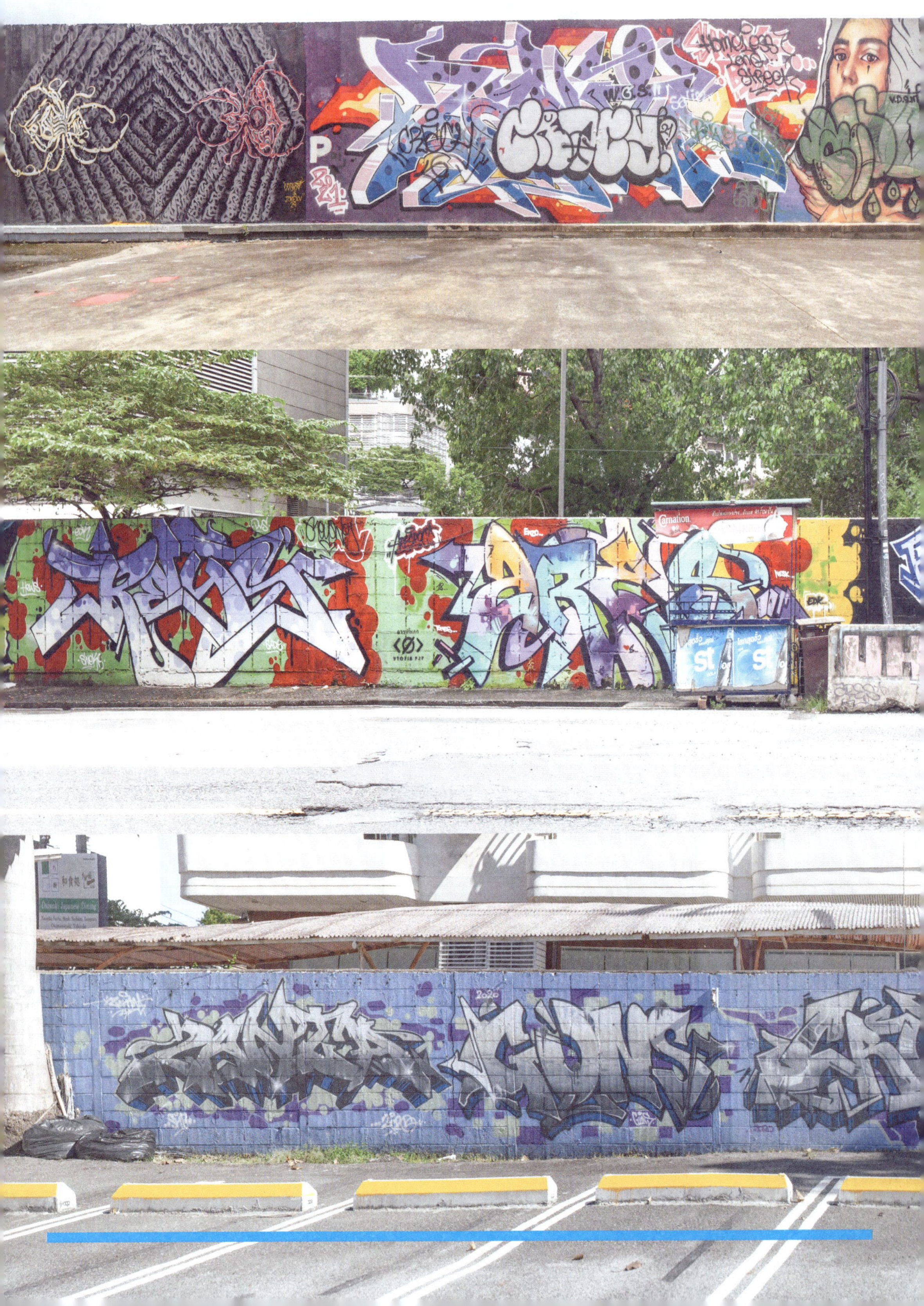

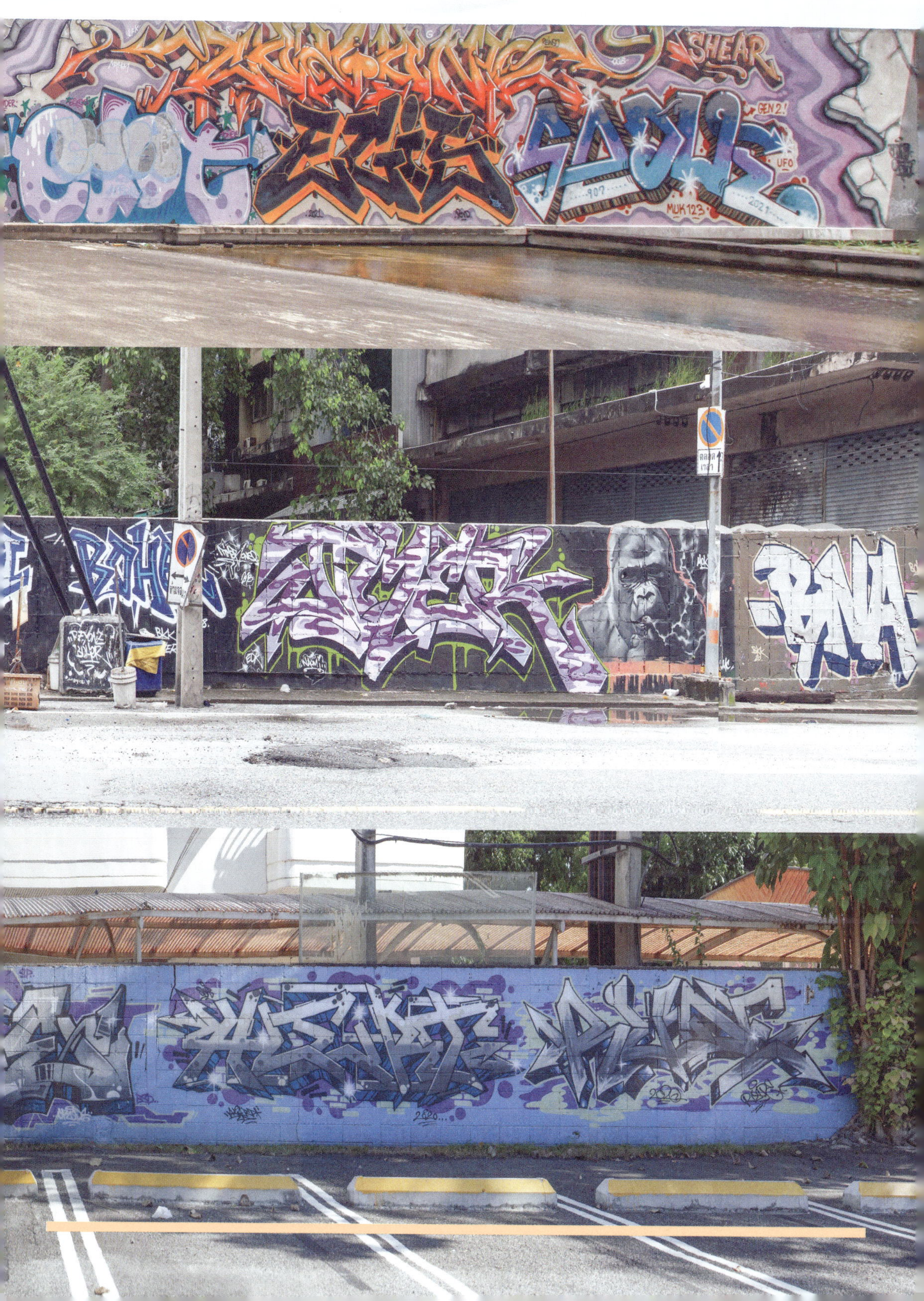
SHEAR
GEN 2!
UFO
MUK 123
2021

06

DISSENT

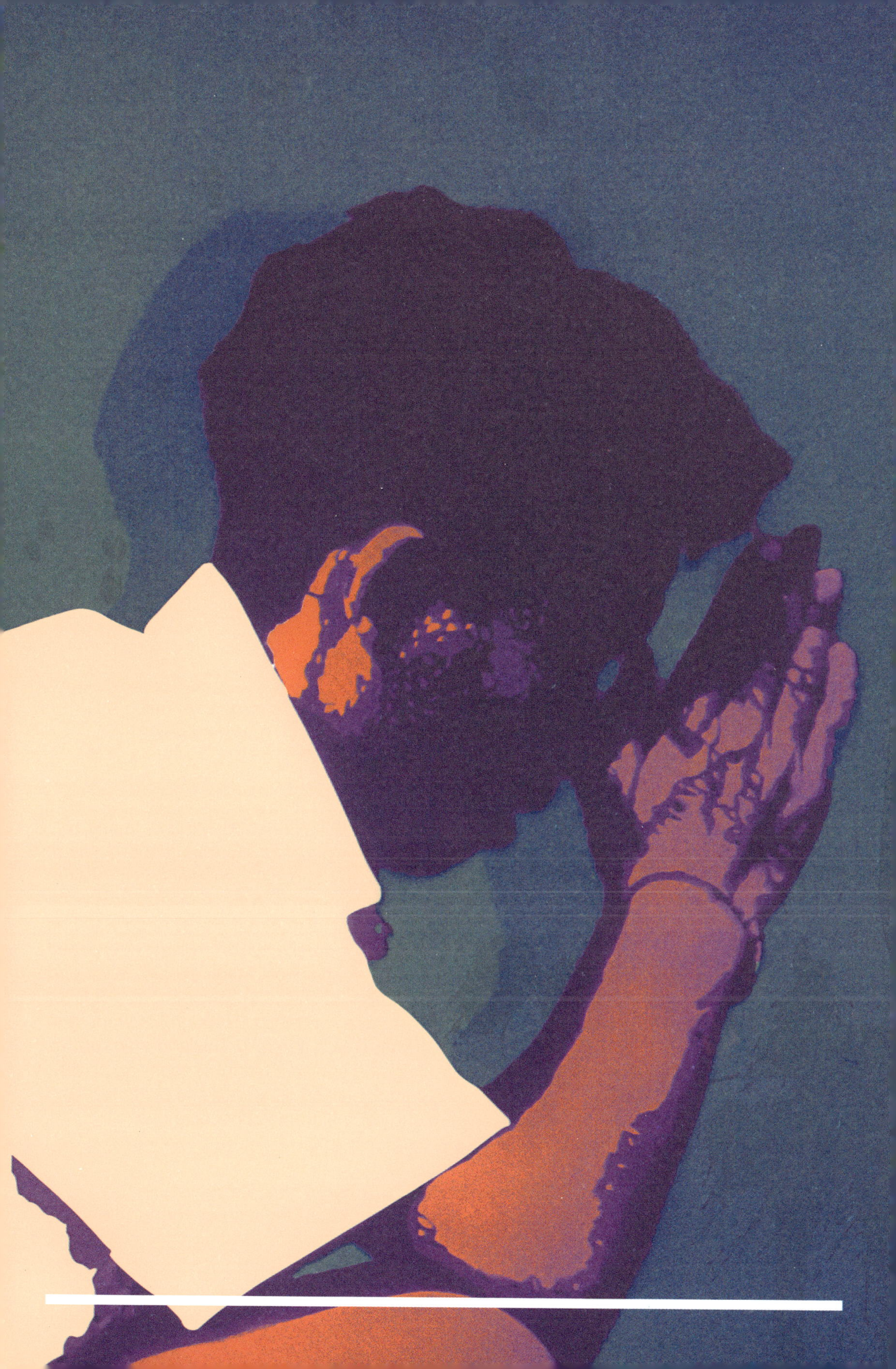

During 2018, as the original promises of the 2014 coup leaders evaporated, a more open willingness to use street art for political purposes was present in Thailand. The art form increasingly became a way to voice political dissent and assert the right to criticise those in power. Unlike during the Hopewell years, by 2018, Facebook, Twitter and Instagram were widespread. This meant that street art was visible to millions online, rather than just those who saw it on the street. Social media's ability to ignite revolution had been demonstrated in many parts of the world. As Thai street art grew more popular with people outside the subculture that created it, its political potency intensified. The combination of street art's wide popularity, social media's ability to disseminate images quickly and a new willingness to paint about politics was a threat to official control of the truth. General Prayut's government was hoping to establish the image of a reluctant and dutiful military, yet again saving the country from collapse. The street artists were offering a different interpretation.

"Street art was booming in the last six to seven years. This was also the time that Prayut and the military government gained power. This doesn't mean that the military government supports street art, it doesn't. There are more political works because street art can be a way for the opposition and dissidents to speak about social issues. That is why street art is so attractive. This makes it appear that there is more political content in street art when actually we disapproved of governments even in the past, but street art wasn't popular then."

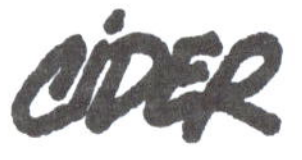

"How can political street art not happen? We've been under military coups for like 30 years now… Shit. And they want to say something about it."

By 2018, Thailand had been under military rule for four years. At first, many had been happy to see the public protests subside after so many tumultuous years, but the military were lingering longer than promised. In 2017, a collection of photos showing Deputy Prime Minister General Prawit Wongsuwan wearing luxury watches began circulating on social media. Journalists calculated that the 20 or so watches he had worn since coming to power were worth more than US$1 million. They asked how a lowly government salary could provide such things. Many people concluded that corruption had been exposed at the top of the new government. And, for Headache Stencil, the perceived hypocrisy was too much. Through his work, and that of other artists at the time, they declared that things in Thailand were not as they should be. Many other Thai people agreed but were fearful of speaking openly, so kept quiet. It's easy to see why, in a culture built on deference and politeness and where censorship is a legal reality that can carry extreme consequences.

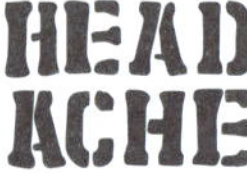

"Why do people here put up with so much? Now we know how other countries stay, how civilisation is… I think many young

people feel the same thing. Why do old people believe in this news? It's crazy. Now we think that Thailand is separated to be two colours, red and yellow. Then the military coup came to make it better. Yeah, they made it better. They separated from two groups to four. Now we have red and yellow and cut each of them in half by age – because the old people are loyal. No hope. I don't believe in this country any more. No way to change. It's not because of the government. It's the system that's shit. The top of the system here is the elites – they're all on the same side. The other side has only workers. That side is 99 percent of people. And one percent of people on the other side have much more money, and they have weapons. How do you fight? No way. The rich get more and more money. No hope. One day, when people have no money anymore, no work, no food. Finally, people won't be able to stand it. People will come out to kill. It's a crisis war that will come. It's not because of some leader or someone ordering them to do it. It's because for Thai people, when nothing is in control, they'll all go crazy. For me, it's really dangerous. Next time will be different because next time it happens, when people have no choice, no food, no money, it will be worse."

Headache Stencil did a piece in January 2018 depicting General Prawit's face in the middle of an alarm-clock dial (see next page). He painted it on a pedestrian overpass outside his apartment block. "It's the alarm clock that wakes up every Thai person in the country," he wrote on Facebook at the time. "Many Thais just opened their eyes and woke up from an unrealistic dream." For the government, Prawit was too important a figure to be tarnished. Headache Stencil's piece was immediately buffed, but not before it was shared widely online. Prawit later claimed that he had borrowed the watches from a friend.

HEAD
ACHE

"After I painted the Prawit face, I had a message on my page: a reporter from AFP, she asked if she could use a photo of the work on the news. After that, I got many messages from Thai reporters. So, after a while, my apartment security called me and said, 'Okay, now I don't think it's reporters – it's police.' I had to go. I posted on my Facebook page that the police are chasing me. I felt angry after that. I did just one artwork. I didn't kill anyone. They sent 13 police to stay at my apartment, 24 hours for three days."

Headache Stencil's ability to speak out comes partially from his bravery and partially from protection afforded by his family connections. Many other artists who don't have such connections, are less willing to take the risk. So, even within the subculture of street art, the long-standing divisions between those who have power, or connections to power, and those who don't, defines who speaks most openly. Unusually, Headache Stencil criticises the same structures that protect him – because of, or despite, them.

·MUEBON·

"I've had a lot of run-ins with politics. It's too bad if your family or father's family isn't honourable. When the police come to you, harass you, follow you, threaten you, bully you with various laws, you can't imagine it. I'm really fed up with this. In fact, I was arrested in 2006 and other times during political events because of my work. Recently, during this current military dictatorship, my work was smashed by the police, they threatened to kidnap me, to use the law against me if I didn't stop creating my art. Can you imagine? Working on art is like breathing for me. It's like the police put their hands over my mouth and told me to stop breathing. It was so bad I was worried that the police were going to harass my family. But I managed to get through it and I'm still breathing through my art." (see opposite)

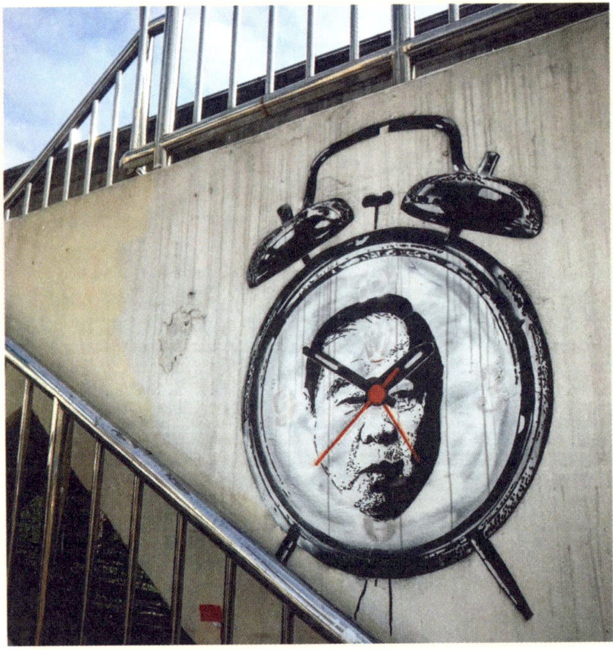

Piece
by Headache
Stencil

HEAD
ACHE

"I have a connection, so I can say more. Yeah, it's a bullshit system."

A month after Headache Stencil's Prawit piece was buffed, street artists would turn their attention to another political controversy. The government's response – to again censor the artworks – would trigger a new wave of political street art in Thailand. In February 2018, one of Thailand's richest men, Premchai Karnasuta, was arrested for hunting wildlife in a World Heritage listed reserve. Premchai is president of Italian-Thai, the company that built the Dark Red Line that replaced the Hopewell columns. Park rangers came across his campsite where they found the pelt of a black leopard, a kalij pheasant, and a red muntjac deer – all protected animals. Premchai was also charged with trying to bribe an official. He was eventually found guilty of crimes related to poaching, after a delayed process, and was sentenced to a prison term. He was immediately released on bail and appealed the conviction. That appeal was rejected and the court extended his sentence. As of December 2021, his most recent appeal has been rejected by the Supreme Court and his jail term of three years and two months has been upheld, perhaps affirming the political role of street art in contemporary Thailand.

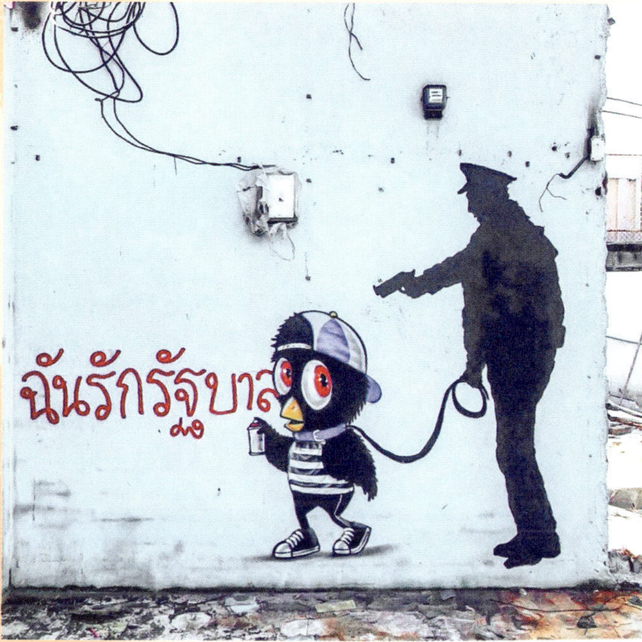

Piece by MUEBON.

The figure writes, "I love the government"

HEAD ACHE

"Believe me, finally Premchai will not have to go to jail. I still believe the law can't do anything to the rich in Thailand. But what he got from society, from social media, for me, is enough. Because he's not the only rich guy going to hunt wild animals, for sure. We still have a series on TV that shows some beautiful girls still love animal hunters, or there are romantic scenes with animal hunters. Because in the past animal hunters are cool, they're strong. I don't care what else he gets. Because, if I was him, I would've committed suicide in the first week, with the black leopard everywhere."

In March 2018, Headache Stencil created a piece showing the slaughtered leopard beside a phone mute symbol. Other artists, such as Pakorn BNA, had done pieces about the black leopard before Headache Stencil. But because of his fame through the Prawit watch piece, and his booming social media following, Headache Stencil's black leopard was shared widely. Again, the authorities quickly buffed the piece.

HEAD ACHE **"The black leopard is not about the government, it's about the guy who sponsors everything, all the organisations, even the elites, Premchai. So this is a worse case."**

Many people expected Premchai's crimes to be hidden, as the transgressions of other wealthy Thais had been before him. The black leopard's death – like Hopewell's – became a symbol. It also came to represent a line where many street artists chose to stand against the creeping incursion of censorship into their work. On behalf of the leopard and a dream of Thailand unchained by corruption, they drew resolve from the animal's murder and open dissent began to rally around its sleek, dark corpse.

HEAD ACHE **"We have a quote in Thai, 'Kill one, and a hundred thousand will be born.' And at that time the street artists used that quote."**

At this time, dozens of artists created works depicting the black leopard, and other animals that were slaughtered by Premchai. Soon after news broke of the poaching, an animal-rights Facebook group worked with graffiti writers and street artists to paint a second black leopard within 100 metres of the Italian-Thai headquarters in Bangkok on 8 March 2018. The artist, Tossraporn Klunkaew said in the Bangkok Post at the time that, "Graffiti sometimes gets a bad rap, but in fact it is a form of expression that can change society for the better. Before the Premchai incident went viral, I didn't even know we had black leopards left in the wild. Once I learned more about the case and realised they were protected in a wildlife sanctuary, I immediately took action and we spent quite some time planning this artwork." Soon after, a pet and aquatic animal hospital invited ten artists to paint a mural of the slaughtered animals in their car park. Bangkok's established street artists, who were rarely political at the time, also got involved. ALEX FACE painted his iconic Mardi figure, with a long Pinocchio nose, wearing a black leopard suit. It was soon buffed. Rukkit painted the leopard in his distinctive style incorporating the Italian-Thai logo, Premchai's silhouette and bullet holes (see opposite).

In attempting to bury the issue, the junta had ignited the street-art community with a new willingness to paint overt political works. In a way not seen since 2013 at the Hopewell site, artists began to riff on a common political theme. This art was shared amongst the general public many times through social media. And the message, like at Hopewell, was contempt for the misuse of wealth and power.

The attention that was generated by the street artists and their work ensured it was far more difficult to hide the black leopard issue. As a result, prosecutors pleaded for the public to keep drawing attention to the case. It may have worked.

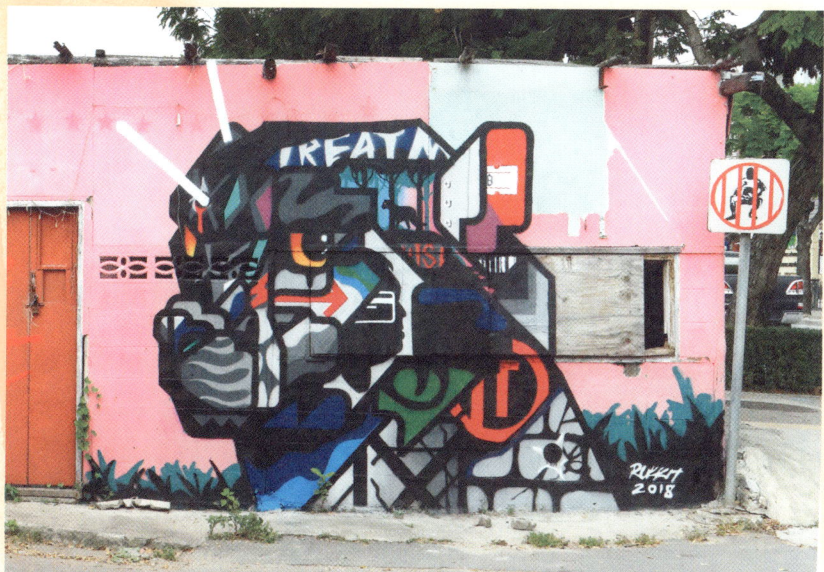

Piece by Rukkit

MALKA

"Normally, I don't paint about people, I paint animals. I felt that the legal process was protecting Premchai from justice. The black leopard incident shows that people with money can escape the hands of justice. People like us, without money, could be compared to the animal in this story. If, one day, Premchai did something like this to a person then he would still escape. I am pitching the rights of living things against the power of money. Money wins. The legal process favours money more than justice. I was so emotional about the story of the black leopard. And I could see that, if money can buy justice, the fate of the black leopard is not that different from ours. When I shared my piece (see next page) **on Facebook, it was the same moment Headache Stencil's work was buffed. People thought my work was an act of revenge against the removal of Headache's piece. That wasn't my intention at all. I create work to serve myself and the public. It's purely coincidental."**

HEAD ACHE

"People felt that this time it's too much. It's about the rich again. The rich are never wrong. And people feel the same thing, 'Shit, this is not cool.' So, after they erased the leopard,

other artists did the same piece. Those artists didn't want to support me. They just wanted to support the truth. They're trying to stand up with their art style."

• • •

Over time, political content in street art has become more overt. Headache Stencil's use of Prawit's face in his alarm-clock piece is more direct and personal than most political street art had been before. Although it was not the first example, many artists are uncomfortable with such directness. Perhaps it betrays the artistic ideal of being poetically oblique or perhaps it was simply the threat of prosecution – or worse – that remains a risk in Thailand.

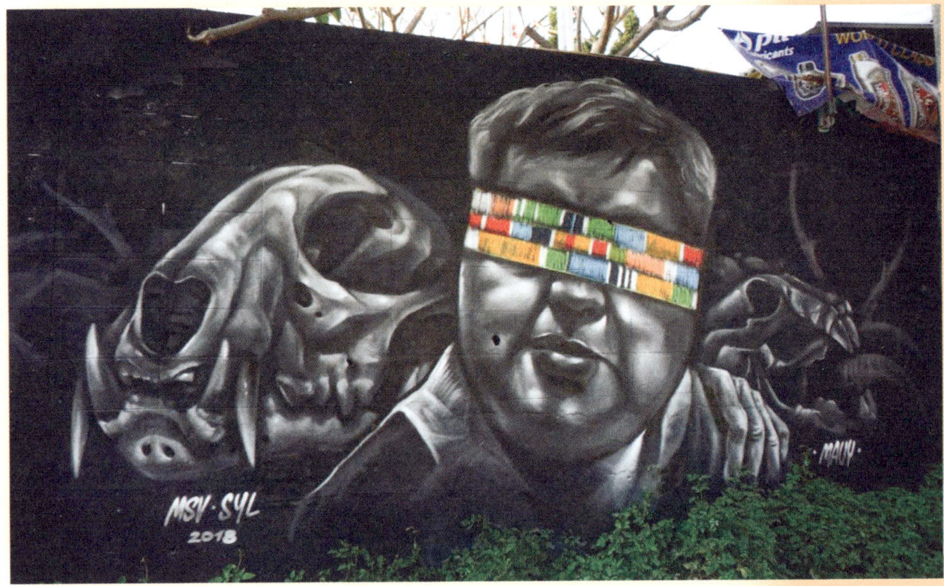

Piece by MAUY

BONUS TMC →

"Many artists put their political views in their own works, but they were not straightforward. The political content in art is everywhere, but it's not obvious, or easy to see."

AS!N →

"Artists painted about politics for a long time. Since the yellow and red shirt protests. But it has become so trendy these days because the subject matter is the people in power now. Around the time the NCPO [National Council for Peace and Order] took over and Prayut banned media such as *Voice TV*, Reuters came and interviewed me. My piece was a chicken holding a megaphone that was cut

in half and there was an unidentified hand reaching for the chicken from behind. The journalist was disappointed that I didn't use Prayut's face. I told them I didn't do this to just satisfy myself."

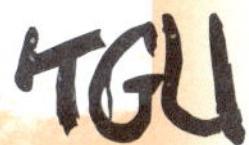

"There are street artists who represent themselves as political artists because they want to be famous. There has always been political street art, but that particular Headache Stencil piece became viral, so a lot more people saw it then. So people might think political street art is more new. But actually less than 10 percent of Thai street art is political. There are so many types of street art, not only political art, characters or graffiti. People perceive that it became more political because it went viral, not because there is more. Many artists already paint what they want to communicate. For example, the black leopard issue, I painted that because I'm interested in animal rights."

HEAD
ACHE

"Some graffiti artists think that I changed the perception of street art or graffiti art here to take the side of politics, or to be one of the tools of politics. So some artists hate me for this reason."

Public street art and graffiti enables direct communication with the public, and that audience is not pre-filtered. These works speak directly with the people who see them, either online or in person. When the content of that art is a widely held, if private, political view, it suddenly resonates. Street art and political dissent become potent allies and the art form arrives back home, where it began.

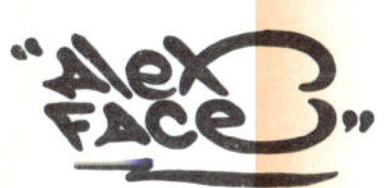

"Street art is a tool to speak out. If the people in this country feel unhappy about politics, then street art can be a tool to say that. But if Thailand was a really good country with no corruption, good politicians, then maybe street art could say something else. I think it's just a tool. Everyone thinks, maybe, the same way. Everyone has an opinion about what's going on, how the situation is about politics in Thailand. But I don't think I'm political. I talk about things in a more layered way. Not just like, Boom! Sometimes it's good to be straightforward with street art, I think that's good too. If you don't have many layers, more people are going to understand what you say. I think that's also good."

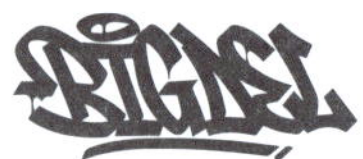

"A lot of artists use politics as their concept because it's easy to connect with the public. When you post something that becomes the news, then it touches people. So it's easier for them to connect with your art. I think a lot of people use this."

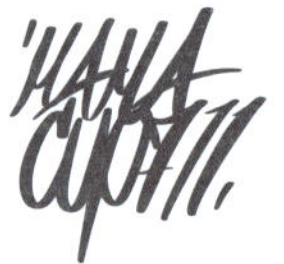

"Politics is something that you can mock or joke around with in Thailand, it's not untouchable. So that's why a lot of artists choose to paint about politics, because it can be easily understood by everyone who sees the work."

Regardless of how direct a street-art piece is, other artists judge its worthiness by the creator's motives. Many street artists, and many more graffiti writers, criticised those who painted about the black leopard during 2018 for being opportunistic and seeking fame. This disagreement exposes a central concern many artists have – whether the people who are involved in creating street art and graffiti are genuine, or whether they're simply trying to get famous.

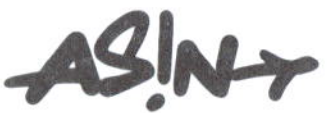

"I wasn't so motivated by the animal rights perspective but by the inequality. I think most artists were talking about animal rights, especially protected and rare animals like the black leopard. But for me, I was looking at it from the perspective of the rich being above the justice system and police are under them. This has been the essence of Thai society forever. Look at the Redbull heir who they say killed a policeman. He just ran away, went abroad. He's chilling there! So, I used the black leopard as a way to speak about inequality. I wanted to suggest that the rich have certain privileges that help them escape the law. It's no surprise why people in this country want to be rich. These rich people can escape justice after killing people, let alone a black leopard. There were people who did black leopard pieces who were really into animal rights and politics. But there were also people who just tried to exploit the trend. The irony is that there were artists who supported those political views and wanted to create work related to the black leopard. But those artists had previously mocked other artists who did political pieces, so they were afraid of being seen as hypocrites and couldn't work."

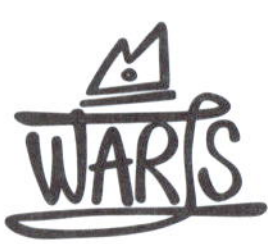

"There are two groups of artists doing political street art. One group really wants to communicate politics to people. The other group does it because it's popular. There is quite a trend against the government at the moment so some artists use this to advance their own career."

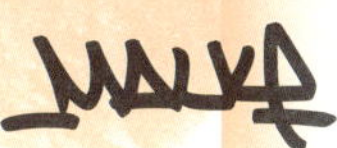

"I sometimes call artists who use political issues to become famous, 'front-page artists.' But I reserve this call-out for those who only pick up popular news, not for those who always use art to mobilise social movements. The front-page artists cater to the Thai audience who might not even appreciate art but who want to insult politicians. Whatever insults speak to them the most – the sassiest, the rudest, even though sometimes rather shallow – gets the largest audience. It is a reciprocal relationship between artists who want to be in the spotlight and the audience who want to snap at the government. This is what makes an artist popular. It is good for these artists that Prayut continued his power because without him, they would miss a big target for insult. Though, it's unwelcome news, I teased them by asking whether they secretly smiled when Prayut won power again."

As the military junta of General Prayut morphed into the military-aligned government of Premier Prayut, street art re-emerged as a tool of open political dissent in Thailand. The art form asserted itself as a way for alternative voices to be heard in public. By 2018, Bangkok's street-art tradition could utilise a sophisticated set of methods and images that distilled political and social messages into popular artworks. Using the power of social media, those artworks were amplified across the country.

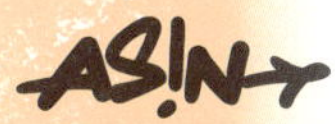

"Street art seems to be more political now because there are more people doing street art. Political expression has also intensified. Not just because of the political situation but also because social media has boomed. Social media has made people more involved in politics. It makes a younger age group interested also. Even secondary school students dig at Prayut on their Instagram accounts, now."

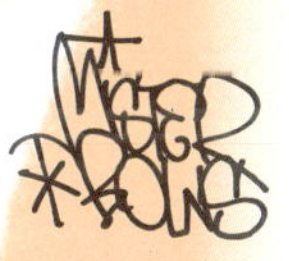

"Most of the time, politicians don't care about graffiti and street art. In the past, these politicians wouldn't have known they're being mocked via street art, so they wouldn't care. But nowadays, people share photos on social media. Now, when the politicians see the photos, they ask staff from that district office to go and remove the street art."

The inevitable result of street art becoming politically potent was the authorities' attempts to censor it. Whether Thai political street art is done for fame or for advocacy, the government took it seriously and by trying to smother the movement, they ignited something far more difficult to extinguish – determination to speak up.

• • •

When martial law was imposed after the 2014 coup, censorship became further enshrined as a part of Thai society. Detention without charge, limitations on public gatherings and censorship of government criticism were all imposed in the early days of Prayut's government. In July 2014, Order 97/2557 demanded that media and social-media users cease all criticism of the NCPO. From the outset, journalists who dared to probe for answers were pressured to fall back in line.

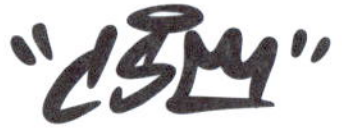

"Many years ago, we actually had more freedom of expression than we have today. Now we are falling off a cliff."

It softened this ban after opposition from media agencies and stated that it only applied to "false information". Of course, that definition was theirs to oscillate. Such threats are often enough to make people think twice about speaking up, even if they are later withdrawn. Many people began to reconsider what they said online and in person. This fear, a cheap and easy way to control people, is the true hand of censorship.

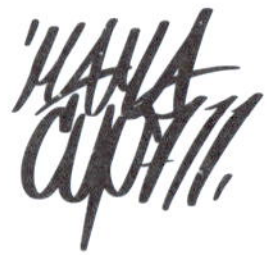

"I don't usually get involved in political things. I noticed that my dad was really stressed by politics. So, we made a promise that after 2016, my dad would stop following political news and I wouldn't do anything political. After that, there was more calm in our family."

"There was a coup in 2014 and from that time onwards, freedom of expression has been restricted. We are oppressed by the military government. So, many artists try to find their own way of expressing political opinions. Some are afraid to speak out. But when one artist speaks out, people are happy to support them because it resonates with what they think and want to say. An artist can be a voice for the people. But many artists are quite afraid to speak or are not interested in talking about these things. In fact, I censor myself quite a bit because there are things in this country we can't talk about. The law is keeping our mouths shut. The right to freedom of expression in this country is at its lowest. Whenever we say things against the government, our lives will be at immediate risk. But speaking up is inevitable. We must speak the truth and side with people who are oppressed by the state. I have never been neutral when it comes to dictatorship versus democracy. Most importantly, I'm a human being and a human being who can't stand still and just live a comfortable life when he can see the suffering of society."

HEAD ACHE

“Artists censor themselves. It’s not just about art, it’s all advertising, TV, radio, no one dares. Censorship works. I think all artists want to make art about politics, but they don’t want a problem because they know that it’s not an easy problem to solve. You have to have some connection so you’re sure you won’t go to jail.”

While street art has become popular over recent years, its’ reach is small compared to that of traditional print and broadcast media in Thailand. The influence of works like those created around the black leopard case is exceptional. The government appears to be most concerned about the audience size and directness of the work. The niche status of street art means most works are able to avoid attention from the censors.

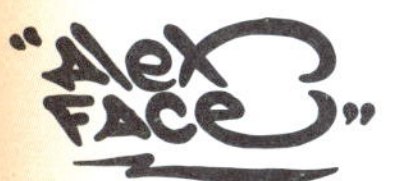

“I don’t think people stop themselves because of censorship, they do whatever they want to do. But it depends. My friend Headache Stencil talked about an individual person. If he talked about the Prime Minister, or some politician – he stencilled that person, like Prawit’s face about the watch thing. That’s very direct. So if you’re talking about a topic, you might not have to be so straightforward about a specific person. But, whether or not an artist is straightforward with their art, it all boils down to their personal technique or their intentions. But being straightforward can be a problem because it can be personal. Many guys around, they have power, so it can cause problems.”

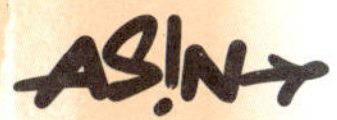

“I don’t think the government cares about censoring art too much. They don’t think it’s a popular medium. For example, a political pantomime won’t get a look, but you might get arrested if you go shouting shit in front of the parliament. So, it’s not just about what you tell, but how you tell it and the medium through which you tell the story. This is why that rap song [*Prathet Ku Mee* by Rap Against Dictatorship], which literally criticises the government and is on Youtube, is so popular. It is much easier to understand than a play or painting. My work is not straightforward. I won’t create a work which directly says ‘Fuck Prayut’ for example. There were a few times when I wanted to do something but changed my mind because I thought it would come out a bit too harshly. I preferred to use more creativity, to throw shade rather than literally snap at something or someone.”

Perhaps for these reasons, many Thai artists, avoid political messages in their art, not necessarily because they have no political views, but because they don't see it as an effective way of changing the situation.

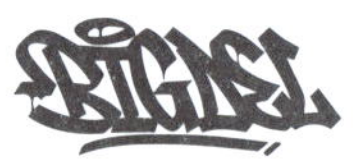

"I just want to see the people's smiles when they look at my work, or glimpse it when they are caught in traffic – just five seconds is all I need. I don't think any of my work can change the world, I just want to do what I love. I just go out painting for fun."

Creativity is intimately linked to the internal world of an artist. The act of writing and painting is the perceivable expression of ideas which go on to influence other ideas in other people. Thoughts gain life when shared. By imprisoning thought in people's heads, censorship can atrophy creativity.

NOLA -NO- LEE

"I don't self-censor. It's better when we speak out, loud and clear and to the point. I just need to be smart how I express it. It's cool to sign your name under your art to show it's your work and your criticism. Without stating your name then it's like you don't really have a voice. By being able to tell who it is that is behind this work and this voice, it states that you have the right of free expression."

Free expression may be stifled by censorship, but many Thai street artists argue that free thought can not be. Censorship may even increase creativity by forcing artists to make their statement without contravening the law. like a Darwinian selection pressure, censorship can force the evolution of new ways of communicating.

"Censorship doesn't stop creativity. It's the opposite, even more censorship means even more stories and inspiration for the artists to paint their work. Artists can find a way. More censorship, so then artists just try to figure a way out to find a way around, it creates more variety."

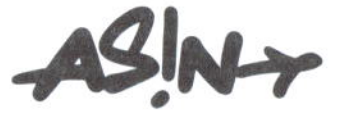

"Censorship helps us to develop our creativity, because we want to get attention from the government. You can't just paint, 'Fuck you' directly, because you will get arrested. But artists also want to get attention from the government, so that's why they create more controversial artworks."

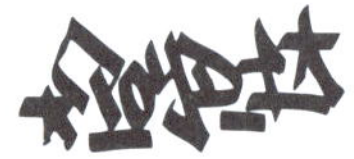

"Yeah, censorship helps creativity because an artist has to find new ways to express their ideas. Creativity is not

just about how they create a piece, it's also about how they present an idea. They have to find a way to not break the law but to use the flaws in the law to present their work and their idea. There is a proverb in Thai, when you are doing something against the law but you don't want to break the law, you have to find a hole in the law in order to break it – *lieng ba li* – creating a piece without breaking the law, but breaking the law at the same time."

Censorship can be regarded as a traditional part of Thai society in the form of the lèse-majesté law that protects the monarch and his immediate family from criticism. There are certain things that even many street artists and graffiti writers regard as beyond the bounds of criticism. This is a political reality for Thai street art and graffiti that makes the scene live in a way not seen in countries where freer speech exists. There are areas of censorship in Thailand that are seen by many as necessary, leaving blind spots in the set of issues Thai street artists and graffiti writers will address. A much deeper tension underlies this – how far to challenge the status quo before conflict's cost is greater than its benefit. Many of Thailand's neighbours also ask this question. And in a region where European and Japanese colonialism, socialism, sudden modernisation, loss of tradition and some of the world's most violent social re-orderings echo through peoples of incalculably varied religions, cultures and histories – destabilising authority is begun cautiously.

Rukkit

"Censorship has its pros and cons. Too much freedom might not always be good. For example, an artist who likes to draw genitalia. If he goes on a spraying spree, the general public could be wondering why they have to put up with this sort of thing on the street. We have freedom of thought but the freedom of presentation needs to be more thought-through by the artist themself. Will it hurt anyone? Is the information correct? But there's a lot of dumb censorship when it comes to politics. There is a lot of pointless street art removal going on because people already saw it on the news before it was removed – just like Headache Stencil's piece about Prawit's watch. The government uses its power to shut people's eyes and ears."

"Don't criticise too much or too deeply. The deeper you go the more the danger comes your way."

At Hopewell, the artists went to work on the columns once it was known they would be demolished. There was no threat of arrest by then, the columns would be destroyed. Rather than the illicit aspect of street art and graffiti attracting people, as it does in many other places, it was the removal of risk that created the blossoming of art there. This reveals how much creativity there is to be unchained in Thailand when legal threat and censorship are removed. Perhaps this is why those in power continue to censor.

For some street artists, censorship is a tranquilizer. For others, a stimulant. Attempts by Prayut's government to silence street artists caused them to become more vocal. As the nation's laws were being bypassed, yet again, by the rich, artists and writers refused to stand by. This is the power of street art and graffiti. And why – unlike their curated, gallery-bound cousins – they provide insights into hidden areas of contemporary Thai society. When the state imprisons its people behind walls of censorship, these art forms push light through the cracks. The more those cracks are patched, the more driven people become to open them up again. Hopewell's street art and that found across Bangkok are rich veins of political and cultural heritage – the revelries and anguish of modern Thailand.

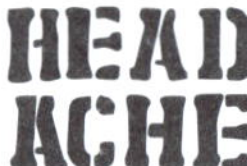

"For me, daring is more helpful than creativity. At that time, during the coup, no one dared to speak. Why do you have to shut your mouth? If you just speak, they'll kill you? No way! We all share the same world. You can't kill me just because I speak. No way. I want to make people feel that."

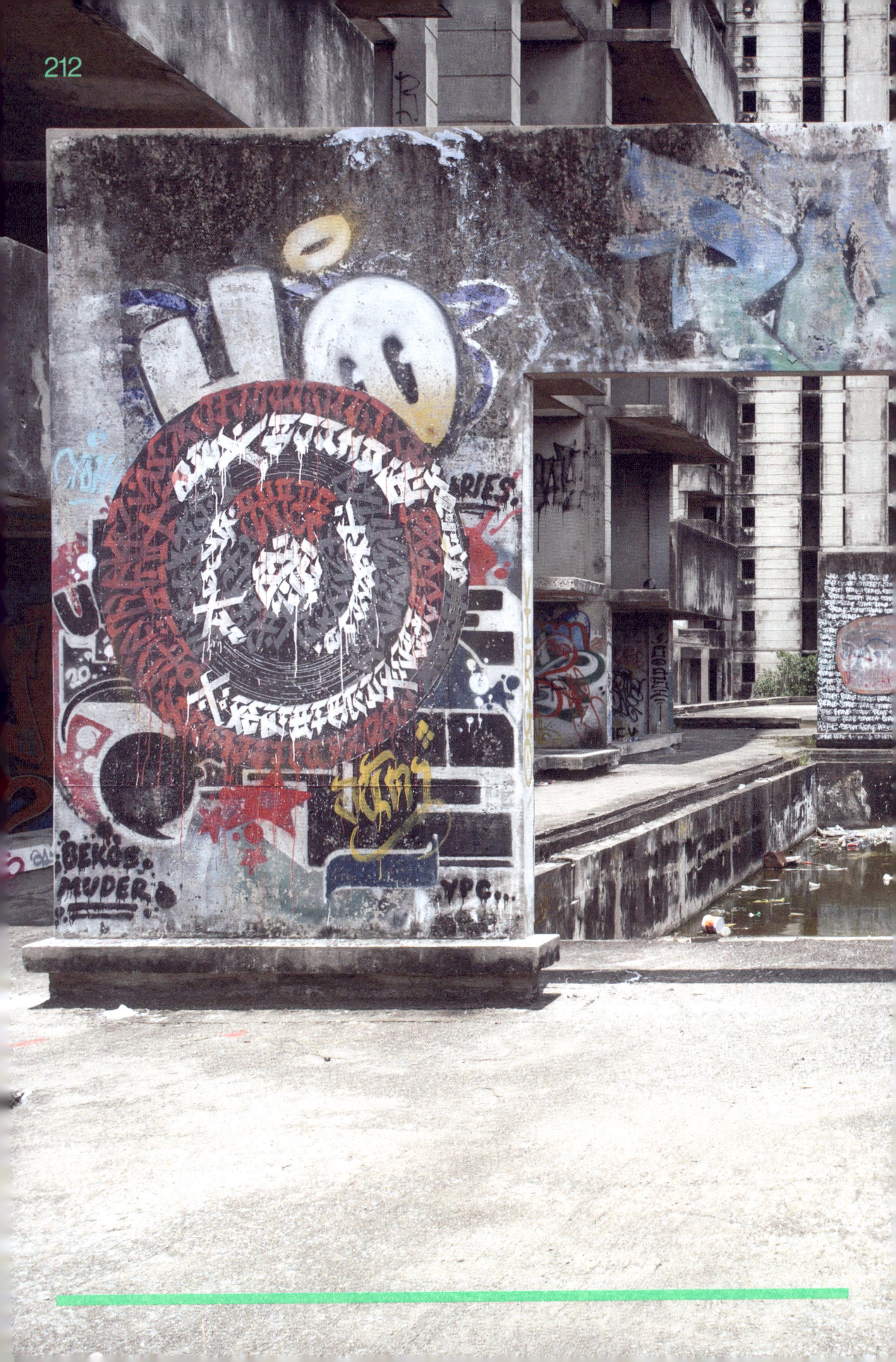
BEKOS.
MUDER
VPC...

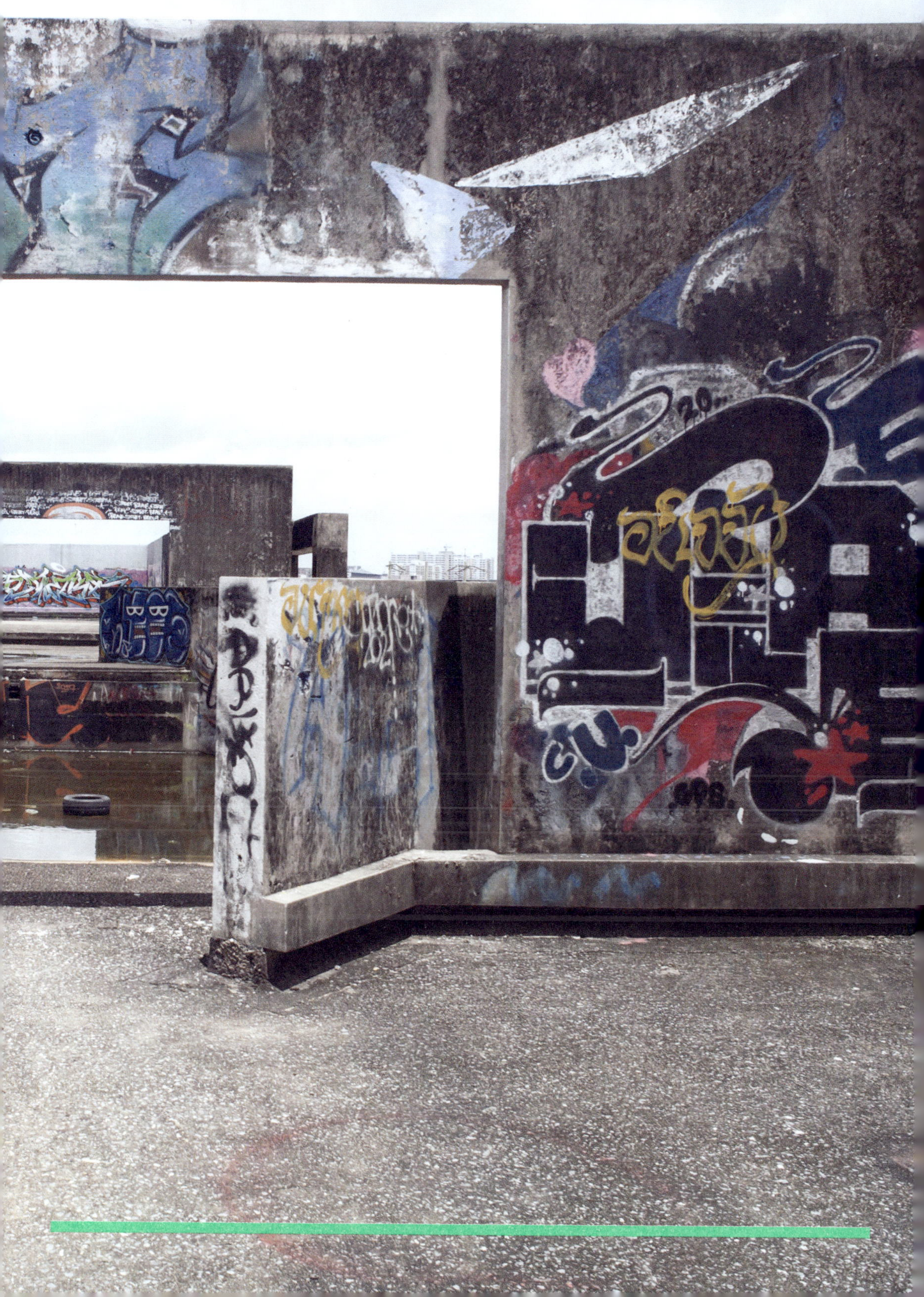

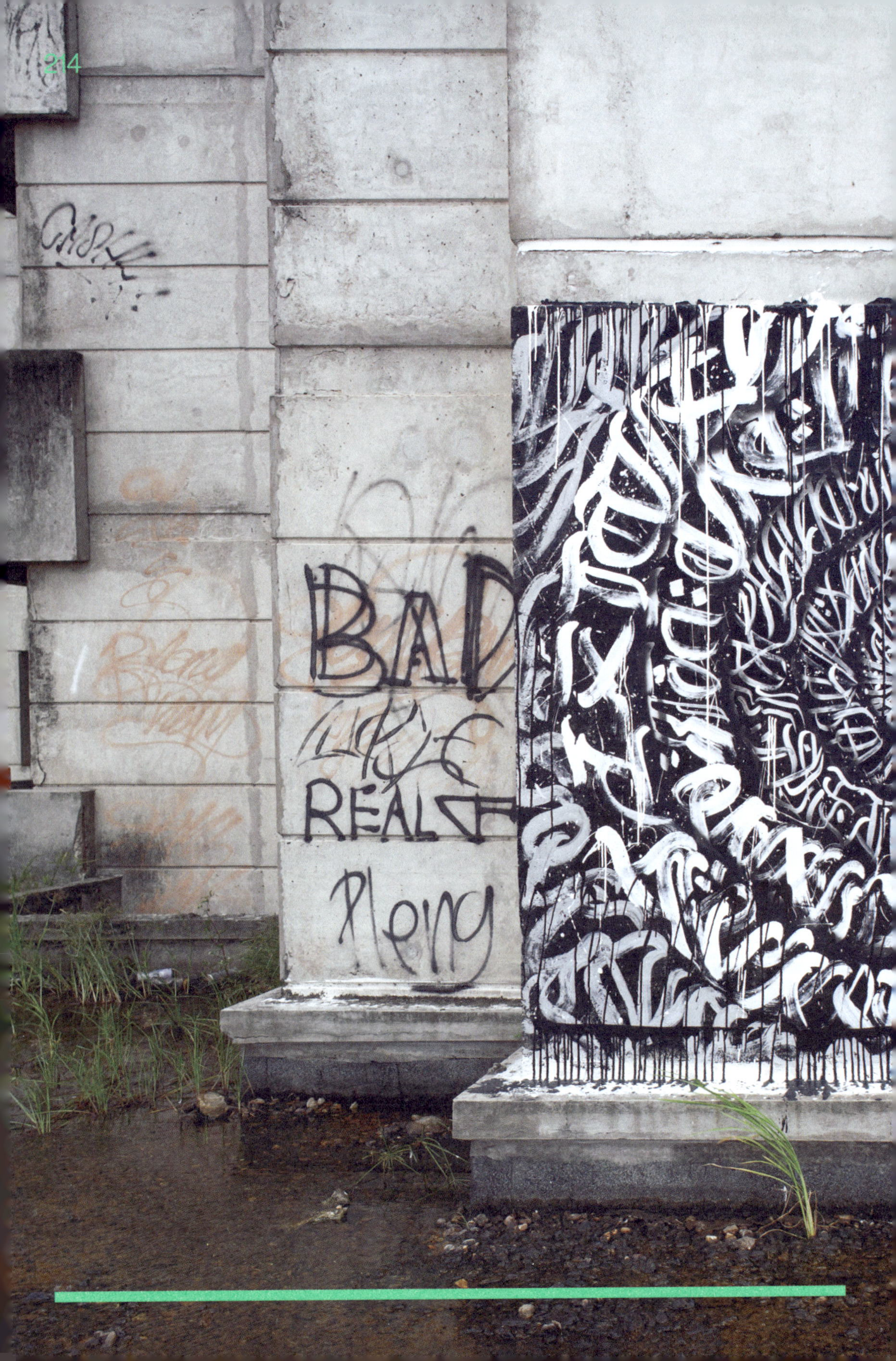
BAD

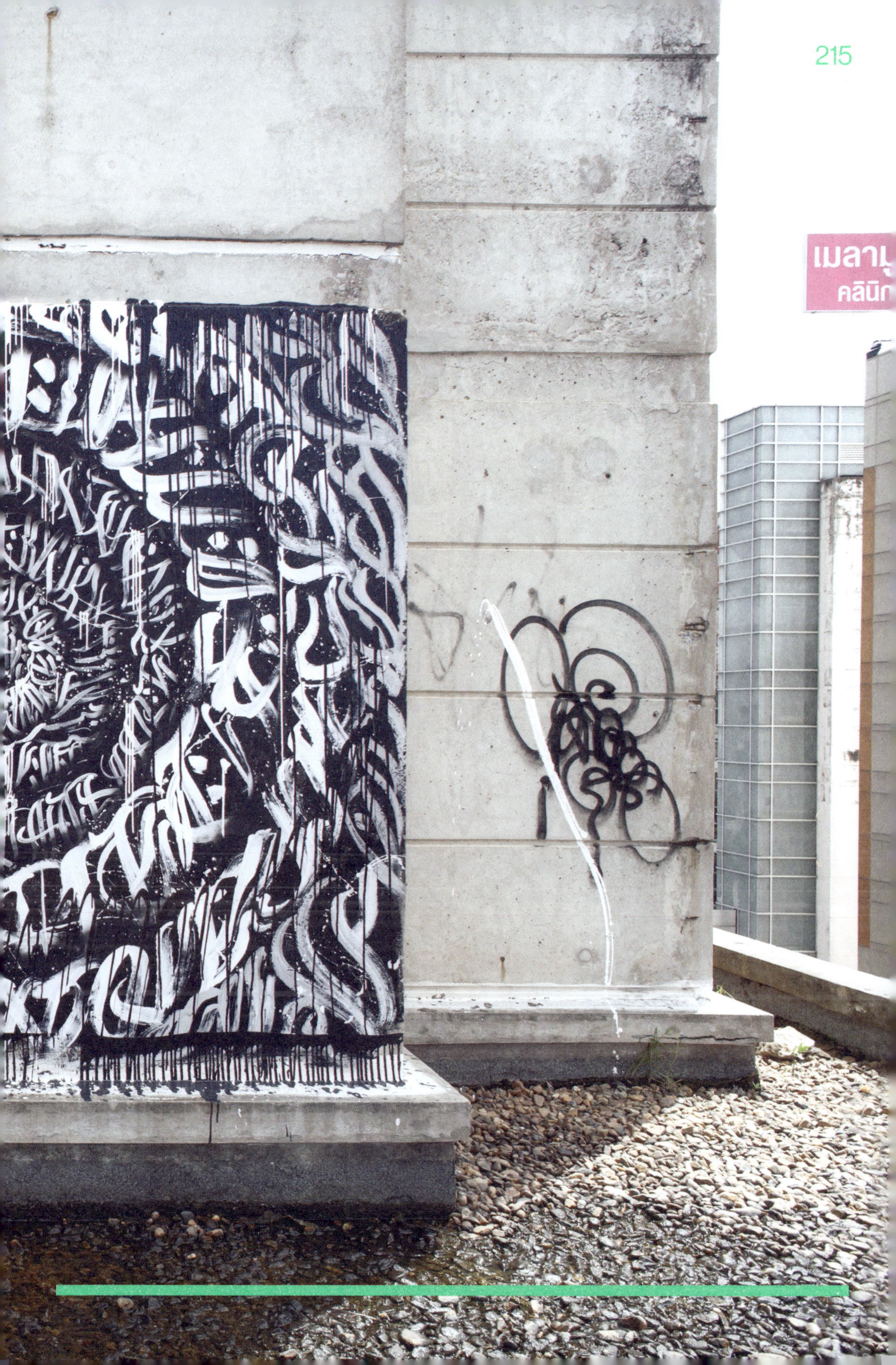

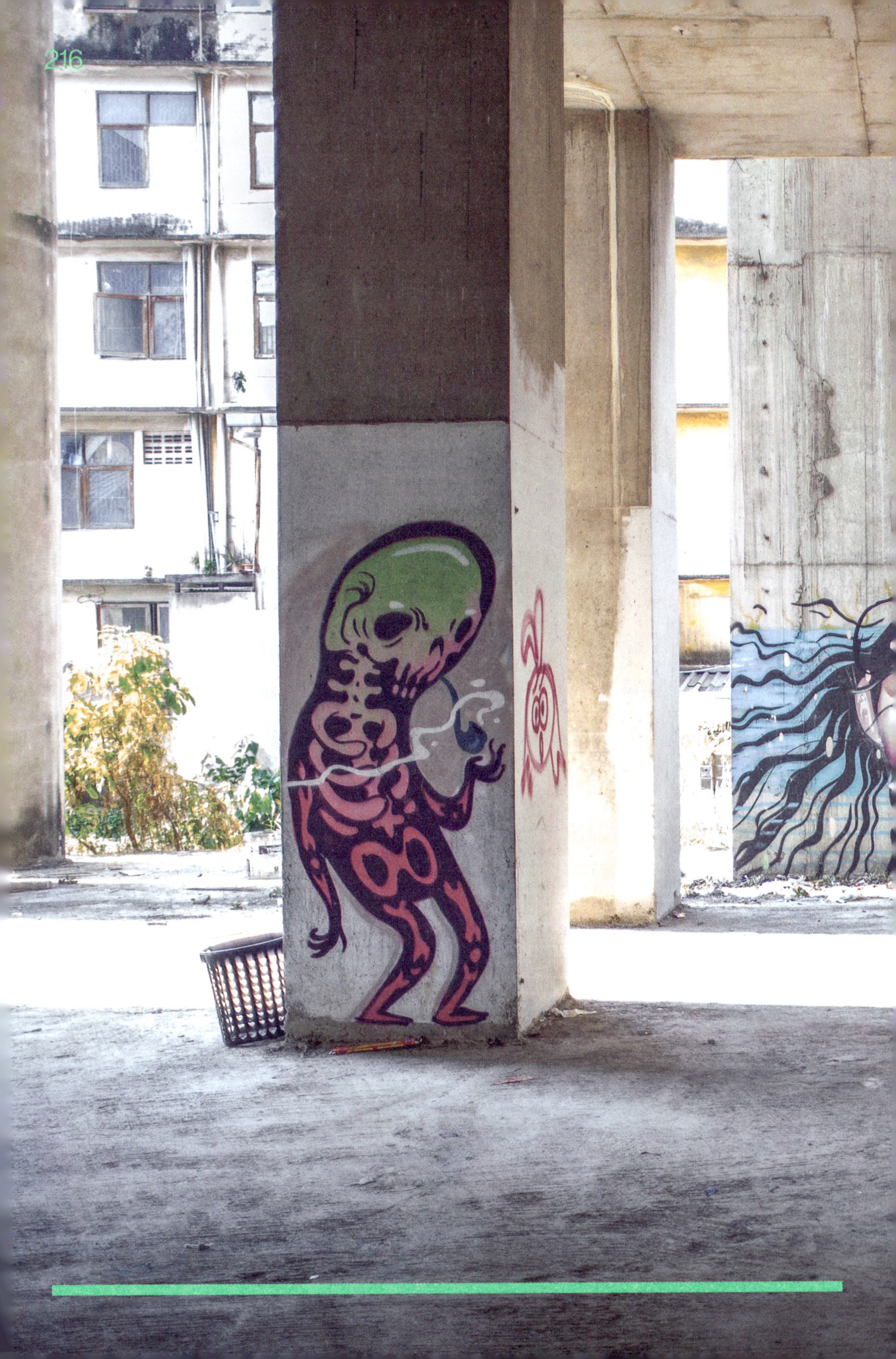

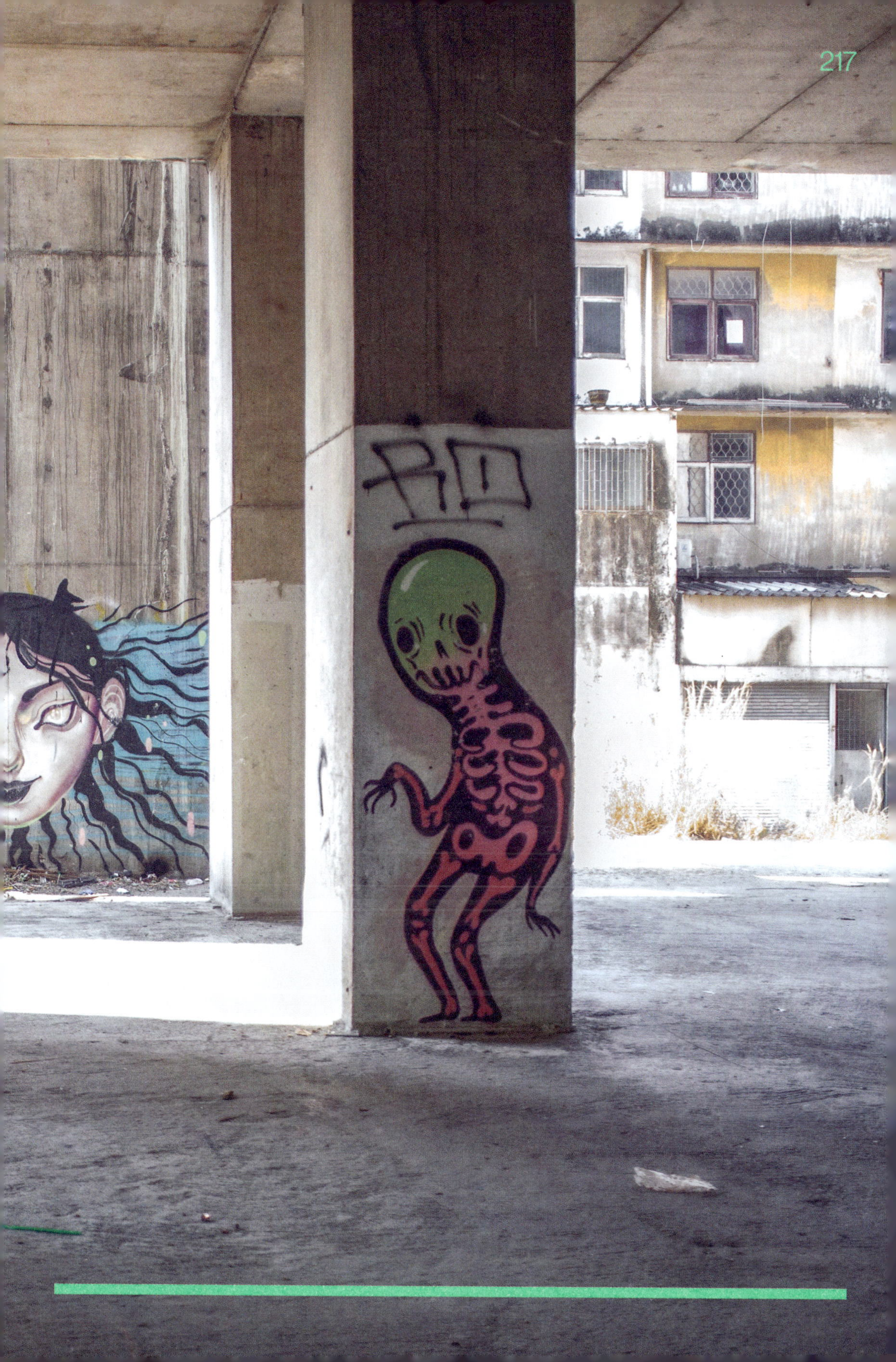

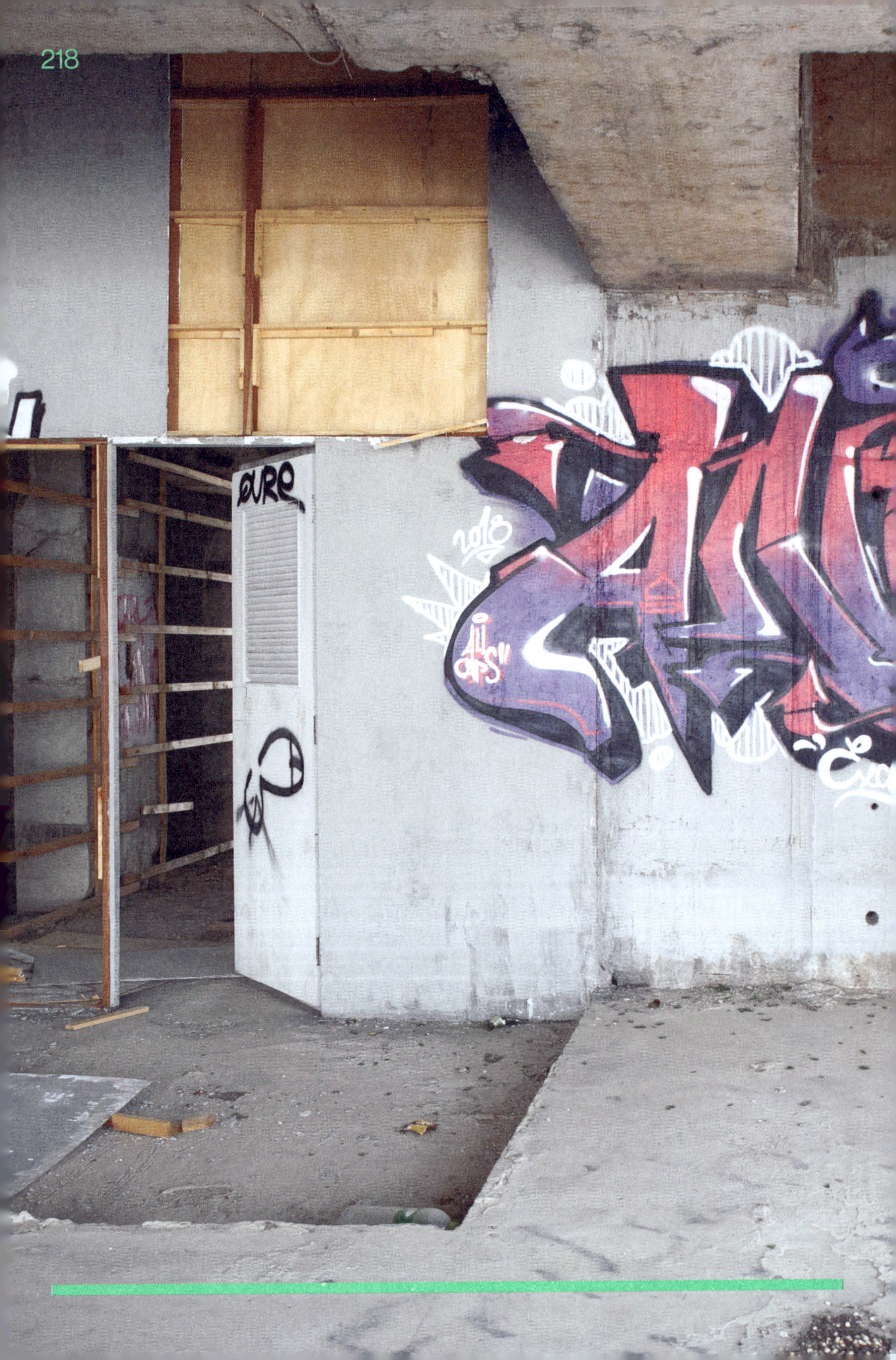

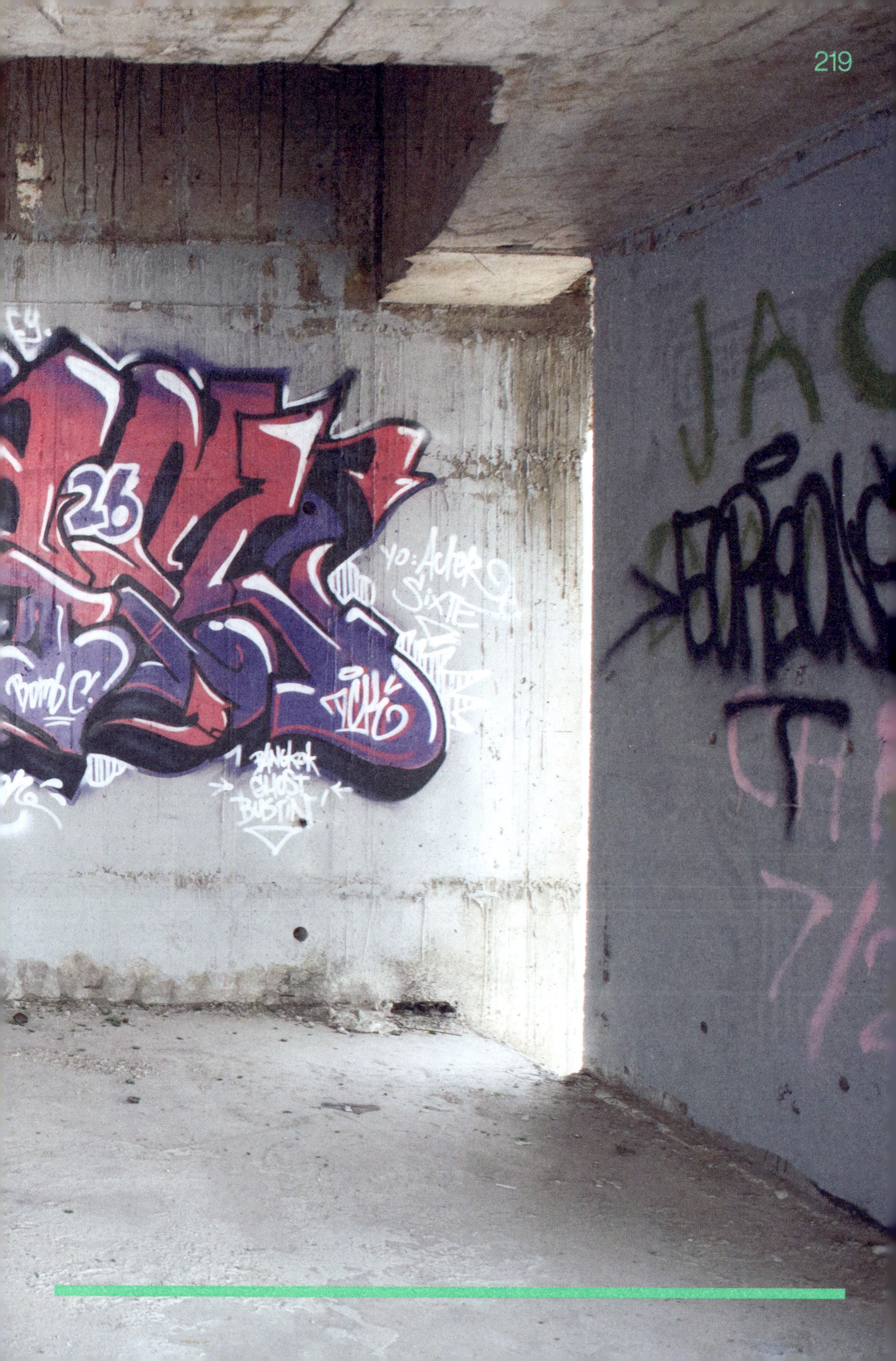
26
BANGKOK
GHOST
BUSTIN

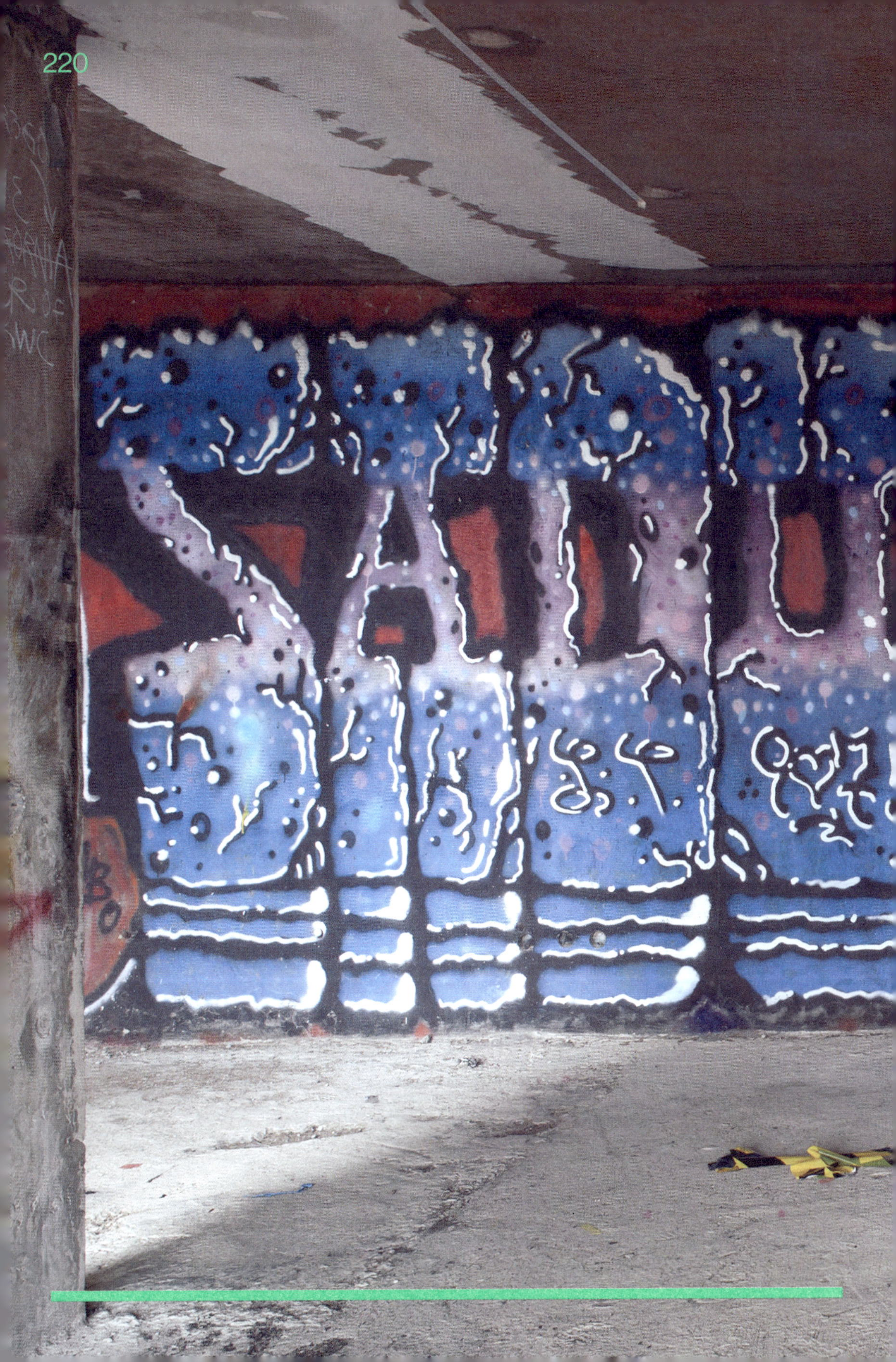

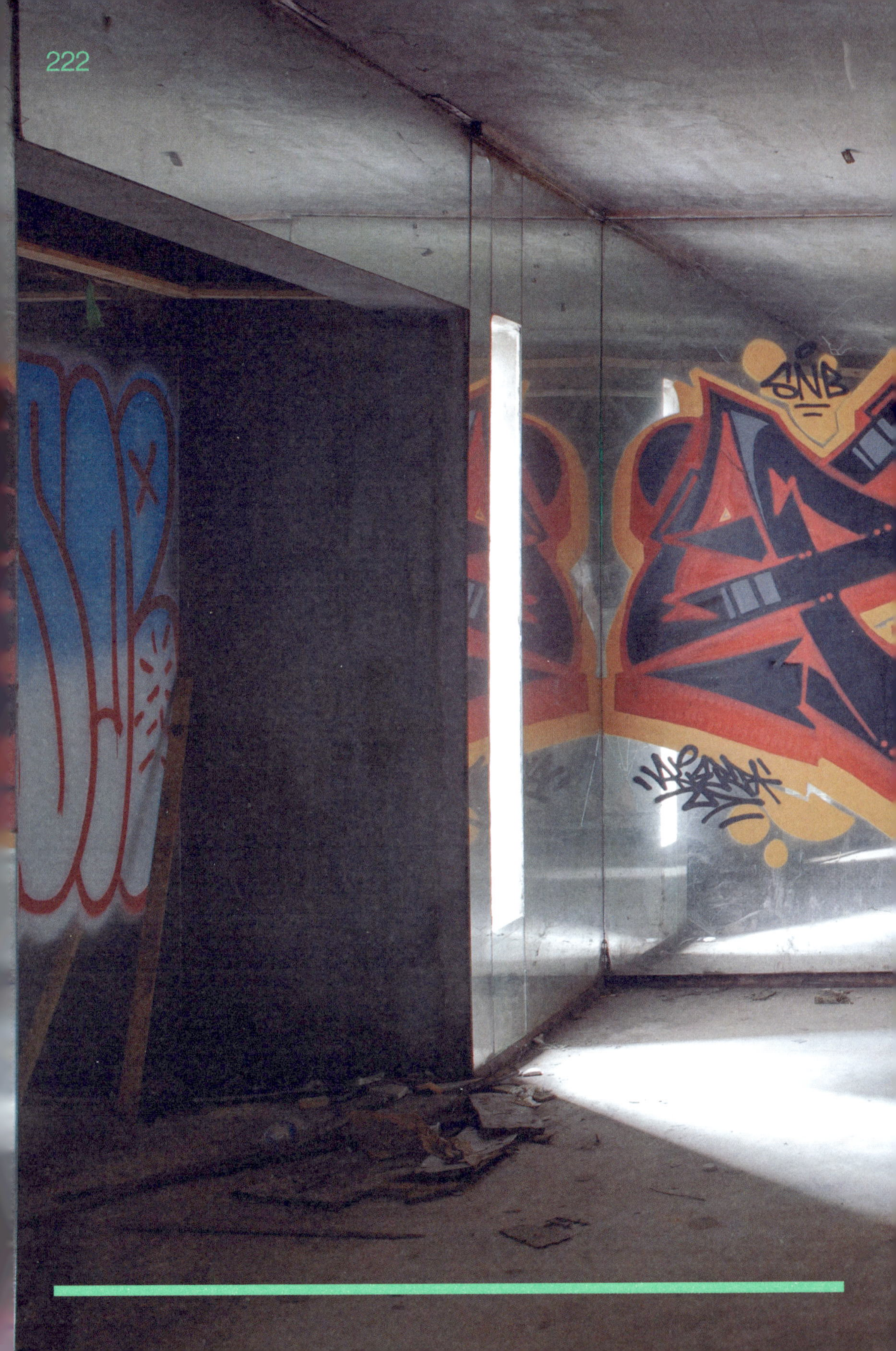
SNB

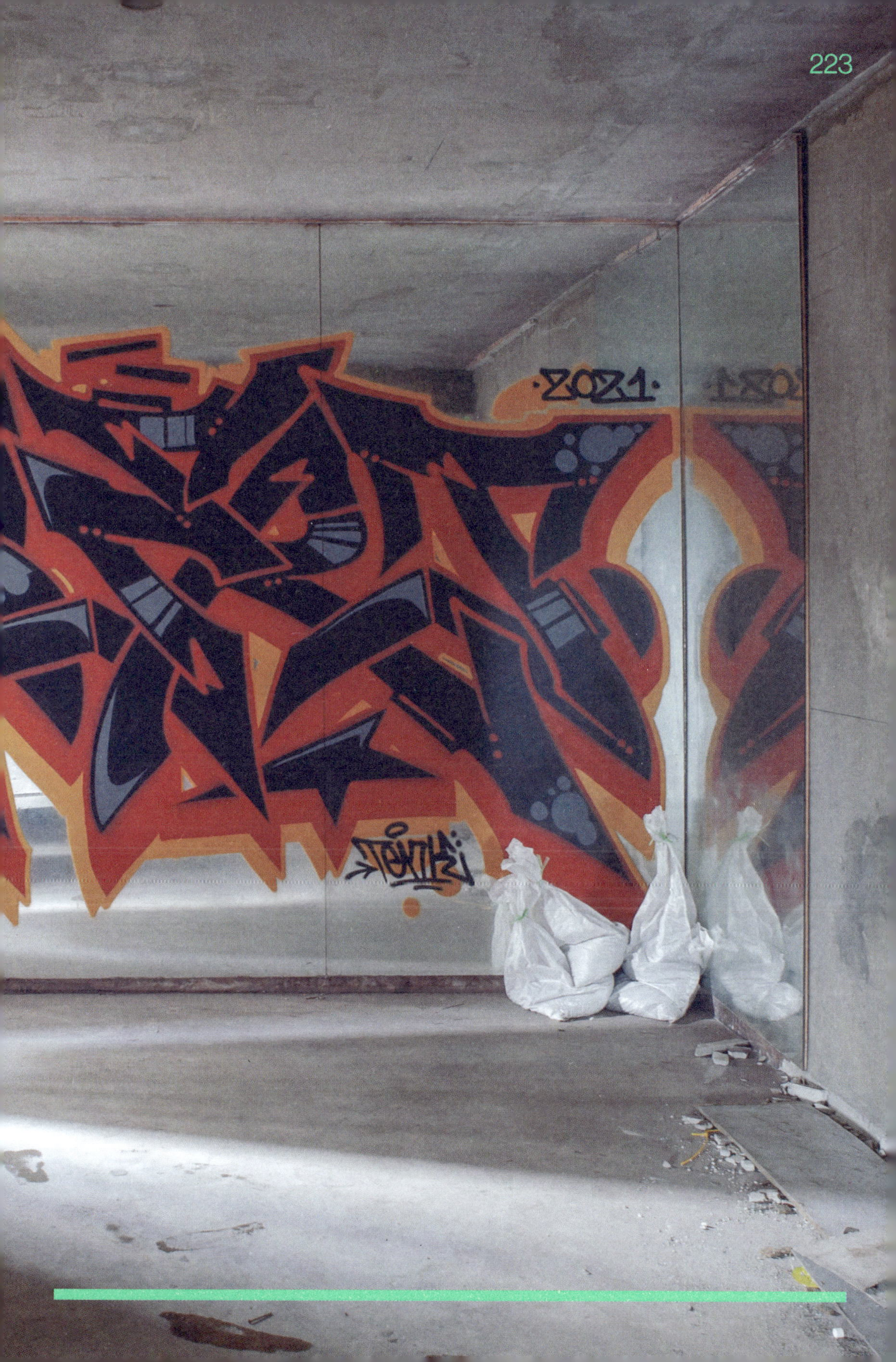
·2021·

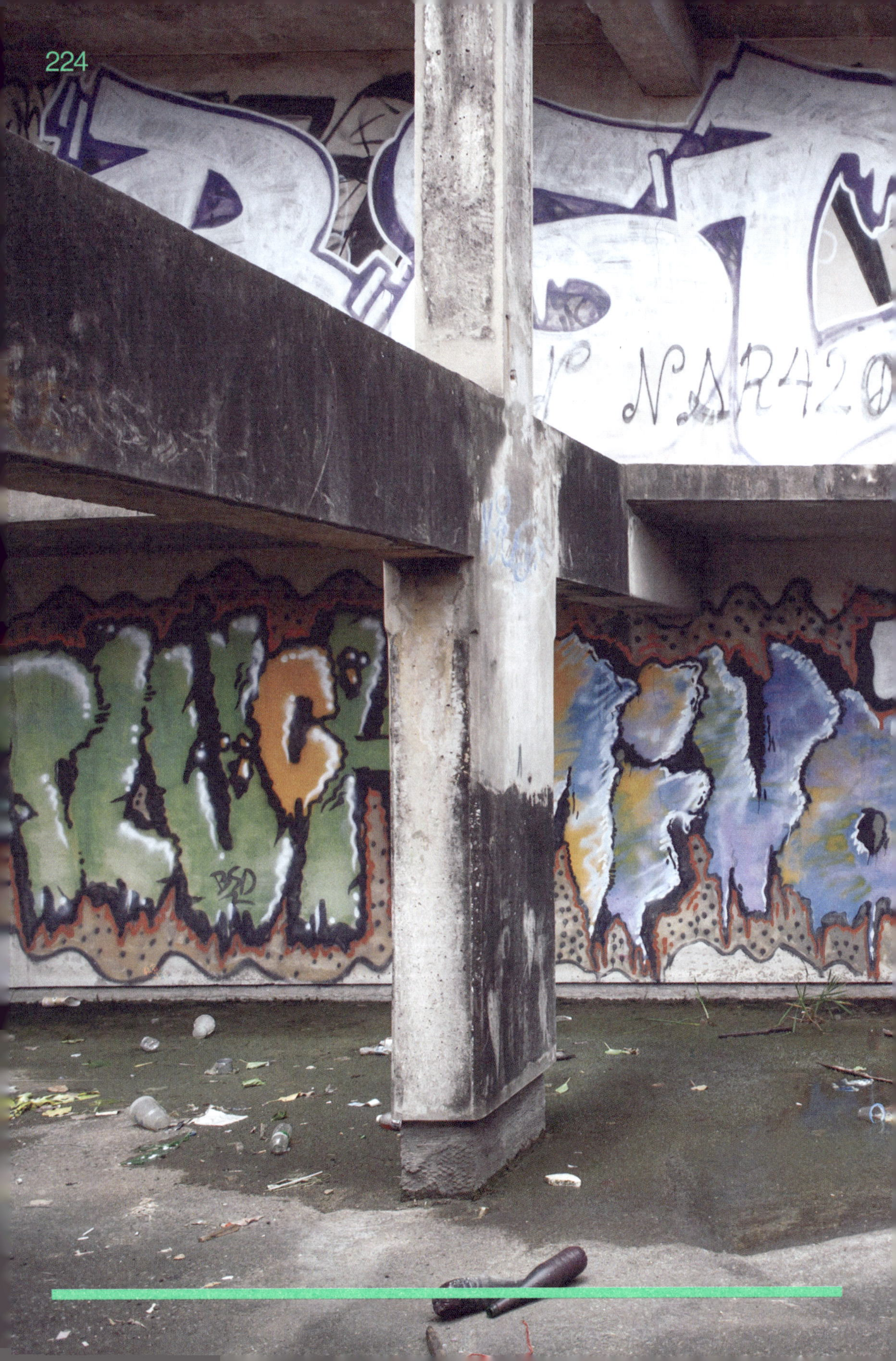
NAR420

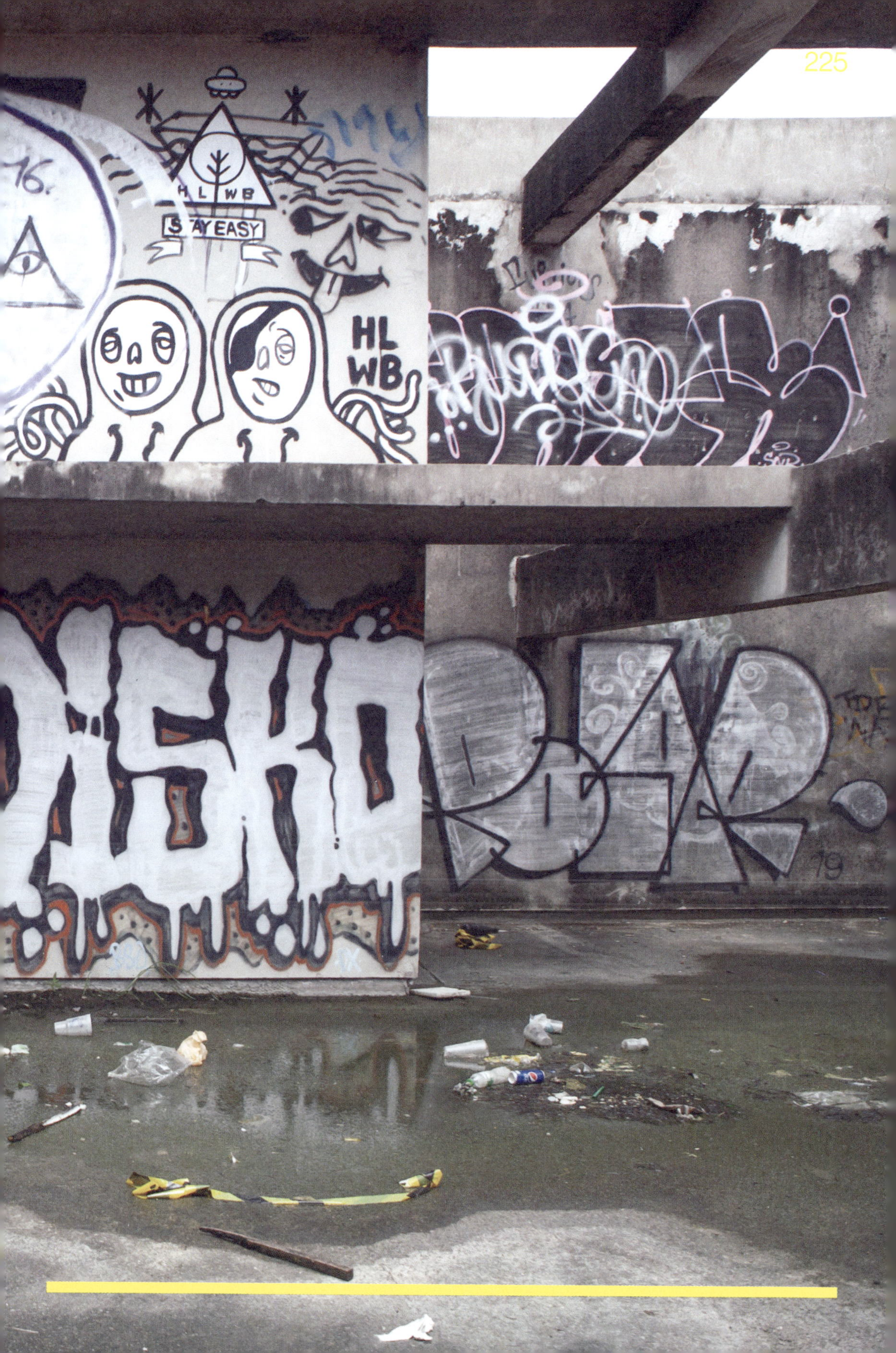
HL WB
STAY EASY
HL
WB

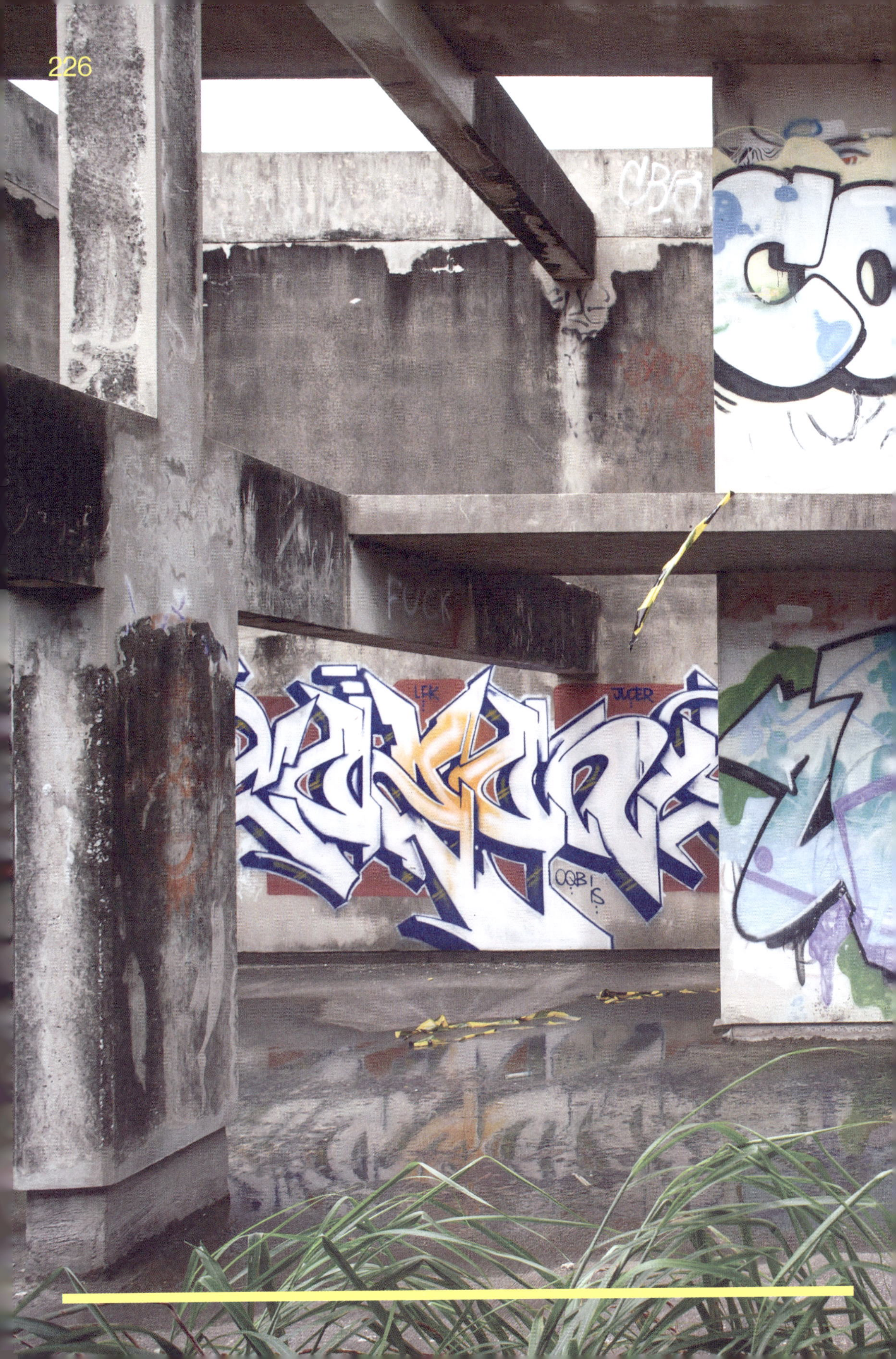
FUCK

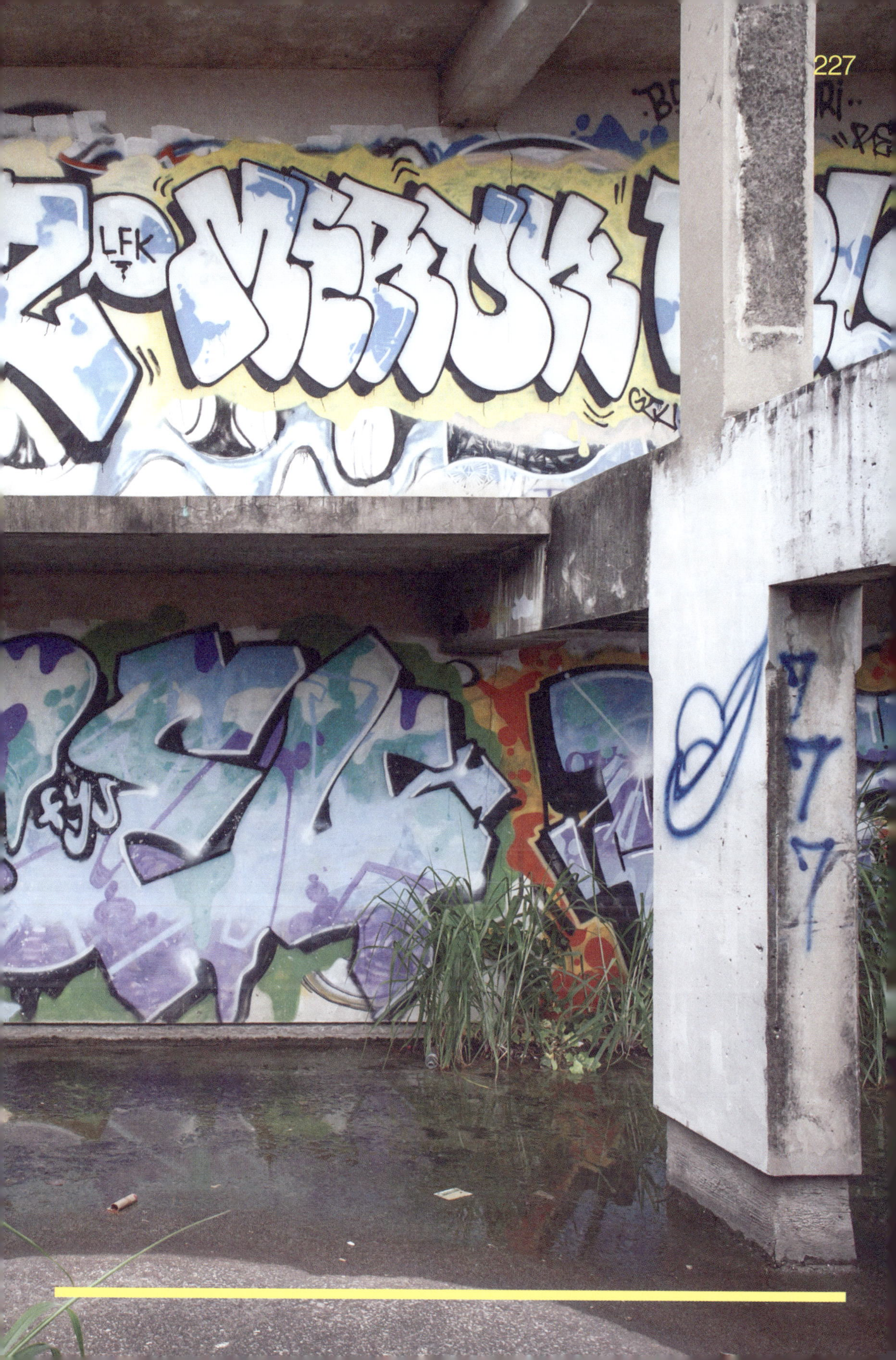
LFK

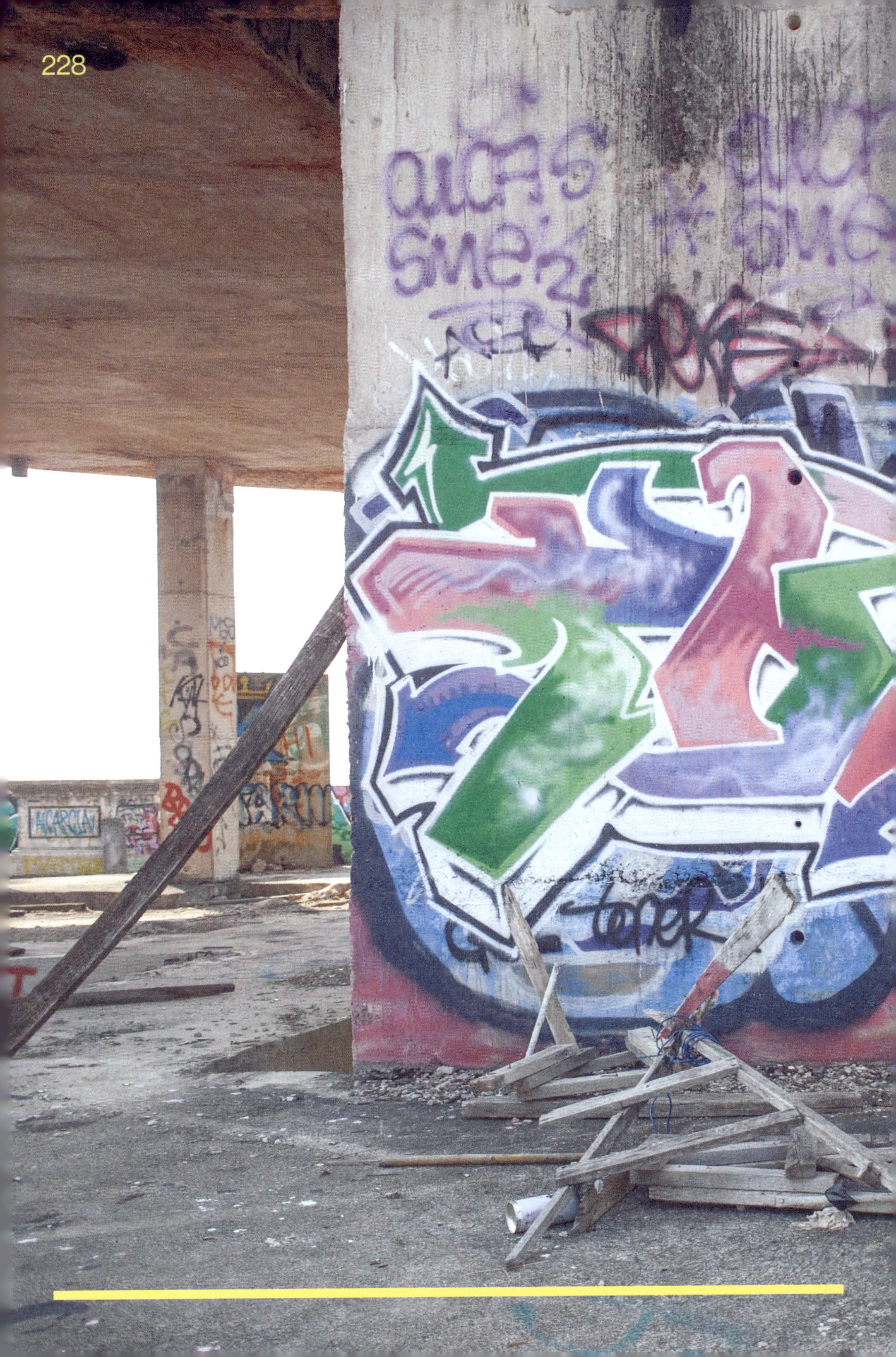

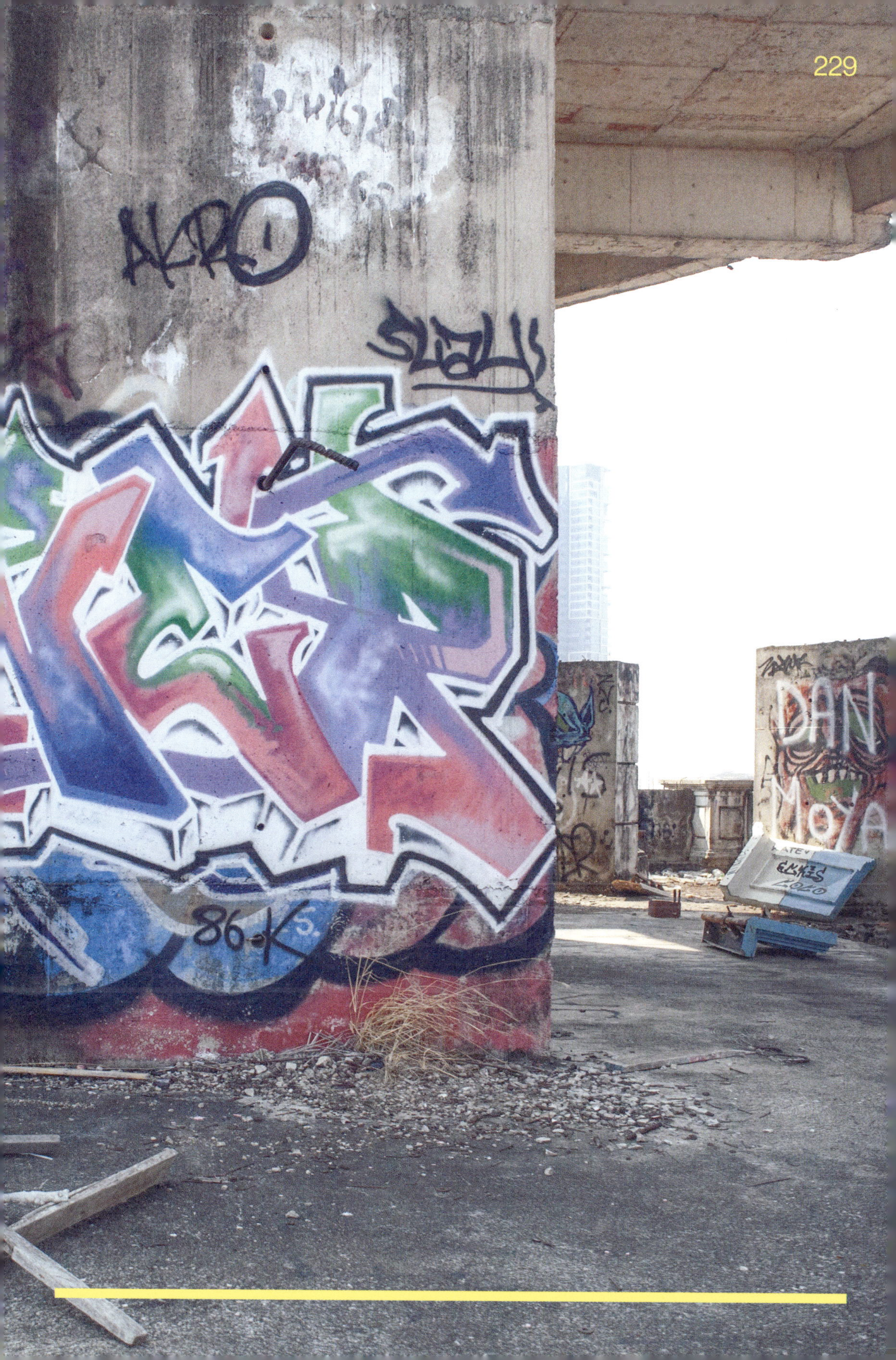
AKRO
86-K
DAN
MOYA

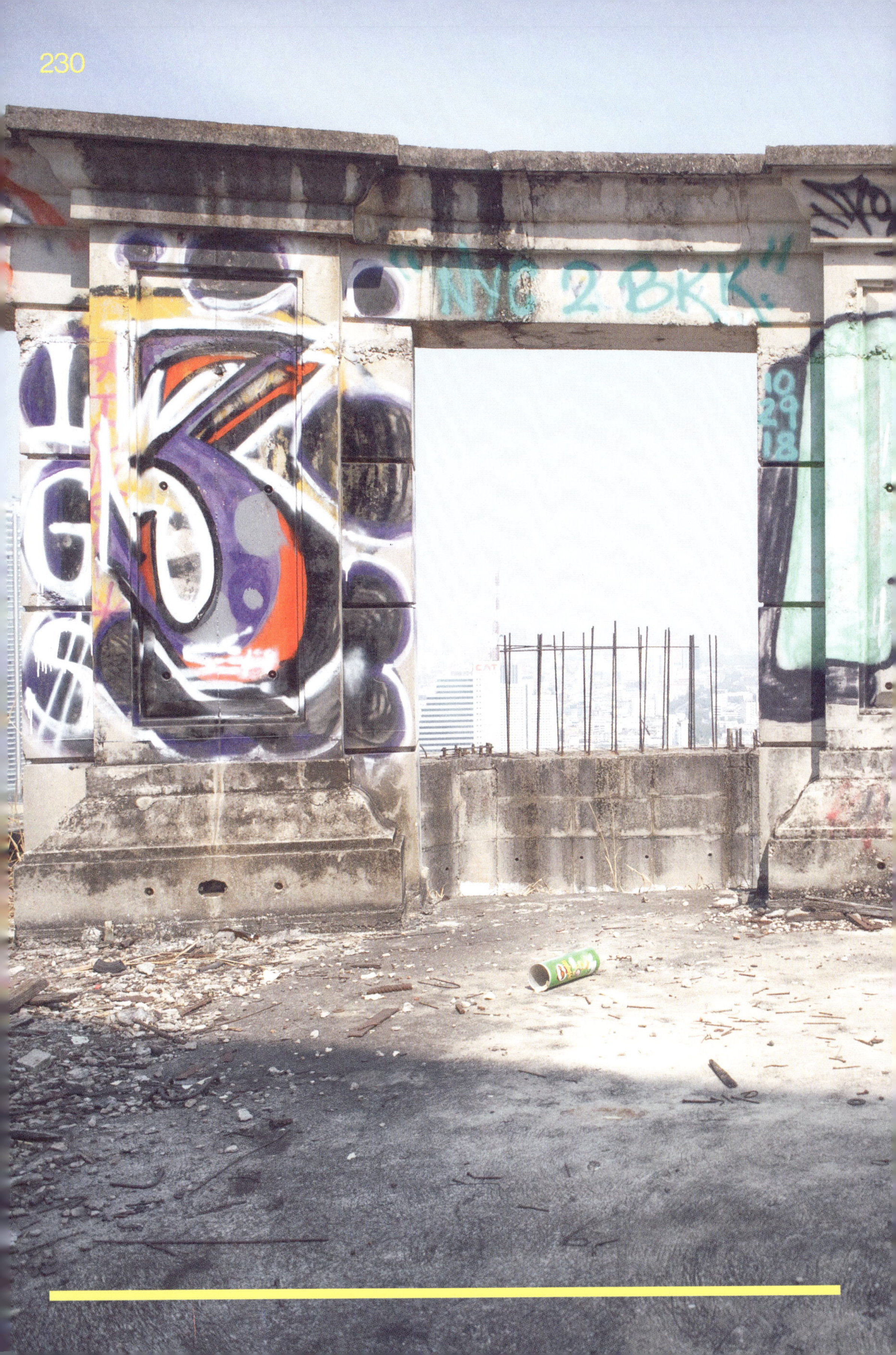
"NYC 2 BKK"
10
29
18

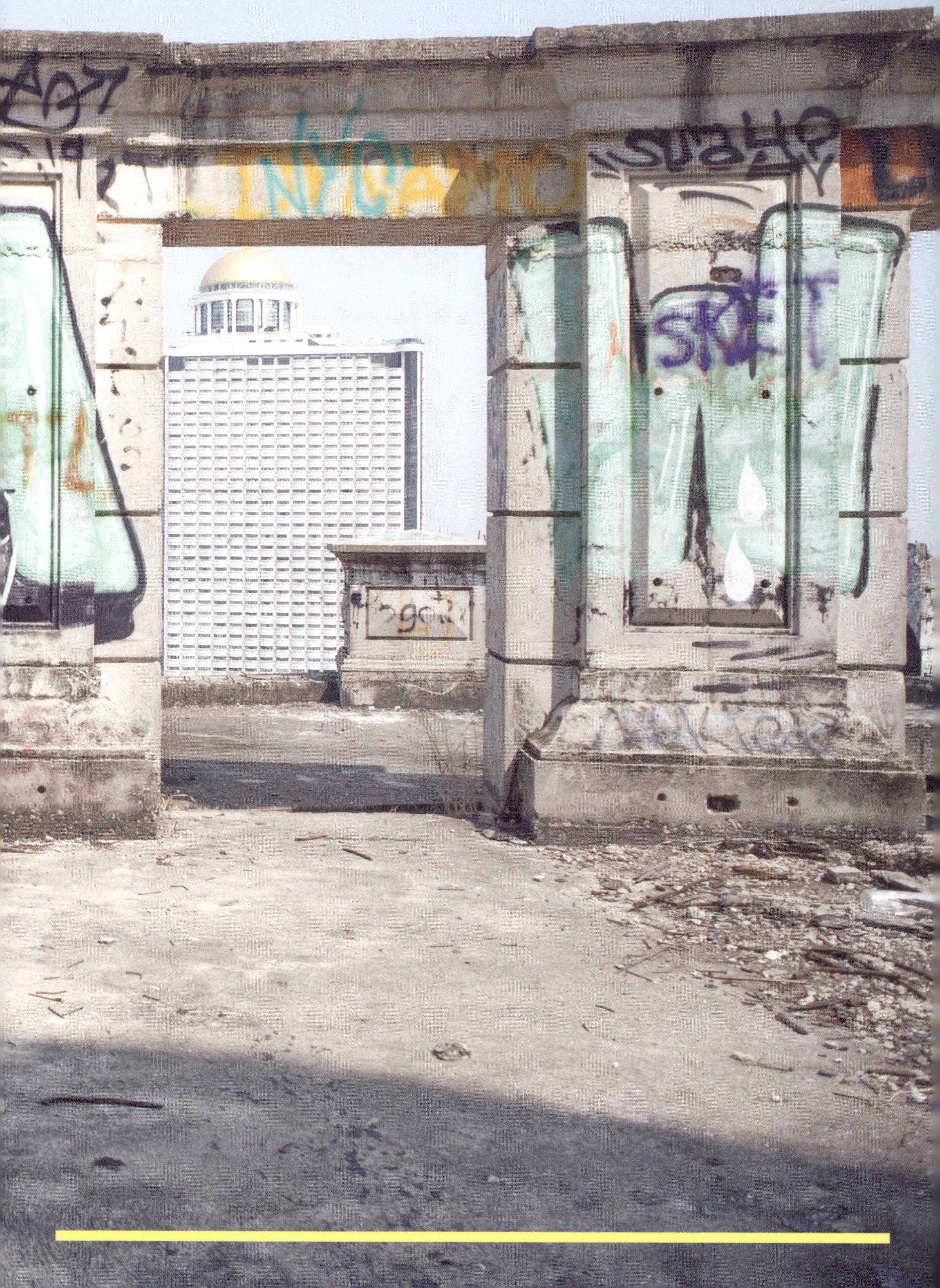

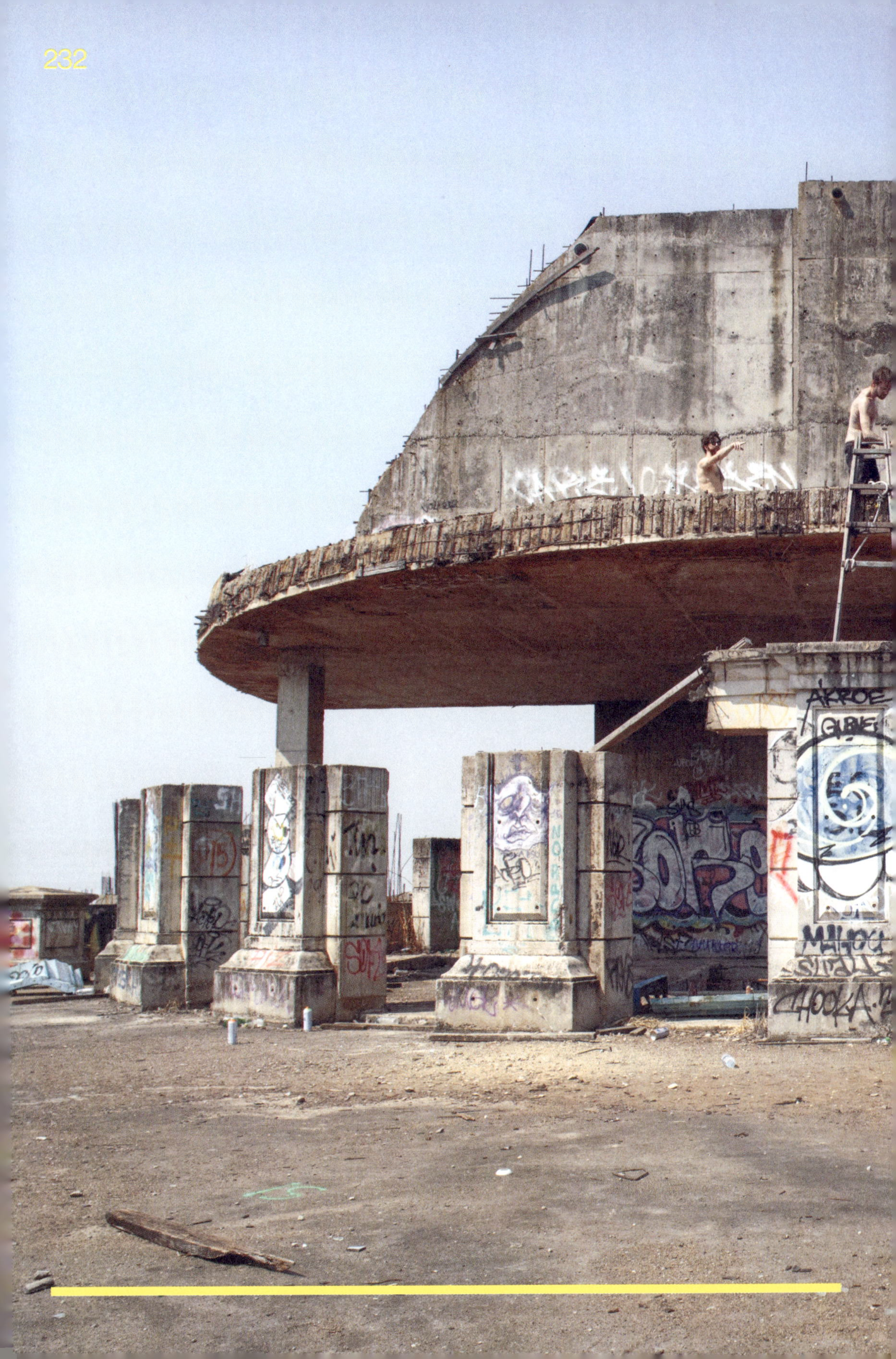

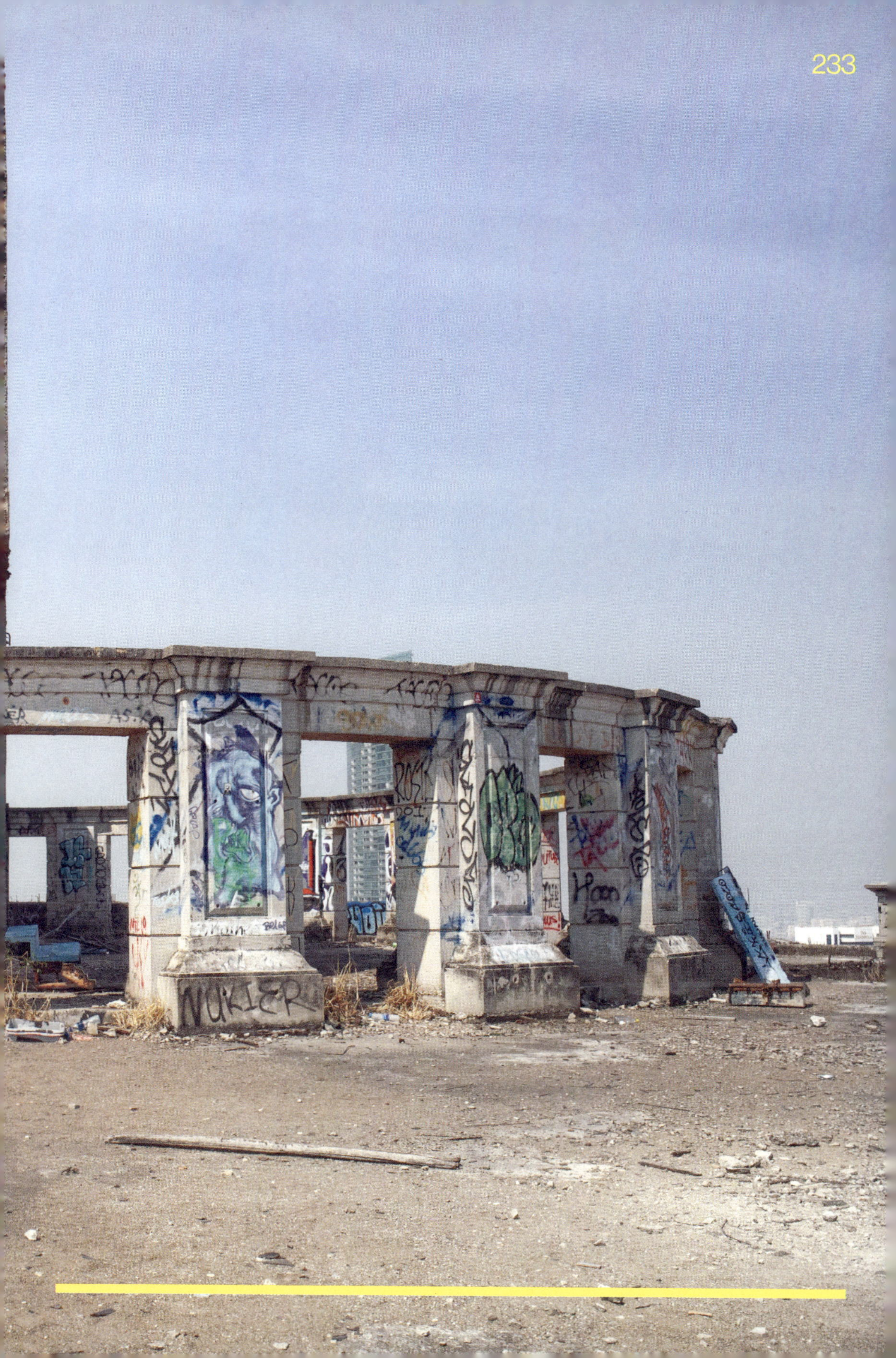
NUKIER

07

HOPE FULL

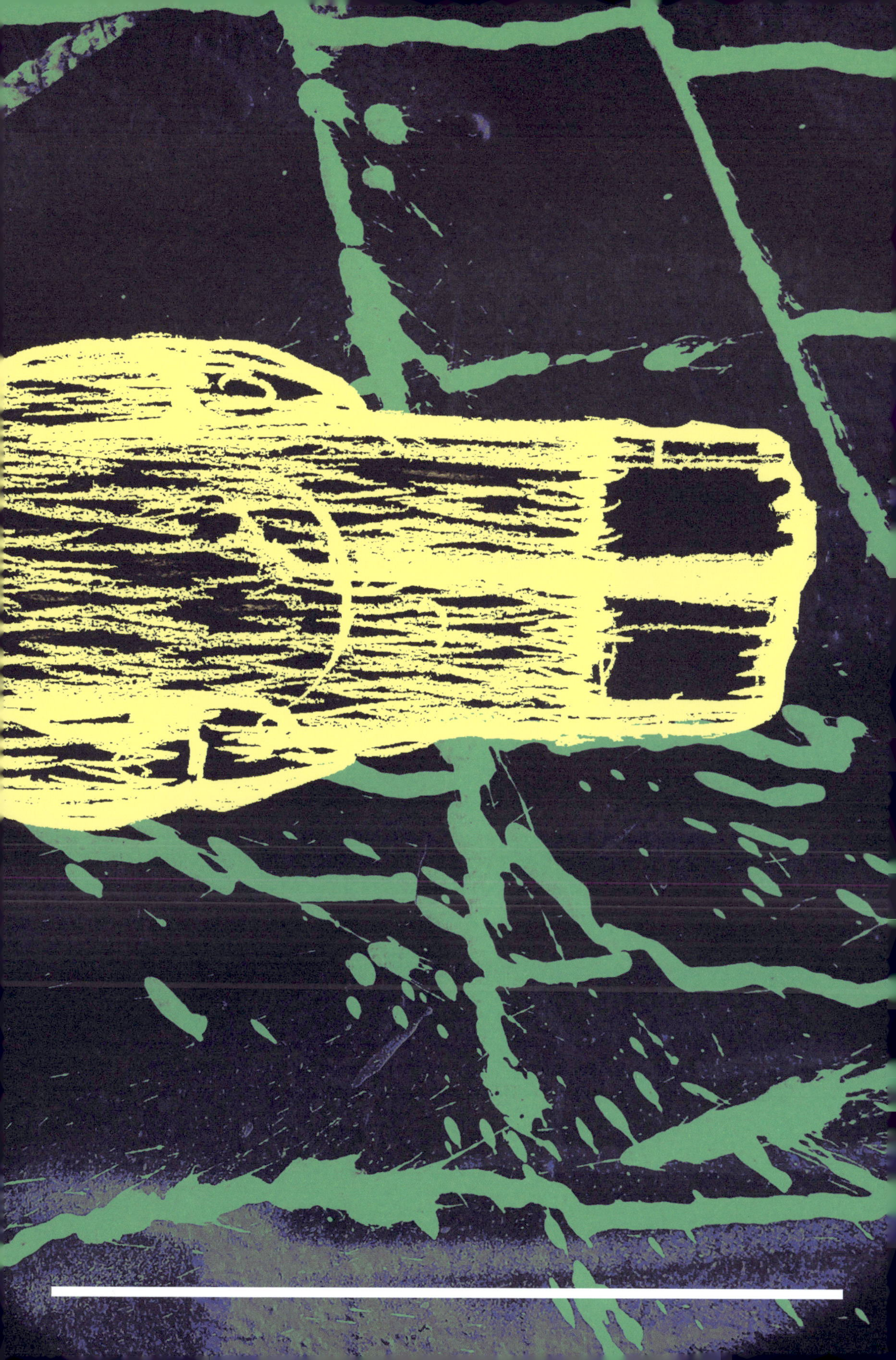

Over the last 70 years, Bangkok strove for a version of progress that took it far from its green, river-bound origins. The city's upward explosion of concrete and steel left many older meanings amputated. This New Bangkok first engulfed a generation of people in the 1960s who were born into a habitat more akin to village than city. By the 1980s, the Hopewell elevated rail project represented Bangkok's first real attempt at re-joining its disparate limbs. Within a few years it had collapsed under the weight of mismanagement. When its useless columns began to disappear, the street artists came – cultural hybrids of the New Bangkok. As an antidote to the blandness of the site's (and the city's) industrial form, and to further the project's symbolism, they created. Their art told of corruption's cost, censorship's consequence and overdevelopment's fallout – how the Old Bangkok, the one their parents knew, was lost. Even during the 2020 protests, as new waves of old grievances regained momentum, people spoke of Hopewell as a symbol of what they opposed.

Thai Street artists and graffiti writers share a repulsion of disingenuousness. They differ in their politics, style, aims, degree of commercialism and willingness to work illegally, but share the belief that to be considered worthy, dedication over time, and allegiance to your beliefs are admirable. Seeking fame, for fame's sake is a sure path to illegitimacy, regardless of which tribe you belong to. These values are the soul of graffiti and street art – a renunciation of the status quo, a rejection of the daylight laws of property ownership, a challenge to the state and those who ordinarily buy and control what people see in public space – a subculture willing to expose uncomfortable truths and trespass social borderlands. By speaking without being asked, they usurp the right to be heard. This is a fundamentally controversial act in a country like Thailand where censorship is ingrained. To become an advertisement for yourself is to abide in the tainted vocation that the scene would denounce – betraying the spirit of the movement. Without representing something bigger than yourself – a crew, a school, a conviction – graffiti and street art fall back into the visual art crowd. The young, the revolutionaries, contrarians and outsiders – those who can see that something is wrong and will say so – are drawn to deface spaces where authority expresses its control and to warn, inform and alarm. If that work doesn't enrage someone, or contravene some law, then it's probably not worth doing.

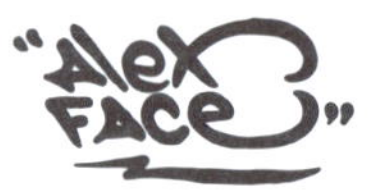

"Graffiti is about small people who want to say something, to spread it out. We don't have any power. Small people have problems in their lives, this is something they can do. They can write it down, to tell to other people who can see their message. Maybe it looks like shit, but you can see what's going on with the city, what the government is doing, political shit. They're saying, 'Please listen to me.'"

Graffiti and street art expose the comforting truth, that, behind the facade, our world is unpredictable. The state can't see everything, the corporations can't buy everything and there is always a way to speak, even with a boot on your neck. Transgressing laws, criticising the powerful, poking fun at society's norms, exposing injustices, revealing secrets, gesturing to hypocrites, beautifying the streets – graffiti and street art are sweet disorder to the horror of a sanitised city. They are concrete's nectar. These artists and writers perform an ancient role as custodians of humanity's memory, the transient tablets where alternative urban history is recorded. This is the scene's essence – subversive communion. Like a recorder left running, Thai graffiti and street art absorb their creators and the city they live in – the stop button hasn't yet been pushed. As they become more accepted and commercially profitable in Bangkok, these art forms fight to maintain their cut as subcultural traditions and their identity in a world swamped by connection and media.

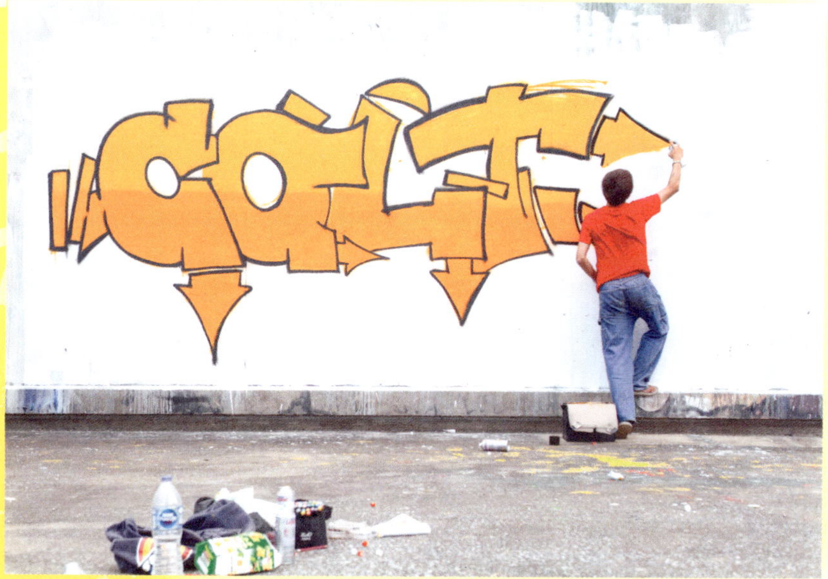

COLT working

The Internet has put an enormous variety of styles within reach of Thai graffiti writers and street artists. This influx is the inevitable result of globalisation and we are too near its impact to see the cultural cost. Of course, there has always been exchange across cultures, however, its volume and speed was far slower before the Internet. That easier pace gave time for local traditions to adapt, rather than be disordered and replaced. With this intermingled pool of styles and influences swirling round, a huge variety of colours mix together. The future will tell if they cancel each other out, leaving grey nothing, or spark new vibrancy.

In the end, as the new elevated Bang Khen station took shape in the months before COVID-19 would change the world, Hopewell's street art was erased by the new rail line's construction. The old columns, too small to be of use, were removed – a few survive today as monuments. The New Bangkok pushes onwards. Thirty years after the Hopewell project's inception, at the point of its demolition, the only good that came of it and the US$794 million cost, was around 300 street-art pieces, visible for a couple of years – US$2.6 million per piece. Today, Gordon Wu sits at the helm of Hopewell Holdings in Hong Kong as the Chinese Communist Party takes the island into its fold, the Thai politicians who approved the project are mostly dead, their children rich, a new king sits on the throne and a new wave of protests, graffiti writers and street artists shake the kingdom's foundations.

·MUEBON·

"I actually try to stay optimistic. I hope that one day it will change, even though in reality it will be hard to reconstruct Thai society. We have to stay optimistic. And we have hope for the new generation, we do what we can do, and don't care about the old generation. The problem is, the rich older generation wants to create a new generation that is similar to them, because no one wants to lose their power. That's why I do a lot with the new generation. They need to be born and make my country new. Please, don't believe everything from your mum and your dad, some stories from your mum and dad, they're shit! Because in Thai culture, seniority plays a major and important role in our culture and society, so the older generation have strong beliefs about politics and society, about work, about eating, and actually about everything. It's hard to change their minds, because of seniority. That makes them firm. But I say to them, you don't need to take your kids to your way. Parents don't know everything about the future, so why do you take your kids to your way? And the world changes every year, it changes a lot."

JAKE working

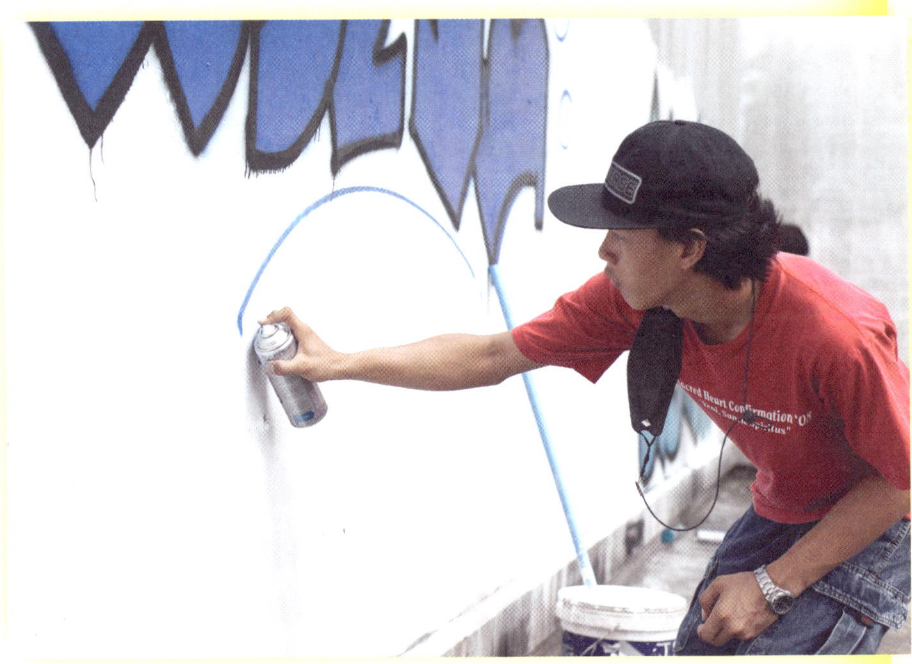

They may not know it, but Bangkok's street artists and graffiti writers are the memory of otherwise lost sub-heritage. The government, the institutions, and their sanctioned histories tell official versions of what it means to live in Thailand. The street artists tell another side. Without permission. They benevolently tarnish the city with subversive declarations. Anointing the concrete carcasses left by economic collapse and government corruption, they record the nation's discarded memory. And under their breath, despite advancing age and increasing popularity, the movement's first generation murmur some of humanity's oldest sutras, and the young repeat them – the anthems of graffiti and street art:

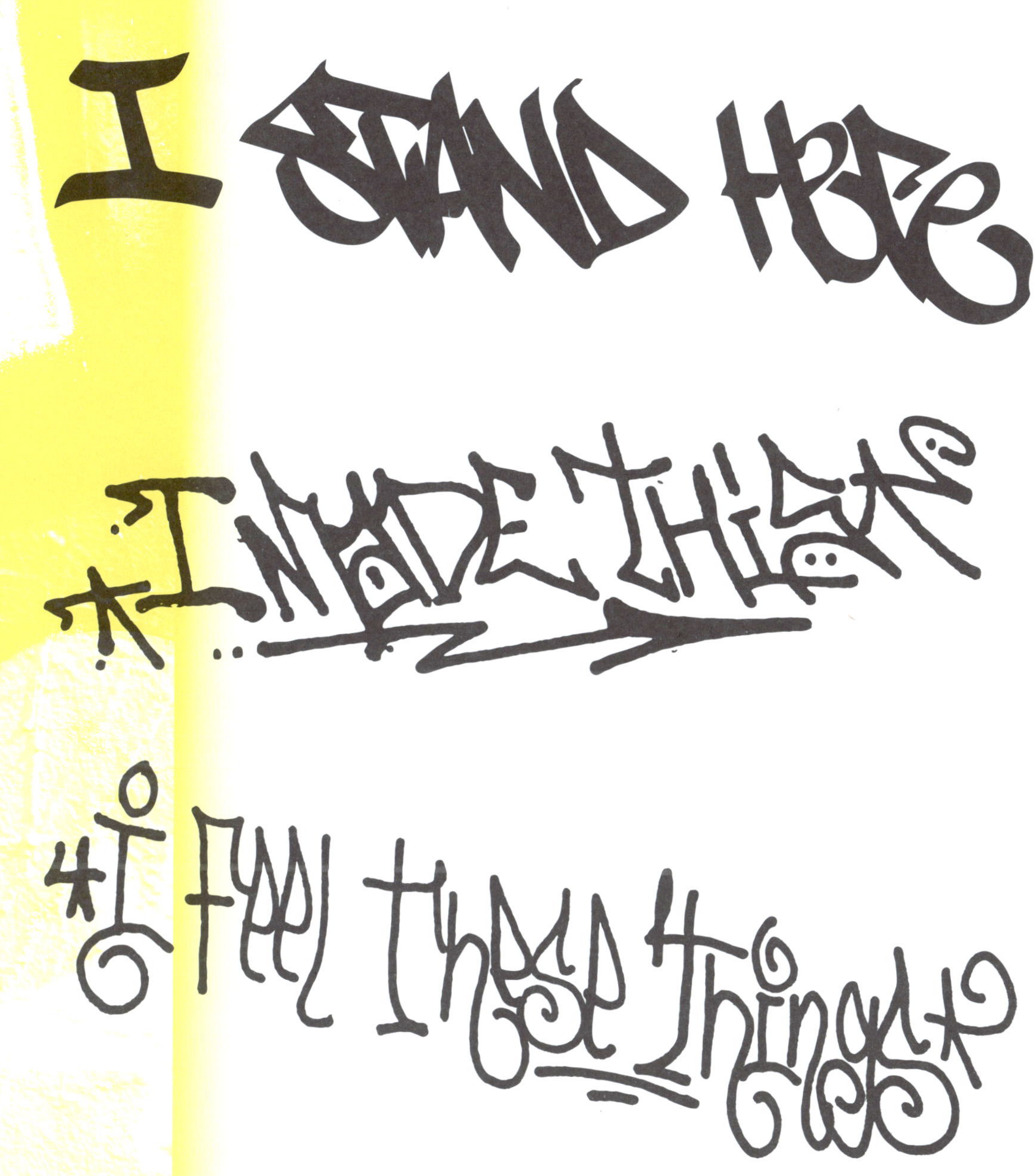

"I DECLARE"

I'm REAL

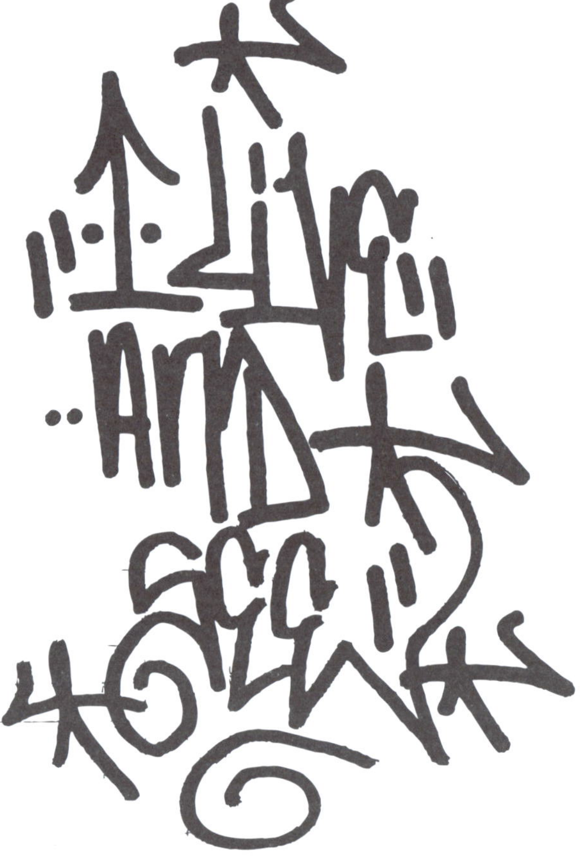

THIS IS WHAT I KNOW

These declarations invoke a million questions and finding just a handful of their answers means a lifetime's fascinating journey:

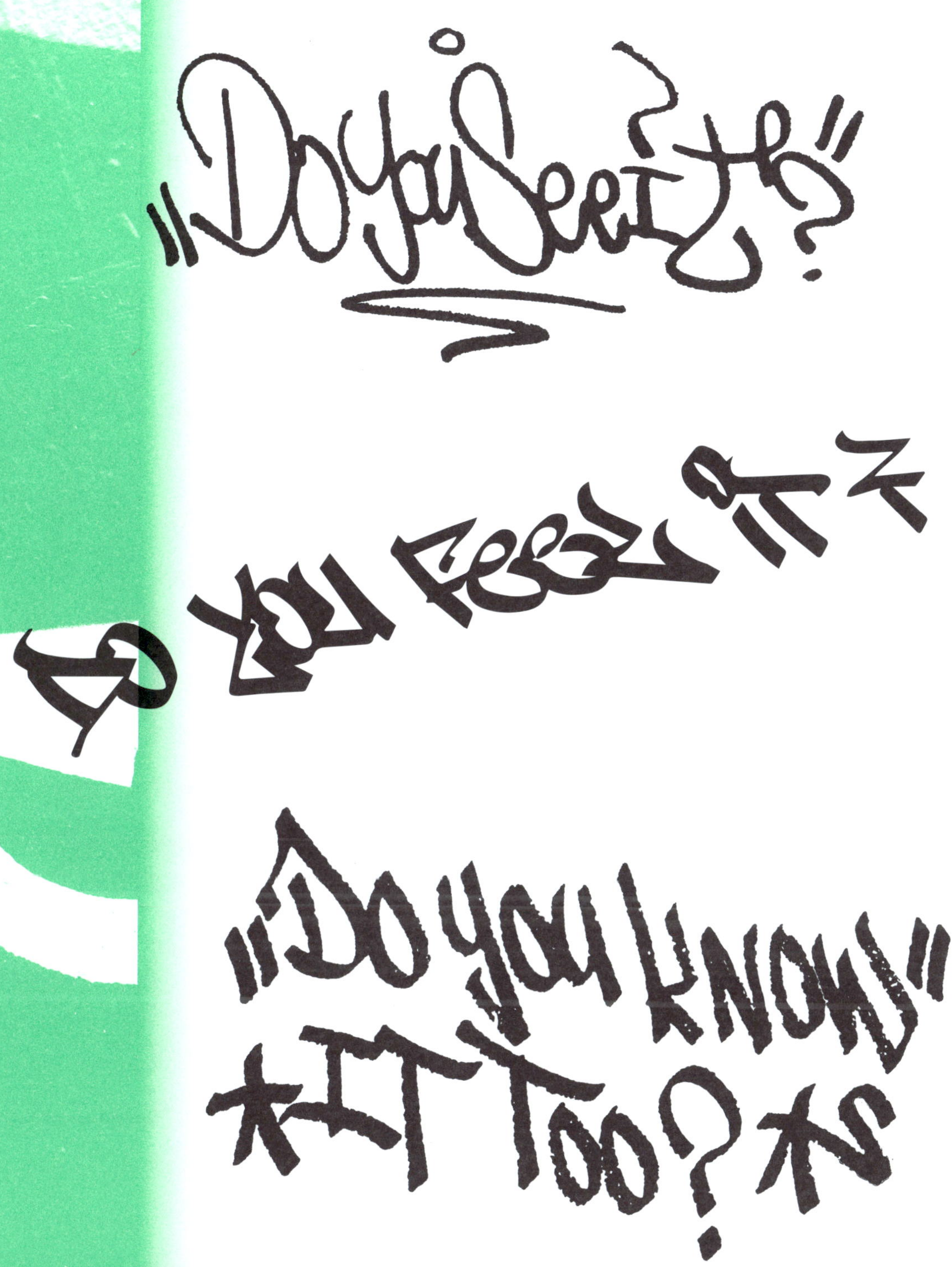

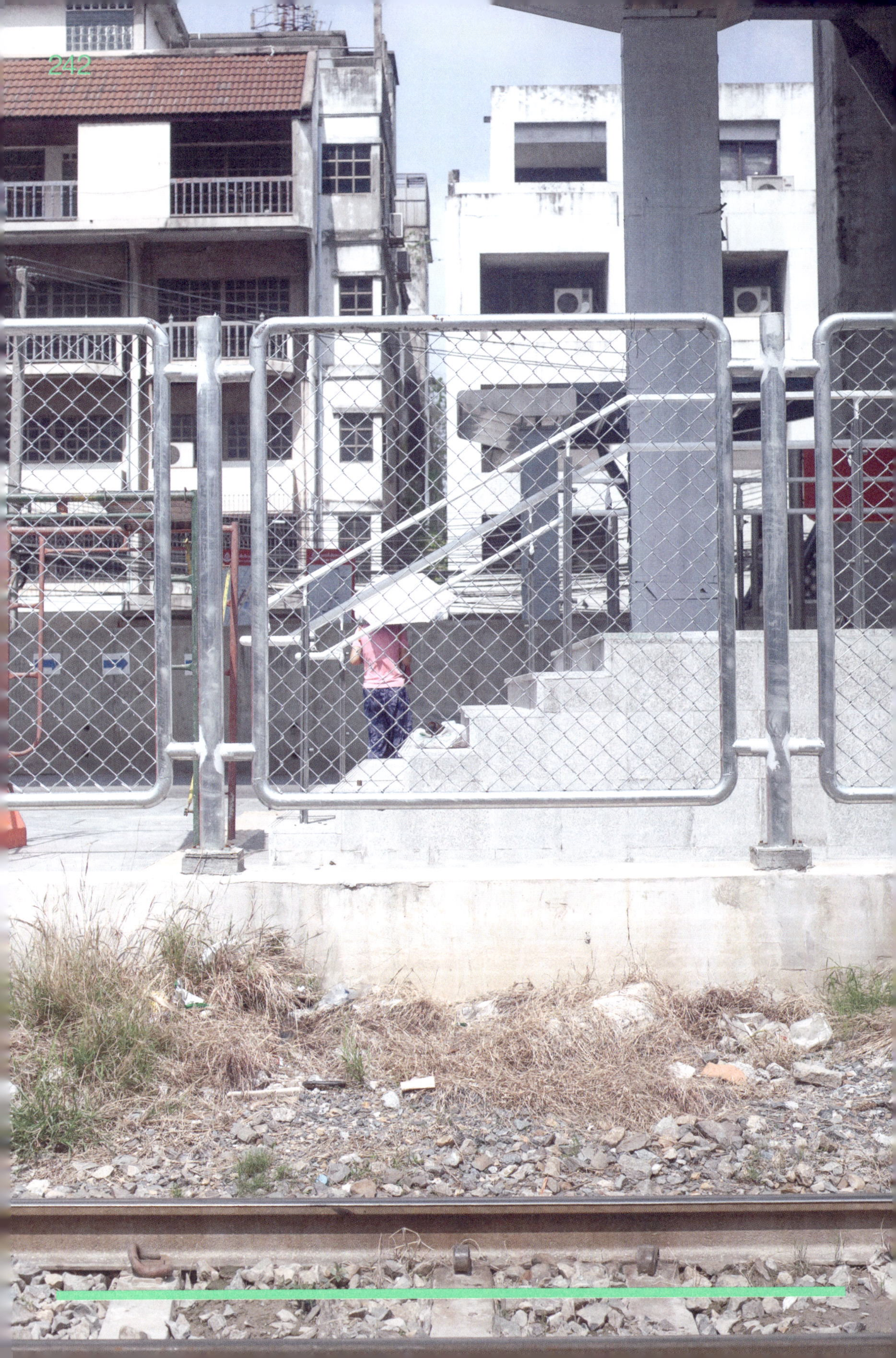

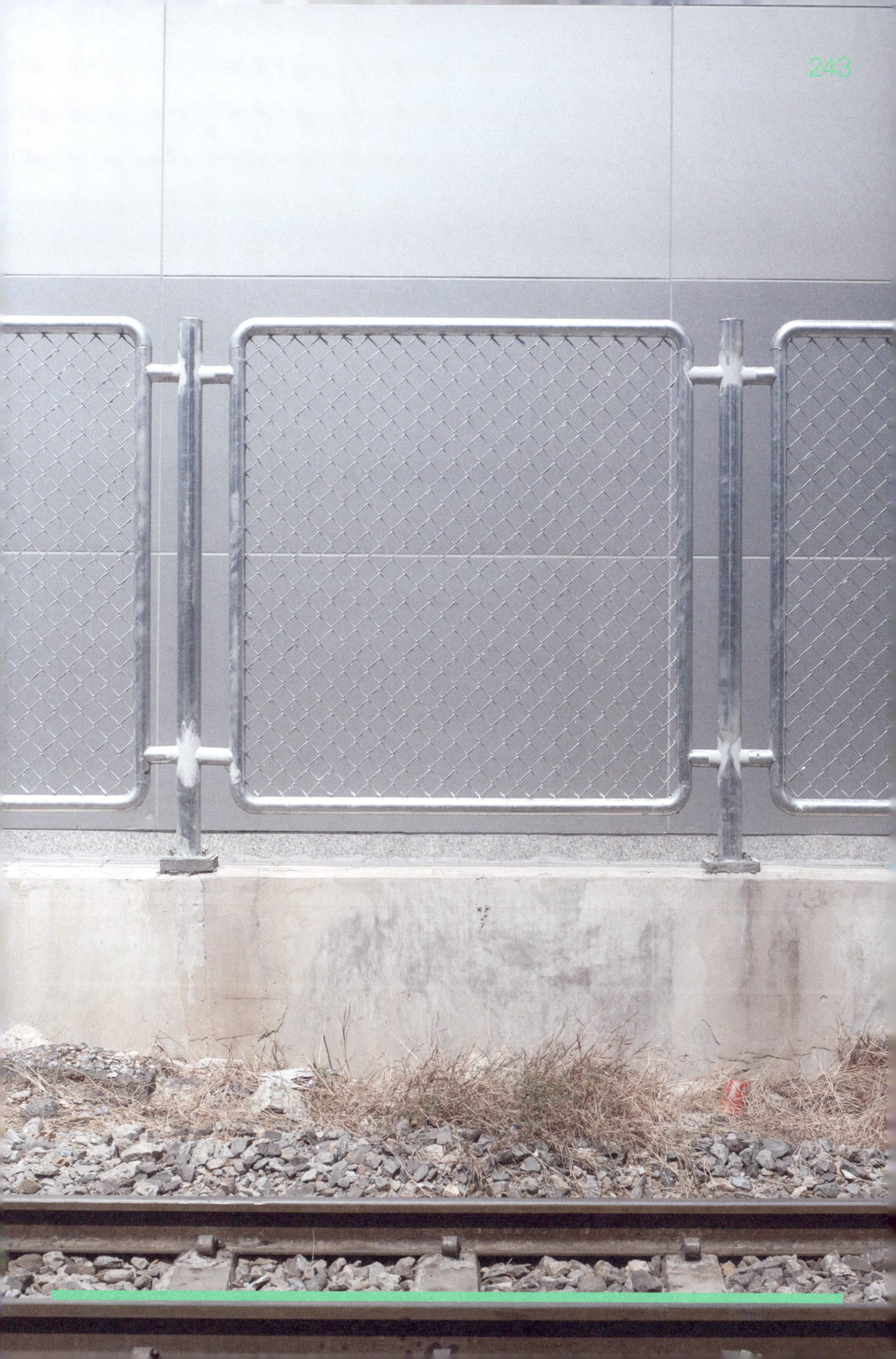

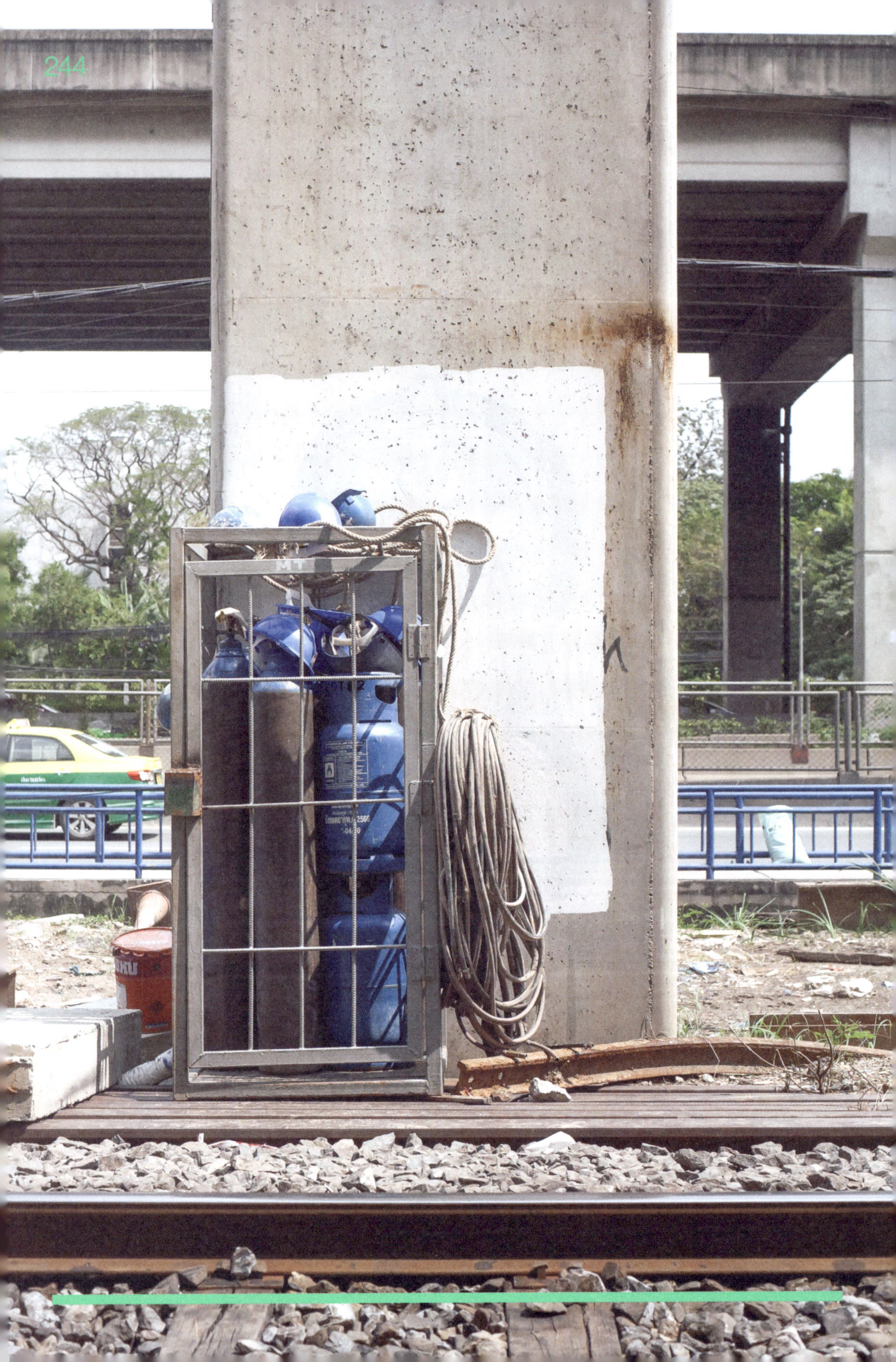

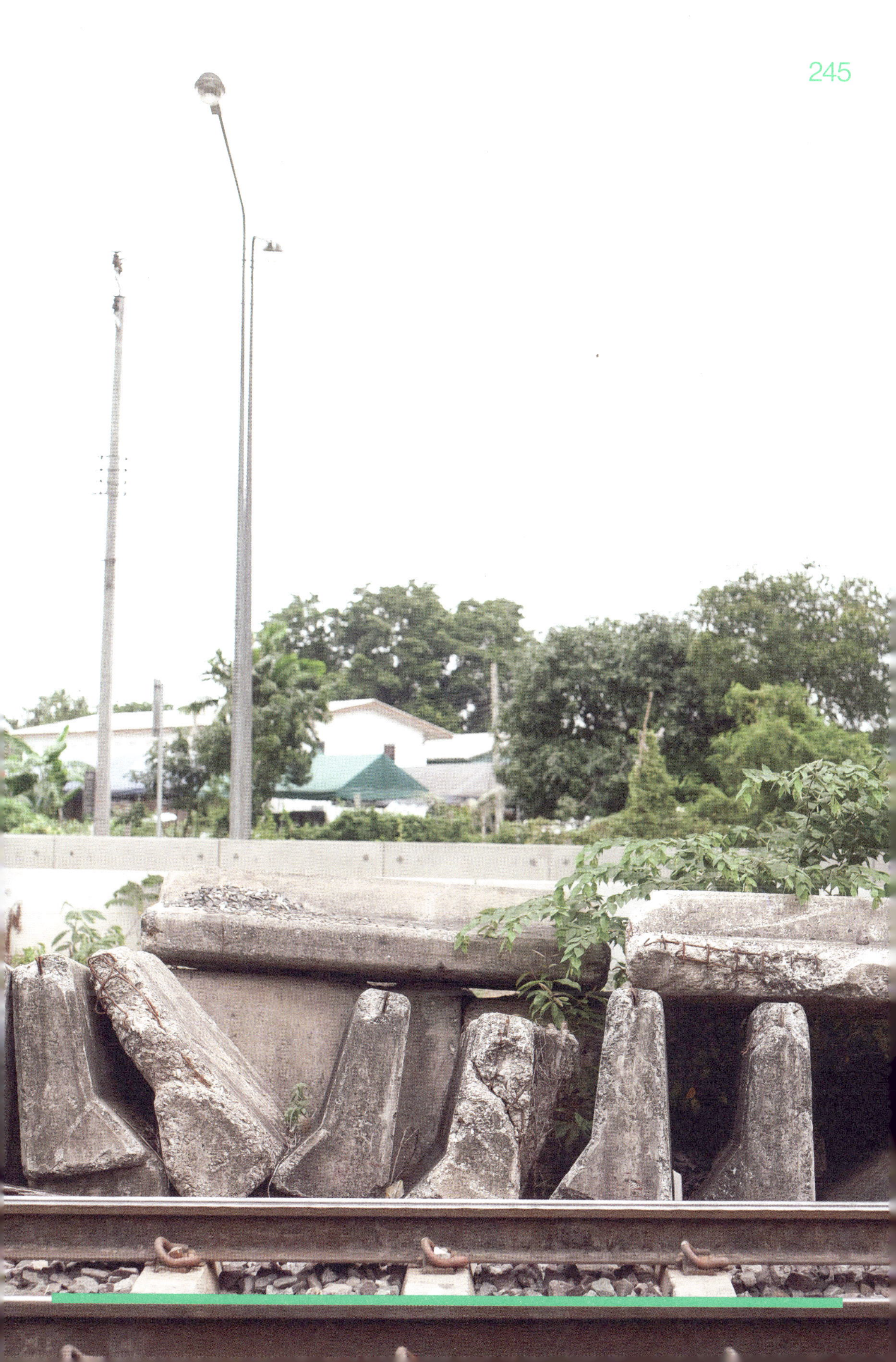

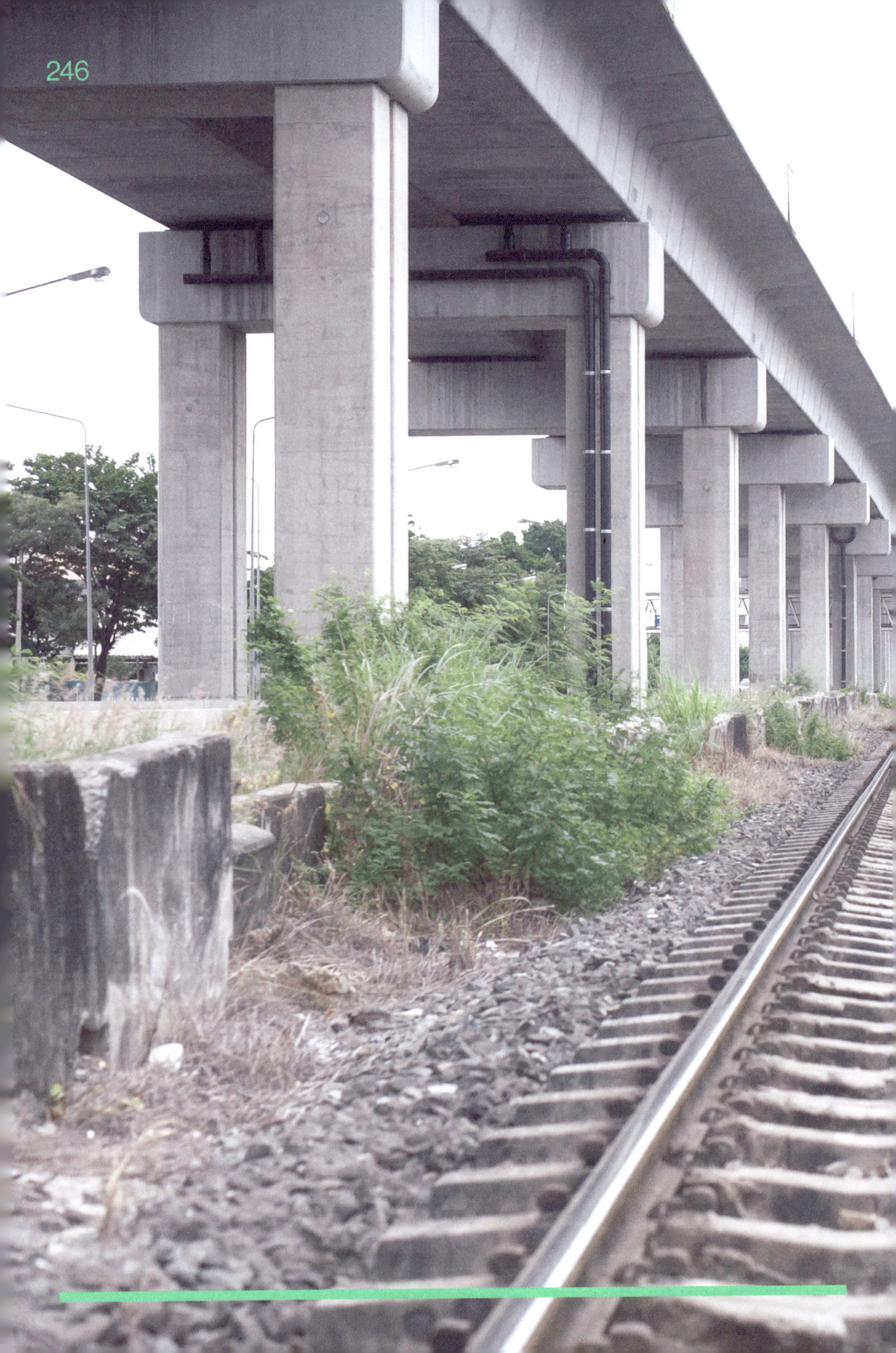

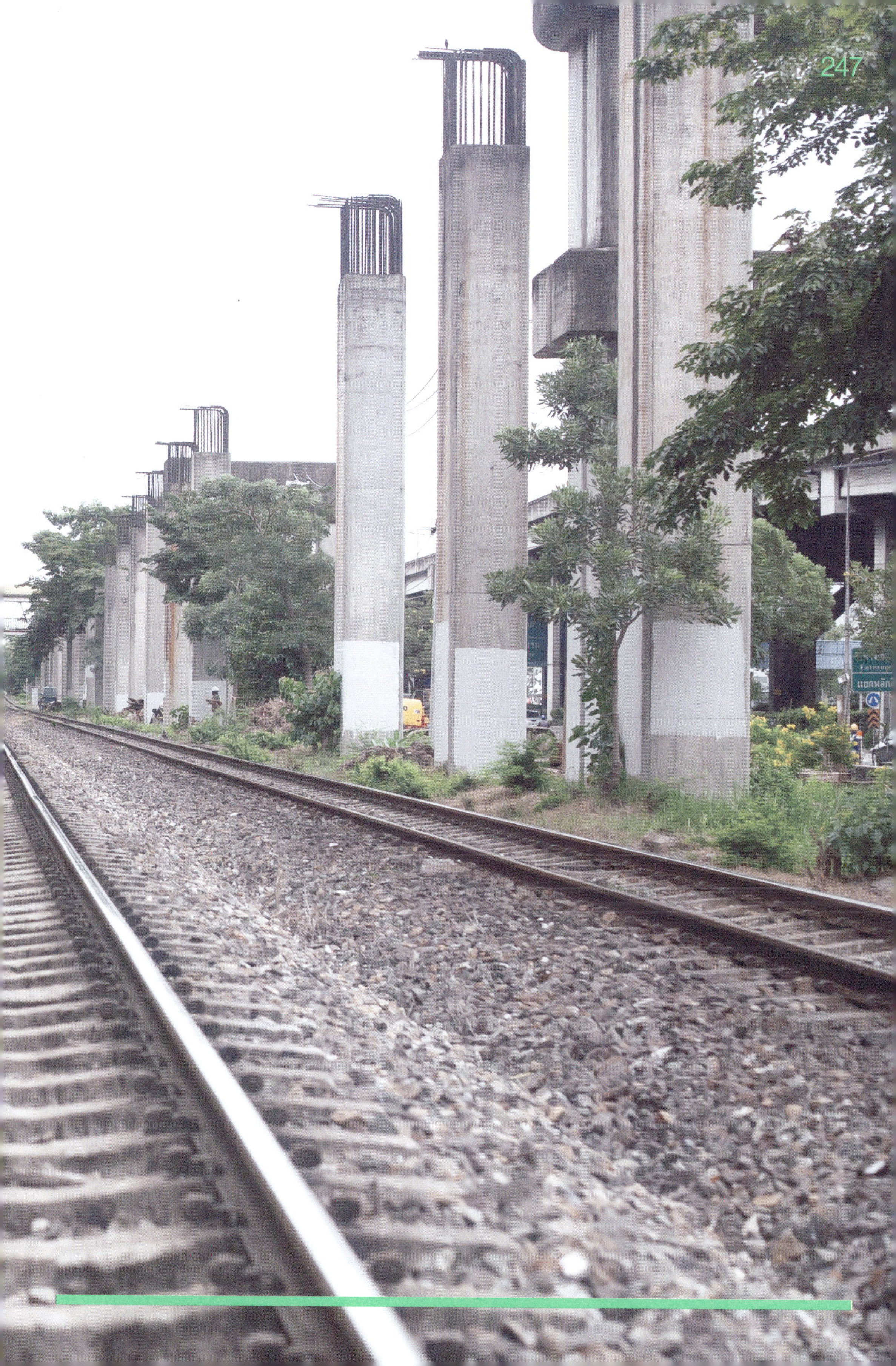

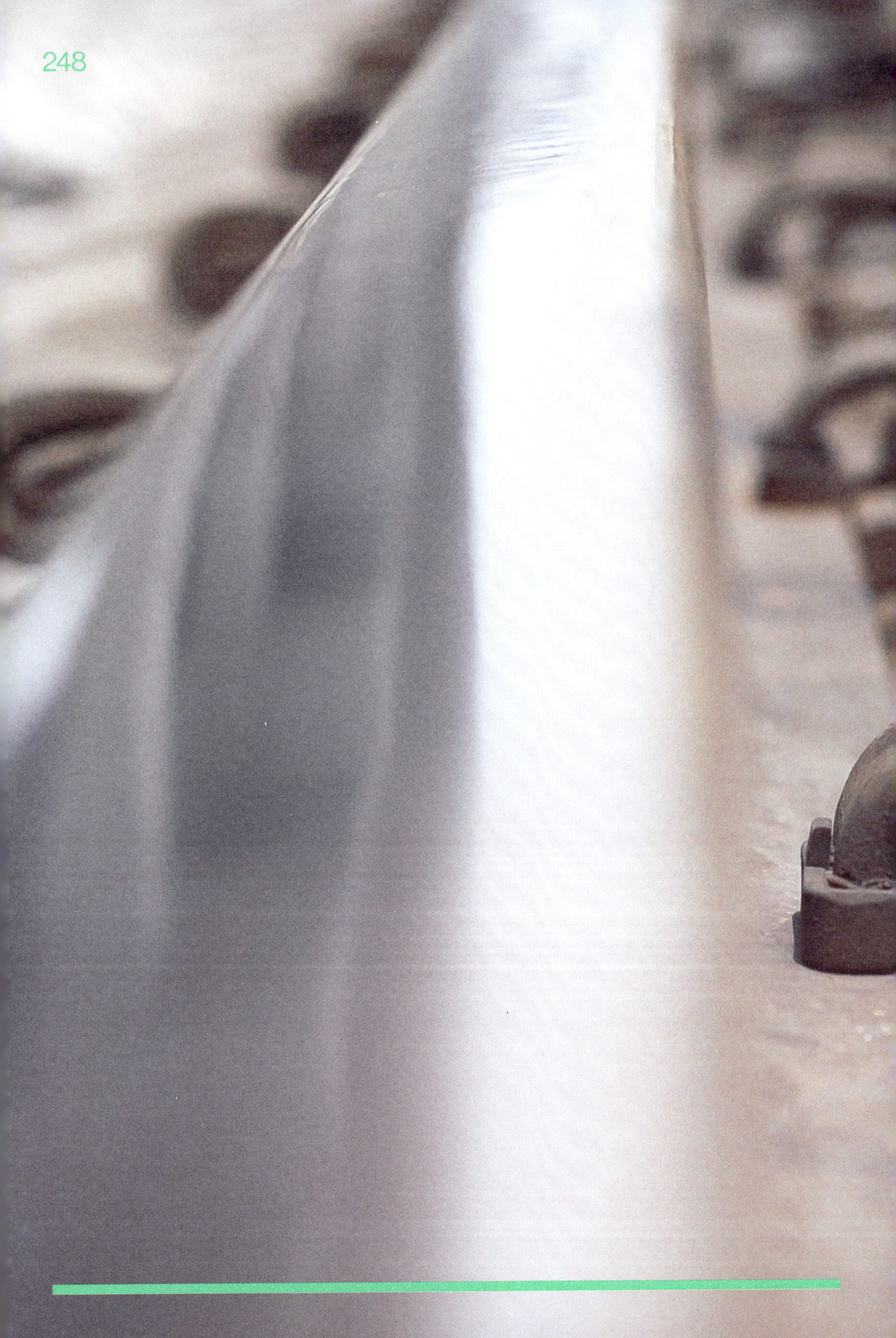

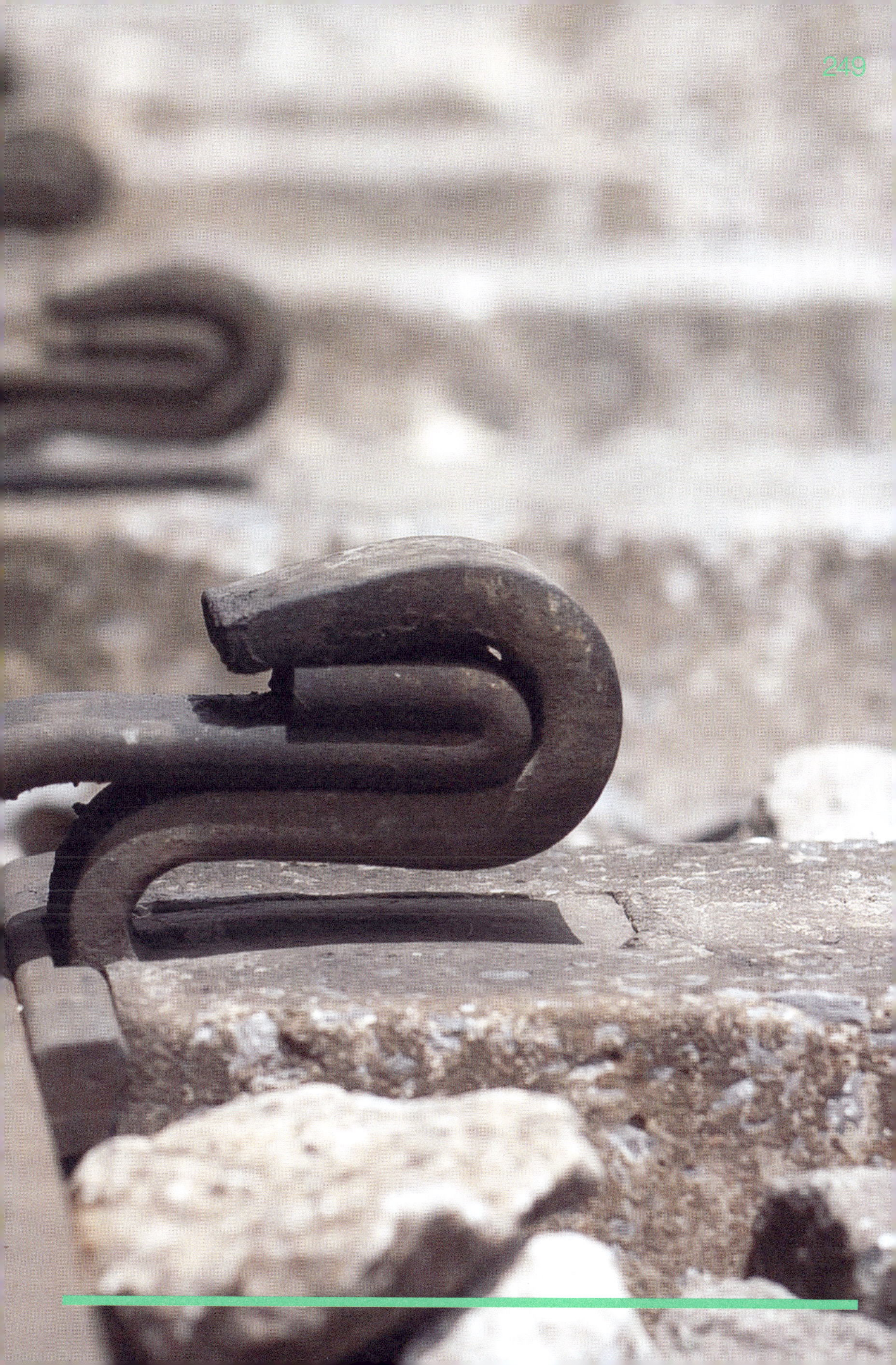

TAG INDEX

This book is built on many hours of recorded interviews with 18 of Bangkok's street artists and graffiti writers. Excerpts of these are shown in bold with the interviewee's tag placed nearby. Some have been credited as ANONYMOUS, where the interviewee requested this. One interviewee, SHEET, doesn't use a tag and so his preferred name is used. For convenience, the tags are listed below. They are shown in the order they first appear in the book;

BONUS TMC

RUKKIT

NOLA NOLEE

AS!N

MUEBON

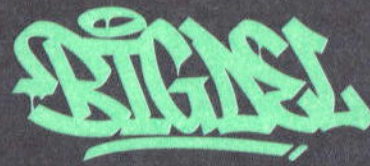

MAUY

CIDER

HEADACHE STENCIL

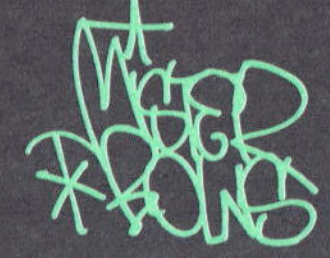

BIGDEL

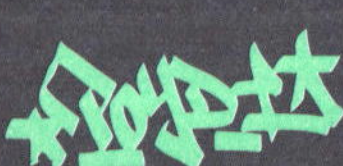

ALEX FACE

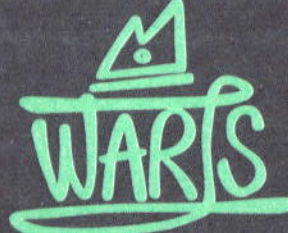

CSM

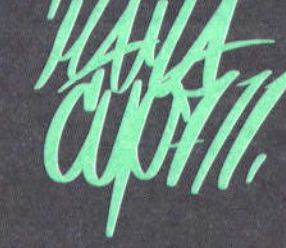

MISTER BOWS

POYD1

WARIS

MAMACUP711

SHEET

SHEET

TORCHER

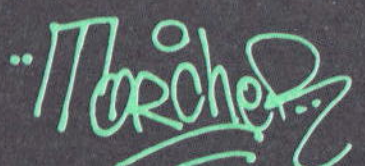

TGU

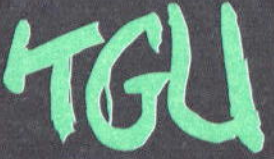

ARTIST CREDITS

The photography in this book documents the street art and graffiti at the Hopewell site and around Bangkok. Best efforts were made to identify and acknowledge the artists and writers whose works are depicted. If a work of yours has been miscredited or not credited, please contact the publisher. The credits below are listed by page, referencing pieces as they appear in the frame, from left to right and then top to bottom.

COVER
NEV3R, CRUDE, POYD1

CHAPTER 1
12 – POYD1
25 – PETE BULLET
27 – ASUI ART
28 – JENG
29 – SMOKE HEAD
31 – P-4
36 – POINT
37 – PUKU
40 – MAMACUP711
41 – TEAS
43 – NICKER SKII
44 – AKE
45 – GONEZK

CHAPTER 2
46 – SHEET
58 – AL
60 – TGU
61 – CRUDE (lower piece)
66 – POB
67 – NOLA NOLEE (left) TOY (right)
68 – BONUS TMC
69 – ALEX FACE
70 – KUANG SOO
72 – MRO
73 – KOUKU
75 – CARNIVOLS
79 – MATT
81 – BLURLER

CHAPTER 3
82 – HEADACHE STENCIL
93 – NINJA (left)
98 – V44
99 – E
102 – ROBIN (left) JAW (right)
103 – L&L
107 – FARO
108 – KANS
109 – KANS
110 – MISTER BOWS
111 – MISTER BOWS
112 – WIDESPREAD (KAJUIKAJAI)
113 – PAAKORN

CHAPTER 4
116 – AS!N
118 – SHEET
138 – ESA Crew (GOH-M, PUK, BIGDEL), BAI Crew (POYD1), DSG Crew (GUMDIK, MONSTER, JUNE, ACID, SUCK1, COLE)
140 – CANTWO, CIDER, CO2
142 – JACE
148 – WEIRD9
149 – P7
150 – POYD1
151 – WEIRD9, SANOT
152 – ALEX FACE (lower)
154 – TONEK, STN, SECUACES
155 – ALEX FACE,
156 – BKK, PAKORN BNA, NEV3R, DOR Crew,
157 – top: GRAFFITI HOLIDAY Crew (DEDO, OMEKA, GORES, PNTX, PRADE) bot: SOME
158 – GFL Crew, DR ONE
159 – QUCAN, KIMES
160 – KULT
162 – BONUS TMC
164 – ALEX FACE
165 – MUEBON
166 – ALEX FACE
168 – P7
169 – JACE

CHAPTER 5
170 – CIDER
172 – BIGDEL
176 – P7
178 – PMT Crew
181 – SIKA (left) DAYOE (right)
182 – MUEBON, ALEX FACE, MAMAFAKA, P7
186 – top: NTA, CATMASK, SOKER, JIM, POYD1, LUXE
186 – bot: COD, SUD, UNKNOWN, ZYKO, UNKNOWN, ZIDS, LANS, CATMASK
188 – top: SAWASDEE, BIGDEL, ZITOK

188 – mid: BKK, SOMER, ALERT, ZANTA
188 – bot: CHIP7, THOR, SOMAR, CIDER, COZ
190 – top: EDOT, COZONE, SAWASDEE, OEK, BKK
190 – mid: COZONE, HEKS, CHIP7, ACNE, CHIP7
190 – bot: DESM, BLEEK, CHIP7
192 – top: UNKNOWN, ZANTA, CRACY, RUDE, EDOT, EGIS, SADUE, COZONE,
192 – mid: REYS, ARES, REY, BOHER, TIMER, JOKER, BOHER
192 – bot: ZANTA, GUNS, CRUDE, ALERT, RUDE

CHAPTER 6

194 – HEADACHE STENCIL
198 – HEADACHE STENCIL
199 – MUEBON
201 – RUKKIT
202 – MAUY
212 – UNKNOWN, PNT, OMEKA, UPAE
216 – SQUID LICKER
218 – ANGEL
220 – SADUE
222 – ALERT
224 – top: BSD
224 – bot: PLUCH, MIVO, DISKO, POLAR
226 – top: COZ, MEROK
226 – bot: COZONE, BEU
228 – TONER
232 – SORE (background)

CHAPTER 7

234 – ALEX FACE
237 – COLT
239 – POYD1, CIDER
240 – POYD1, CIDER
241 – POYD1, CIDER

PHOTOGRAPH CREDIT AND COPYRIGHT

All photographs are by the author, unless indicated below.

15 – Bangkok Elevated Road and Train System (BERTS) or Hopewell Project at Bangkok Thailand By Anirut Thailand, Shutterstock
48 – Bangkok Floating Market From the Warren Smith Collection (COLL /5713) at the Archives Branch, United States Marine Corps History Division
50 – Vehicles on the street in Bangkok, Thailand, 1951 by Dmitri Kessel/The LIFE Picture Collection /Shutterstock
85 – Sia Thairath
118 – Sarah Rooney
121 – IG: Nisamanee.nutt
124 – Cave of the Hands by Buenaventura, Shutterstock
126 – Henry Chalfant
127 – Henry Chalfant
132 – Anonymous
138 – LANS
140 – LANS
178 – LANS
182 – Vincent Lim
186 – top: LANS
186 – bot: LANS
198 – Headache Stencil
199 – MUEBON
201 – RUKKIT
202 – MAUY

TRANSLATIONS

42 – "The good guys always win, the bad guys always lose"
43 – "All the time"
63 – "Politician"
72 – "Montree"
85 – Clockwise from top left: "The government is full of debt. Will someone who loves me, please help"
"Will he survive?"
"Hopewell wasted taxes"
"I like paying wasted taxes"
"More bad karma is coming for him"
"Wasted taxes on the Akara gold mine"
102 – "Jao"
104 – "Bang your cock"

ACKNOWLEDGEMENTS

A chance encounter with the Hopewell columns began this book – a journey shared with my brother, Ottar Olivera. May there be many more adventures.

To all the street artists and graffiti writers, credited and uncredited, with work in this book – thank you for picking up the cans and heading out – don't stop, keep going, ignore the hateful ones and get your work up.

Thank you to the artists and writers interviewed – BONUS TMC, RUKKIT, NOLA NOLEE, AS!N, MUEBON, MAUY, CIDER, HEADACHE STENCIL, BIGDEL, ALEX FACE, CSM, MISTER BOWS, POYD1, WARIS, MAMACUP711, SHEET, TORCHER, TGU – for your generosity and honesty. You welcomed me into your scene, I hope this book provides an honest portrait of it.

Thanks to NEV3R, CRUDE, POYD1, AS!N, HEADACHE STENCIL, SHEET, CIDER, and ALEX FACE for generously providing the cover and chapter title pages' artworks.

Special thanks to POYD1, BIGDEL, CIDER, ALEX FACE, HEADACHE STENCIL, THISONE and RUKKIT for your additional advice and support.

Thanks to Pat and Pae (Studio150) for creating such an innovative design that captures the essence of the city and the scene, also for your professionalism and dedication.

To Yui and Nong for your support – especially to Fon for your professionalism and fine work.

To Narisa Chakrabongse for publishing the book and believing in its value. Thank you for safeguarding its integrity and for sage guidance on design and editing. Thanks also for safe harbour in the final months of the book's creation.

To Sarah Rooney for many things. Firstly, for early support and encouragement. Secondly, for conscientiously editing such a complex manuscript. Thirdly, for the fascinating conversations, the book has benefitted enormously from your nuanced perspective.

To Jaem Prueangwet for your fine translation and enduring support. Also, for many discussions that provided valuable insights.

To Alice Aomtip Kerdplanant, this book would not have happened without you. Thank you for your unfailing dedication and your dignity and good humour in working on such a complex project. Also, for your friendship and conversation as we traversed Bangkok.

Thank you to, LANS, Nutt Nisamanee and Vincent Lim for providing their fine photographs. And to Henry Chalfant, wonderful to have your images in the book, thank you.

Thank you to friends; Maram Aung Mai, Wendy Joy Morrissey, Shoko Sakuma, Gaye Paterson, Katsuya, Li Jia Li, Harry Roovers, Theingi Lynn, Kyan Dyne Aung, Hugo Chan, Kyaw Naung Khant, Phillip Cannizzo for your valuable conversation and support while the book was written.

Thanks to Wan, Ma Lay, Ohm and Atom for your kind welcome.

Thank you to my parents, Jane and Spencer, for your love and support. And my brothers, Oliver and Paddy.

MAP

The map opposite shows where you can find most of the street art and graffiti depicted in this book. Others, you will have to find yourself. These are not precise directions, so take your time to explore and discover these pieces where the creators intended them to be seen. Some may be gone and new pieces will be in their place. There are thousands of other places to find street art and graffiti not on this map. As you find new pieces, you can mark them here.

SITE 1 CHALOEM LA PARK

From BTS Ratchathewi Station, walk south along the east side of Phayathai Road until you see the park on your left. From here, you can walk under the nearby bridge over Phayathai Road to the next site.

SITE 2 SAEN SAEP CANAL BY CHALOEM LA 56 BRIDGE

Walk from Chaloem La Park or catch the BTS to Ratchathewi Station and walk south down the west side of Phayathai Road and go under the bridge. On your right side, down a narrow path, you will find your way onto the tow paths of the canal. Many pieces on both sides of the canal, east of the bridge.

SITE 3 SAEN SAEP CANAL NEAR RAMKHAMHAENG MALL

Catch the water ferry from Hua Chang (Siam Square) Ferry Terminal and get off at The Mall 3 Ferry Terminal. You will find lots of pieces in the area on both sides of the canal.

SITE 4 SALAK HIN ALLEY

From Hua Lamphong Station, walk to the building's east side. Enter Salak Hin Soi from the Rong Mueang Road.

SITE 5 BESIDE PORTUGUESE EMBASSY

From Hua Lamphong Station, walk south down Mahaphruttharam Road into Charoen Krung Road. From there, turn right into Charoen Krung Soi 32.

SITE 6 SATHORN UNIQUE TOWER

It may not be possible to enter this place as it's private property. From the last site, walk south down Charoen Krung Road and underneath the highway overpass, you will see the tower on your left. Or catch the BTS to Saphan Taksin, see the tower as you look south from the platform.

SITE 7 A CAR PARK

From BTS Thong Lo Station, walk north up Sukhumvit Soi 53, then turn right into Thong Lo Soi 5, and then left into Pai Di Ma Di Klang Soi, keep walking north and you will see the car park on your left just near Thong Lo Soi 11.

SITE 8 HOPEWELL COLUMNS

Catch the SRT Dark Red Line to Wat Samian Nari and walk north along the footpaths beside the railway line all the way to Don Mueang Station. By 2022, almost all the pieces had been buffed, but some new ones are appearing.

SITE 9 MUANG THONG THANI TOWERS

Search online for the building owner's contact details and let them know you will come first. Get a train to SRT Dark Red Line Lak Si Station and then get a taxi to the corner of Bond Street and Popular Road. Or ask to be taken to the M Society Condominiums, the ghost towers are to the north. Ask locals if you have trouble finding the entrance.

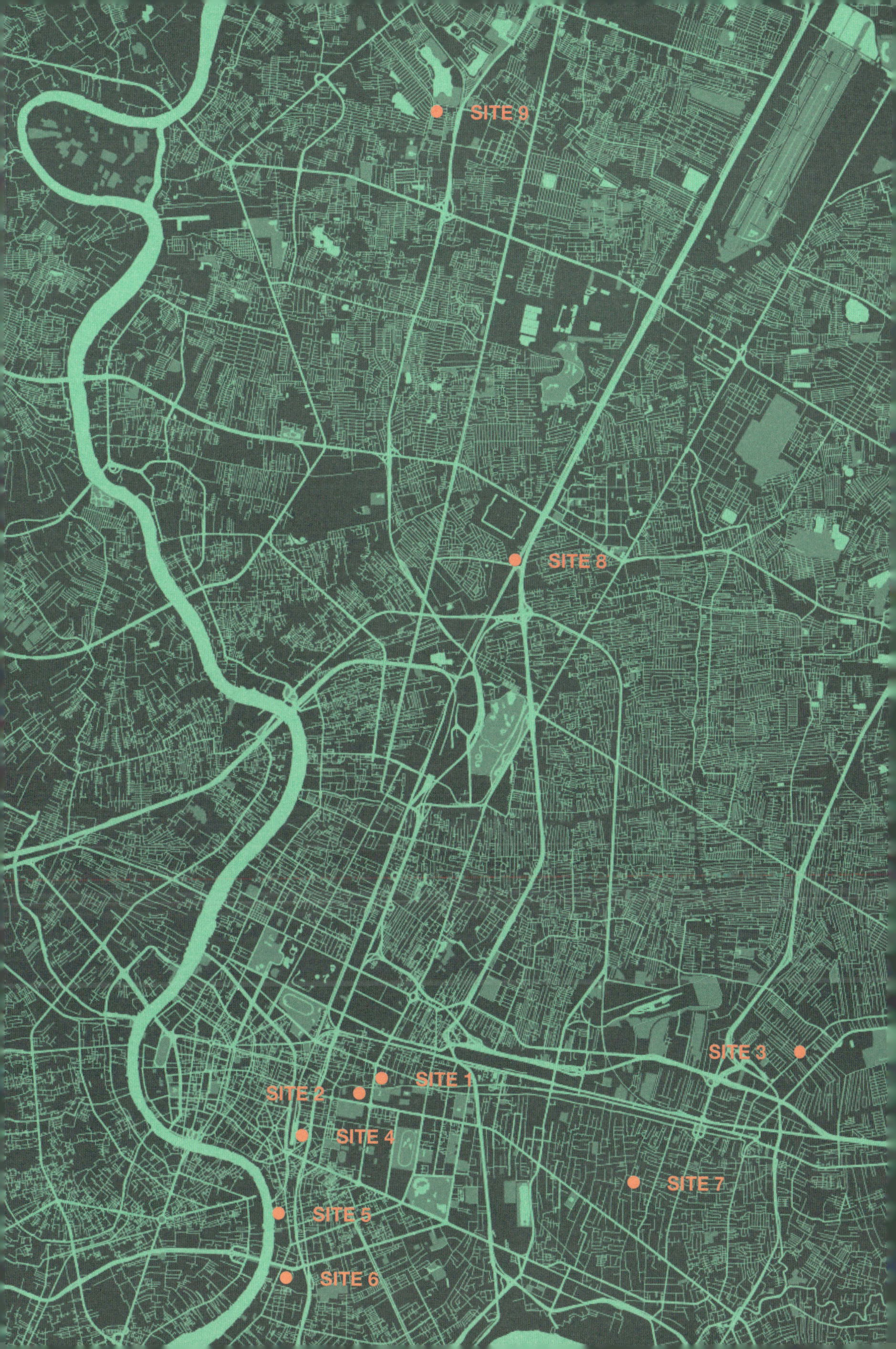
SITE 9
SITE 8
SITE 3
SITE 1
SITE 2
SITE 4
SITE 7
SITE 5
SITE 6

DABS1
JOE COOL
JOE COOL
YIA POP